ROLF BAGINSKI

Design & Building of
Split-Bamboo Flyrods

1st Edition

English Translation and Editing: Timothy A. Anderson and William A. Harms (USA)
Layout-Graphic Design: Lounès Kessi (Hamburg, Germany)
Pre-print Preparation: Team Media: Raini Sicher (Switzerland)
CD: Studio Ton, Bremen, Germany
Music: Burkhard Hartmann and Rolf Baginski
Printed in Switzerland
ISBN 978-3-033-01312-4

The English edition of this book is a limited edition of 1500, and includes a CD.
This is book number:

Rolf Baginski, Hildesheimerstrasse 2, 28205 Bremen, Germany

Contents

Historical reels go well with split-bamboo rods, including the new ones.

Acknowledgements

"This book is dedicated
to my grandfather and father.
When I was a child,
they allowed me to build things
and went fishing with me!"

When I began this book, I intended to spend no more than six to eight months on it. As with so many things, however, greater involvement always teaches how much the content and material need to exceed the original concept. It soon became clear to me that I would need help in gathering the information needed for the book. I'm particularly grateful to the American Museum of Fly Fishing and its then-director, Gary Tanner, who first opened the doors and, in the truest sense, placed the treasures of the museum in my hands. Many helpful colleagues in the USA, such as Thomas Dorsey, A. K. Best, Rick Gottdenker, Paul Schmookler, and many others helped me with their knowledge and information.

Although he doesn't know it, I must also thank Lon Deckard. True to my fear of flying, on my first trip to the USA to show my rods at a convention, everything went wrong. On the evening before departure, my airline informed me that its partner company would be having a strike, so the total flight plan had been changed. Now, I had to fly to London alone on a turboprop, instead of joining my friend, Michael, in Amsterdam for our flight the next afternoon across the Atlantic. The plane from London took me to Toronto, so, pressed into my seat and flying alone, I was allowed to indulge my fears without interruption. From Toronto, I flew to Cincinnati, Ohio, where I was to wait five hours for my connecting flight to the final destination in Salt Lake City, Utah. In the meantime, I guess I couldn't have cared less. I just wanted to arrive somewhere!

While waiting in the airport, I had leaned a large leather tube containing my rods on my seat when a friendly, heavy-set gentleman next to me asked, "Golf clubs or fishing rods?" I replied truthfully and briefly, "Split-bamboo rods." He replied, "Unpack them," which I actually did. It would be a long time before the connecting flight departed anyway. With a critical eye, he took his time and inspected my rods, piece by piece. Finally he put everything away and said, "Not so bad." Then he gave me his card which read: "Lon Deckard – Thomas & Thomas – Owner." I must have looked flabbergasted, but then he clapped me on the shoulder and said we probably had the same destination and should sit together to talk about split-cane rods. More than anything, I wanted to avoid focusing on the plane's takeoff and landing, and thanks to our spirited conversations, these passed with little attention. No more fear of flying!

I also owe many thanks to my friends in Germany who assisted in word and deed – especially Michael Werner with his many useful suggestions and Claas Hutschenreiter, who provided a number of watercolors. Antje Bertram and Hille Wigand offered voluminous corrections and edited the German text, and I was delighted to receive a wide range of pictures and photos from my old friend, Lars Østergaard, in Denmark. Leen Huisman from Holland contributed wonderful drawings and headings and gave helpful tips. Lastly, I cannot thank my Swiss friends, Philipp and Raini Sicher, enough – without whom the project could not have been finished.

From this list, one can see that the bamboo community is an international group, and its many participants act that way, too. I first met Bill Harms four years ago at a convention near New York, but when we met for a second time, he had heard about my book project and volunteered, without restriction, to read and edit the English translation. Some months later, and out of the blue, I received an email from Tim Anderson in California, asking if I needed the book to be translated from the German. And how!! In only a few months, they finished their first draft.
It was very difficult to obtain important information in our German-speaking region because very few of our records can be considered as documentation. Without some of the "old masters" providing many valuable tips (such as Heinz Weiland in the Franconian hills), this book could not have been written. I particularly want to thank Bernd Krogmann, Olav Koch, Christian Budday and Rudolf Huber for helping me to reconstruct the development of fishing equipment in Germany. These men have been collecting equipment and information for many years, and each has generously supported me with his knowledge. I was able to inspect and photograph their many collected treasures, realizing that a large part of German fishing history would have been lost without them.

Once infected with the "Bamboo virus," one soon becomes acquainted with others suffering the same condition. New friendships arise and invitations are extended. It's always a pleasure for me to meet with these people; to exchange ideas, learn, try new rods and foremost, to fish.

6

7

Rolf Baginski - always involved with bamboo.

The Beginning

Evidently, people first fished with rod and line about 4000 years ago. Artificial flies were used more than 2000 years ago, and the first "feather fishing" was mentioned about 800 years ago. Nevertheless, it would still be a very long time before the first split-cane rod was to appear.

Unfortunately, the full history of the split-bamboo rod cannot be determined, for too much documentation has either been lost or was never written at all. Also, because fishing in recent centuries was often considered a leisure-time activity, the first tackle producers offered rods only as a sideline, and unlike economics, politics and other serious things, leisure activity usually didn't receive much attention. I often regret that this remains the case.

In my research, therefore, I was restricted to the available literature, but I also interviewed as many people as I could and visited several museums. And, too, I made extensive use of the two-volume work, *Trout*, by Ernest Schweibert.

Gary Tanner and the author in front of the American Museum of Fly Fishing in 2001.

"You are warmly invited to visit our little museum, and I'll make it completely available to you." Once again, I was taken-aback by the friendly fashion of extending invitations in the USA. I met Gary Tanner (then, the Director of the American Museum of Fly Fishing) at a show in New York, and a few days later I was standing at the museum's door. Garry greeted me with the words, "Just ask if you want to know something." Well, I wanted to know a lot. A little uneasy, I stood before the many rods by those famous masters I had only read about – plus, cases full of historical tools, reels, and wonderful pictures. In the truest sense, Gary placed the treasures of the museum in my hands. My visit lasted three days, but I'm sure I saw only a small fraction of everything on hand.

I'm grateful for the many details provided by individuals who were kind enough to share their knowledge, either personally or through their books and publications. Even so, it became clear during my progress on this book, that a complete overview would be impossible. After all, two World Wars had occurred during the most significant eras in the development of split-bamboo rods, causing irretrievable loss of important documents and artifacts. Other reasons for incomplete coverage come from my own choice to represent the period after 1970 only in selected segments. Far too many new and outstanding rod-builders (several of whom are my friends) share the lime-light in our modern era, and it's just not possible to represent all of them or to acknowledge their accomplishments. Fortunately, a very large group has developed (most notably, in the USA) – makers who are willing to share their knowledge with others. Nowadays, there are small, specialty magazines, Internet forums, and in some states, annual rod-makers' meetings where new building methods and rod designs are presented..

Inside the museum: historical tools and rods.

Brief Overview

2000 B.C.

The first depictions of people using fishing rods and lines appear in Egypt.

200 B.C.

Aelian, in his *De Naturea Animalium*, describes a fishing method in Macedonia, "They wrap dark wool around the hook, and on the wool, fasten two feathers which grow under the neck of a rooster and have the color of wax..."
Most historians interpret this passage as the first evidence of fly-fishing.

1210

Wolfram von Eschenbach writes a story describing a young man who catches both trout and grayling with a "feather rod." The term "feather rod" appears commonly in German literature until the Seventeenth Century.

1496

The first description of fly-fishing is published by Dame Juliane Bernes in her *The Treatyse of Fysshynge wyth an Angle*.

Here begynnyth the treatyse of fysshynge wyth an Angle.

Salamon in his parablys sayth that a good spyryte
makyth a flourynge aege / that is a fayre aege & a
longe. And syth it is soo: I aske this questyon / whi
che ben the meanes & the causes that enduce a man
in to a mery spyryte.: Truly to my beste dyscrecon
it semeth good dysportes & honest gamys in whom a man Joy
eth wythout ony repentaunce after. Thenne foloweth it y go=
de dysportes & honest games ben cause of mannys fayr aege &
longe life. And therfore now woll I chose of foure good dispor
tes & honeste gamys / that is to wyte: of huntynge: hawkynge:
fysshynge: & foulynge. The beste to my symple dyscrecon why
che is fysshynge: callyd Anglynge wyth a rodde: and a lyne

First-page facsimile of
Berners' *Treatyse of Fysshynge wyth an Angle*, 1496

The first known description of fly-fishing was published by Dame Juliane Bernes in 1496 in "The Treatyse of Fysshynge wyth an Angle."

1558
The physicist and teacher, Conrad Gessner of Zurich, describes various artificial flies in *De picinum natura*, the fourth volume of his *Historia animalium*. Here, he describes patterns and presentation methods used in German-speaking countries.

1624
Thirty-three fly patterns for fishing are described between January and June in *El Mauscrito de Astorga*. This manuscript is considered to be the beginning of fly-fishing as a sport in Spain.

1653
Isaak Walton writes *The Compleat Angler*. For the first time, fishing is presented as a lyrical and philosophical ideal, and the book has since influenced innumerable generations of fishermen. Walton's is the third most published book in English after the *Bible* and the works of Shakespeare.

1747
The Art of Angling, by Richard Bowlker, marks the beginning of modern fly-tying and becomes a standard for tying and fishing techniques during the second half of the Eighteenth Century.

1747-1841
Spanish silkworm "gut" begins to replace horsehair as leader material. Fly lines are now commonly made from silk, and the first, simple reels are used – these, allowing greater casting-distances and better hand-control of the line.

1766
The English teacher, Joseph Banks, travels to America and attests to wonderful fishing for large trout in his diary. He describes the particularly successful "gold-ribbed" fly patterns.

1777
The first advertisement for a silk line appears in America.

1830
Alfred Ronalds writes *The Flyfisher's Entomology*, a well-illustrated reference book about the insects eaten by trout and grayling in English waters.

1843
An anonymous angler, writing in the English magazine, *Bell's Life of London*, reports that he has fished with flies in fresh and saltwater for years. This is the first mention of saltwater fly-fishing.

1850
The Mormons and various railway workers seem to have been the first to fish with flies west of the Mississippi. They soon discovered how to catch Pacific steelhead and salmon as well, and thereby opened a new world for American fly-fishermen.

1840-1870
Samuel Phillippe, Ebeneezer Green, and Charles Murphy begin using bamboo for rod-building. Samuel Phillippe is probably the first to make six-strip rods from bamboo.

1857-1870
The first hooks, designed with eyes for attaching the leader, are invented and quickly accepted.

1864
Thaddeus Norris publishes *The American Anglers Book* and offers, for the first time, a description of fishing with a dry fly

1870
Oil-impregnated silk lines (reportedly invented in America) simplify fishing with a dry fly. These lines helped to achieve far greater casting distances.

1874
The first, modern, fly-fishing reel is developed by the American company, Orvis. It's perforated, has a narrow spool, is very light in weight and retrieves the fly line rapidly.

1875
Max von dem Borne writes the *Illustrated Handbook of Angling*, in which he describes the advantages of a split-cane rod.

1877
Rainbow trout from California are stocked in waters throughout America, and with great success.
The classical salmon fly, as described by George M. Kelson, gains wide popularity.

1882
Jakob Wieland builds the first split-cane rod in Germany. Its details and construction plans probably came to Munich via Max von dem Borne.

1883
Fred Mather and Seth Green transport brown-trout eggs from Germany to New York. These are raised in a hatchery in Michigan and the fish develop very well.

1886

Frederick M. Halford writes *Floating Flies and How to Dress Them*. In this book, Halford describes his patterns and how to tie them, arguing that fishing with dry flies is the only ethical way to catch a trout. Even today, most of his tying recipes remain valid for modern patterns.

1890

Theodore Gordon, a talented fly-fisher on the Neversink River (New York's Catskill region), receives a number of dry flies from Halford in England – February 22, 1890. Gordon, also an excellent author, develops a new fly-fishing "ethic" in his writings, creating a strong influence in America. In his view, fishing should always be recreation and never a compulsion for success.
He establishes new fly-tying techniques in America with such famous patterns as his "Quill Gordon."

1870-1890

The former rifle maker, Hiram Leonard, brings rod-building to new heights. In the mid-1870s, and with his newly-invented machine, bamboo strips are given a perfect taper and can be replicated at any time. In 1881, Leonard opens his first rod factory in New York.

1892

Mary Orvis Marbury's *Favorite Flies and their Histories* is published, showing a wonderful collection of American fly patterns and what they imitate. For the first time, names and patterns are standardized, including even saltwater flies.

1914

George M. La Branche writes *The Dry Fly and Fast Water*. His casting abilities and experience were outstanding, and his book greatly influenced the American fly-fishing public. La Branche was a glowing defender of fishing with dry flies.

1920-

Rainbow trout are introduced and raised in England. Their growth is strong and their success extends through all of Europe.

1921

G. E. M. Skues, initially a good friend of Halford, engages in a bitter fight with him about whether wet flies and nymphs are better than dry flies for fishing. Skues' book, *The Way of a Trout with a Fly*, emphasizes all of the advantages of wet-fly and nymph fishing. More books on this theme would follow, while Halford writes that dry-fly fishing is the only acceptable method. Both authors influenced the continuing discussion of these ideas in Europe and America.

1929

The "German Fishing-Tackle Manufacturer" (D. A. M.) applies for a patent to impregnate bamboo rods.

1939

Lee Wulff, in his *Handbook of Freshwater*, writes for the first time, "A trout is too valuable to be caught only once," and, at once, becomes the pioneer of "catch and release."

1948

The Shakespeare company introduces the first fiberglass rod. Lighter, cheaper, and in some ways stronger than a bamboo rod, fiberglass establishes a new milestone in rod-building technology.

A fly-fisher in the Nineteenth Century might have looked like this.

Historical and modern equipment. Old and new still go well together.

History

*"It's difficult to say who first had the idea
to split bamboo into splines and
glue them together to make a rod.
It was first mentioned
sometime between 1795 and 1810
in English publications."*

It is hard to imagine a fisherman without a fishing rod. The rod extends his arm, allowing him to cast the line with hook and lure to the presumed location of the fish.

The beginnings of fishing with a pole or rod are hidden in history, but the first documents and drawings appeared in China and Egypt about 2000 years B.C. Catching fish for food is probably as old as mankind, and it's certain that Egyptian drawings depict catching fish with both nets and fishing poles.

Because there's no doubt that fishing with a net is more effective than with a rod, this could mean that pleasure or recreational fishing with a rod is more than 4000 years old.

Fishing plays a role in the mythologies of many ancient cultures, and even Plutarch, in *The Life of Antony*, describes how Cleopatra and Antony fish from a boat on the Nile.

Rod and line were used for fishing more than 4000 years ago.

The Ancient Egyptians Had an Advantage

Out of respect for its long tradition, we should view the heritage of modern fishing with reverence. Our rods are the result of thousands of years of development, and it's easy to imagine the endless experiments with various materials. Just picture two Roman legionnaires standing along the Rhine, debating the advantages of certain, selected hazel branches, for we know their fishing poles were made from small trees.

Anglers in Asia and Egypt had the advantage of fishing with various species of bamboo or cane. These would have been very light in comparison to wood, chiefly because of being hollow.

The wheel had long since been invented, but not in the form of a fishing reel for storing line. Previously, a line was simply tied to the end of a long pole in order to reach out as far as possible. Fishing poles as long as to 16 to 20 feet were not unusual. Well-known descriptions from the Fifteenth and Sixteenth Centuries report fishing poles having their butt ends burned out with glowing, metal rods to reduce excessive weight. Poles of this type would have weighed between five and 10 pounds, and while the burning may have made them lighter, it couldn't have been easy to manage such tackle with a fish at the end of the line. Surprisingly, however, tackle makers (commonly, blacksmiths, wheelwrights, or cabinetmakers who made poles on the side) continued to use solid materials in building fishing poles, and this basic concept did not change much, even with the rise of the British Empire and greater access to exotic materials.

First: Experimentation

At last, the time arrived for experimenting with various types of wood. English rod-makers dominated the industry for nearly 150 years, and a great many multi-piece rods derived from these experiments. We read Dame Juliana Bernes, even back in 1496, as she explains her preferred rod in her *The Treatyse of Fysshynge wyth an Angle*. The butt section was hazel, willow, or aspen and the tip section was blackthorn, crabtree, medlar, or juniper. In 1676, almost 200 years later, Charles Cotton speaks of his 15 to 18-foot Yorkshire pole with a butt section of fir and a tip section of thornwood, juniper or yew.

Many exotic woods were imported from the English colonies, and the woods' qualities were tested for suitability as fishing poles. For a brief period, hickory was the preferred material.

After the middle of the Eighteenth Century, rods were frequently made of lemonwood (*Pittosporum engenoides*) coming from New Zealand, lancewood (*Pseudopanax crassifolius*) from British Guyana, or greenheart (*Nectandra rodiaei*). In the Nineteenth Century, an African greenheart species (called *Piptadenia africana)* dominated, along with various Jamaican species.

In following decades, most rods would be made of these two species because they're very hard and flexible. Some manufacturers continued with hardwoods even into the Twentieth Century. From our modern point of view, however, these woods are far too heavy and relatively brittle.

A fly rod made of greenheart – from about 1900.

The First Rods Were "Heavyweights"

Rods for salmon and trout continued to be made from greenheart for a surprisingly long time. If I recall correctly, an English company produced a small series of "greenhearts" even in the 1980s, and in Scotland or England it's still possible to find these "heavyweights" in antique or second-hand stores. Perhaps the manufacture of wooden rods persisted because the material is easily shaped into a taper.

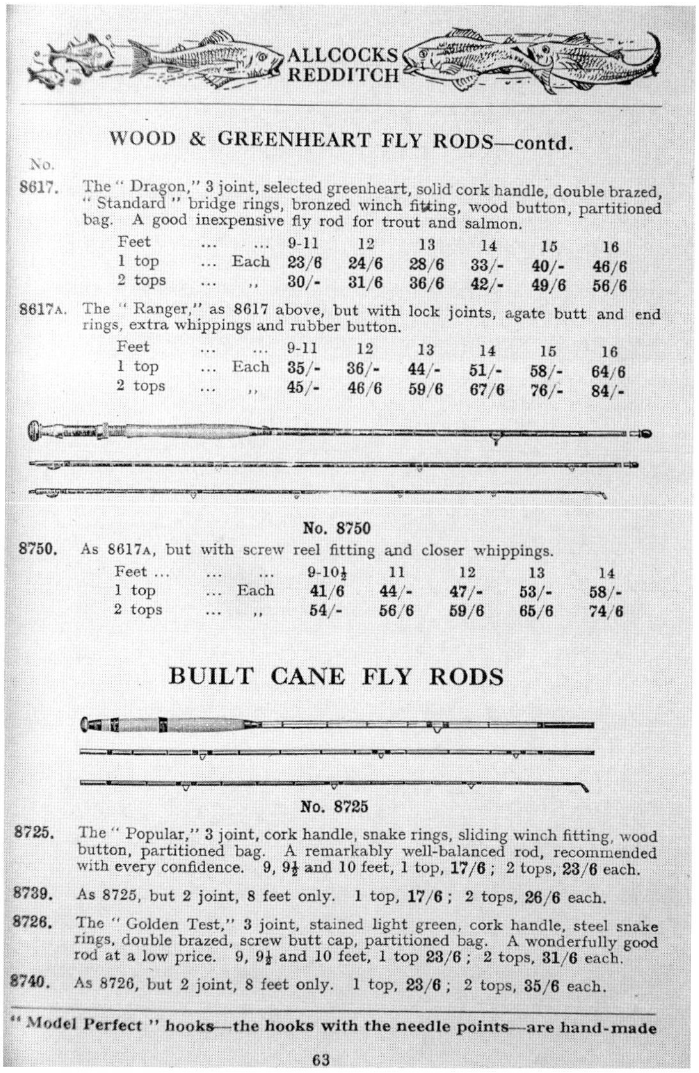

ALLCOCKS
REDDITCH

WOOD & GREENHEART FLY RODS—contd.

No.

8617. The " Dragon," 3 joint, selected greenheart, solid cork handle, double brazed, " Standard " bridge rings, bronzed winch fitting, wood button, partitioned bag. A good inexpensive fly rod for trout and salmon.

Feet ...	...	9-11	12	13	14	15	16
1 top ...	Each	23/6	24/6	28/6	33/-	40/-	46/6
2 tops ...	,,	30/-	31/6	36/6	42/-	49/6	56/6

8617A. The " Ranger," as 8617 above, but with lock joints, agate butt and end rings, extra whippings and rubber button.

Feet ...	...	9-11	12	13	14	15	16
1 top ...	Each	35/-	36/-	44/-	51/-	58/-	64/6
2 tops ...	,,	45/-	46/6	59/6	67/6	76/-	84/-

No. 8750

8750. As 8617A, but with screw reel fitting and closer whippings.

Feet ...	...	9-10½	11	12	13	14
1 top ...	Each	41/6	44/-	47/-	53/-	58/-
2 tops ...	,,	54/-	56/6	59/6	65/6	74/6

BUILT CANE FLY RODS

No. 8725

8725. The " Popular," 3 joint, cork handle, snake rings, sliding winch fitting, wood button, partitioned bag. A remarkably well-balanced rod, recommended with every confidence. 9, 9½ and 10 feet, 1 top, **17/6**; 2 tops, **23/6** each.

8739. As 8725, but 2 joint, 8 feet only. 1 top, **17/6**; 2 tops, **26/6** each.

8726. The " Golden Test," 3 joint, stained light green, cork handle, steel snake rings, double brazed, screw butt cap, partitioned bag. A wonderfully good rod at a low price. 9, 9½ and 10 feet, 1 top **23/6**; 2 tops, **31/6** each.

8740. As 8726, but 2 joint, 8 feet only. 1 top, **23/6**; 2 tops, **35/6** each.

" Model Perfect " hooks—the hooks with the needle points—are hand-made

63

A page from the Allcock catalog of 1939 shows many wooden rods still being offered.

It's uncertain who first devised the idea of splitting bamboo and making a rod by gluing the resulting strips together, but publications mentioning the method appeared in England sometime between 1795 and 1810. In his book, *The Angler's Bamboo*, Luis Marden refers to an English publication dating back to 1801 which reports,

"...the bamboo cane...is cut into joints, thick enough when divided lengthways into four pieces, to form the tip" and then "the sections of cane are glued together, after which they are properly tapered with double tooled planes and fine rasps; finished off with sandpaper and the joints wrapped with silk, well waxed."

Unfortunately, Marden does not cite the actual source, but I would very much like to read it.

Marden was probably quoting a certain W. D. Coggeshall (a member of England's prestigious Fly Fishers Club of London), finding the passage in a copy of *The Young Angler's Companion*. At least, this is the suggestion of George Leonard Herter in his preface to *Rod-Building Manual and Manufacturer's Guide*. Unfortunately, the publication date of the *Companion* is not known.

Who Invented It?
It was the English!

The first split-cane rods were made from two, three, or four pieces of bamboo, with the actual taper being shaped or planed after assembly. Most rods were turned into a round shape, while others remained polygonal. Various experiments oriented the "power fibers" both to the inside and the outside, and all in all, it took a long time for bamboo to become established as a rod-building material.

The "Variopower" model of Pezon et Michel. Its butt is made of tubular fiberglass, but the tip is split bamboo. The designation "HS/HL" on the butt indicates (Highspeed-Highline)

Many types of composite rods are known, as for example, the practice of building only the tip section of split bamboo, while making the butt and middle sections from earlier-mentioned, exotic woods.

Surprisingly enough, composite rods (built of bamboo, mixed with other materials) were offered even into the 1960s. After the introduction of hollow fiberglass, it was also common to assemble rods with butt sections of bamboo and tip sections of fiberglass – or the reverse.

Long after bamboo rods became commonplace, several catalogs continued to promote rods of other materials. Customers just didn't completely trust the "new" material – as evidenced by some manufacturers whose rods even showed alternating strips of hardwood and bamboo. Anglers and tackle manufacturers, alike, were quite conservative.

Although England's rod-builders have the honor of discovering how to assemble a rod from strips of bamboo, the final development (leading to our modern rods) would be unthinkable without American rod-builders.

Samuel Phillippe of Easton, Pennsylvania must be seen as the father of American rod-building, but he, too, experimented with "hybrid" rods, using various types of wood, combined with all-bamboo tip sections. Before long, he settled on four-strip construction and, by 1846, began building rods with both butt and tip sections of bamboo. As a trained gunsmith and musical-instrument maker, he had become technically proficient, and easily transferred these skills to his rod-building. Additionally, Phillippe was an outstanding trout fisherman and his own best critic – able to use his experience to devise new rod designs. His first rod using six-strip, bamboo construction probably emerged in 1859, with even a few eight-strip models being built later. Between that first six-strip rod and 1870, he produced a number of six-strip rods, the construction also adopted by such famous rod-builders as Ebenezer Green, Charles Murphy or Hiram Leonard. Phillippe died in 1877, but his son, Solon, continued on with the business.

In short time, similar rod construction developed in England, and although the six-sided principle appeared in nearly all fishing catalogs, it had not yet completely taken over.

Many American rods from this era were exported to England and Scotland by "Andrew Clerk and Company." Eventually, the new designs were accepted enthusiastically, and of course, also copied.

Samuel Phillippe (1831-1877) is considered the "father" of American rod-building. He was probably the first to build an entire, six-strip rod of split cane.

Other famous makers at this time were Charles Murphy, Ebinezer Green, William Mitchell and Thaddeus Norris. It was particularly Charles Murphy, however, selling his rods in 1863 through "Andrew Clerk and Company," who developed new trends in theory and construction, and who influenced so many later rod-builders. The quality of his later rods, especially, is still remarkable. One of his masterpieces (from the Kaufmann collection) is on display in the American Museum of Fly-Fishing, and left me with the impression that I could use it for fishing anytime. Of surprisingly modern design, Murphy's rods showed the way to the future.

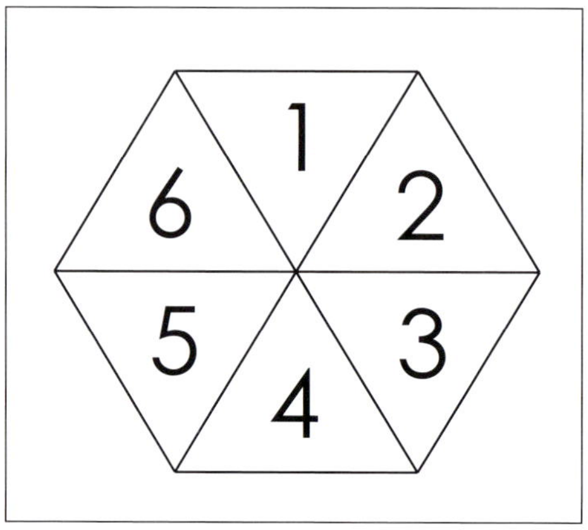

The principle of the hexagonal rod.

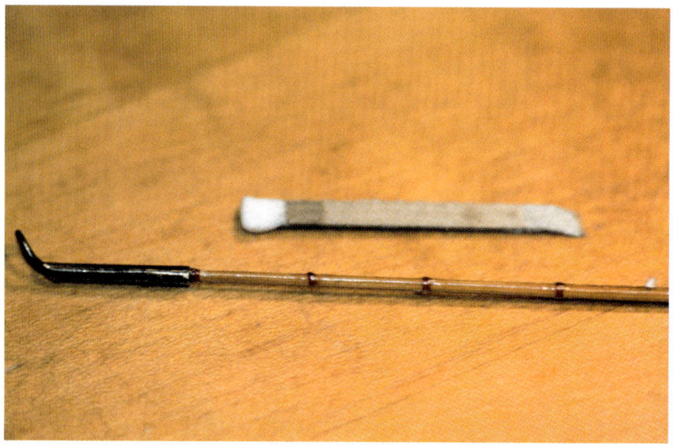

The extremely thin tip of a Murphy rod – built before 1900!

No record of the roots of modern rod-building would be complete without mention of Charles F. Orvis of Manchester, Vermont.

Born near the Battenkill River in 1831, he fished it as a youth, and records show that Orvis undertook the repair of clocks and toys before rod-building became his profession.

His first rods appeared sometime around 1854, and his split-bamboo rods were first mentioned in 1874, these, soon to become famous through his company's many catalogs. Depictions of those rods reveal that the first cork grips began to appear in the USA after 1880. Prior to that time, it was more usual for grips to be wrapped with rattan, leather, or turned wood.

The founder of a company known around the world: Charles F. Orvis.

Not Just for Ladies – the Cork Grip

Initially conceived as a weight-reduction advantage for "ladies' rods," it took a mere 10 years before most grips were built with cork as the preferred material. Among the first modern, light fly rods in hexagonal form were those appearing at Orvis in 1900. Here, too, and for the first time, Orvis used English snake guides rather than the "hanging rings" (dangling loops, attached to the rod blank with tiny metal bands) that had been the standard for so long.

Even before Leonard opened his famous factory, Charles Orvis had been offering split-bamboo rods on his own. His company thrives even today in Manchester, Vermont where it was founded.

Before the general acceptance of cork, grips of wood or rattan-wrapped wood were standard.

A rattan grip. This type of grip was common before cork became dominant.

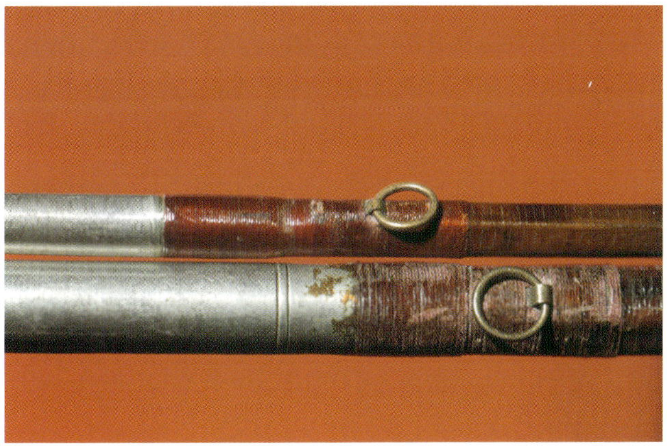

The precursors of today's snake guides – rings attached to the blank with small metal bands.

Initially, the Orvis company became known because of the exceptional quality of its flies – tied by Mary Orvis Marbury. Modern iterations of her many patterns remain in almost every flybox. An example would be the "Royal Coachman," first tied in 1878!

Mary Orvis Marbury soon took over the fly-tying division of Orvis and trained as many as 7 women in this art.

Orvis was the first company to include color pictures of flies in its catalog, making it easier for the customer to select the correct fly.

As Old as the Fishing Rod Itself: The Question of the Right Taper.

D. C. Corkran took over the company in 1938, and soon enticed Wesley Derrel Jordan away from South Bend to join him at Orvis – Jordan, the man who would preside over the production of Orvis' bamboo rods for the next 35 years.
Before he came to Orvis, Wes Jordan helped to establish the reputation of another large manufacturer, Cross Rod and Tackle Co. Working later for South Bend Co., he influenced the design of many of that company's rods. Born in 1894, Jordan worked more than 50 years (1919-1971) in the split-bamboo, rod-making industry. Jordan describes his several ideas for a "proper" rod in the following:

"I have always preferred a rod with a smooth action that works down to within three or four inches of the grip. I think most fisherman also prefer this type of action, judging from the acceptance and popularity of the rods I designed and built at Cross and at South Bend. Rods that work well down into the butt section are more comfortable to cast and provide better line control because the caster can feel what the line is doing all the time. This makes it easier to get the timing right, which is the secret to successful casting.

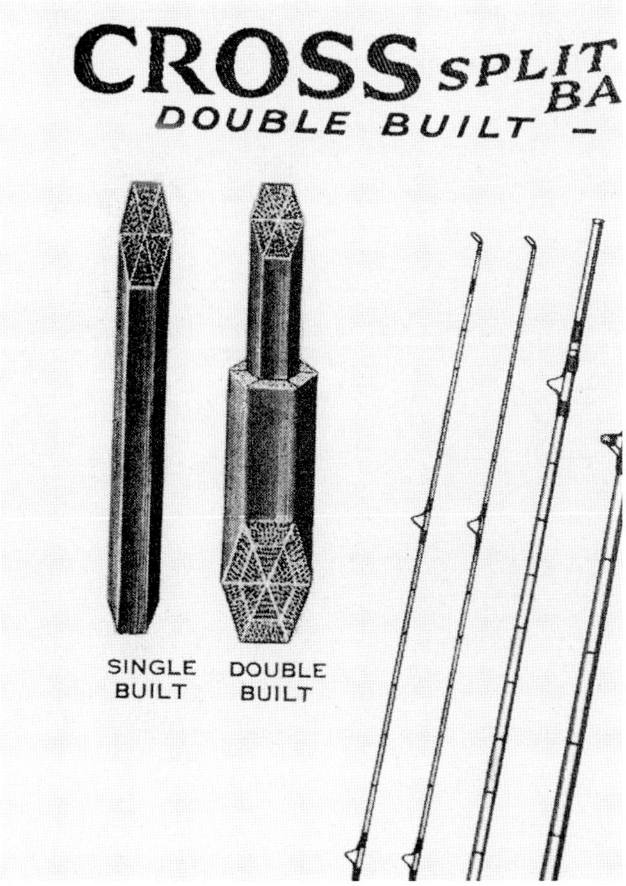

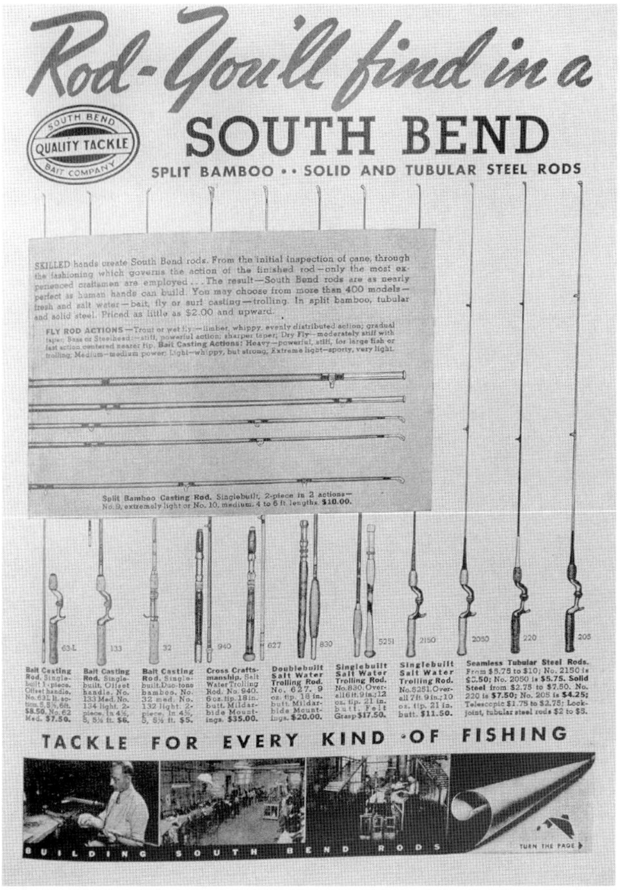

Cross, later South Bend, was a well-known producer of everyday rods. Wes Jordan worked for both firms before moving to Orvis and enhancing its reputation.

"I taught myself to cast. There were no books on casting back when I was learning and I didn't know any of the good fly-fishermen who could help me learn. I was always lucky to have a natural instinct and timing for casting. This was a great help in designing rod tapers because it allowed me to cast any rod and know precisely what changes were needed to make the rod cast better. There is an old maxim that says, all other things being equal, a big man can always cast farther than a smaller man. And I suppose this is basically true. However, Mr. Forsyth was a big man, well over six foot and 200 pounds, and he never could figure out how I could cast farther than him using the same rod. Part of it was timing. The other part, which I didn't realize until years later when I read a description of it in a fishing magazine, was the double haul. I had instinctively started using a single or a double haul to increase distance without ever knowing there was a name for this technique.

"The main reason I'm partial to the full-working style of rods is that they tend to be more durable and hold up under tough fishing conditions. Everywhere I worked I emphasized quality and durability in my rods. I tested every new taper under extreme situations. I always felt if a design had weakness and was going to break it should show up before it left the shop, not after someone bought it and took it fishing.

"Rods with a so-called dry fly action have a stiff butt section and then a relatively flat taper up to within about six inches of the tip where the taper drops very dramatically. These types of rods are the least durable of all. They place far too much stress on certain parts of the rod. Quite a few rods of this style were built by Jim Payne; I think they were designed or at least influenced by Edward Hewitt. I'd hate to tell you how many of these rods I've had in for repair with the top five or six inches just snapped off.

"Another influence on my preference for full-working rods is their improved ability to strike and play fish. These rods provide a cushion effect that protects both the rod and the fine tippets required to catch fish. Also with these rods it is much easier to use larger flies since more of the rod is involved in doing the work. It is like throwing a ball; you can use just the wrist or you can improve you performance by using your entire arm."

Wes Jordan's preferences in rod action produced several outstanding examples, equally well-suited to split-cane, spin/casting rods!

Jordan planed his first rods by hand, but soon developed his own machines to produce bamboo strips (or "splines") faster. Even during his years at Cross (as early as 1924 and 1925), the Cross Company had become famous for high-quality rods, and could produce as many as 60 rods per week. Most were fly rods, but several models were for saltwater fishing. Many of these were produced as rod blanks and made available to various companies such as Abbey & Imbrie, Abercrombie & Fitch, and Edward von Hofe, all in New York.

Wes Jordan was one of the most innovative rod-builders of all time. Among other experiments, he began research into various methods of staining bamboo, one of which ultimately led to his patent for bamboo impregnation (United States Patent Office No. 2,532,814).

In the early 1980s, I met an English colleague, Mike Brooks, at the Dutch "Fly Fair" – then, a playground for professional, European rod-makers. When we found each other two years later at the next Dutch show, he invited me to join him for a little fishing trip in England. In those "early" years, many of the secrets of rod-building were unknown in Europe, and I accepted the invitation, eager to learn more from the English makers, while getting in a little fishing on the island.

In the 1950s, Wes Jordan produced a rod series carrying his own name. His grips were ergonomically shaped.

I set off in my motorhome and arrived safely at my destination in Derbyshire (though I had to drive on the "wrong" side of the road). We fished, first, on a small private stream near the little town of Bakewell and caught a few lovely brown trout. In the evening, our plan was to meet with Tom Moran, but somehow we missed one another. Tom is another rod-builder from the UK – at the time, working occasionally for Partridge of Redditch, but later, joining Thomas & Thomas in the USA. Nevertheless, we had all agreed to meet on the next day to fish the Derbyshire Wye, a beautiful chalk stream. We arrived promptly, only to dawdle-about, awaiting the river keeper who would give us our permits. So of course, there was a lot of shop-talk and discussions of rod-building. I still remember Mike suggesting I visit the Partridge company because they impregnated all their rods. Then, with slight disgust, Moran added at the end, "...but doing that is like pissing in the church." Surely, he meant the process and not the impregnation itself....

In addition to his impregnation patent, we also owe Wes Jordan and his co-workers thanks for the later developments in nickel silver ferrules, and for sizing these in increments of 1/64 inch – still the standard today. We note, too, Jordan's patented, threaded reel seats, developed to assure a solid attachment for the reel. These, as well as his special, grip-shape (with a cutout for the thumb) are only a few examples of his searching mind.

Shortly after Wes Jordan joined South Bend, he made the acquaintance of Paul Young (Detroit, Michigan), for in its early years, the Paul H. Young Rod Company bought most of its blanks from South Bend, finishing them with Young's own hardware and wrappings. Wes and Paul became good friends in the years following 1928 and helped each other a great deal. The rod-building master offered immeasurable support when Young decided to make rod-building a part of his new company. Paul, in return, had become a superb fly-tier, and introduced Wes to the secrets of nymph fishing on Michigan's storied Au Sable River.

As Wes Jordan once said, he was not ashamed of the many fine, utility rods produced by Cross and South Bend. With regard to accessories and finish, however, their rods were never the equal of those built by H. L. Leonard – nor those built by Leonard's many famous workers who, later, established their own companies.

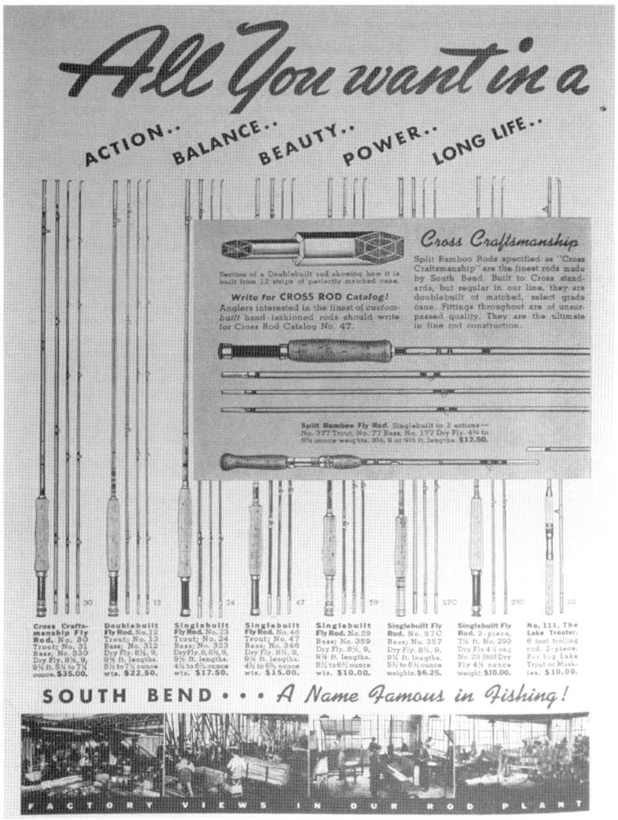

South Bend produced a very wide range of rods, also supplying un-branded versions to other companies.

Charles F. Orvis died in 1915, and his sons, Robert and Albert, took over the company – although with very different aims and interests.

The stock market crash of 1929 led many companies into bankruptcy, and those that survived, suffered badly during the subsequent, Depression years. Once-prosperous companies lost everything between one day and the next, and even Orvis bottomed-out financially in 1939, retaining only two employees.
There was essentially no income, production was limited to fly-tying, and the company belonged to the bank.
It was Dudley C. Corkran, however, who wanted to preserve this tradition-rich company, so he found a few investors on the East Coast and bought the company from the bank for $4500.

At that point, Orvis badly needed a rod-maker who could build production up again, and found that man in Wes Jordan – whose good reputation preceded him. But his first impressions at Orvis must have been horrible. A thick layer of dust coated the workshop, and the milling machine was disassembled into parts. It took a week to rebuild the mill and get it running properly, but finally production could start again. To his credit, Corkran must have been a good businessman because, by 1942, Orvis was firmly back in the game, already employing seven workers. And thanks to the contributions of Jordan, the company reestablished its strong reputation for bamboo rods. A tradition was saved.

In their best times, Orvis produced the astonishing number of 15,000 bamboo rods annually – an average of 41 rods per day!

The most famous series, the "Battenkill" (named for the river flowing through Manchester), was produced for line weights of 6 through 9, and a few 3-piece versions were developed as travel rods. Among other rods produced later, were the Orvis "Flea," Orvis "Nymph," and the "Limestone Special," most of these in various lengths and line weights – and, of course, there was the famous "Wes Jordan" series.

An Orvis rod from the famous, impregnated "Battenkill" series.

A commemorative rod given by Orvis to the American Museum of Fly Fishing on the occasion of its 25th anniversary.

In comparison to America, little is known about individual rod-builders in England, as these were all employed by such larger companies as Hardy, Allcock or Farlow.
S. Allcock and Company, Ltd., Redditch, represented itself in catalogs as being, "The world's largest and oldest fishing tackle manufacturer." A purely production and wholesale company, Allcock delivered only to retailers, later founding subsidiaries in Paris and Maçon, France.
Other English companies producing high-quality rods were John Forrest in Kelso-on-Tweed, Westley Richards in Birmingham, Walker Falcon in Redditch, Farlow in London, and J. S. Sharpe in Aberdeen, to mention only a few.

A Great Tradition Begins and Continues to Today

William Hardy founded his famous company in 1872 on Paikes Street in Alnwick, Northumbria. The Hardy family had always enjoyed a tradition of sporting activities, so it was only a question of time until they became professionally involved in the production of rods. But, because several family members were already proficient in metal-working, Hardy's long history actually began as a producer of rifles .
Unfortunately (or perhaps fortunately, from the fisherman's point of view), gun production in those years was dominated by the larger companies in London. The market for a small, local, firearms-producer was limited, so Hardy soon turned its attention fully to the production of fishing equipment.

During the 1880s, sport-fishing became popular everywhere in England, and Hardy was to benefit from this new trend as well. Shortly after William founded Hardy, his brother, John James, joined the company and the new venture soon became well-established. Although American rods had grown in popularity in the UK, Hardy worked to re-claim England's earlier position of dominance by offering its own, full line of rods.

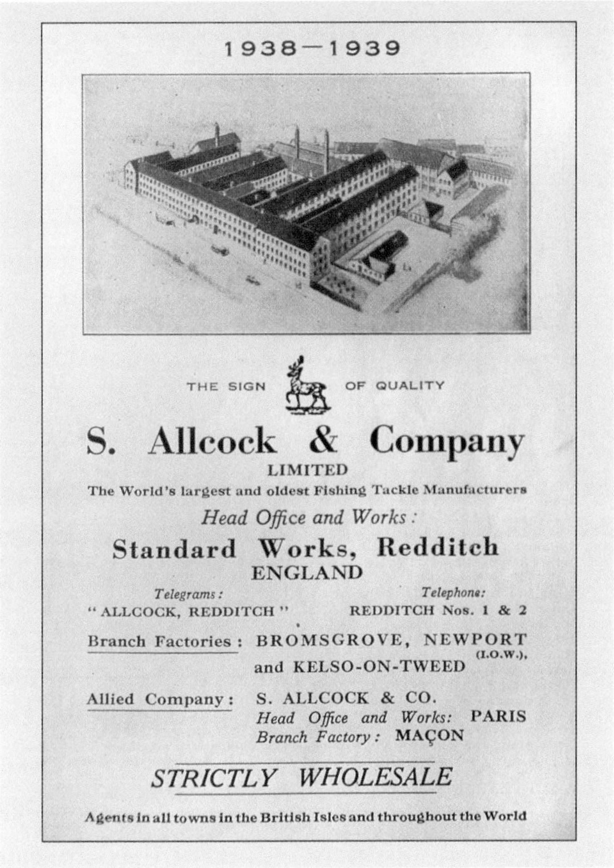

Almost forgotten today, the Allcock company in England made top-quality tackle, but only for the wholesale market.

In 1883-1885, Hardy mounted an impressive display for the great, London, fishing exhibition, eager to demonstrate to the world what the company had achieved. Evidently, their efforts were met with great success, for Hardy took several medals and received large numbers of orders.
Much of their success was due to the fact that J. J. Hardy was a very good tournament caster. His expertise was applied to the company's products, and the many resulting ideas and patents clearly showed Hardy's innovative strength. In the beginning, the company concentrated on rod-production, although Hardy is perhaps best known today for their excellent reels.

Members of the Hardy dynasty in 1908.

Then as today, Hardy produces "By Appointment to the King" (or Queen).

In 1911, Hardy introduced the new "C.C. de France" rod which, at 2 3/4 ounces (in its 7-foot version), was said to be the lightest rod in the world. This was contested abroad, however, because of the competitive battle between the American companies, Leonard and Payne. In any case, Hardy had become the undisputed leader in England, leaving all other companies (Allcock, Farlow and others) behind. One factor accounting for Hardy's dominance in England was its strong emphasis on the quality of the products. I'm unable to say if the story is true, but a tale, still circulated at Hardy, is that, during the days of L. R. H. Hardy in the 1930s, a retired employee was told to check the products at several work stations during lunchtime, when the workers would be away. The man was instructed to carry a hammer and immediately to destroy every piece that showed a fault. We don't know if the cost for these pieces was to be deducted from the workers' salaries, but unfortunately, it seems probable.

About Casting Distance

I can't explain it rationally, but I take great pleasure whenever I'm able to surprise my friends.

For many years, I've driven to Denmark's eastern coast to catch sea-run, brown trout (or other fish), and for a very long time, I was the sole, upright citizen fishing exclusively with a fly. That is, until the time I couldn't fish for almost a week because of a strong, onshore wind. Gritting my teeth, I tried and tried, but each time, the fly would stick in the beach behind me. With my irritation growing ever more apparent, I asked a friend for his spin/casting rod – which he gave to me along with an astonished look. Of course, everyone had to make great fun of me, each having a sarcastic remark to offer. I took careful note of all this and swore I'd get my revenge. But, the only problem was – how? With thoughts kept to myself, fishing against that strong wind made me ponder how to build a bamboo spin/casting rod when I returned home. It needed to be about 8 feet long, but I had no idea how to calculate its action or casting weight. So, I found an old reel and fastened it with rubber bands to a cheap, 8/9-weight rod from England. The result was surprising. The old rod flexed elegantly and delivered a 1/2-ounce lure an impressive distance. I thought, "This would be a good start for my first spin/casting rod," and began to measure the old piece. The next step was simply to build it, and then to get help from some old, English catalogs to determine the design and size of the grip, reel seat, and guides. When finished, my first practice-casts on the grass made me think, even then, "Now there's a pretty good shot...!"

But soon, my new project disappeared into a dusty corner of my workshop – that is, until the rod came back to mind while packing for my next trip to Denmark. Back at the shore, we were the same "team" once again, and once again, we distributed ourselves along the beach. As was often the case when we fished together, my friends made cast after cast with their spin/casters, meeting with only modest success. At some point, I grabbed my "new" project and made a cast as well, but not without a great deal of razzing about my ancient, Swedish casting reel. I chose to ignore the abuse and continued fishing – but like my companions, making cast after cast without success. Suddenly, I noticed! My lure was flying far greater distances than those of my companions!

The next day we tested all this on the beach, making elaborate comparisons with just one reel and one lure. Sure enough, my split-bamboo rod cast much farther – in some cases, up to 65 feet more. After that, there were no more remarks about my "old stuff." Now, I was a hero: I was rehabilitated and I had my revenge.

Even through I arrived at the dimensions for my rod through lucky coincidence, apparently, it's the "mass" of a split-cane, spin/casting rod that's responsible for such great acceleration potential. But these rods don't respond like a graphite rod, and they require a different casting technique. The split-cane rod must be accelerated more slowly, and its trajectory needs to be aimed higher than when using the modern, synthetic rod. Additionally, the cane rod should be brought to a sharp "stop" just as the line is released. The rod is now loaded deeply into its grip, and the sudden release of energy provides the great casting distance.

Since then, my spin-fishing equipment has won many a bet on distance-casting. I did lose one wager against an Irishman, however. This fellow maintained he could throw his 7 1/2-foot rod 130 feet. Then he grabbed his rod, with its grip facing forward, and in the style of a javelin-thrower, he chucked it as truly as he promised. In the pub that evening, I happily paid my friend, if only because the other "secrets" he revealed were indeed valuable.

Working Conditions a Century Ago

Individual workshops at Hardy's; ca. 1900. Some machinery was in use, but much still needed to be done by hand.

Hardy's fishing gear became so famous in Europe that, not only did the company attain the coveted, "By Appointment to the Queen," but also received orders from royalty abroad, such as the German Kaiser and the King of Belgium.

Reportedly, however, Hardy was unhappy about one order it received from Queen Mary. The Queen had built a giant doll house in Windsor Castle, with the dolls in each room of this miniature building displaying a different theme. To represent the "fishing" theme, Hardy was commissioned to make a scaled-down, miniature, salmon rod about 10 inches long. I don't think I would have wanted to hear what the workers muttered as they turned the ferrules for this three-piece rod!

Of all the many rods developed by Hardy (beyond the excellent salmon fishing gear), their "light" models, in particular, stand out. Examples are the previously mentioned "C. C. de France" series (offered in 7, 8, and 9-foot lengths and named for the famous Casting Club of France), as well as the Hardy "Marvel," made only in a 7 1/2-foot length. The 2 3/4 ounce weight of this rod was achieved only because it was built hollow.

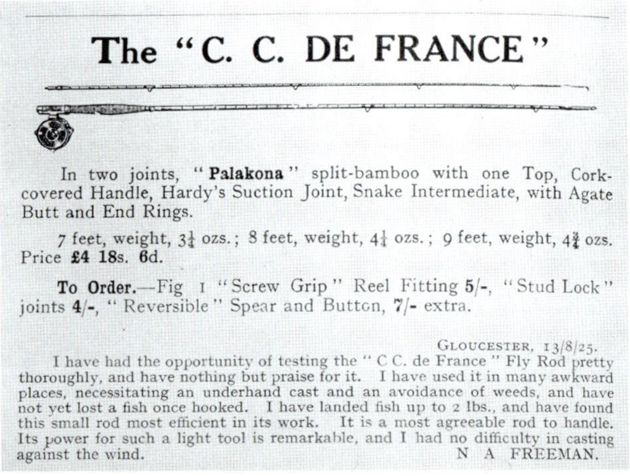

The "C. C. DE FRANCE"

In two joints, "**Palakona**" split-bamboo with one Top, Cork-covered Handle, Hardy's Suction Joint, Snake Intermediate, with Agate Butt and End Rings.

7 feet, weight, 3¼ ozs.; 8 feet, weight, 4¼ ozs.; 9 feet, weight, 4¾ ozs. Price **£4 18**s. **6**d.

To Order.—Fig I "Screw Grip" Reel Fitting **5**/-, "Stud Lock" joints **4**/-, "Reversible" Spear and Button, **7**/- extra.

GLOUCESTER, 13/8/25.

I have had the opportunity of testing the "C C. de France" Fly Rod pretty thoroughly, and have nothing but praise for it. I have used it in many awkward places, necessitating an underhand cast and an avoidance of weeds, and have not yet lost a fish once hooked. I have landed fish up to 2 lbs., and have found this small rod most efficient in its work. It is a most agreeable rod to handle. Its power for such a light tool is remarkable, and I had no difficulty in casting against the wind. N A FREEMAN.

The C. C. de France announcement in the Hardy catalog of 1927.

In good company: A Hardy "Marvel" and two "C. C. de France" rods, all with serial numbers from the 1950s.

A Vast Number of Models

Hardy's 1956/57 catalog describes 40 different models in various lengths (including spin/casting rods)! This means that more than 160 different rod models were made from bamboo. Hardy's production of bamboo rod models ended in the 1970s, and at once, all existing rods became collector's items to be sold for very high prices. The continuing requests for bamboo, coming from customers around the world, however, led to resumed production in the 1990s. After a bit of a wait, even today, one can have a new, Hardy, split-bamboo rod.

Hardy's production is a good example of developments throughout the "Old World." This company has received numerous prizes and awards throughout its history, and there's good reason for Hardy to remain proud of producing "By Appointment."

It is hard to explain why, at the turn of the Twentieth Century, American rods were dismissed by the English market as being "cheap." It's true, one notable source rightly denigrated certain, low-quality, American rods coming onto the market in England, but this opinion was then used to downgrade all American rods in general. In 1892, the Military Equipment Stores and Tortoise Tents Co., Ltd. in London (49, Pall Mall, S. W.) spoke venomously about rods from the "New World," saying:

"It should be remembered that Hardy's rods have proved to be the best, and won the Gold Medal in 1883 ... As has been pointed out there are firms who are buying cheap American Rods, and offering them as English make, guaranteed to stand two years, &c., &c., and we caution unwary buyers against them.... Remember that Hardy's is the only make of any value, and the name of Hardy Brothers is security for the quality."

Additional assertions that Hardy's rods are the best in the world are given elsewhere:

"The reason is very simple. In the first place, 15-16ths of all the rods offered are either factory-made or imported, and there is not that careful detail given to construction which is so necessary, the goods being made to price without attention to quality, and naturally very different to their production.... Bamboos may be had in almost any quality, but they have, after trying almost every district and many samples sent them by the Indian Forestry Department, found that there is one particular district which produced canes of a quality superior to all others. This cane they now use exclusively, and have appointed agents on the spot, who buy up all the choicest, and have them seasoned under their instruction - not burned until the fibre is destroyed as is usually the case - but properly oiled, fired and seasoned in a special manner.... This then, is the secret of the great spring, toughness and durability of these rods."

Cited as evidence of the low quality of American rods, were a number of letters to the editor in *The Field*, a well-known hunting and fishing magazine – letters which report breakage or complain of barely-used rods falling apart after standing in the rain.

But, even admitting to the high quality of English rods in those days (evidenced by the many outstanding examples still in existence), the many complaints about American rods probably weren't based solely on differences in quality. The alarm about American rods must have had other causes, perhaps grounded in the very different fishing styles between the Brits and the Yanks.

Preferred fly-fishing practices in England usually involved broad and slow water and casting wet flies with long rods – the line often being returned upstream with a roll-cast. During this same era in the States, however, dry-fly fishing on the smaller and faster East Coast streams had gained rapid popularity. For "dries," different rods were necessary! They had to be shorter and faster than wet-fly rods, and "false-casting" became the order of the day – both to shake water from the fly and to deliver line by "shooting" it. In addition, rod-makers were asked to produce lighter blanks. By 1900, the average length of a rod in England was still 10-14 feet (for trout models), while the "standard" length in the USA had been reduced to 9 feet.

Once, when I tried casting a 6-weight, 10-foot Hardy rod from this period, the weight of the rod and its flexing were so great that I had difficulty staying on my feet during the back-cast.
Just as did Farlow, Hardy, too, first presented hexagonal rods at an 1883 international fishing show. The initial response was very modest, and not until the end of the 1890s would the hexagonal, split-bamboo rods became dominant. Despite the eventual success of six-strip bamboo, rods made of wood continued to be shown in many catalogs.

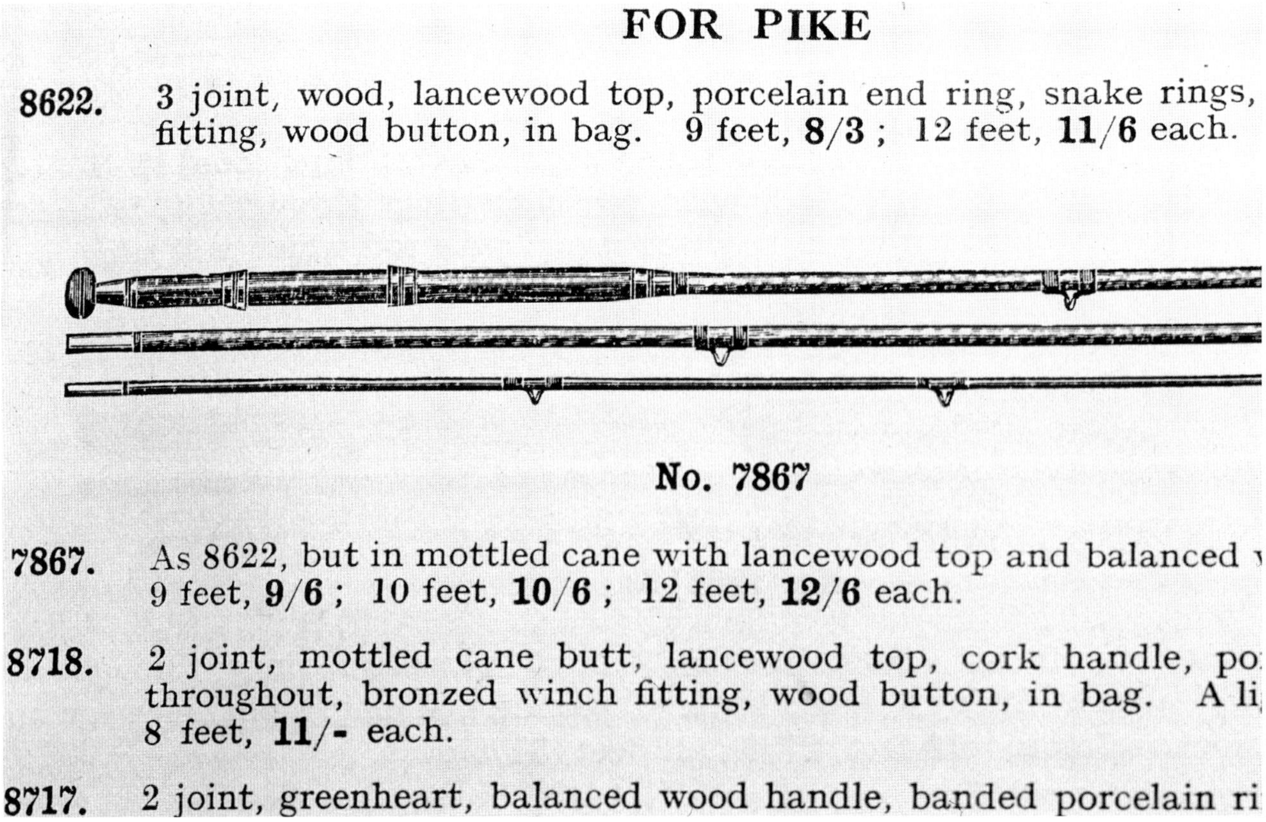

FOR PIKE

8622. 3 joint, wood, lancewood top, porcelain end ring, snake rings, fitting, wood button, in bag. 9 feet, **8/3** ; 12 feet, **11/6** each.

No. 7867

7867. As 8622, but in mottled cane with lancewood top and balanced
9 feet, **9/6** ; 10 feet, **10/6** ; 12 feet, **12/6** each.

8718. 2 joint, mottled cane butt, lancewood top, cork handle, po
throughout, bronzed winch fitting, wood button, in bag. A li
8 feet, **11/-** each.

8717. 2 joint, greenheart, balanced wood handle, banded porcelain ri

Wooden fishing rods were made in England even into the 1940s. They were simply cheaper to produce and cost the customer less than a split-bamboo rod.

Hexagonal Is Ugly

At first, the public found the "hexagonals" quite ugly, because, according to tradition, a rod should be round. Consequently, many hexagonal rods continued to be sanded round, although the practice was abandoned once makers discovered that rounding ruined the rod's action.

From our modern point of view, the general weak-point and disadvantage of split-bamboo rods during the early years was the inferior quality of glue (hide-glue, essentially, from rabbit, fish, etc.). Problems of delamination were rampant, but a number of ideas emerged to hold the strips together more permanently. One extreme measure was to wrap a rod with silk from butt to tip and then varnish, or to apply a more open, spiral-wrapped thread along the blank. One can easily imagine how heavy these treatments would cause a rod to be. Soon, so-called "intermediate wraps," spaced one inch apart, became the standard. Even when improved glues appeared, however, many English companies continued to use intermediate wraps – though apparently only for decorative and nostalgic reasons. The fashion continued even into the 1950s, while American rod-builders, long-since, had abandoned such embellishments to save weight.

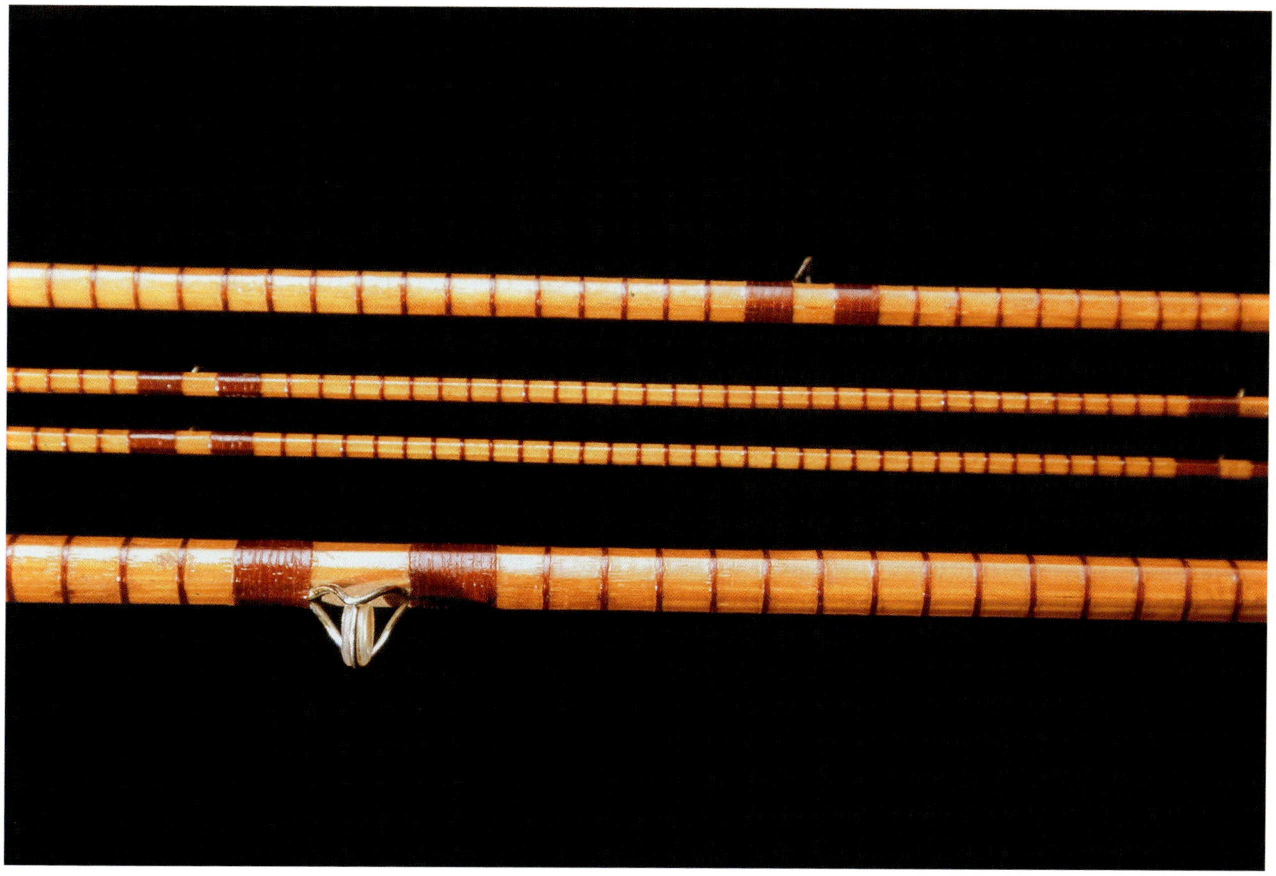

Very closely-spaced, intermediate wraps on a well-preserved German rod from 1910.

The development of ferrules became yet another great difference between English and American rod-makers.
Before the first metal ferrules were developed, separate rod pieces were simply tied together, either with strips of leather or a strong linen thread – the joined surfaces having been planed to matching angles.

A typical "pin" ferrule on an old Hildebrand rod from Germany.

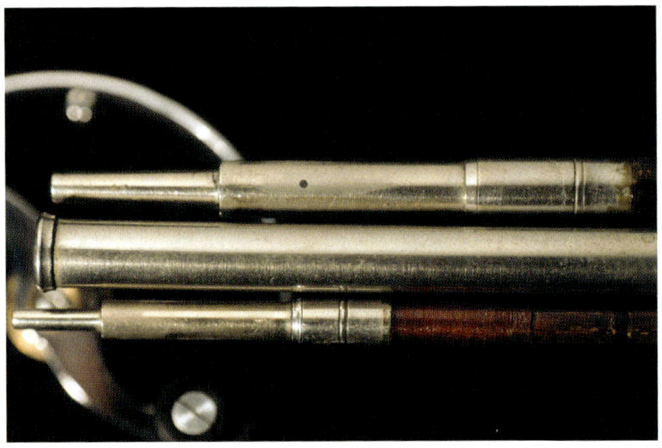

For comparison, an American Leonard rod with pin ferrules.

The earliest ferrules were made out of rolled and soldered metal strips, and were called "dowel" or "pin" ferrules.
At first, copper or brass was the preferred material, but soon, nickel-silver (or "German silver") was considered the ideal choice. This alloy is actually composed of copper, nickel, tin, and a small amount of lead, but it has remained, ever since, the favorite choice for ferrules on split-bamboo rods. The alloy was first produced in German factories, and rods fitted with "German silver" ferrules became known in the USA after about 1850. At first, these were just simple tubes without a bottom to protect the bamboo, but that deficiency soon became apparent when the bamboo ends within the ferrule began to rot from exposure to moisture.

Hiram Leonard was the first to register a patent for a waterproof ferrule in 1875, and in 1890, a certain George Varney (working for Leonard) announced his patent for a "lamellar" ferrule, featuring an end that was slotted and thinly tapered. It would still be a long time before the modern, "suction" ferrule appeared, and although America had already developed relatively light ferrules, back in England, these remained both heavy and complicated.

Heavy Ferrules – Much Weight

Rods built in the "Old World" frequently had ferrules with threaded closures and complicated overhangs. In addition to excessive weight, such ferrules became stuck very easily. Depending on the alloy, nickel silver can easily oxidize, and twisting the threaded ferrules often leads to "overturning," that is, damage caused by forcing the corroded threads. But still greater damage occurred if the forcing were to break the bamboo just where it enters the stuck ferrule. Both threaded ferrules ("Lockfast Joints") and those that snapped together with a spring-loaded knob ("Studlock Joints") remained in Hardy's catalog of 1957, but these were also offered alongside the lightweight, suction-fit ferrules.

To compensate for the extra weight of these ferrules, English rods had to be designed with a somewhat stronger taper, thus rendering them heavier than American rods of comparable length and line weight. It wasn't until after the Second World War that a new ferrule (called the "Swiss-type," though probably developed in Bavaria or Austria) became the standard of the industry. Available references on its actual origin are ambiguous.

In America, Luis Feierabend became the man responsible for the "Super-Z" version of the original "Swiss-type." His design remains, to this day, as the standard for nearly all first-rate rods. Feierabend had been an engineer for most of his working life, and his ferrule was patented in 1952. He lost his job during the Second World War, and subsequently opened a small fishing store, Rockland Tackle Co., in Hillburn, New York. Through his store, he regularly came into contact with great numbers of anglers, including a few local, rodmakers. In the years following the war, he came to work briefly with Nat Uslan – the maker known for his pentagonal rods. Later still, Feierabend is thought to have worked for Jim Payne.

With the appearance of fiberglass rods, Feierabend recognized that the standard ferrules of the day (constructed with inside-diameters of different sizes for the female and male parts) wouldn't fit on fiberglass rods. The glass rods were built with identical diameters at the join of the butt and tip, and needed a similar ferrule.

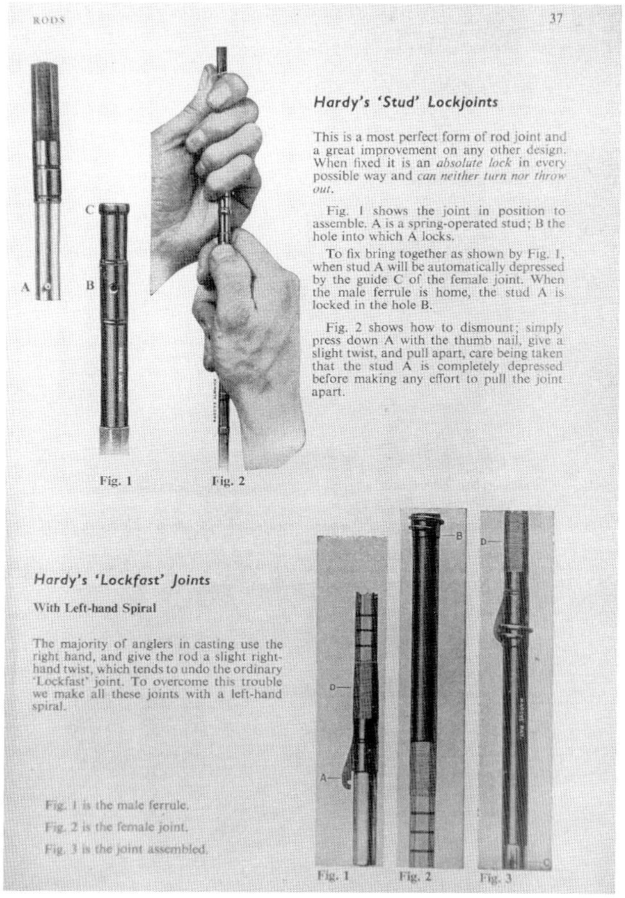
RODS 37

Hardy's 'Stud' Lockjoints

This is a most perfect form of rod joint and a great improvement on any other design. When fixed it is an *absolute lock* in every possible way and *can neither turn nor throw out.*

Fig. 1 shows the joint in position to assemble. A is a spring-operated stud; B the hole into which A locks.

To fix bring together as shown by Fig. 1, when stud A will be automatically depressed by the guide C of the female joint. When the male ferrule is home, the stud A is locked in the hole B.

Fig. 2 shows how to dismount; simply press down A with the thumb nail, give a slight twist, and pull apart, care being taken that the stud A is completely depressed before making any effort to pull the joint apart.

Fig. 1 Fig. 2

Hardy's 'Lockfast' Joints

With Left-hand Spiral

The majority of anglers in casting use the right hand, and give the rod a slight right-hand twist, which tends to undo the ordinary 'Lockfast' joint. To overcome this trouble we make all these joints with a left-hand spiral.

Fig. 1 is the male ferrule.
Fig. 2 is the female joint.
Fig. 3 is the joint assembled.

Fig. 1 Fig. 2 Fig. 3

Hardy used complicated, heavy ferrules even as late as the 1950s.

Just one of the advantages of the new "Super-Z" was that its internal diameters would mate the sections of a fiberglass rod perfectly (see drawing). U. S. Patent number 2,600,629 was registered on June 17, 1952, and manufacturing began at the Super Z Manufacturing Co. in Pearl River, New York.

The other strengths of this ferrule were instantly recognized by Garrison, whose shop was across the Hudson River, and from then on, Garrison used the "Super-Z" on all his rods. Other rod-makers drawn to these new ferrules were "Pinky" Gillum, Paul Young, and Orvis (used mostly on their "Model 99" and "Wes Jordan" models). The ferrule-making business was not large enough to provide much of a living, however, so Luis Feierabend eventually sold his patent and moved to Colorado to work for IBM.

The patent was bought by the Conolon Company, with the intention to mass-produce ferrules. This new company failed to obtain the exact tolerances needed, however, just as did Garcia, buying the company later. The third company to buy the patent was Rodon, who had the good sense to make their ferrules such that its final fit would be provided by the purchaser. Most ferrules are made in a similar manner to this day, though Rodon has since been purchased by the Cortland Line Co.

A present-day set of "Super-Z" ferrules for a three-piece rod with two tips.

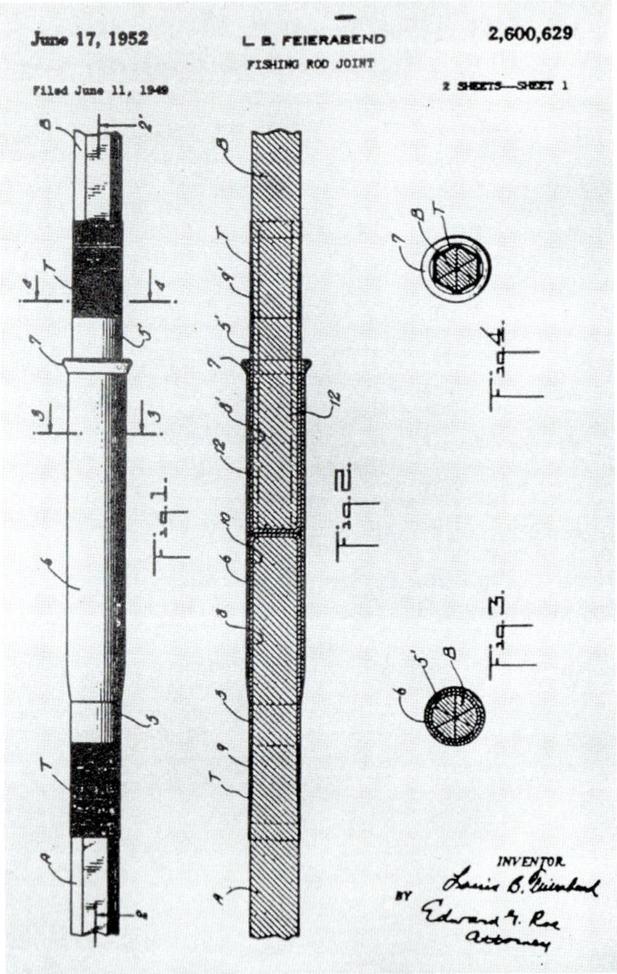

The patent drawing for the "Super-Z" ferrule, as invented by Luis Feierabend.

An American Legend

Hiram Lewis Leonard. Hardly another company influenced rod-building so extensively.

The art of American rod-building could not have developed without Hiram Lewis Leonard, whose name continues to stand for the beginning of the modern, bamboo, fishing rod. Born in 1833 in Maine, Leonard's early work was with metal, but he was also a furniture maker, and from this experience, he learned most of the needed wood-working techniques. His career as rod builder began in 1871 in Bangor. An enthusiastic fisherman, he first built rods for himself, tested them on the rivers in his immediate area, and continued with improvements until he became satisfied with the results. Leonard, too, began his rod-making with woods of various sorts. Even those first rods must have been successful, however, because friends took notice and showed them to the famous sporting goods store, Bradford & Anthony, in Boston.

This company began to market his products and encouraged him to develop rods of bamboo – the first of which were four-sided.

Apparently, not only did Leonard have the ability to apply practical fishing experience to his rod-making, but he was also able to communicate these ideas to others and make his concepts understandable. There must have been large numbers of sympathetic fisherman in Bangor because, within a short period of time, several young people came to work at Leonard's shop, producing rods under his direction and control.

In later years, each of these would become a famous rod-maker – with names like Edward Payne, Eustis Edwards, Thomas Chubb, Fred Thomas, and the Hawes brothers. Although Ernest Schweibert maintains, in his reference book, *Trout*, that Fred Divine also was part of this team, this appears to be very unlikely. As Michael Sinclair discovered in his research on Divine, the announcement of Fred D. Divine's own rod-making and tackle company (Utica, New York) appeared as early as 1882.

Family-like conditions must have characterized Leonard's company, and some historians rumor that it was important to be able to play a musical instrument to work there. It's been said that, during breaks and after work, the staff would sit together and play music. I'd give a lot to hear a tape of this band with such star players....

A Leonard rod made before 1900.

The Leonard logo on a reelseat butt cap – ca. 1925...

...and the still-fishable rod it belongs to.

After a short period, however, economic conditions and the need to find a better market forced the company to move to the New York area, and the "star team" soon fell apart. Leonard formed a partnership with William Mills & Son, and in 1881, moved to Central Valley, New York. Most of its best makers left the company before 1900, but despite this, Leonard continued to build excellent rods. When looking into the literature, we learn that nearly everything concerning high-quality, American rod-making began at this time, and almost all the leading makers were once with Leonard.

When Hiram Leonard died in 1907, his son, Reuben, took over the business. Upon his death, Reuben was succeeded by the general manager, Reynolds. He ultimately retired in the 1960s, however, when a terrible fire nearly wiped out the entire company, severely damaging the famous Leonard machines that prepared bamboo strips. In today's collectors' catalogs, Leonard rods are frequently described as being built "pre" or "post" fire.

During Reuben Leonard's era, most rods were built in three-pieces and were 8 or 9 feet long, although some shorter and very light versions were produced after 1914. The best-known rod, both before and after the Second World War, was the "50DF," with the "Catskill" series becoming popular when lighter and shorter rods grew fashionable. Additional models built before the fire, such as the "Letort," "Ausable," "Miramichi," and the impregnated "Duracane," came in various lengths and editions and found favor with fly-fishermen throughout the world. Famous models built after the fire were the "37," "38," "38 ½," "50 ½," "65," and "66." Many collectors maintain that the rods built before the fire were of higher quality, and today's prices seem to reflect that belief.

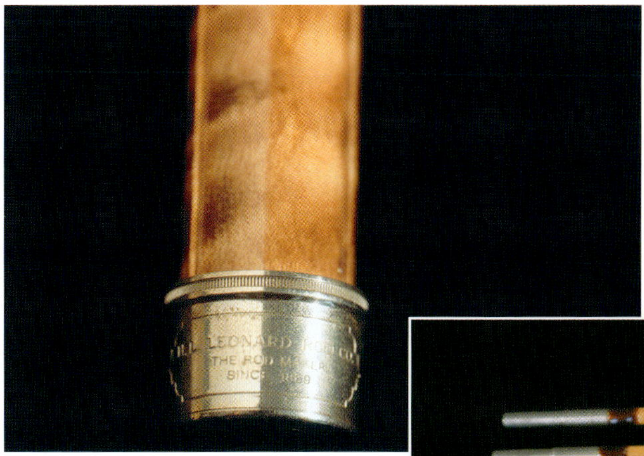

The later Leonard logo: A little more modern, but still traditional.

A legend: A Model 39 from the "Ausable" series, built in the early 1970s.

An Englishman Fishes with American Rods!

It's said that the famous English author and fly-fisherman, G. E. M. Skues, fished for half his career with a Leonard rod, despite the best English rods that were available to him. Understandably, this must have been very disappointing for English rod-makers, and when Dermot Williams once asked Skues about this while fishing, he answered, "Oh yes, that has irritated them very much."

Leonard catalog covers from 1974 and 1976. Today, these are rare collectors pieces.

Skues received his first 10-foot Leonard from Walter Durfee Coggeshall in 1903. The rod must have pleased him greatly because, in 1904, Skues quickly ordered a shorter version. The shorter rod would allow him to cast comfortably and slowly without drying the small nymphs he preferred, a method explained more exactly in his book, *Nymph Fishing for Chalk Stream Trout*.

An uncommon picture today. Five, different, Leonard rods – all from the 1970s and 1980s, including Models 37, 38, and 39 from the "Ausable" and "Hunt" series.

A Marriage of Giants

Thomas Chubb opened his own company in Vermont, while at nearly the same time, Thomas, Edwards, and Payne left Leonard to found "Kosmic" – one of the most legendary, if short-lived companies. In 1890, these three men began to design very modern rods (even by today's standards) under this new name. Some notable characteristics were the new ferrule design and the very narrow cork rings on the grips. Unfortunately, cooperation between these three greats lasted only about 3 years. Today, only a very few of their products survive, and when sold, go for very high prices.

After leaving Kosmic, Edward Payne (together with Frank Oram, a foreman with Leonard), opened his own business only a few miles distant from Leonard in Highland Mills. Their first rods were so good that they won the gold medal in Chicago in 1893. This is all the more surprising when we consider that Payne had been responsible only for making ferrules while with Leonard. When E. W. Payne died shortly after the First World War, the company went to his son, James, who had worked in his father's workshop since childhood.

With the exception of the period during World War Two, Jim Payne worked his entire life on split bamboo rods – so loved for their design and workmanship that even during his career, the used market brought prices nearly equal to his new rods. When Jim Payne died in 1970, many people tried to hoard the remaining rods at Abercrombie & Fitch – they had risen so in value. Surely, the discussion will continue as to whether his rods or those of Everett Garrison were the best ever built.

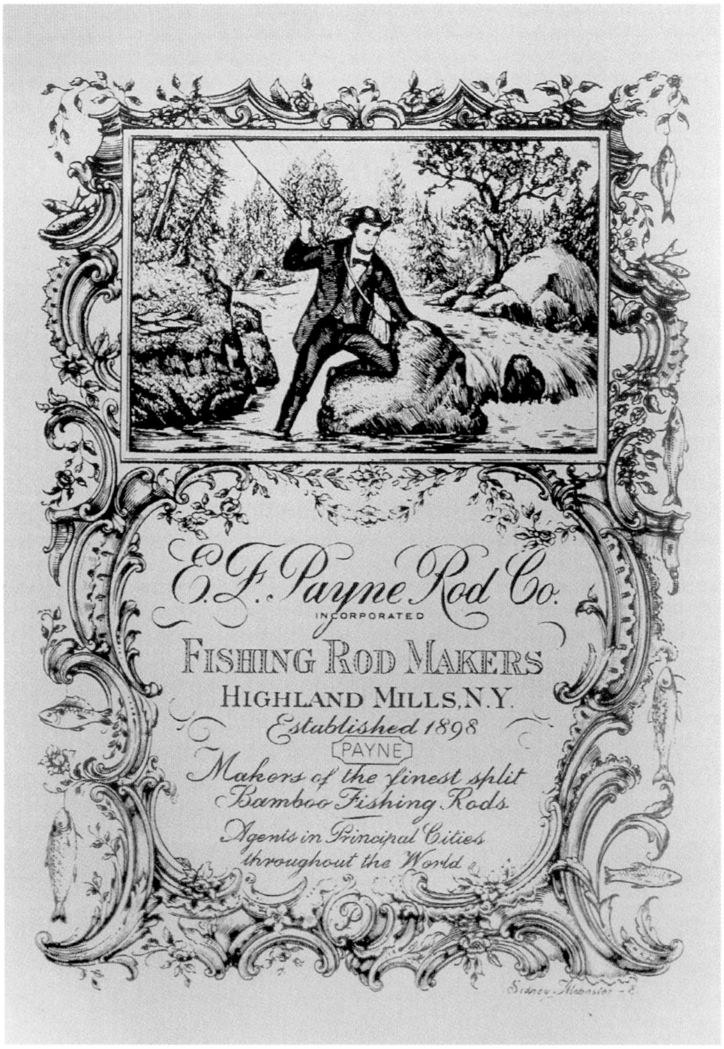

The cover of a Payne catalog. The company was founded in 1898 and located only a few miles from the Leonard workshops.

Lightweights

The elder Payne made relatively heavy rods in two and three-pieces, some flamed quite dark, and with agate stripping and tip-top guides. The younger Payne changed the tapers completely and included some relatively short rods in his product-line (a 7-foot rod in 3-pieces, and a number of 7 1/2-footers) that were particularly light in weight. After 1916, he experimented with high temperatures to temper the bamboo and produce a darker color. After perfecting the process, he offered both dark and light-colored rods, with the darker ones costing 20% more. The light-colored rods were discontinued in the mid-1930s, and only rods with the incomparable, medium-brown shade were offered. These were the models responsible for the Payne Rod Company's fame.

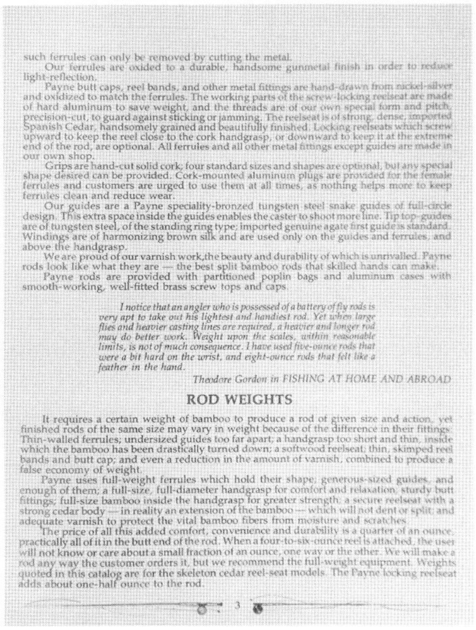

such ferrules can only be removed by cutting the metal.

Our ferrules are oxided to a durable, handsome gunmetal finish in order to reduce light-reflection.

Payne butt caps, reel bands, and other metal fittings are hand-drawn from nickel-silver and oxidized to match the ferrules. The working parts of the screw-locking reelseat are made of hard aluminum to save weight, and the threads are of our own special form and pitch, precision-cut, to guard against sticking or jamming. The reelseat is of strong, dense, imported Spanish Cedar, handsomely grained and beautifully finished. Locking reelseats which screw upward to keep the reel close to the cork handgrasp, or downward to keep it at the extreme end of the rod, are optional. All ferrules and all other metal fittings except guides are made in our own shop.

Grips are hand-cut solid cork; four standard sizes and shapes are optional, but any special shape desired can be provided. Cork-mounted aluminum plugs are provided for the female ferrules and customers are urged to use them at all times, as nothing helps more to keep ferrules clean and reduce wear.

Our guides are a Payne speciality-bronzed tungsten steel snake guides of full-circle design. This extra space inside the guides enables the caster to shoot more line. Tip top-guides are of tungsten steel, of the standing ring type; imported genuine agate first guide is standard. Windings are of harmonizing brown silk and are used only on the guides and ferrules, and above the handgrasp.

We are proud of our varnish work,the beauty and durability of which is unrivalled. Payne rods look like what they are — the best split bamboo rods that skilled hands can make.

Payne rods are provided with partitioned poplin bags and aluminum cases with smooth-working, well-fitted brass screw tops and caps.

I notice that an angler who is possessed of a battery of fly rods is very apt to take out his lightest and handiest rod. Yet when large flies and heavier casting lines are required, a heavier and longer rod may do better work. Weight upon the scales, within reasonable limits, is not of much consequence. I have used five-ounce rods that were a bit hard on the wrist, and eight-ounce rods that felt like a feather in the hand.

Theodore Gordon in FISHING AT HOME AND ABROAD

ROD WEIGHTS

It requires a certain weight of bamboo to produce a rod of given size and action, yet finished rods of the same size may vary in weight because of the difference in their fittings. Thin-walled ferrules; undersized guides too far apart; a handgrasp too short and thin, inside which the bamboo has been drastically turned down; a softwood reelseat; thin, skimped reel bands and butt cap; and even a reduction in the amount of varnish, combined to produce a false economy of weight.

Payne uses full-weight ferrules which hold their shape; generous-sized guides, and enough of them; a full-size, full-diameter handgrasp for comfort and relaxation; sturdy butt fittings; full-size bamboo inside the handgrasp for greater strength; a secure reelseat with a strong cedar body — in reality an extension of the bamboo — which will not dent or split; and adequate varnish to protect the vital bamboo fibers from moisture and scratches.

The price of all this added comfort, convenience and durability is a quarter of an ounce, practically all of it in the butt end of the rod. When a four-to-six-ounce reel is attached, the user will not know or care about a small fraction of an ounce, one way or the other. We will make a rod any way the customer orders it, but we recommend the full-weight equipment. Weights quoted in this catalog are for the skeleton cedar reel-seat models. The Payne locking reelseat adds about one-half ounce to the rod.

3

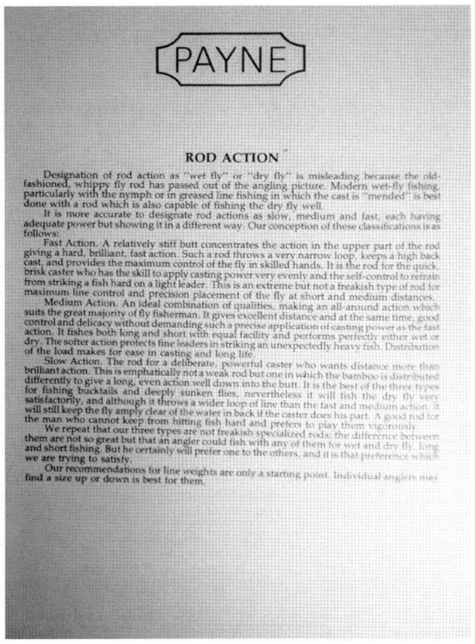

PAYNE

ROD ACTION

Designation of rod action as "wet fly" or "dry fly" is misleading because the old-fashioned, whippy fly rod has passed out of the angling picture. Modern wet-fly fishing, particularly with the nymph or in greased line fishing in which the cast is "mended" is best done with a rod which is also capable of fishing the dry fly well.

It is more accurate to designate rod actions as slow, medium and fast, each having adequate power but showing it in a different way. Our conception of these classifications is as follows:

Fast Action. A relatively stiff butt concentrates the action in the upper part of the rod giving a hard, brilliant, fast action. Such a rod throws a very narrow loop, keeps a high back cast, and provides the maximum control of the fly in skilled hands. It is the rod for the quick, brisk caster who has the skill to apply casting power very evenly and the self-control to refrain from striking a fish hard on a light leader. This is an extreme but not a freakish type of rod for maximum line control and precision placement of the fly at short and medium distances.

Medium Action. An ideal combination of qualities, making an all-around action which suits the great majority of fly fisherman. It gives excellent distance and at the same time, good control and delicacy without demanding such a precise application of casting power as the fast action. It fishes both long and short with equal facility and performs perfectly either wet or dry. The softer action protects fine leaders in striking an unexpectedly heavy fish. Distribution of the load makes for ease in casting and long life.

Slow Action. The rod for a deliberate, powerful caster who wants distance more than brilliant action. This is emphatically not a weak rod but one in which the bamboo is distributed differently to give a long, even action well down into the butt. It is the best of the three types for fishing bucktails and deeply sunken flies, nevertheless it will fish the dry fly very satisfactorily, and although it throws a wider loop of line than the fast and medium action, it will still keep the fly amply clear of the water in back if the caster does his part. A good rod for the man who cannot keep from hitting fish hard and prefers to play them vigorously.

We repeat that our three types are not freakish specialized rods; the difference between them are not so great but that an angler could fish with any of them for wet and dry fly, long and short fishing. But he certainly will prefer one to the others, and it is that preference which we are trying to satisfy.

Our recommendations for line weights are only a starting point. Individual anglers may find a size up or down is best for them.

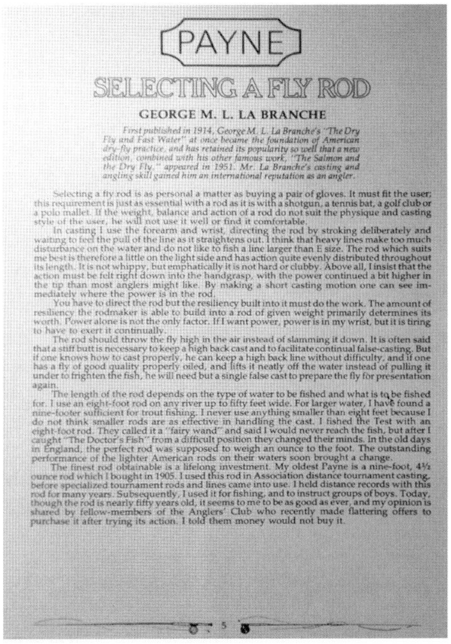

PAYNE

SELECTING A FLY ROD

GEORGE M. L. LA BRANCHE

First published in 1914, George M. L. La Branche's "The Dry Fly and Fast Water" at once became the foundation of American dry-fly practice, and has retained its popularity so well that a new edition, combined with his other famous work, "The Salmon and the Dry Fly," appeared in 1951. Mr. La Branche's casting and angling skill gained him an international reputation as an angler.

Selecting a fly rod is as personal a matter as buying a pair of gloves. It must fit the user; this requirement is just as essential with a rod as it is with a shotgun, a tennis bat, a golf club or a polo mallet. If the weight, balance and action of a rod do not suit the physique and casting style of the user, he will not use it well or find it comfortable.

In casting I use the forearm and wrist, directing the rod by stroking deliberately and waiting to feel the pull of the line as it straightens out. I think that heavy lines make too much disturbance on the water and do not like to fish a line larger than E size. The rod which suits me best is therefore a little on the light side and has action quite evenly distributed throughout its length. It is not whippy, but emphatically it is not hard or clubby. Above all, I insist that the action must be felt right down into the handgrasp, with the power continued a bit higher in the tip than most anglers might like. By making a short casting motion one can see immediately where the power is in the rod.

You have to direct the rod but the resiliency built into it must do the work. The amount of resiliency the rodmaker is able to build into a rod of given weight primarily determines its worth. Power alone is not the only factor. If I want power, power is in my wrist, but it is tiring to have to exert it continually.

The rod should throw the fly high in the air instead of slamming it down. It is often said that a stiff butt is necessary to keep a high back cast and to facilitate continual false-casting. But if one knows how to cast properly, he can keep a high back line without difficulty, and if one has a fly of good quality properly oiled, and lifts it neatly off the water instead of pulling it under to frighten the fish, he will need but a single false cast to prepare the fly for presentation again.

The length of the rod depends on the type of water to be fished and what is to be fished for. I use an eight-foot rod on any river up to fifty feet wide. For larger water, I have found a nine-footer sufficient for trout fishing. I never use anything smaller than eight feet because I do not think smaller rods are as effective in handling the cast. I fished the Test with an eight-foot rod. They called it a "fairy wand" and said I would never reach the fish, but after I caught "The Doctor's Fish" from a difficult position they changed their minds. In the old days in England, the perfect rod was supposed to weigh an ounce to the foot. The outstanding performance of the lighter American rods on their waters soon brought a change.

The finest rod obtainable is a lifelong investment. My oldest Payne is a nine-foot, 4½ ounce rod which I bought in 1905. I used this rod in Association distance tournament casting, before specialized tournament rods and lines came into use. I held distance records with this rod for many years. Subsequently, I used it for fishing, and to instruct groups of boys. Today, though the rod is nearly fifty years old, it seems to me to be as good as ever, and my opinion is shared by fellow-members of the Anglers' Club who recently made flattering offers to purchase it after trying its action. I told them money would not buy it.

5

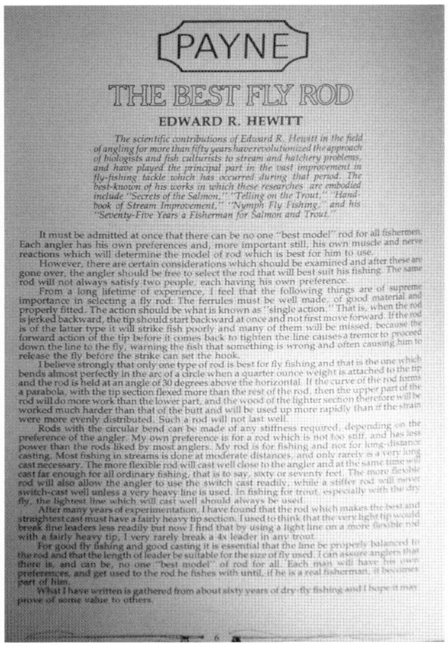

PAYNE

THE BEST FLY ROD

EDWARD R. HEWITT

The scientific contributions of Edward R. Hewitt in the field of angling for more than fifty years haverevolutionized the approach of biologists and fish culturists to stream and hatchery problems, and have played the principal part in the vast improvement in fly-fishing tackle which has occurred during that period. The best-known of his works in which these researches are embodied include "Secrets of the Salmon," "Telling on the Trout," "Handbook of Stream Improvement," "Nymph Fly Fishing," and his "Seventy-Five Years a Fisherman for Salmon and Trout."

It must be admitted at once that there can be no one "best model" rod for all fishermen. Each angler has his own preferences and, more important still, his own muscle and nerve reactions which will determine the model of rod which is best for him to use.

However, there are certain considerations which should be examined and after these are gone over, the angler should be free to select the rod that will best suit his fishing. The same rod will not always satisfy two people, each having his own preference.

From a long lifetime of experience, I feel that the following things are of supreme importance in selecting a fly rod: The ferrules must be well made, of good material and properly fitted. The action should be what is known as "single action." That is, when the rod is jerked backward, the tip should start backward at once and not first move forward. If the rod is of the latter type it will strike fish poorly and many of them will be missed, because the forward action of the tip before it comes back to tighten the line causes a tremor to proceed down the line to the fly, warning the fish that something is wrong and often causing him to release the fly before the strike can set the hook.

I believe strongly that only one type of rod is best for fly fishing and that is the one which bends almost perfectly in the arc of a circle when a quarter ounce weight is attached to the tip and the rod is held at an angle of 30 degrees above the horizontal. If the curve of the rod forms a parabola, with the tip section flexed more than the rest of the rod, then the upper part of the rod will do more work than the lower part, and the wood of the lighter section therefore will be worked much harder than that of the butt and will be used up more rapidly than if the strain were more evenly distributed. Such a rod will not last well.

Rods with the circular bend can be made of any stiffness required, depending on the preference of the angler. My own preference is for a rod which is not too stiff, and has less power than the rods liked by most anglers. My rod is for fishing and not for long-distance casting. Most fishing in streams is done at moderate distances, and only rarely is a very long cast necessary. The more flexible rod will cast well close to the angler and at the same time will cast far enough for all ordinary fishing, that is to say, sixty or seventy feet. The more flexible rod will also allow the angler to use the switch cast readily, while a stiffer rod will never switch-cast well unless a very heavy line is used. In fishing for trout, especially with the dry fly, the lightest line which will cast well should always be used.

After many years of experimentation, I have found that the rod which makes the best and straightest cast must have a fairly heavy tip section. I used to think that the very light tip would break fine leaders less readily but now I find that by using a light line on a more flexible rod with a fairly heavy tip, I very rarely break a 4x leader in any trout.

For good fly fishing and good casting it is essential that the line be properly balanced to the rod and that the length of leader be suitable for the size of fly used. I can assure anglers that there is, and can be, no one "best model" of rod for all. Each man will have his own preferences, and get used to the rod he fishes with until, if he is a real fisherman, it becomes part of him.

What I have written is gathered from about sixty years of dry-fly fishing and I hope it may prove of some value to others.

6

Pages from a Payne catalog, explaining the company philosophy.

Shortly before the Second World War, Payne introduced a threaded reelseat on his rods, most of them including a walnut insert, and he also developed a "parabolic" model. The influence of several famous fisherman of the time are noticeable – men like George La Branche and Edward Hewitt.

Three-piece rods under 7 1/2 feet were no longer built; two-piece rods became more common; and even by today's standards, remarkably light weights were achieved. The 6-foot rod weighed only 1 5/8 ounces, the 7-foot only 2 3/4 ounces, the 7 1/2-foot weighed 3 1/4 ounces, the lightest 8-foot was 3 1/2 ounces, and their famous 8 1/2-foot rod was a mere 4 5/32 ounces. I'm not certain if these indicated-weights are for the blanks alone or if they represent the finished rods, but if one considers the weight of nickel-silver ferrules, reelseat hardware, accessories, and wooden insert, Payne's scales probably would have been tipped only by the blanks. I've weighed a number of these rods and arrived at other values, though it's possible my scale was improperly adjusted. On the other hand, because many American rods from this period had very small and light cork grips (and similarly delicate reelseats), it's possible the stated weights could have been for these models. Anglers of today, however, would not accept grips of this type.

An American colleague, Marc Bourgea, provided me with a good explanation. The weights given in Payne's catalogs allowed for a variation of ¼ ounce, so the literature probably cited the lightest version of each model. Such a range could easily result from variations in bamboo quality, so we might safely add ¼ ounce to any particular model. And, if a customer ordered a threaded reelseat and longer grip, probably ¾ ounce could be added to the weight given in the catalog.

A Model 37 from Leonard's "Hunt" series, built ca. 1980 during the Tom Maxwell era. Notice the particularly small grip.

The parabolic taper, developed by Charles Ritz in Europe, was transformed by Alden Knight into an American version. To reduce weight, these rods were usually provided with cork reelseats, and the flexing action continued down into their grip. Alden Knight explained later in a Payne Co. catalog:

"When Charles Ritz came to this country in 1936, we compared notes and rods. Then we went to the E.F. Payne Rod Company plant at Highland Mills, and had a talk with Jim Payne. He set up the first American rod in the true parabolic action. This rod, like Ritz's rods, demanded perfect timing but it was a surprising tool for angling. Soon, however, he modified the patterns and produced a rod more acceptable for general use, and for which, I understand, there is an ever-increasing demand....

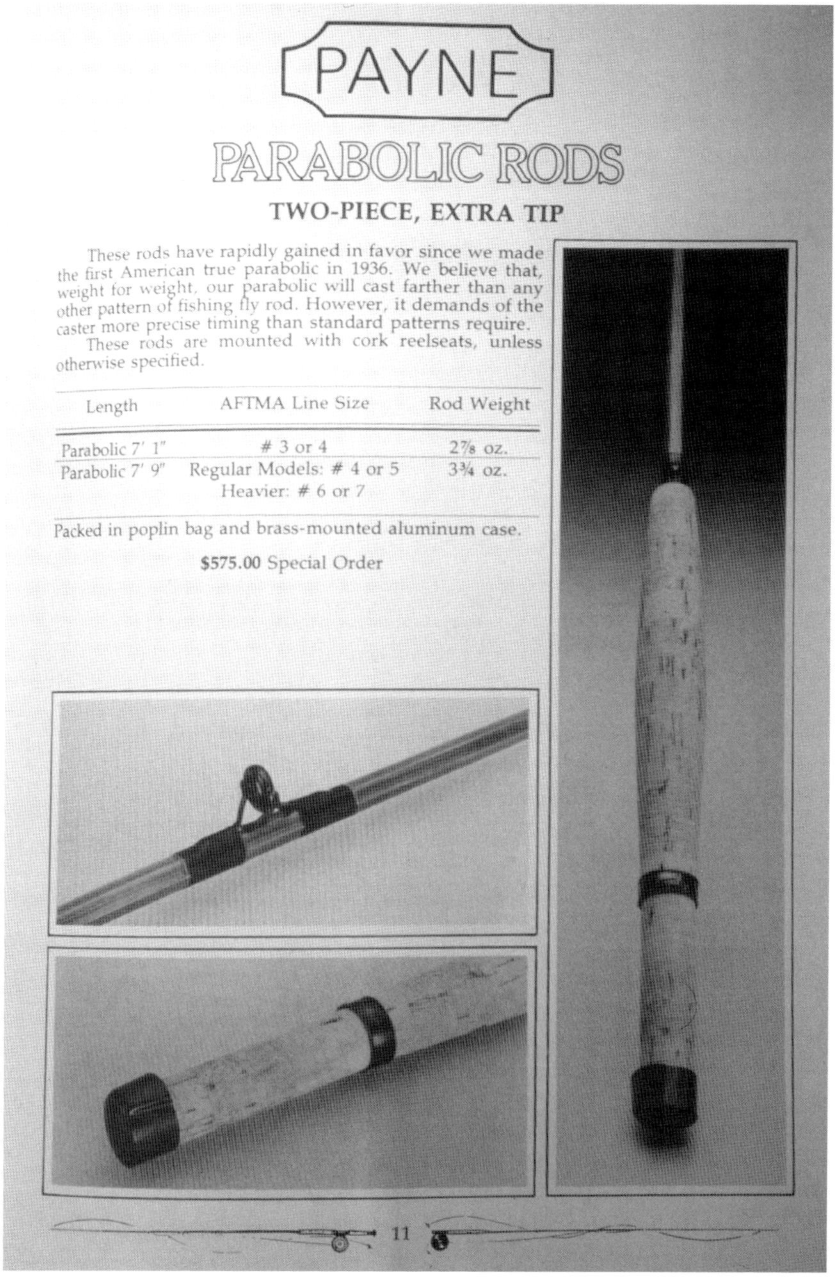

PAYNE

PARABOLIC RODS

TWO-PIECE, EXTRA TIP

These rods have rapidly gained in favor since we made the first American true parabolic in 1936. We believe that, weight for weight, our parabolic will cast farther than any other pattern of fishing fly rod. However, it demands of the caster more precise timing than standard patterns require.

These rods are mounted with cork reelseats, unless otherwise specified.

Length	AFTMA Line Size	Rod Weight
Parabolic 7′ 1″	# 3 or 4	2⅞ oz.
Parabolic 7′ 9″	Regular Models: # 4 or 5 Heavier: # 6 or 7	3¾ oz.

Packed in poplin bag and brass-mounted aluminum case.

$575.00 Special Order

11

This page from one of the last Payne catalogs describes the parabolic rod.

"True parabolic action is not satisfactory for the average angler. It demands too much in the way of timing and is not a pleasant rod to use. The parabolic rods that are being turned out today are, in effect, semi-parabolic in that they are not top-heavy, and permit a certain laxity in timing. They are delightful rods to use in that they handle both short and long casts equally well, in addition to having a high ratio of power to weight."

There's an interesting story relating to the development of the famous 8 1/2-foot rod. It happened by accident when Jim Payne (together with the famous Roy Steenrod) was casting with only the middle and tip sections of a long salmon rod belonging to A. E. Hendrickson. The result of this stunt was the annunciation of a new taper!

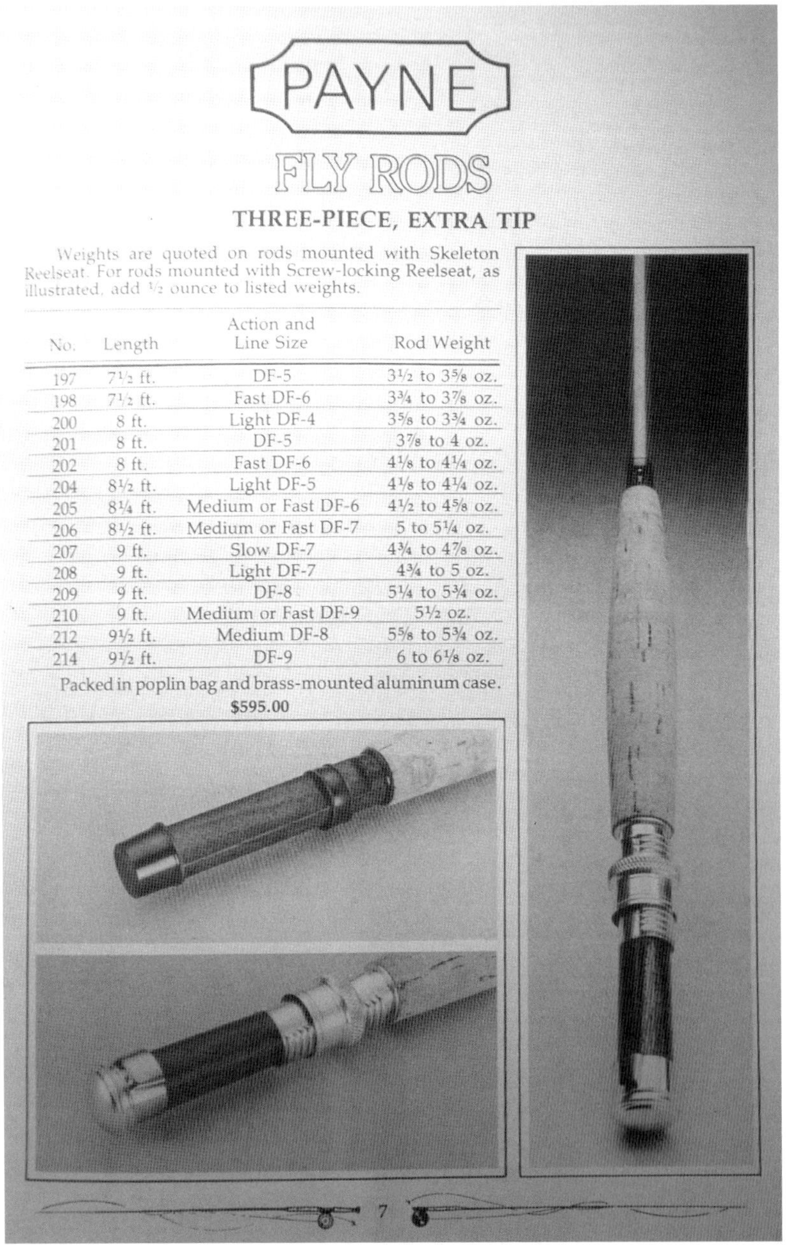

PAYNE

FLY RODS

THREE-PIECE, EXTRA TIP

Weights are quoted on rods mounted with Skeleton Reelseat. For rods mounted with Screw-locking Reelseat, as illustrated, add ½ ounce to listed weights.

No.	Length	Action and Line Size	Rod Weight
197	7½ ft.	DF-5	3½ to 3⅝ oz.
198	7½ ft.	Fast DF-6	3¾ to 3⅞ oz.
200	8 ft.	Light DF-4	3⅝ to 3¾ oz.
201	8 ft.	DF-5	3⅞ to 4 oz.
202	8 ft.	Fast DF-6	4⅛ to 4¼ oz.
204	8½ ft.	Light DF-5	4⅛ to 4¼ oz.
205	8¼ ft.	Medium or Fast DF-6	4½ to 4⅝ oz.
206	8½ ft.	Medium or Fast DF-7	5 to 5¼ oz.
207	9 ft.	Slow DF-7	4¾ to 4⅞ oz.
208	9 ft.	Light DF-7	4¾ to 5 oz.
209	9 ft.	DF-8	5¼ to 5¾ oz.
210	9 ft.	Medium or Fast DF-9	5½ oz.
212	9½ ft.	Medium DF-8	5⅝ to 5¾ oz.
214	9½ ft.	DF-9	6 to 6⅛ oz.

Packed in poplin bag and brass-mounted aluminum case.
$595.00

7

Another page from the same catalog. These rods are worth about ten times as much today and regarded as rarities. To Mr. Payne's credit, he explains that rods with screw-locking reelseats would be heavier than the weights stated in the catalog.

After the Second World War, Abercrombie & Fitch tried several times to take control of the Payne Co., but Payne resisted strongly because he did not want his rods to be sold by just one company.

James Payne died in 1970, but even in his latter decades, he had little regard for fiberglass rods – reportedly, because they involved too little hand work. A friend of the company said after his death, "Jim was a king of craftsmen, a true friend, and a real gentleman."

The last Payne catalog to appear listed 14 three-piece rods between 7 1/2 feet and 9 1/2 feet, in addition to 13 different two-piece models between 6 feet and 9 feet. All but two among the parabolic models had disappeared, and these two would reveal tapers almost identical to the Charles Ritz "PPP" series – models, "Featherlight" and "Colorado," as built by "Pezon & Michel" in France.

After Payne's death, David Decker took over the company and built rods under his own name, using the same material and tools. A short time later, however, he changed the company name back to E. F. Payne Rod Company.

An early Payne rod, built by the master himself.

Threaded reelseat showing the Payne logo: A rod from the 1980s.

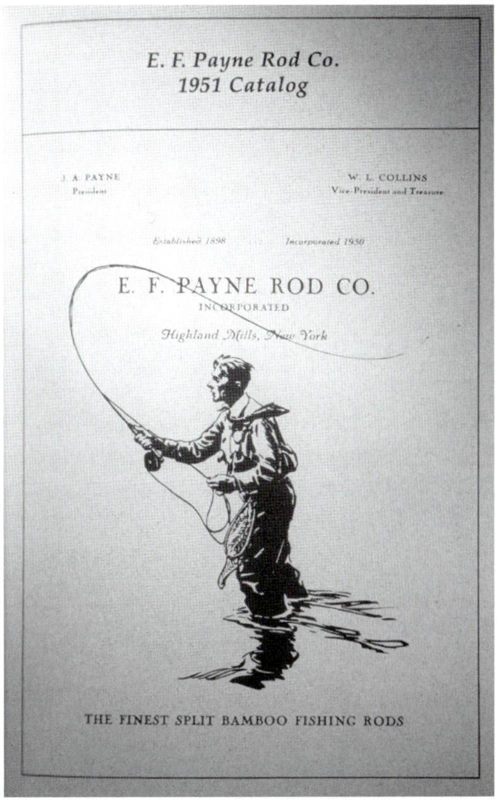

After leaving Leonard, Fred Thomas went back to Bangor and, together with Eustis Edwards, began building rods under his own name – later still, including his son, Leon Thomas. The F. E. Thomas Rod Co. produced a wide spectrum of models in a similarly wide a range of prices. These price differences weren't meant to reflect the variety of tapers, but the quality of finish and accessories on the rods. The most expensive model was the "Browntone Special" (the first versions of this model were called "Mahogany"), followed by the "Special," and then the less expensive "Dirigo" and "Bangor" models. Another model worth mentioning was the "Streamer" series.

The 1951 Payne catalog shows a curiously exaggerated rod action.

The company produced rods in two colors, the normal straw-yellow and a deeper brown. Thomas typically retained the more exemplary features of Leonard's rods, except that the grips on most Thomas rods were a little more generous. Fred Thomas retired in 1937 and his son, Leon, headed the company until 1958. Ernest Schwiebert characterized Thomas rods saying, "Many people who own such a rod would not want to sell them for a blank check."

The company name and nearly all of its equipment were sold to the very able rod builder, C. W. "Sam" Carlson. Sam used the Thomas name for an additional 15 years, even after he began making his world-famous, four-sided "Quad" rods, and did not change it to Carlson until 1970.

The F. E. Thomas logo on the butt cap of a cork reelseat.

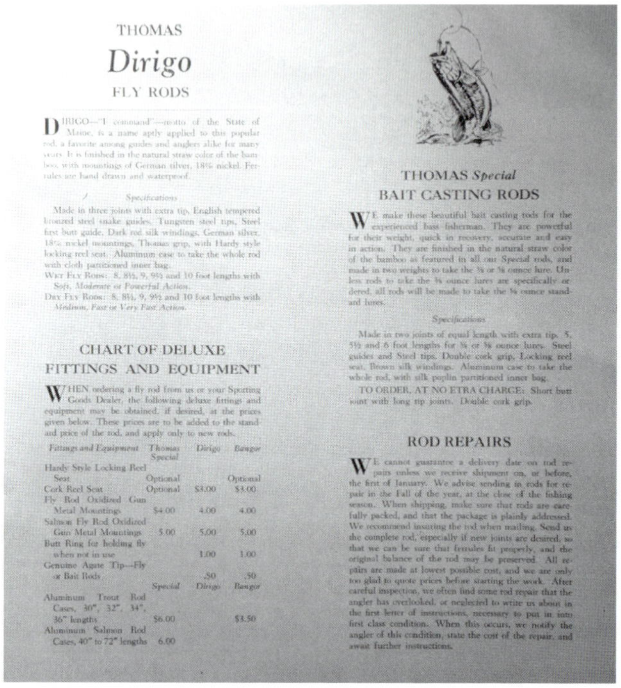

THOMAS

Dirigo

FLY RODS

DIRIGO—"I command"—motto of the State of Maine, is a name aptly applied to this popular rod, a favorite among guides and anglers alike for many years. It is finished in the natural straw color of the bamboo, with mountings of German silver, 18% nickel. Ferrules are hand drawn and waterproof.

Specifications

Made in three joints with extra tip. English tempered bronzed steel snake guides. Tungsten steel tips. Steel first butt guide. Dark rod silk windings. German silver, 18% nickel mountings. Thomas grip, with Hardy style locking reel seat. Aluminum case to take the whole rod with cloth partitioned inner bag.

WET FLY RODS: 8, 8½, 9, 9½ and 10 foot lengths with *Soft, Moderate or Powerful Action.*

DRY FLY RODS: 8, 8½, 9, 9½ and 10 foot lengths with *Medium, Fast or Very Fast Action.*

CHART OF DELUXE FITTINGS AND EQUIPMENT

WHEN ordering a fly rod from us or your Sporting Goods Dealer, the following deluxe fittings and equipment may be obtained, if desired, at the prices given below. These prices are to be added to the standard price of the rod, and apply only to new rods.

Fittings and Equipment	*Thomas Special*	*Dirigo*	*Bangor*
Hardy Style Locking Reel Seat	Optional		Optional
Cork Reel Seat	Optional	$3.00	$3.00
Fly Rod Oxidized Gun Metal Mountings	$4.00	4.00	4.00
Salmon Fly Rod Oxidized Gun Metal Mountings	5.00	5.00	5.00
Butt Ring for holding fly when not in use		1.00	1.00
Genuine Agate Tip—Fly or Bait Rods		.50	.50
	Special	*Dirigo*	*Bangor*
Aluminum Trout Rod Cases, 30", 32", 34", 36" lengths	$6.00		$3.50
Aluminum Salmon Rod Cases, 40" to 72" lengths	6.00		

THOMAS *Special*

BAIT CASTING RODS

WE make these beautiful bait casting rods for the experienced bass fisherman. They are powerful for their weight, quick in recovery, accurate and easy in action. They are finished in the natural straw color of the bamboo as featured in all our *Special* rods, and made in two weights to take the ⅜ or ⅝ ounce lure. Unless rods to take the ⅜ ounce lures are specifically ordered, all rods will be made to take the ⅝ ounce standard lures.

Specifications

Made in two joints of equal length with extra tip. 5, 5½ and 6 foot lengths for ⅜ or ⅝ ounce lures. Steel guides and Steel tips. Double cork grip, Locking reel seat. Brown silk windings. Aluminum case to take the whole rod, with silk poplin partitioned inner bag.

TO ORDER, AT NO ETRA CHARGE: Short butt joint with long tip joints. Double cork grip.

ROD REPAIRS

WE cannot guarantee a delivery date on rod repairs unless we receive shipment on, or before, the first of January. We advise sending in rods for repair in the Fall of the year, at the close of the fishing season. When shipping, make sure that rods are carefully packed, and that the package is plainly addressed. We recommend insuring the rod when mailing. Send us the complete rod, especially if new joints are desired, so that we can be sure that ferrules fit properly, and the original balance of the rod may be preserved. All repairs are made at lowest possible cost, and we are only too glad to quote prices before starting the work. After careful inspection, we often find some rod repair that the angler has overlooked, or neglected to write us about in the first letter of instructions, necessary to put it into first class condition. When this occurs, we notify the angler of this condition, state the cost of the repair, and await further instructions.

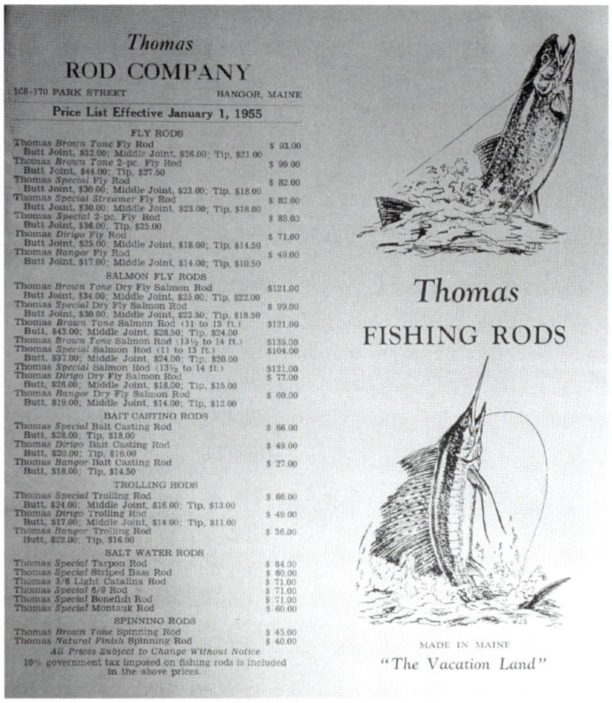

Thomas

ROD COMPANY

168-170 PARK STREET — BANGOR, MAINE

Price List Effective January 1, 1955

FLY RODS	
Thomas *Brown Tone* Fly Rod	$ 93.00
Butt Joint, $32.00; Middle Joint, $26.00; Tip, $21.00	
Thomas *Brown Tone* 2-pc. Fly Rod	$ 99.00
Butt Joint, $44.00; Tip, $27.50	
Thomas *Special* Fly Rod	$ 82.00
Butt Joint, $30.00; Middle Joint, $23.00; Tip, $18.00	
Thomas *Special Streamer* Fly Rod	$ 82.00
Butt Joint, $30.00; Middle Joint, $23.00; Tip, $18.00	
Thomas *Special* 2-pc. Fly Rod	$ 88.00
Butt Joint, $36.00; Tip, $25.00	
Thomas *Dirigo* Fly Rod	$ 71.00
Butt Joint, $25.00; Middle Joint, $18.00; Tip, $14.50	
Thomas *Bangor* Fly Rod	$ 49.00
Butt Joint, $17.00; Middle Joint, $14.00; Tip, $10.50	
SALMON FLY RODS	
Thomas *Brown Tone* Dry Fly Salmon Rod	$121.00
Butt Joint, $34.00; Middle Joint, $25.00; Tip, $22.00	
Thomas *Special* Dry Fly Salmon Rod	$ 99.00
Butt Joint, $30.00; Middle Joint, $22.50; Tip, $18.50	
Thomas *Brown Tone* Salmon Rod (11 to 13 ft.)	$121.00
Butt, $43.00; Middle Joint, $28.50; Tip, $24.00	
Thomas *Brown Tone* Salmon Rod (13½ to 14 ft.)	$135.00
Thomas *Special* Salmon Rod (11 to 13 ft.)	$104.00
Butt, $37.00; Middle Joint, $24.00; Tip, $20.00	
Thomas *Special* Salmon Rod (13½ to 14 ft.)	$121.00
Thomas *Dirigo* Dry Fly Salmon Rod	$ 77.00
Butt, $26.00; Middle Joint, $18.00; Tip, $15.00	
Thomas *Bangor* Dry Fly Salmon Rod	$ 60.00
Butt, $19.00; Middle Joint, $14.00; Tip, $12.00	
BAIT CASTING RODS	
Thomas *Special* Bait Casting Rod	$ 66.00
Butt, $28.00; Tip, $18.00	
Thomas *Dirigo* Bait Casting Rod	$ 49.00
Butt, $20.00; Tip, $16.00	
Thomas *Bangor* Bait Casting Rod	$ 27.00
Butt, $18.00; Tip, $14.50	
TROLLING RODS	
Thomas *Special* Trolling Rod	$ 66.00
Butt, $24.00; Middle Joint, $16.00; Tip, $13.00	
Thomas *Dirigo* Trolling Rod	$ 49.00
Butt, $17.00; Middle Joint, $14.00; Tip, $11.00	
Thomas *Bangor* Trolling Rod	$ 36.00
Butt, $22.00; Tip, $16.00	
SALT WATER RODS	
Thomas *Special* Tarpon Rod	$ 84.00
Thomas *Special* Striped Bass Rod	$ 60.00
Thomas 3/6 Light Catalina Rod	$ 71.00
Thomas *Special* 6/9 Rod	$ 71.00
Thomas *Special* Bonefish Rod	$ 71.00
Thomas *Special* Montauk Rod	$ 60.00
SPINNING RODS	
Thomas *Brown Tone* Spinning Rod	$ 45.00
Thomas *Natural Finish* Spinning Rod	$ 40.00

All Prices Subject to Change Without Notice

10% government tax imposed on fishing rods is included in the above prices.

Thomas

FISHING RODS

MADE IN MAINE

"The Vacation Land"

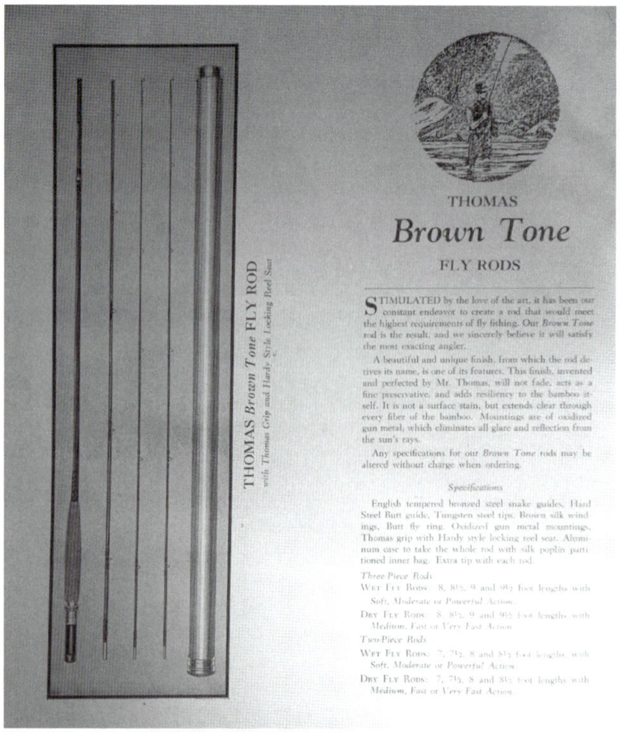

THOMAS

Brown Tone

FLY RODS

STIMULATED by the love of the art, it has been our constant endeavor to create a rod that would meet the highest requirements of fly fishing. Our *Brown Tone* rod is the result, and we sincerely believe it will satisfy the most exacting angler.

A beautiful and unique finish, from which the rod derives its name, is one of its features. This finish, invented and perfected by Mr. Thomas, will not fade, acts as a fine preservative, and adds resiliency to the bamboo itself. It is not a surface stain, but extends clear through every fiber of the bamboo. Mountings are of oxidized gun metal, which eliminates all glare and reflection from the sun's rays.

Any specifications for our *Brown Tone* rods may be altered without charge when ordering.

Specifications

English tempered bronzed steel snake guides. Hard Steel Butt guide, Tungsten steel tips. Brown silk windings, Butt fly ring. Oxidized gun metal mountings. Thomas grip with Hardy style locking reel seat. Aluminum case to take the whole rod with silk poplin partitioned inner bag. Extra tip with each rod.

Three-Piece Rods

WET FLY RODS: 8, 8½, 9 and 9½ foot lengths with *Soft, Moderate or Powerful Action.*

DRY FLY RODS: 8, 8½, 9 and 9½ foot lengths with *Medium, Fast or Very Fast Action.*

Two-Piece Rods

WET FLY RODS: 7, 7½, 8 and 8½ foot lengths, with *Soft, Moderate or Powerful Action.*

DRY FLY RODS: 7, 7½, 8 and 8½ foot lengths with *Medium, Fast or Very Fast Action.*

Price list from the 1955 Thomas catalog and a description of the famous "Brown Tone" rod series.

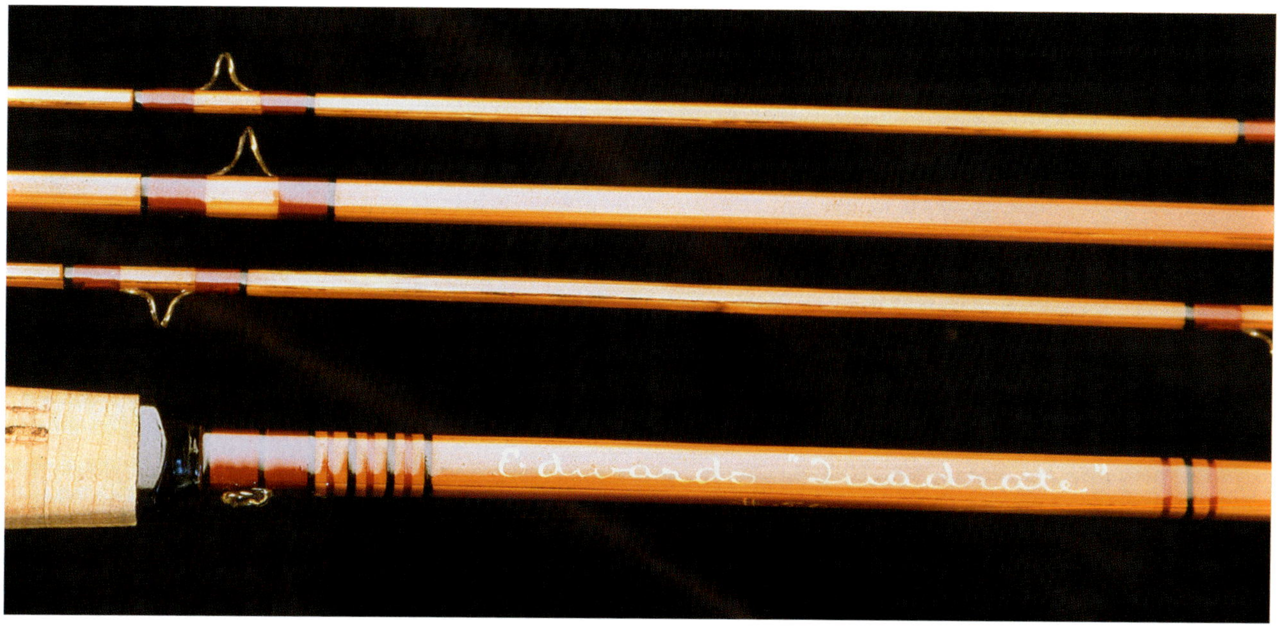

William Edwards produced the "Quadrate" rods.

Eustis Edwards, another early worker at Leonard, also produced rods under his own name for a number of years. As in so many other cases, however, this company's rod-building only came into full bloom under his sons, William and Eugene. The first Eustis Edwards rods were very reminiscent of those of his former employer, Leonard, and were relatively heavy, three-piece models. Later, Edwards began to produce blanks for various sporting goods companies and fishing stores. In addition to those built for other companies, he made a series of 7 1/2-foot blanks for the Winchester Repeating Arms Company, which became a sensation on the Catskill rivers because of their superb casting abilities. Indeed, the popularity of 7 1/2-foot rods in the USA is, to a great extent, due to these rods.

His son, William, broke with tradition and produced a number of square (four-strip, or "Quadrate") models, soon to became famous for their low weight and excellent casting characteristics. Today, these rods are sought by collectors and fishermen alike.

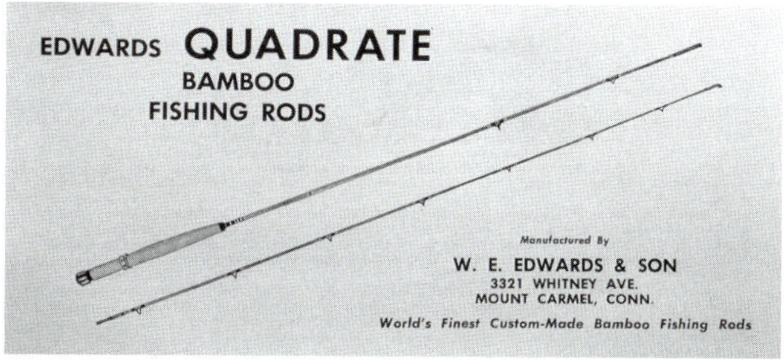

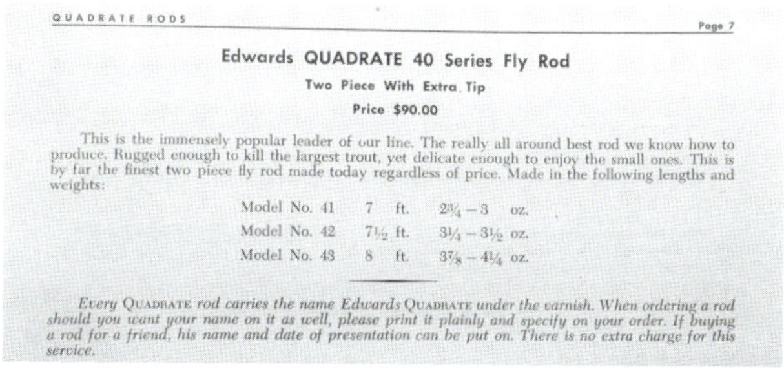
QUADRATE RODS — Page 7

Edwards QUADRATE 40 Series Fly Rod

Two Piece With Extra Tip

Price $90.00

This is the immensely popular leader of our line. The really all around best rod we know how to produce. Rugged enough to kill the largest trout, yet delicate enough to enjoy the small ones. This is by far the finest two piece fly rod made today regardless of price. Made in the following lengths and weights:

Model No. 41	7 ft.	2¾ – 3 oz.
Model No. 42	7½ ft.	3¼ – 3½ oz.
Model No. 43	8 ft.	3⅞ – 4¼ oz.

Every Quadrate *rod carries the name Edwards* Quadrate *under the varnish. When ordering a rod should you want your name on it as well, please print it plainly and specify on your order. If buying a rod for a friend, his name and date of presentation can be put on. There is no extra charge for this service.*

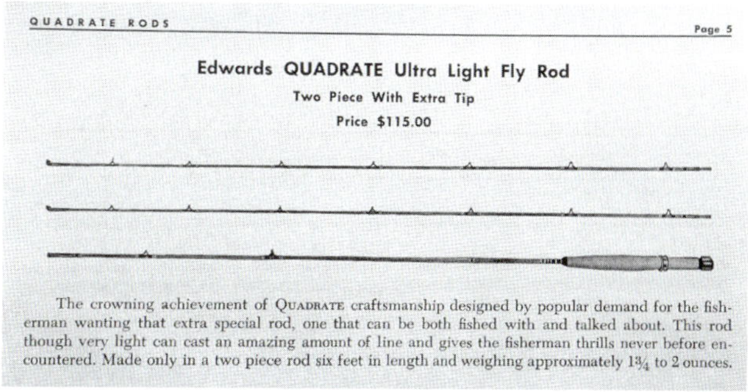
QUADRATE RODS — Page 5

Edwards QUADRATE Ultra Light Fly Rod

Two Piece With Extra Tip

Price $115.00

The crowning achievement of Quadrate craftsmanship designed by popular demand for the fisherman wanting that extra special rod, one that can be both fished with and talked about. This rod though very light can cast an amazing amount of line and gives the fisherman thrills never before encountered. Made only in a two piece rod six feet in length and weighing approximately 1¾ to 2 ounces.

An Edwards catalog from the 1950s lists the "Ultra Light" as weighing from 1 ¾ to 2 ounces. A very light rod, even considering that it was only 6 feet long. The 40 Series was a favorite of Edwards' customers.

There were many more companies producing good rods in these glorious days of American fly-fishing. Some examples are Montague, Heddon, and South Bend. The best of their products nearly approached those of the master rod-builders, but these companies could only survive by producing rods under the various names of large catalog companies of the day. Sewell Dunton worked at Montague and later established his own workshop in Greenfield, Massachusetts. Upon retirement, he sold out to two able, young men, Thomas Maxwell and Thomas Dorsey. These two established the Thomas & Thomas Co., having learned rod-building in their youth from Maxwell's grandfather. Tom Dorsey told me that, as students, they used to build rods for friends and acquaintances, but their orders continued to increase, and after finishing their university education, they decided to build rods professionally. Thomas & Thomas, split-bamboo rods were built, initially, in Turner Falls, but the company continues today in Greenfield, Massachusetts. It didn't take long for the good reputation of their rods to become known, and not just in the USA. The first series of rods was impregnated in a light-brown color, although varnished models were soon included among their offerings. In the beginning, T&T took advantage of the large volume of rods needing repair (rods built by other makers) and Tom Dorsey says today, "I regret it greatly that we never had time to photograph the many famous rods that passed through our hands."

The major rod series from Thomas & Thomas are the "Classic Series," with the models, "Gnat," "Paralight," "Limestone," "Cahill," and "Coachman." The "Individualist" series is divided into the "Midge," "Hendrickson," and "Montana" rods.

Rolf Baginski and Thomas Dorsey at Thomas & Thomas in Greenfield in 2001.

The Thomas & Thomas logo on a threaded reelseat. The company developed this oval-shaped cutout in the threaded tube to provide a snug fit between the reel and the reelseat.

A typical T&T with a strongly-swelled butt at the transition to the grip. This is a "Hendrickson" from the "Individualist" series.

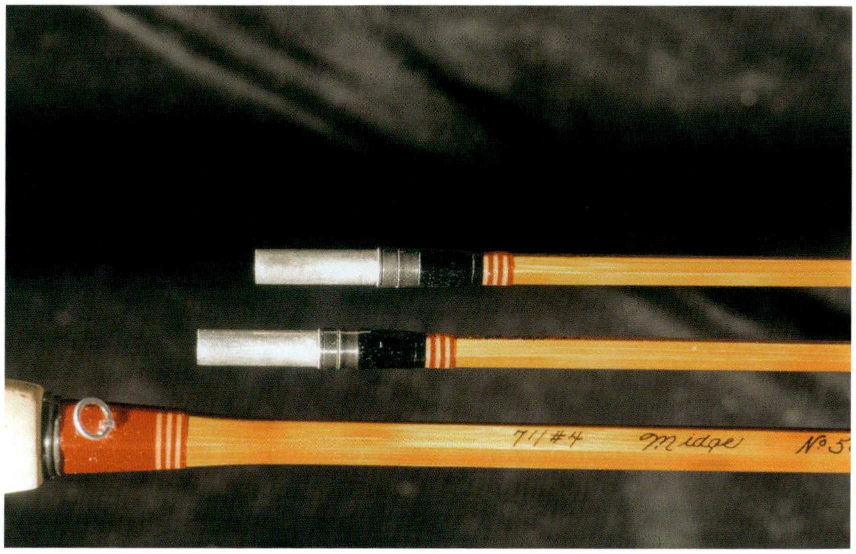

A "Midge," also from the "Individualist" series. The decorative wraps are especially striking.

A New Beginning

It borders on the amazing that, just shortly after the death of Jim Payne (and long after fiberglass rods had dominated the market), two young men could come from nowhere, overcome the risks of starting a new company, and carry forward the tradition of American split-cane rod-building. I think we all owe a large debt of gratitude to Thomas & Thomas for establishing so many friends of split-cane rods throughout the world. They smoothed the way for many young rod-builders to follow.

In addition to the early companies and their successors on the East Coast, many excellent rod-builders, such as Stoner, Powell, and Granger established themselves farther to the west.

Tom Dorsey standing before an impressive stash of bamboo in T&Ts attic...

...and proudly in front of the company sign.

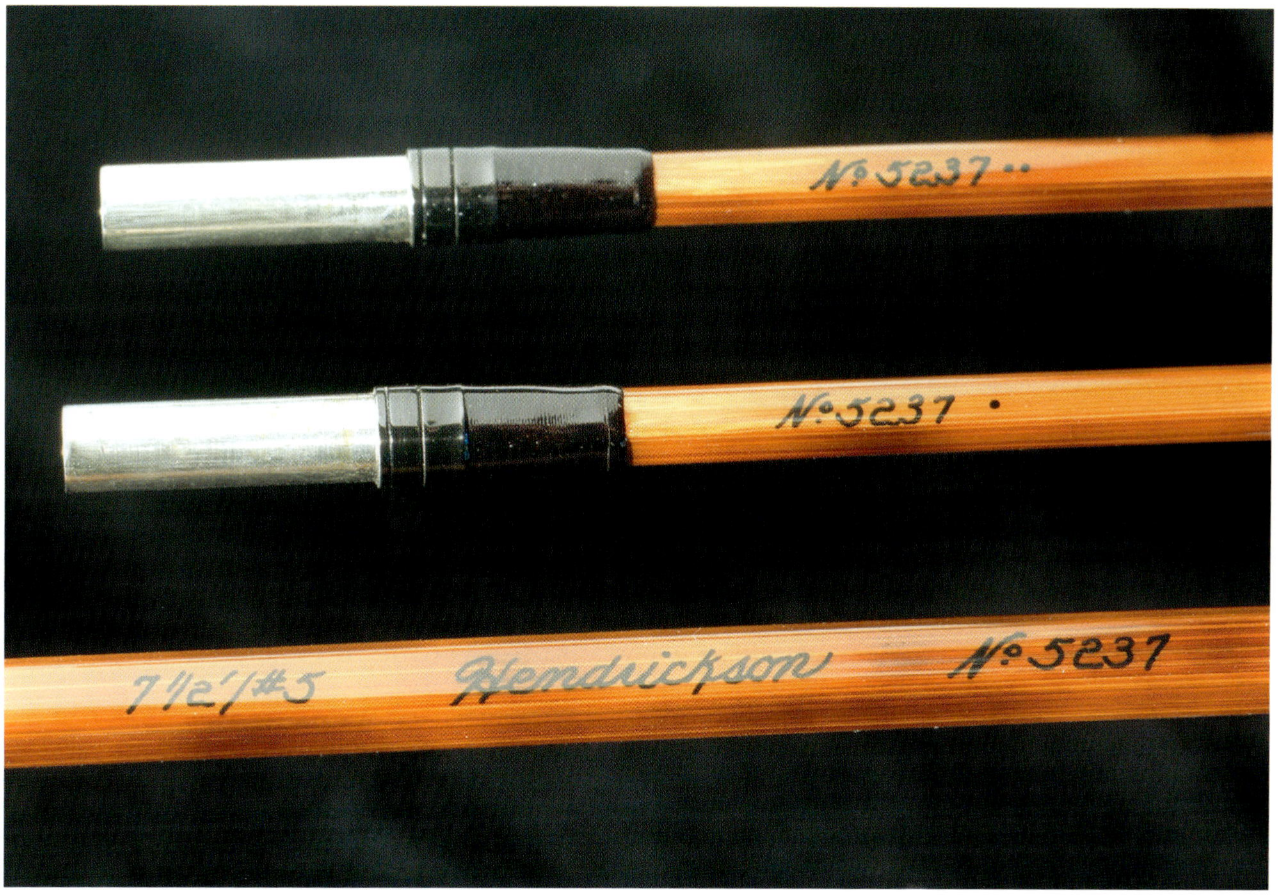

A wonderful "all 'round" rod: The 7 ½-foot "Hendrickson" from T&T.

Edwin C. Powell began to build his first rods in 1912, and, shortly after the First World War, opened his business in Marysville, California. All Powell's rods were hexagonal, "solid" rods until 1933 when he took out a patent for "hollow construction" – a method which would reduce weight and greatly change the action of the rods by making them faster. Influenced by the Hardy rods of the time, Powell developed a new construction method. He reduced the inner side of each bamboo strip to only a few thirty-seconds of an inch, leaving just a thin band of power fibers. Then, he glued a light strip of cedar wood to the thin layer of fibers, and after the glue was dry, the strip would be given its triangular shape. Finally, the inner apex was cut down, but punctuated by small dams at certain intervals. Powell tempered his bamboo culms by hand over an open gas flame, making his rods somewhat delicate, and the presence of intermediate wraps on many of his models (particularly the hollow-built ones) is not just for decoration. These intermediate wraps truly prevented separation of the individual splines – a common risk with the glues used at the time. Tony Maslan, Powell's son-in-law, took over the company later, continuing to produce the rods under the name "E. C. Powell."

Powell's son, Walton Powell, opened his own workshop and used tools similar to those of his father, but produced an entirely different line of rods and tapers.

Lewis Stoner, another rod-building genius from the West Coast, was one of the two men responsible for the establishment and growth of R. L. Winston Rod Company. As with many of his contemporaries, he also learned woodworking from his father while still a child.

In 1926, Stoner developed a very fast milling machine to prepare his bamboo strips. (It was approximately during this same time that Hardy, in England, decided to give up hand-planing in favor of a milling machine – again, to achieve greater speed and precision in their production.) Despite many financial difficulties at the beginning, Lewis Stoner found a partner, Robert Winther, who brought new capital to the company, and **Win**ther and **Ston**er formed the R. L. Winston Company in 1927. Stoner decided to continue the company under this same name when the Depression caused Winther to lose his interest, leaving the company in 1933. In 1945, an outstanding fly-fisherman and well-known tournament caster arrived at the company's door to buy himself a new rod. His name was Douglas Merrick. Stoner and Merrick spoke briefly about what a good rod should be, and that very same evening, Merrick resigned from his better-paying job to begin work the next morning at Winston. These two artists of rod-building complemented each other perfectly, and their time together has been described as Winston's "Golden Era." But it was Merrick who provided for the future of the company when Stoner suddenly and prematurely died in 1957.

During Merrick's tenure, Winston was located on Harrison Street in San Francisco. One day, another young man came into the workshop to buy a number of seasoned, bamboo strips – a fellow who'd begun building bamboo rods back in 1947 and had received much advice over the years from both Stoner and Merrick. His name was Gary Howells, and this young man began working for the company the day after Stoner's death. Winston gained another excellent craftsman.

As already mentioned, Lewis Stoner invented a method of hollow construction, devised by routing a "U-shaped" channel, full-length, along each bamboo strip.

A Winston catalog from the 1970s. Its simple appearance forms a contrast to the wonderful rods produced by this company.

A "modern" Winston rod: An 8-footer from the 1970s, showing the typical, fully-wrapped ferrules.

As a result of Stoner's methods, Winston rods came to be characterized by their lightness. First, Stoner shaped the separate strips to their dimensions, followed by routing concave channels along their inner surfaces, and lastly, the strips would be glued together. A few years ago, I was fortunate enough to visit Winston's present location in Twin Bridges, Montana, and there, I inspected the old machines with my own eyes.

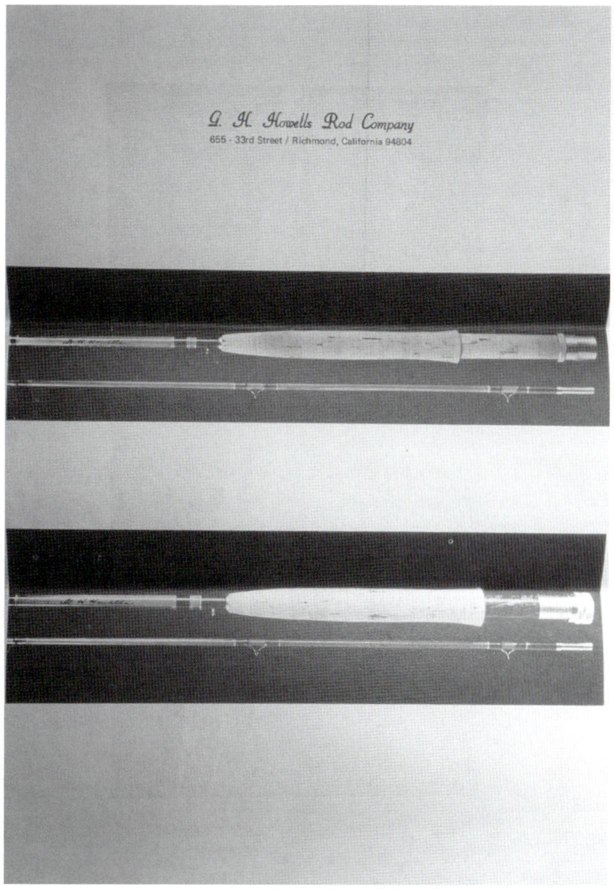

Even today, Winston rods are greatly admired and are particularly popular in the USA. With these rods, even on the many windy days in the American West, you can cast a line cleanly over the famous trout waters. But it shouldn't be forgotten that the heavier Winston rods, 9 feet and longer, are considered to be among the best rods of all time for burly steelhead.

In 1969, Howell left Winston to start his own rod-building career and offered models under his name. These rods (uniting the best experience of two rod-building generations) are now among the most highly-desired by collectors and fishermen, alike.

A page from the Howell catalog. In the American market it was unusual to show rods with only one tip.

Little Known, but Good

I believe some of the best (but also most under-appreciated) rods in the USA came from makers in Denver, Colorado – lying exactly one mile above sea level. In contrast to their more famous counterparts on the East Coast, the outstanding rods emerging from Denver received little attention from fly-fishers. If mentioned at all, these latter were called good, "utility" rods. They rarely appeared in tests or reviews, and this was unfortunate because, both in construction and in action, many Denver rods were at least the equivalent of their better-known contemporaries.

As did many so many of his West-Coast colleagues, Goodwin Granger (one of the first rod-makers in Denver) began his career as a hobby in 1918, shortly after the First World War. Considering the fabulous waters in the vicinity, it's no wonder that his rods were quickly discovered and prized by his customers, and Granger's company remained active until 1942. In 1938, Granger took out a patent for an up-locking, threaded reelseat and used this on nearly all subsequent rods. One needed only to turn a simple, knurled wheel at the end of the seat to advance the mechanism inside and fasten the reel securely.

The quality of a Granger rod sold itself, if only because (in contrast to most other manufacturers) Granger's bamboo was split by hand to keep the fibers running straight along the strip. Typical models were the "Premier," "De Luxe," "Favorite," and "Special," all available in lengths from 7 1/2 to 10 feet.

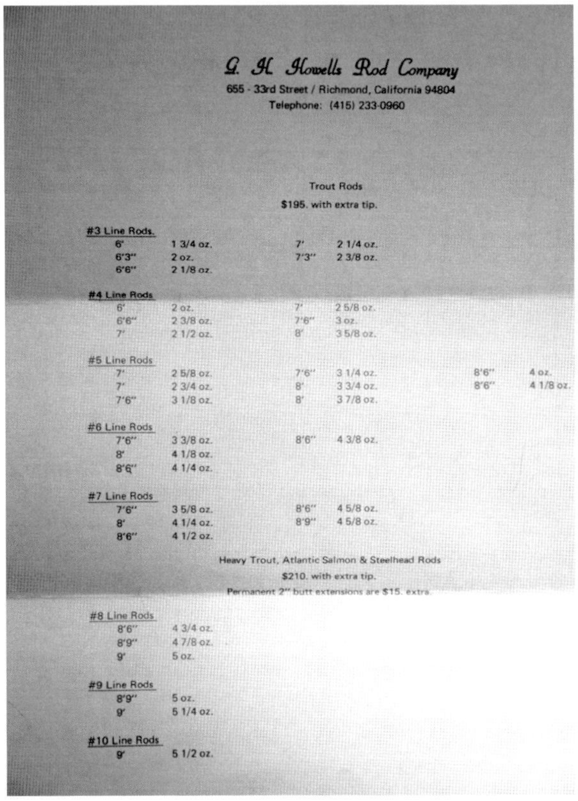

G. H. Howells Rod Company
655 - 33rd Street / Richmond, California 94804
Telephone: (415) 233-0960

Trout Rods
$195. with extra tip.

#3 Line Rods.

6'	1 3/4 oz.	7'	2 1/4 oz.		
6'3"	2 oz.	7'3"	2 3/8 oz.		
6'6"	2 1/8 oz.				

#4 Line Rods

6'	2 oz.	7'	2 5/8 oz.		
6'6"	2 3/8 oz.	7'6"	3 oz.		
7'	2 1/2 oz.	8'	3 5/8 oz.		

#5 Line Rods

7'	2 5/8 oz.	7'6"	3 1/4 oz.	8'6"	4 oz.
7'	2 3/4 oz.	8'	3 3/4 oz.	8'6"	4 1/8 oz.
7'6"	3 1/8 oz.	8'	3 7/8 oz.		

#6 Line Rods

7'6"	3 3/8 oz.	8'6"	4 3/8 oz.		
8'	4 1/8 oz.				
8'6"	4 1/4 oz.				

#7 Line Rods

7'6"	3 5/8 oz.	8'6"	4 5/8 oz.		
8'	4 1/4 oz.	8'9"	4 5/8 oz.		
8'6"	4 1/2 oz.				

Heavy Trout, Atlantic Salmon & Steelhead Rods
$210. with extra tip.
Permanent 2" butt extensions are $15. extra.

#8 Line Rods

8'6"	4 3/4 oz.
8'9"	4 7/8 oz.
9'	5 oz.

#9 Line Rods

8'9"	5 oz.
9'	5 1/4 oz.

#10 Line Rods

9'	5 1/2 oz.

Rod listings by the G. H. Howell Rod Company - about 1972.

After Granger died in 1931, William Phillipson assumed management of all production. Phillipson was born in Sweden, came to Denver in 1923, and worked for Granger from 1925 onward – attempting, but failing, to buy the company in 1945.

In 1946, following the Second World War, the Wright & McGill Company in Denver bought Goodwin Granger. The new company continued to use Granger's equipment and produced excellent rods under the same name and tradition. Just as was the case at Heddon and South Bend, large numbers of essentially "production" rods were turned out, but Granger's were held to a surprisingly high level, and perhaps their quality would rank among the best production rods ever built.

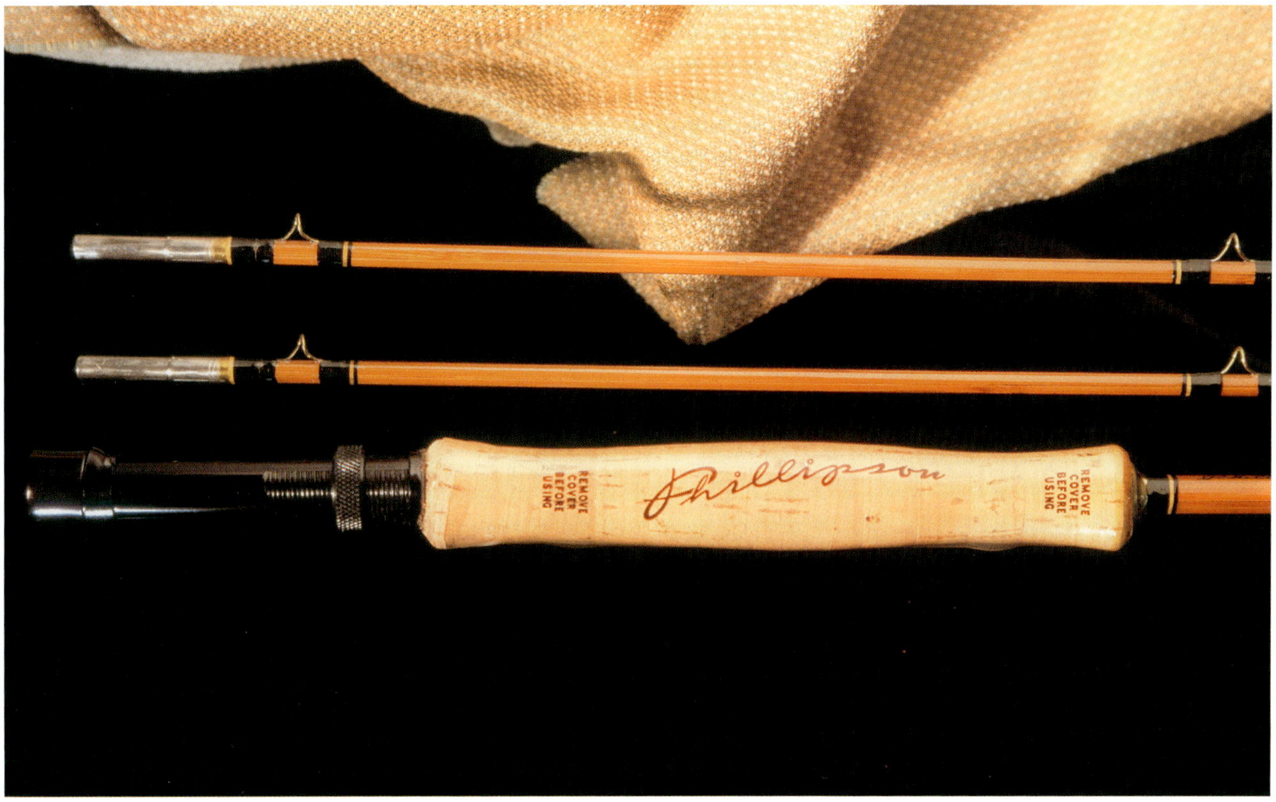

A magnificently preserved Phillipson rod, never used and still with its plastic cover on the grip. This is an example from the "Premium" series, displaying a grip shaped like a hammer handle.

After the failed attempt to purchase Granger, Phillipson started his own company, its first rods being produced in 1946. His long-accumulated ideas and experience showed quickly in the new models, and for the first time, Phillipson used completely new, waterproof glues. The rods had a cork grip, shaped like a hammer handle – that is, oval in cross-section.

The best known of his series are probably the "Peerless," the "Paragon," "Powr-Pakt," "Paramount," and "Premium." Also, with his relatively inexpensive series, the "Pacemaker" or the "51," moderately-priced rods in various lengths became available to the average person living beyond Colorado. In 1952, even a multi-piece "Smuggler" rod was introduced, and after 1953, Phillipson produced impregnated models as well. In the meantime, many Phillipson blanks were also provided to Abercrombie & Fitch.

Phillipson's total inventory of stored bamboo was destroyed in a fire in 1960, and the company then decided to switch completely to fiberglass. The only bamboo rod made by the company after the fire was the impregnated "Peerless." Minnesota Mining and Manufacturing Corporation bought the Phillipson Rod Company in 1972.

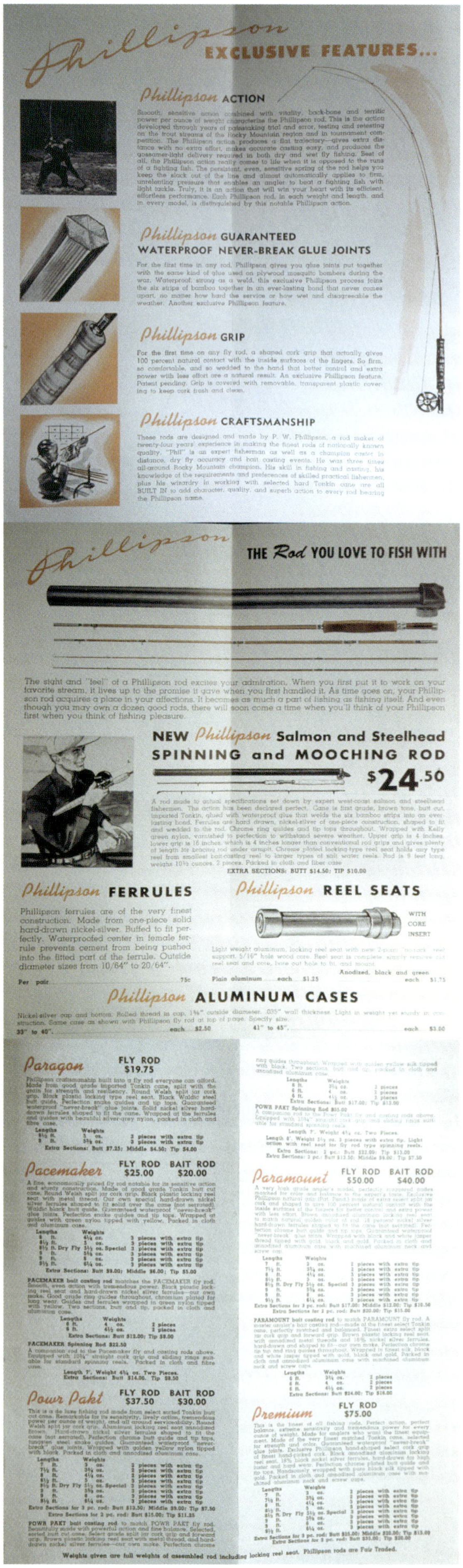

Phillipson EXCLUSIVE FEATURES...

Phillipson ACTION

Phillipson GUARANTEED WATERPROOF NEVER-BREAK GLUE JOINTS

Phillipson GRIP

Phillipson CRAFTSMANSHIP

Phillipson THE Rod YOU LOVE TO FISH WITH

The sight and "feel" of a Phillipson rod excites your admiration. When you first put it to work on your favorite stream, it lives up to the promise it gave when you first handled it. As time goes on, your Phillipson rod acquires a place in your affections. It becomes as much a part of fishing as fishing itself. And even though you may own a dozen good rods, there will soon come a time when you'll think of your Phillipson first when you think of fishing pleasure.

NEW Phillipson Salmon and Steelhead SPINNING and MOOCHING ROD $24.50

Phillipson FERRULES

Phillipson ferrules are of the very finest construction. Made from one-piece solid hard-drawn nickel-silver. Buffed to fit perfectly. Waterproofed center in female ferrule prevents cement from being pushed into the fitted part of the ferrule. Outside diameter sizes from 10/64" to 20/64".

Phillipson REEL SEATS

Phillipson ALUMINUM CASES

Paragon FLY ROD $19.75

Pacemaker FLY ROD $25.00 BAIT ROD $20.00

Pow'r Pakt FLY ROD $37.50 BAIT ROD $30.00

Paramount FLY ROD $50.00 BAIT ROD $40.00

Premium FLY ROD $75.00

A surprisingly modern presentation: pages from the Phillipson catalog of 1949. These rods were inexpensive and good!

Other rod-makers in Denver were the Arend Rod Co., DeBell Fishing Tackle Co., Ed Sisty Rod Co., L. B. Simmons, Courtney Ryley Cooper, Aladdin Rod Co., Old Faithful Rod Co., Pioneer Rods, and the Jenkins Rod Co. Obviously, the seed sowed by Granger following the First World War bore much fruit and accelerated interest in Denver rod-building.

Today, the Denver area boasts many outstanding fly-fishermen – and no wonder, with this landscape and the profusion of trout streams. Many anglers fish with the local, "classic" rods, and upon arriving at almost any beautiful river on a weekday, you'd have to wonder if anyone is still at work.

Quite a Store

Even the Denver International Airport becomes an interesting experience. When entering the USA, one is normally asked about the reason for the visit, but if you're an international traveler and you've arrived for fly-fishing, it's likely you will make enemies among the travelers behind you in the line. First, you'll be asked to unpack your rod, but then, the officer at the counter will want to provide all kinds of fishing tips, and before you can help yourself, you're caught up in a fly-fishing conversation. Eventually, you agree to meet the officer at his "secret" spot, joining with his other fishing buddies who'd be delighted to meet their German brethren. And, once, a female officer even whistled after me – alas, only to say, "Nice rod case."

Last year, while doing some research for this book, I found an astonishing store – "Rick's Rods" in Denver. I've never seen a store with such a selection of equipment, much of it dating from the 1940s, '50s, and '60s. In the warehouse behind the shop, hundreds of blanks from Wright & McGill were piled high. There must have been several thousand fiberglass rods and split-cane blanks, in addition to guides, reels, and assorted materials for rod-building. Rick and his wife Marilyn allowed me to rummage to my heart's content, and kindly encouraged me to ask any questions. The experience at Rick's Rods became invaluable to my research.

Marylin Richter and Rick Gottdenker in front of their remarkable store in Denver.

Boxes of split-cane and impregnated blanks.

Only a few of their many drawers filled with reels.

How many rods could be fitted-up with the guides in this bottle?

A Dickerson "Guide Special." The workmanship is a feast for the eyes.

There are two additional masters of the art who must not be forgotten: Lyle Dickerson and Paul Young, both from Michigan. Dickerson lived between 1892 and 1982, and got his start as a rod-maker shortly after 1929. The American stock market crash caused him to lose his job between one day and the next, and he was forced to begin something new. Dickerson produced about 1350 rods for trout and salmon fishing between 1931 and 1972 – a most remarkable achievement when we consider that he received no assistance and built his own rod-building tools and machines. It was very difficult to sell rods during the Depression years, so companies were very careful to keep their production methods secret. Certainly no one wanted to generate additional competition. As a result, Dickerson made his own planing forms, constructed his own milling machines and everything else necessary for building rods.

As pointed out in the book, *Dickerson, The Man and His Rods* (Gerald S. Stein and James W. Schaaf), Dickerson's poor sense of business did not simplify his beginnings. His first rods sold for only $35, and were unusually stiff and fast for the time.

His standard rod-offerings included 10 different, three-piece models from 7 1/2 feet to 10 feet, plus a variety of two-piece rods between 7 and 9 feet. This one-man operation received its first real recognition when the well-known author, Ray Bergman, arrived in Michigan to fish with a few of his friends. He ordered a rod from Dickerson, was enthusiastic about its action, and mentioned this rod in his book, *Just Fishing*. Bamboo was generally unavailable during the Second World War, but after the hiatus, Dickerson resumed rod-making in 1946. He retired in 1972 and sold his workshop to Tim Bedford. After Bedford's death, the company was sold to its present owner, James Schaaf, who still produces a few models almost identical to Dickerson's rods.

Very rare, a Paul H. Young catalog from about 1950.

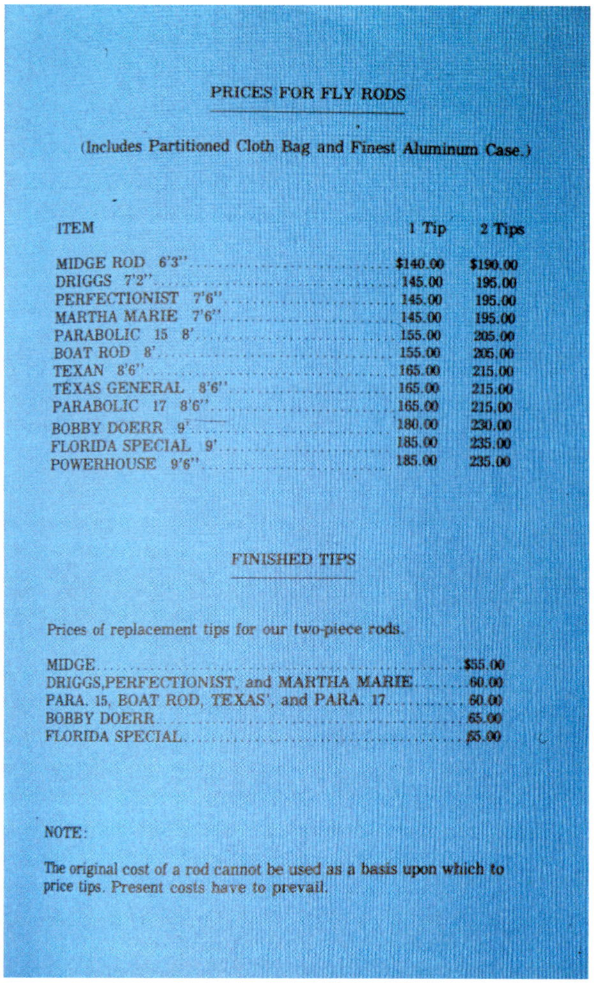

PRICES FOR FLY RODS

(Includes Partitioned Cloth Bag and Finest Aluminum Case.)

ITEM	1 Tip	2 Tips
MIDGE ROD 6'3"	$140.00	$190.00
DRIGGS 7'2"	145.00	195.00
PERFECTIONIST 7'6"	145.00	195.00
MARTHA MARIE 7'6"	145.00	195.00
PARABOLIC 15 8'	155.00	205.00
BOAT ROD 8'	155.00	205.00
TEXAN 8'6"	165.00	215.00
TEXAS GENERAL 8'6"	165.00	215.00
PARABOLIC 17 8'6"	165.00	215.00
BOBBY DOERR 9'	180.00	230.00
FLORIDA SPECIAL 9'	185.00	235.00
POWERHOUSE 9'6"	185.00	235.00

FINISHED TIPS

Prices of replacement tips for our two-piece rods.

MIDGE	$55.00
DRIGGS, PERFECTIONIST, and MARTHA MARIE	60.00
PARA. 15, BOAT ROD, TEXAS', and PARA. 17	60.00
BOBBY DOERR	65.00
FLORIDA SPECIAL	65.00

NOTE:

The original cost of a rod cannot be used as a basis upon which to price tips. Present costs have to prevail.

The Young price list from this same period.

Paul Young (living from 1890 to 1960) traveled extensively through the USA and Canada, eager to fish every available stream wherever he went. When he set up his own rod-making operation and sold the first rod in 1933, he knew from experience what a customer finds important in a good rod – it should weigh as little as possible.

Young carried out seemingly endless experiments, among which was a special oven to temper his bamboo culms within an open flame. Many of his rods are characterized by a bamboo surface that appears to be nearly carbonized. Additionally, Young developed a method of impregnating bamboo that's remained a secret to this day. His process protected the blank against moisture, but without making the rod heavier, as has been the downfall of so many other impregnated rods.

An outstanding model in his offerings is the "Midge," an ultralight rod, 6 1/2 feet long, but differing in design from other comparable rods. This rod is much thinner through its lower butt area than is ordinarily seen, and it would be an understatement to describe its tip as "fine." The rod casts a 4-weight, double-taper line perfectly, and can be fished with the finest tippets. Another notable rod is the "Parabolic 15," a model that could be ordered with different tips – either for dry-fly fishing or for distance casting.

After Paul Young passed away in 1960, the business was carried on by his son, John, and Robert Summers, who had worked in the company since 1956. In 1972, Summers opened his own highly successful company, and today, Paul's grandson, Todd Young, works in the shop.

Harold Steel Gillum was born at the turn of the century, and lived until 1969. He first learned rod-building from Eustis Edwards, but like so many of his generation, he was also strongly influenced by the Payne rods. Gillum produced about 1000 rods during his lifetime, but because he never standardized his numbering system, it's difficult to establish a chronology .

Gillum constantly experimented with his tapers, probably more than any other rod-builder of his time. Some rods employed ferrules from the Payne workshops, while others, he made himself.

A seldom-seen Gillum original. His lifetime production amounted to something like 1000 rods.

His rods were highly regarded by fishermen of the day and an article in *The Fly and the Fish* ranks Gillum's rods as among the best ever built. Not so, however, at the beginning of his career in Connecticut, for his business partner was using a glue of such low-quality that, in short time, the joints of those rods simply "dissolved." Anxious to find a solution, Gillum asked Garrison for help, and was quickly convinced to use a synthetic rather than natural glue.

The Book about Him Influenced Europe

No other American rod-builder had an impact in Europe equal to that of Everett Garrison. Garrison lived from 1893 to 1975, and his book, *A Master's Guide to Building a Bamboo Fly Rod* (written by Hoagy B. Carmichael and published in 1977, after Garrison's death), was the first, modern, step-by-step manual for constructing split-bamboo rods. Called "The Bible" among specialists, this book stimulated a large number of younger people to begin building rods. In fact, I'd go so far as to say that this book was responsible for rejuvenating the public's interest in bamboo, and gave rise to an entire generation of American rod-makers – and soon after, to take hold in Europe as well. The book's impact in Europe is even more remarkable when one recalls that, by the mid-1970s, D.A.M. had already overwhelmed the entire tradition of split-bamboo rods by introducing the first graphite rods to the "Old World" market. I had begun rod-making several years before obtaining Garrison's book (in 1978 or '79), but soon recognized that much of what I had done before was simply wrong or could have been done more easily.

Garrison called himself an "amateur" rod builder because many of his rods were made during the evenings or weekends. Despite this, his rods, like those of Payne, are considered some of the best split-cane rods made in the entire world.

Unlike the rods built by nearly all his famous colleagues, Garrison's rods were planed entirely by hand, and he never used a milling machine.

After earlier schooling in Yonkers, New York, Garrison studied engineering, and for several years following 1916, he held a position with the New York Central Railroad. Apparently, in those years, he often enjoyed a round of golf, and one day when he became unhappy with the shaft on one of his clubs, he asked his brother (an able craftsman) to help with its repair. The story has it that this brother recently obtained a copy of Dr. George Parker Holden's book, *The Idyl of the Split-Bamboo* – the only book published at that time on the construction of hexagonal, bamboo rods.

Garrison learned extensively from Dr. George Parker Holden.

One of the legendary Garrisons. This well-preserved "Model 228" is still ready to use.

By very good fortune, Holden lived in Yonkers (just as did Garrison), and once the two men began working together, they remained the best of friends until Holden's death.
Garrison gained his basic knowledge about the details of rod-building from Holden, but because of Garrison's technical education, he quickly uncovered the theoretical basis for that knowledge. In 1927, Garrison borrowed an 8-foot Payne for measurement and evaluation, but shortly after, he designed his own, new tapers, and put these into production instead.
When the Great Depression reached its peak in 1932, Garrison lost his job with the railroad and decided to withdraw to his workshop to build rods for the market. In 1933, he took an entire bundle of rods to a lecture being held at the Angler's Club of New York, and by the end of the evening, all the rods had been sold. According to Kienbusch's forward to the Garrison book, however, "...it is doubtful whether he received more than $45 for each of the rods."

Sometime later, he obtained a position with another railroad and, after 1940, became a civil engineer for a number of companies until his retirement in 1970. Garrison's friends described him as a gentleman who loved fun, good conversation, good food, and attractive women. He was ready at any time to take a customer behind his house, "armed" with various rods and reels for testing. Many a customer learned the proper method of casting with a split-bamboo rod directly from Garrison.

You simply can't imagine how I felt when I first held a Garrison rod in my hand. The circle had closed.

Just When You Think You Know Everything

It really wasn't really a fishing vacation and we had no special destination, but the trip from Zurich, (where we had visited friends) to Austria wouldn't take long. Somehow, we – that is, my blond girlfriend, her enchanting and similarly-blond daughter, and I – ended up at a small hotel near a little mountain stream. Purely by happenstance, of course, I had some fishing equipment along, so, once we settled in, I could no longer contain my impatience for a little closer look at the creek.

We all know that feeling when approaching a new stretch of water. There's joy and excitement to lighten your step; the sound of water in the distance; the sharp smell of the woods and damp stream banks; the first silvery flashes showing through the trees, and then a little bridge.

But, this creek was rushing through the valley foamy and yellowish-gray. Fishing? Impossible! Well, I consoled myself, it really wasn't a fishing vacation anyway, and the brochure did mention a mountain lake. Tomorrow would be another day, but…darn!

On the next day, however, the weather was most unfriendly and the surrounding mountains were barely visible. Take out the umbrella, take a walk, eat...and maybe, ask how to get to the lake. At the entrance to our hotel, I spotted a notice-board, covered with a variety of information. One, in particular, brought me screeching to a halt – a color photo of a trout, and written beneath I read, "Brown trout, 4 3/4 pounds, caught by Mr. S. on 22 June." Unfortunately, where our Mr. S. had caught this dream-fish wasn't mentioned, but judging by its size, I was sure it could only have come from one of the many ponds we had seen, both left and right, while driving into the village.

Now, such a photo doesn't offer much encouragement when it's pouring down rain, and the creek that we crossed several times on our way to the lake was even higher, foamier, and grayer than the day before.

The lake, however, at an elevation of 5600 feet, was a revelation. Set in a valley, closed off at its upper end, the lake glittered and flashed in the sunlight from turquoise to dark green. We had left the clouds behind us at 5000 feet. A few rises at the other end of lake made my heart skip a little, and because my two princesses wanted to walk up to a higher meadow, I only had to pull on my boots, rig up the rod, and I could get going. Choosing the fly didn't take much study because a glance into the water revealed caddis nymphs. Amazing, at this elevation! I fired my back-cast into a space between some trees ("Wow, didn't hang up!") and let the fly settle gently on the water. A rise just next to my fly, a little tug on the sedge, and my rod bent for the first time on this gorgeous, high mountain lake. A little later, a good-sized lake-char was landed and released (meals were included in the room price), but I thought I was seeing things when two blonds waved at me from the opposite shore. How long had I been fishing? How could I be standing on the other side? Had I really walked halfway around the lake in this short time? My two ladies quickly informed me that more than two hours had passed.

Who says that God counts the hours you fish as part of your lifetime?

The excellent food in the hotel's dining room ended our day with full satisfaction and set me to hoping for the coming days. Sure enough, on the next morning even the far mountain peaks were visible. Returning from a quick run down to the stream at noon, I reported breathlessly, "The water looks really good – I have to fish that creek over lunchtime!" One blue and one brown pair of eyes showed understanding, so I bolted down my coffee and made myself ready.

I got to the bridge and stared into the water. It had cleared somewhat during the previous hours and I could now see the bottom in many places, but no movement was visible anywhere. I watched for a long time because experience taught me that fish only become discernable here or there after the eye has adjusted. I must have stood there for nearly ten minutes (providing entertainment for hikers and passers-by) until I gave up and crept downstream, attempting to locate the incognito creek-dwellers. Over the years, I've investigated many rivers and creeks, finally becoming pretty good at spying fish behind big rocks – or searching out their feeding spots at the edge of a current or the in-flow of little riffs, or the tails of pools, and...and...

I learned to hide behind every kind of cover, to consider the position of the sun, to be careful of my shadow, and to sneak up on hands and knees. At one promising spot, the creek made a sharp bend. The bank on the outside of this curve was deeply cut, and a gravel bank on its opposite side, half covered by a side-branch of the creek, sloped down into a beautiful pool. I moved my head slowly and carefully around a large tree trunk, hoping at last to see a fish. They must be here! If not, then nowhere. Slowly, I looked from rock to rock, from the gravel bed into the pool, and I saw...nothing! No fins, no red spots, no shadows, absolutely nothing. Disappointed, I stood up (the devil with all my experience!) and wandered farther downstream to the edge of the access, still looking into the water and hoping. Nothing.

A dipper on the opposite bank looked up, and I could've sworn it watched me with pity as I shuffled back upstream. On top of everything else, a number of those darned little pebbles made their way into my boots. Each step became so painful that I had to stop, jumping around on one foot while I took them off – one-by-one – and shook them out. I won't bother to repeat the remarks made by the couple walking past: In Europe, the type is well known – green hats, brown walking sticks with all the little nailed-on shields, and clack-clack-clack. My mood dropped to a new low, and in frustration, I sat down at the creekside to smoke my pipe. No fish in the stream where I had to end up.... The beauty of the mountain scenery consoled me, although some distant clouds suggested the weather could turn foul again. I looked at my special, small-stream rod. I had thought of everything, 4X tippet (strong current), weighted nymph (dry fly, useless because of the current), but I hadn't anticipated a lack of fish. With faint interest, I stripped out some line and watched as the current pulled my fly downstream, the drag bending the rod tip a little rudely. I let out more line, just allowing the reel to turn without its drag, and the strong current slowly took the line out. Then, re-lighting my now-cold pipe and holding the rod with one hand, my nymph got hung-up on a branch.

"So, now we have that, too," I thought. Then, the branch jumped into the air and showed its deep red spots before taking off downstream. The photo in the hotel came back to mind, and even though the weather was now distinctly cooler, I began to sweat – this creek dweller had shown itself to be big! A lot of line had already been stripped from my reel, and the current's drag created a large, half-circle bend in my rod. I had to get into the water because, even though the tippet was strong, hauling this fish in would be impossible. I couldn't follow it along the shore because of all the overhanging branches, not to mention the big rocks waiting at the next bend. So, I stumbled and splashed downstream as best I could and tried to keep contact while gaining back a little line. Each time I thought I was bringing him closer, the heavy fish used the current and shook hard. When I finally managed to get within about 15 feet, I was astonished at its size! I thought my fish had become tired, but obviously, I had no idea. Until now, it had only been playing with the current and was rested. Then, recognizing its opponent, the trout used its full strength, no doubt, well-trained in the rapid flow of this creek. A quick leap, a powerful run, then he and my nymph said goodbye.

On the way back to the hotel I kept asking myself how a fish as huge as that could hide so that **even I** couldn't see it.

As I entered the hotel, I declined to glance at the photo of "Mr. S." with his fish, nor, as I ate my dinner in silence, did I choose to take notice of the concerned looks coming from those blue and brown pairs of eyes across the table.

An enormous inventory of rods, stored on the top floor of the American Museum of Fly Fishing and waiting to be put on display.

At a show in New York, the Director of the American Museum of Fly Fishing invited me to come for a visit. I set out in my rental car, and after driving many miles too far (there must be at least five towns in New England named "Manchester"), I arrived late in the evening in Manchester, Vermont. The next morning, I stood punctually in front of the museum and received a friendly greeting.

A quick tour through the small rooms provided a general overview, and after brief instructions, I was left alone to examine everything at my leisure. Reverently, I looked in the display cases and read the little signs underneath. I couldn't believe my luck as I read all those famous names, and I was allowed to photograph everything! Then, of course, a problem arose, because it's difficult to photograph through display-case glass. What should I do? Disheartened, I knocked on the door to Garry Tanner's office and asked timidly if I could perhaps open the cabinets to... "Sure," was his quick answer. In the next moment, he stood next to me with a screwdriver, and soon we were lifting a heavy cover from one of the cases. He took the rods from their display mounts, put them in my hands, and returned to his office.

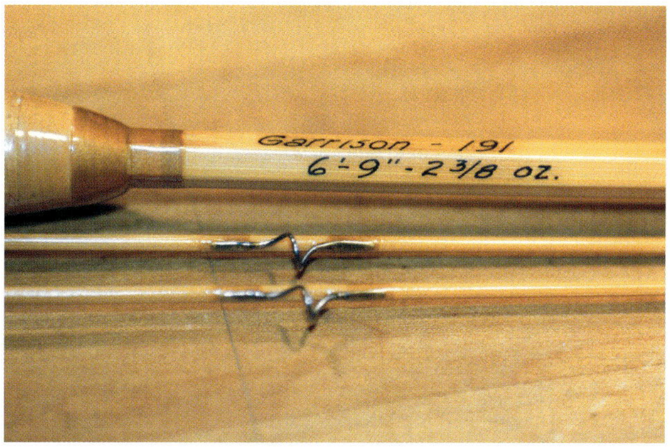

A 6 foot 9 inch Garrison "191" at the museum.

Typical Garrison cork reelseat with hardware he produced himself.

Astonished, I was standing there with a Garrison, a Payne and a Gillum in my hands. Carefully, very, very carefully, I laid them on a table that had been provided for my photography. As I looked down at these rods, it seemed like a dream to be holding things I had only read about, or seen in photos and drawings. In truth, I felt a shiver along my spine.

Garrison preferred two-piece versions for his trout models. His tapers have long been legendary, and many rod-builders throughout the world have copied them. The splendid "206" at 7 1/2 feet can hardly be improved, but the delicate "193" at 6 1/2 feet and the "212" at 8 feet also provide a perfectly-balanced casting response.
Garrison preferred hexagonal rods, and he supported his reasons with detailed theory in his 1952 article for *Field and Stream*. I recommend to anyone interested, that they start on page 238 of Garrison's book and go completely through his mathematical bases and calculations. These certainly exceed the requirements of the book.

A French Wonder

In 1860, a small fishing store opened in Amboise in the Loire Valley, France. This was taken over in 1865 by Gustave Pezon and became the start of Pezon and Michel. In 1924, Pezon and Michel bought Sellier and Robillard, which sold split-bamboo rods imported from England. In 1930, they also took over Garreau, which produced its own split-bamboo rods. But Pezon and Michel first attained international recognition through Charles Ritz (born in 1891). The name, "Ritz," was already well-known because of Charles' father, Cesar, who founded the famous hotels. In 1916, young Charles arrived in America, but was required to learn the hotel business under difficult conditions. He received little financial support from his father – at first, earning pocket money by repairing and restoring rods he bought second-hand.

In those first years, Charles occupied small working and living quarters in the basement of the famous hotel, and during his lunch breaks, he often walked down the next block to visit the Abercrombie & Fitch sporting goods store. There, he grew familiar with the rods of Thomas, Edwards, Hawes, and Payne, all of which, of course, were completely beyond his means.

It was also in those early years that the young Ritz experimented with a variety of inexpensive rods by shortening a tip-section or altering the length of its butt. He analyzed how the action would change and kept the most successful rods for his own fishing. Later, he described his beginnings in his book, *A Fly Fisher's Life* (the German version first published in 1956 as *Erlebtes Fliegenfischen*). A selection follows:

The first German-language version of Charles Ritz's classic A Fly Fisher's Life. This edition appeared in 1956 and numbered 3000 copies.

"The salesmen always seemed to be busy when I appeared [at Abercrombie & Fitch], but nothing could discourage me and, in a very short while, I knew better than they did what the departments contained.
"My salary of a hundred dollars a month prevented my being an important client of theirs and obliged me to slum by frequenting the pawnshops on Fourth Avenue where, for two dollars, ten at most, I was able to gratify my passion for fishing rods! For a few cents I could proudly buy from Abercrombie and Fitch rod varnish, silk for whippings and cement for ferrules. Then, in my little office, which I had transformed into a workshop to the considerable disapprobation of the manager of the hotel, who only put up with my impudence because I was my father's son, I devoted myself to renovating my finds. I scraped them, I took the ferrules to pieces, I shortened the weak joints and strengthened my 'new' rods throughout with extra fine white silk that became invisible when varnished. I then showed my masterpieces to the salesmen in the big shop, who were astonished but interested! My rods had taken on a new life."

New Ideas

By this time, Ritz had discovered that reasonable action in a fly rod would require relative stiffness through its last, uppermost inches. A visit to Jim Payne reinforced this opinion, and it's ironical that this company was later influenced Ritz himself.
Charles Ritz returned to Europe in 1937, where he became deeply involved in building bamboo rods. It was then that Roger Pujo, editor of a fishing magazine, suggested that Ritz visit Pezon and Michel for a look at their production of split-bamboo rods. As he remarks laconically in his book, "A month later, I became their Technical Advisor."
After 1938, cooperation between Charles Ritz, Edouard Plantet (production supervisor), and Pierre Creusevaut (world casting champion) produced the series of rods that would secure their reputation in the annals of bamboo rod-making, even to this day. Ritz was a perfectionist who left nothing to chance, and after several false starts, he developed a series of six models, including the famous "Super-Parabolic P.P.P." (*Puissance Pendulaire Progressive* – continuously increasing power).
In addition to calculating their tapers, Ritz's rod-development required long sessions of pragmatic testing. These sessions called for subjective appraisals of his rods' casting behavior, obtained from both good casters and poor – and included distance-casting over water. Following his tests, Ritz concluded that the best casting characteristics would be achieved by locating the ferrules as far away from the rod tip as possible, and for this reason, Pezon and Michel produced no three-piece models. It was also because of these tests that Ritz developed his unevenly-segmented rods, designed with butts being significantly shorter than the tip sections. These models were called the "staggered ferrule," and for safe transport, an extension was included with the rod. This was simply inserted into the ferrule of the butt section to make its length equal to the tip.

Ritz was very defiant in his opinions about rods, and accepted no other views:

"There are not dozens of types of actions, but one only, whose rigidity varies according to the length of the rod, and it must work progressively from the point to the handle without the slightest weakness, however used."

Ritz originated an artificial designation for his rods, called "parabolic action." He explained this, saying:

"This is the action which I have called 'Parabolic,' though the term is only a figure of speech, and the curve of the rod has absolutely nothing whatever to do with a parabola."
Despite Ritz's disclaimer, his designation still holds today, and rods continue to be described as "half-parabolic" or "full-parabolic." Apparently, many fly-fishermen want to assign meaning to the term – but what meaning?

Ritz was similarly unambiguous about the shape of his grips, rejecting any form of cigar grip, and insisting, instead, that a fisherman must use the "thumb grip" for casting. That is, the thumb should be placed on top of the grip. For him, everything else was simply wrong and damaged the correct casting style.
Interestingly, and particularly for collectors, no Tonkin cane was available during the Second World War. In Europe, "French" bamboo was used in its place, but unfortunately, this species had only a very thin layer of power fibers, and the rods that emerged during these years needed to be built "stronger" (that is, thicker) in order to retain similar action.

Pezon and Michel first produced three different series of parabolic rods, the "Parabolic Speciale," the "Parabolic Supreme," and, the most expensive series, the "Super Parabolic P.P.P." The first two were two-piece rods, with butt and tip sections of the same length, while the "Super Parabolic" employed the un-equal sections described above. Additionally, a number of models were designed for specialized purposes, including the "Parabolic Special Competition" for tournament, distance-casting.

This picture from an older Pezon & Michel catalog shows the milling machine used to cut splines to their final dimensions.

Most rod-builders developed their tapers through testing and altering, but sometimes, tapers also arise by accident, and the story of the "Fario Club" rod is famous. Originally built as a 9-footer, it was delivered by a courier to the Hotel Ritz. Unfortunately, being protected only by its cloth bag, when the rod became tangled in the spokes of the courier's bicycle, fatal breaks occurred at the tip and the ferrule. Saying not a word, the courier left the broken rod at the hotel reception desk and disappeared. Charles Ritz, without looking at it, took the rod on a fishing trip to the River Lech in Germany, noticing the catastrophe only upon unpacking at the river's edge. He had no extra tip and no substitute rod, so the only solution was to repair the rod. Tip-top and ferrule were heated, removed, and newly-attached at the breaks, and the 9-foot rod became an 8 1/2-footer. After Ritz made his first few casts, he was forced to conclude that the "new" rod was much better than the original. A new taper was born! Unfortunately, it's not known what happened to the courier responsible for the accident.

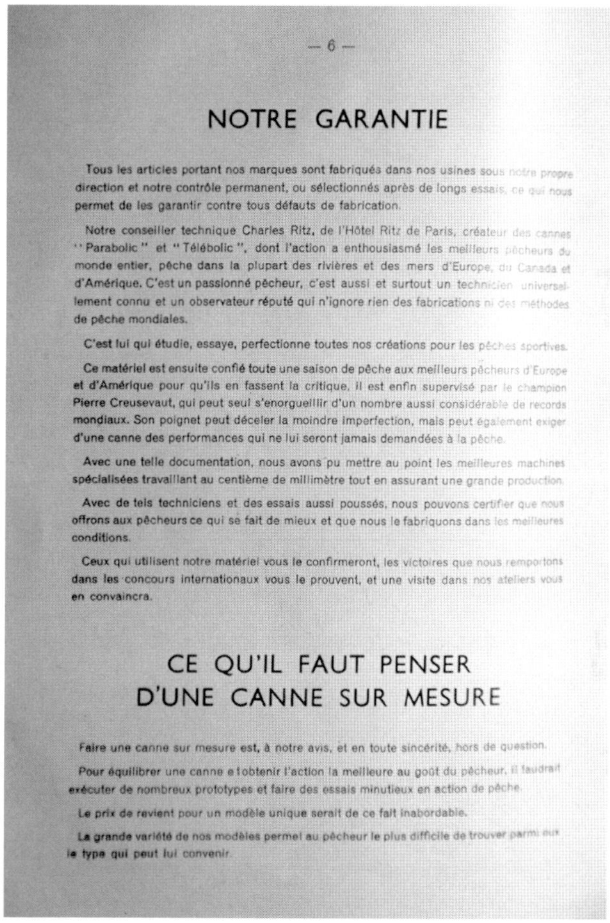
— 6 —

NOTRE GARANTIE

Tous les articles portant nos marques sont fabriqués dans nos usines sous notre propre direction et notre contrôle permanent, ou sélectionnés après de longs essais, ce qui nous permet de les garantir contre tous défauts de fabrication.

Notre conseiller technique Charles Ritz, de l'Hôtel Ritz de Paris, créateur des cannes "Parabolic" et "Télébolic", dont l'action a enthousiasmé les meilleurs pêcheurs du monde entier, pêche dans la plupart des rivières et des mers d'Europe, du Canada et d'Amérique. C'est un passionné pêcheur, c'est aussi et surtout un technicien universellement connu et un observateur réputé qui n'ignore rien des fabrications ni des méthodes de pêche mondiales.

C'est lui qui étudie, essaye, perfectionne toutes nos créations pour les pêches sportives.

Ce matériel est ensuite confié toute une saison de pêche aux meilleurs pêcheurs d'Europe et d'Amérique pour qu'ils en fassent la critique. Il est enfin supervisé par le champion Pierre Creusevaut, qui peut seul s'enorgueillir d'un nombre aussi considérable de records mondiaux. Son poignet peut déceler la moindre imperfection, mais peut également exiger d'une canne des performances qui ne lui seront jamais demandées à la pêche.

Avec une telle documentation, nous avons pu mettre au point les meilleures machines spécialisées travaillant au centième de millimètre tout en assurant une grande production.

Avec de tels techniciens et des essais aussi poussés, nous pouvons certifier que nous offrons aux pêcheurs ce qui se fait de mieux et que nous le fabriquons dans les meilleures conditions.

Ceux qui utilisent notre matériel vous le confirmeront, les victoires que nous remportons dans les concours internationaux vous le prouvent, et une visite dans nos ateliers vous en convaincra.

CE QU'IL FAUT PENSER D'UNE CANNE SUR MESURE

Faire une canne sur mesure est, à notre avis, et en toute sincérité, hors de question.

Pour équilibrer une canne et obtenir l'action la meilleure au goût du pêcheur, il faudrait exécuter de nombreux prototypes et faire des essais minutieux en action de pêche.

Le prix de revient pour un modèle unique serait de ce fait inabordable.

La grande variété de nos modèles permet au pêcheur le plus difficile de trouver parmi eux le type qui peut lui convenir.

The Pezon & Michel guaranty card.

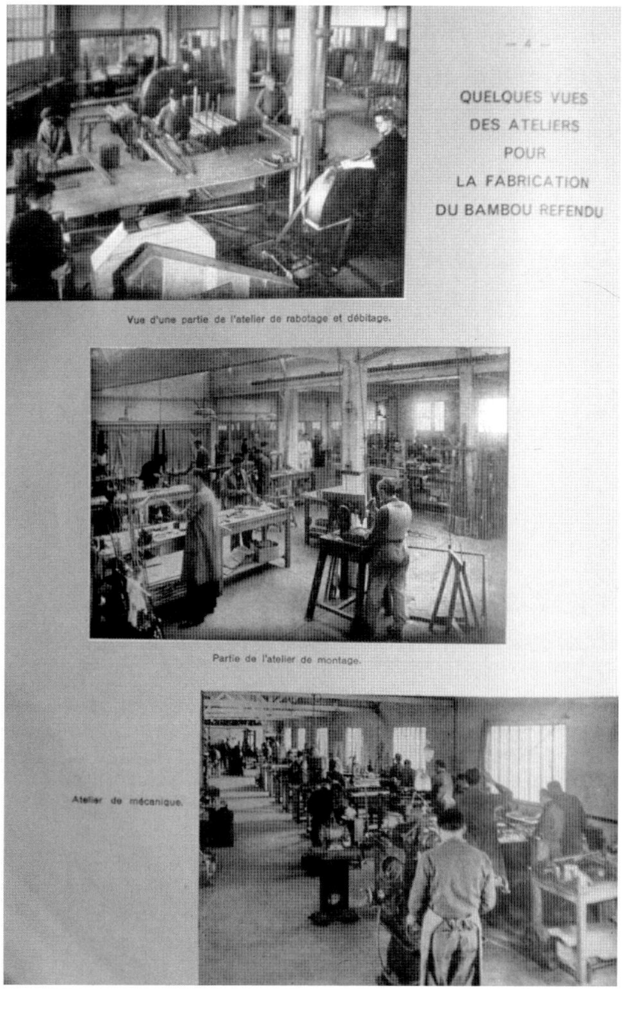

Photos of the workshops demonstrate that the company produced large numbers of rods.

Charles Ritz's line of fly rods and his casting abilities soon generated an international reputation, acclaim that brought him in touch with nearly every famous fisherman of his time. Ernest Hemingway and Frank Sawyer will serve to represent the many other names of equal repute. There were hardly any waters on this earth left un-fished by Ritz and his friends, and many of his special rod creations were derived from discussions with these famous fishermen.

Several of his tapers found their way to England, although many of these were supplied with cigar-shaped, modified grips – even Orvis used some of Ritz's ideas in its own series. Pezon and Michel remained the only large and significant company on the continent able to compete with the big English and American firms, with more than 300 employees working in its plant. In the 1970s, however, the gates in Amboise slowly closed, and the company stopped production in the 1990s. Then, in 1999, the name "Pezon et Michel" was bought by a company in Paris, continuing on with a few split-cane rods under the old name.

The Pezon & Michel logo with the Tricolor.

An 8 ft. 6 in. Pezon & Michel with its typical red wraps. The doubled decorative wraps at the guides were common.

Cultural Revolution and Bamboo

The years between 1930 and 1960 are generally thought of as the "golden years" of the split-bamboo rod. Many jewels in the art of rod-building were produced during this period, but it's certain that the greatest influence and development came from rod-builders in the USA. It's assumed that the more famous companies would have accumulated enormous supplies of Tonkin bamboo, but because of limited storage space and cost, this was only partly the case. Following 1940, the areas of Canton and Fatsan were occupied by the Japanese (thus, restricting most Chinese exports), and trade in Tonkin bamboo was later interrupted during the Second World War. Bamboo deliveries stopped completely after the Japanese attack on Pearl Harbor, and the product was not cultivated at all during the war. But, war returned after 1946 -- this time between Chiang Kai-shek and Mao Tse-tung, and lasting until 1949 with Mao's defeat of Chiang Kai-shek. President Harry S. Truman announced the "Truman Doctrine" after Mao's takeover, accusing the Communist states of endangering world peace, and thus, began the years of the China Embargo. In the years following 1949, American companies obtained bamboo indirectly, but were no longer able to purchase from China. Most supplies came through England, once that country resumed formal relations with China in 1950.

It is documented that, during the time of the Embargo, English firms such as Hardy, Sharpes, or Millward retained the best bamboo for themselves, with the USA receiving only second-class material. American companies had to work with whatever they could get, whether the canes were seasoned or not.

The English company, Fosters, similarly kept the best bamboo for its own rods.

Back to the Future

It used to be simple to go fishing -- that's what was so good about it! You'd agree to meet, at most, one or two fishing friends on the water or at a restaurant, or maybe you'd spend a fishing-weekend together. If the weather gods cooperated and everything else fell into place, you might even catch a fish or two. But, if not, you'd just enjoy some local restaurant or hotel and philosophize (over a few drinks) on the topic of fishing. Such weekends were the source of many of today's legends.

That's how it was. I can attest to it from long years of being one of those who fishes for the sea-run, brown trout, so beloved here in North Germany. But, today, just the plans, alone, for a weekend demand knowledge of modern technology. "What!? Whaddya mean, drive to Denmark? Are you crazy!? We gotta check the web sites to see if anyone's catching anything!" This was what I heard when I asked a friend if he wanted to take off for a weekend. The next morning, his very tired voice was on the phone, "I spent the night at the computer, checking everything. Seems to be okay right now." Well, this was just fine! I'd been fully informed, by email, about the water temperature, catch reports, and the exact weather forecast. So, with his web-site tip to tie a bunch of blue-green patterns (the only thing working at present), our departure time was set.

We drove off in the right direction, at least until we passed Hamburg. Then, the cell phone rang, and on the line was another fishing buddy, telling us that he'd just caught a 19-inch trout on the island of Als. Apparently, he was still standing in the water as he described the thrill of victory. So, instead of driving straight ahead, as originally planned, we turned eastward at Flensburg. Then, the cell phone rang again with its merry little tune. A 20 1/2-incher was reported, and, thank God, also from Als -- but this time on the other side of the island. Twenty and one-half is better than 19 inches, so, with heightened anticipation, we changed our destination again.

That enthusiasm sank a bit, however, when we arrived at the parking spot, for there were five (count 'em, 5!) cars with German license plates. Adding up the customary two people per car, plus us, that made 12 fishermen. Apparently, the fellow with the cell phone was up to speed on his modern technology and had made a conference call.

I was even more disturbed when two more cars appeared from nowhere, driving in our direction, and before we could set up our gear, we greeted still four more fishermen from Lübeck and Oldenburg. It didn't take long to solve the parking problem: We organized the cars into two, neat rows in the tiny parking area.

When we finally got around to tying on our flies, we heard the confirmation, "Yes, that's right, the blue-green pattern!" A short walk brought us to the lucky spot, but what we saw took our breath away -- not to mention all remnants of hope. I counted 14 people, spaced about 35 feet apart, so, together with us late-comers, we now had a total of 20 fishermen! Turn around after driving that long distance and trudging all the way out here in full get-up? Never! So, we get into line (that is, we get into the water), but then our situation suddenly improved. From about 200 yards away, I heard that familiar little melody, and with that, six people departed in a flash. Obviously, they'd just received a call about some other fishing success and I thought, "Some people just fish on the road."

I hoped their car wasn't blocked-in by the others, but finally we're down to 14. Soon, it began to rain, and only one fish was caught, but we all made our way over to the guy to express great admiration for this 16-incher -- a fish, by the way, that was caught on a red-and-black pattern. When everybody got back into the water, I began to wonder about all this cell-phone business. It was nearing evening now, and I was just standing there, but by dusk, only the two of us remained. The rain had let up, and finally we could enjoy the peace and quiet and a view of the horizon. We were somewhat conciliated by the scenery (even without fish), and when we found our way back to the car, it was already dark. Although we were tired by then, we drove to the next town to find lodging. After two hours of hearing only, "Everything's booked: You should have phoned ahead earlier," we realized we'd be in for a long night in the car. What I wouldn't have given for a nice, little hotel -- just like it used to be...!

Special Developments

Fred Divine was an early pathfinder.

Fred Divine was the first to develop the spiraled bamboo rod, built with a continuous twist along its entire axis. The idea was to produce greater stiffness, although from today's point of view, it's questionable whether this procedure produced the desired result. Divine's technique must have been very difficult to accomplish, considering that the spiral had to be formed so the guides would all line up at their designated locations. Unfortunately, the public showed little interest and these rods found very few customers. Divine's spiral rod production ended, but an amateur builder, Letcher Lambuth, is to be thanked for preserving this art. He resurrected and improved Divine's idea a number of years later, leaving a precise description of his altered method to history in his remarkable book, *The Angler's Workshop*.

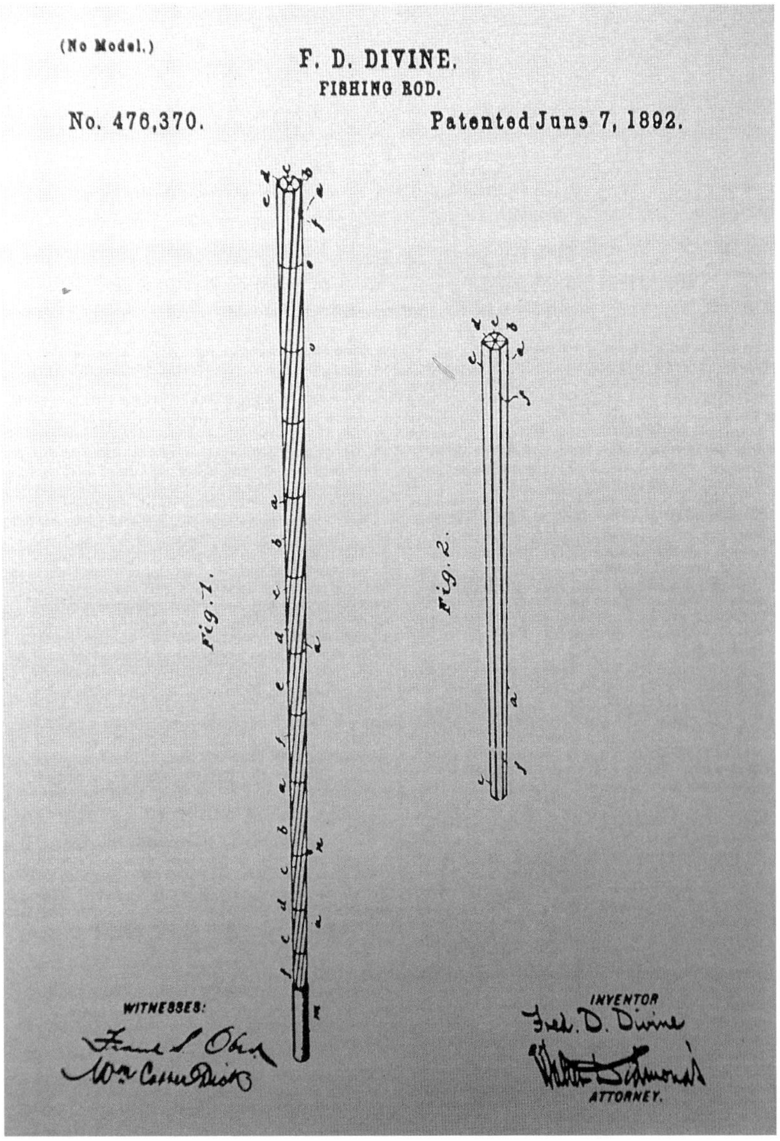

Fred Devine's patent drawing for a "spiral" rod.

Tangible history: Letcher Lambuth's plane and form.

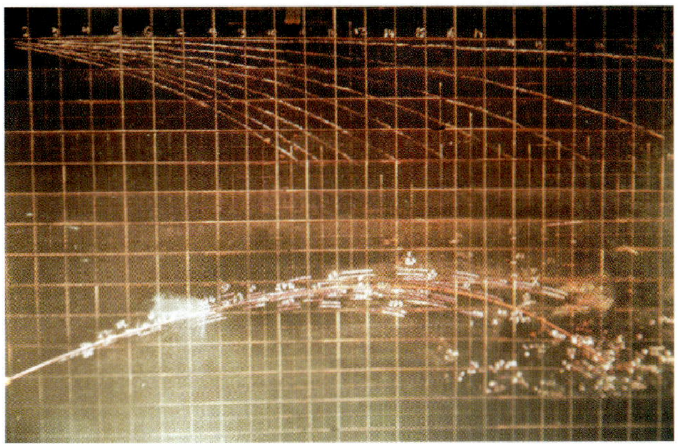

Theory and practice: Various weights are attached to a rod tip, with its resulting bends compared to theoretical curves.

"Holy tools" and rod-building materials once belonging to Hiram Leonard, Hiram Hawes, and Letcher Lambuth: Displayed in the American Museum of Fly Fishing.

Some of his tools still exist and are displayed in the American Museum of Fly Fishing.

Over the years, great numbers of rod-builders have labored to make their products faster or stiffer, so it was necessary to have some method of measuring a rod's relative resilience. One solution was to fasten a rod parallel to a board, nailed on the wall. The rod would be mounted at a slight upward angle and with a line fed through its guides. Lastly, the line would have some fixed, known weight attached to its end.

The resulting flex-curve could easily be drawn on the board, making comparisons to other variations possible. No bamboo culm is completely like another and there are always slight differences, even among rods built to the same length and taper. Some companies tested their products in this way, with the purpose of culling rods that deviated too far from their standard.

Only Power Fibers

It was already clear to early rod-builders that the "speed" of a rod depended largely upon the bamboo's power fibers, while the "backing" material (that is, the inner pith of the bamboo culm) was viewed as a necessary evil and only added weight to a rod. Many makers experimented by gluing two or more outer layers of fibers directly on top of one another, but without seeing much benefit. Nevertheless, rods began to appear with double or multiple-laminations, including several models from American companies. The first patents for double-laminated rods were issued in 1885, while in England, Hardy, too, developed its own multiple-lamination techniques.

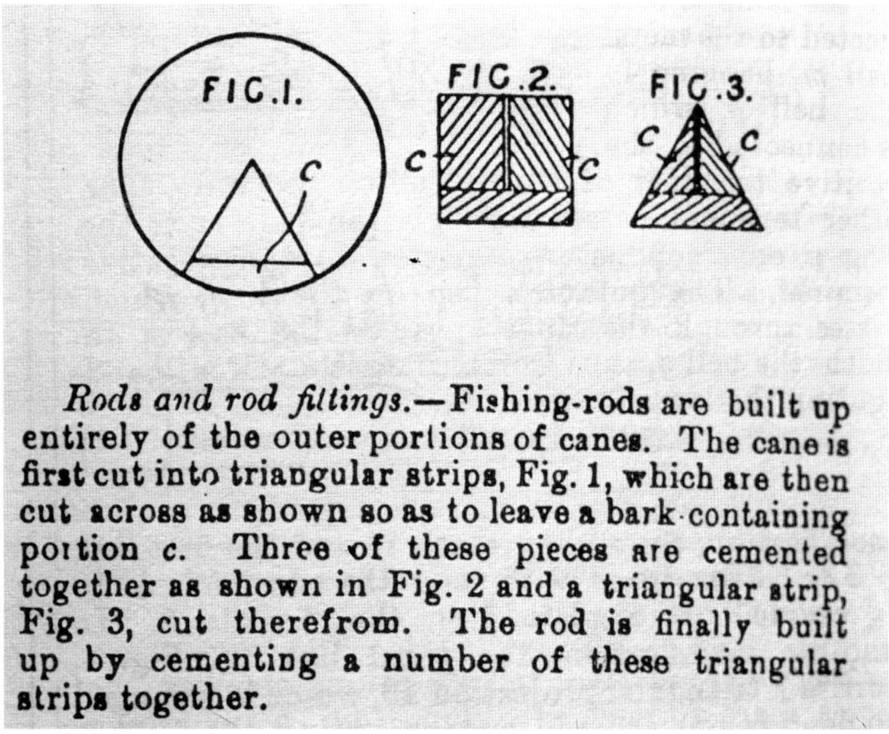

Rods and rod fittings.—Fishing-rods are built up entirely of the outer portions of canes. The cane is first cut into triangular strips, Fig. 1, which are then cut across as shown so as to leave a bark-containing portion *c*. Three of these pieces are cemented together as shown in Fig. 2 and a triangular strip, Fig. 3, cut therefrom. The rod is finally built up by cementing a number of these triangular strips together.

One of many patent drawings showing how a single spline can be fabricated from various segments of a culm's power fibers.

Mistakes and Confusion

Yet another effort to improve a rod's stiffness was the so-called "steel center" design, introduced in England. This involved inserting a thin, steel rod within a hollow blank. Apparently, the taper of the steel rod was achieved by drawing it slowly from a bath of hydrochloric acid. The longer the steel was in the acid, the thinner it became. In this way, the steel's own taper would reach all the way to the tip of the rod. The rods were supposed to be unbreakable, but their overall appeal to the public was only mediocre because they had become slow and, of course, heavy. I've found no records to document the method of producing the steel-cored rod, and even Hardy is no longer certain how it was done. In any event, after a period of time, residue from the hydrochloric acid would react with the rod's glue, and the steel core simply turned to rust. Take one of these "steel center" rods in your hands today and shake it, and you'll hear something like maracas in rod-form.

In the USA, rules limiting the weight of rods for tournament casting stimulated new efforts to lighten rods, and one significant step was made in 1933. Winston's Lew Stoner became the first to develop a process for building hollow-fluted, split-bamboo rods, later receiving a patent for this. The Winston method, still employed today, calls for a U-shaped trough to be routed along the inner side of each bamboo strip. This process leaves a wide area on the mating surfaces for glue, while achieving considerable weight reduction.

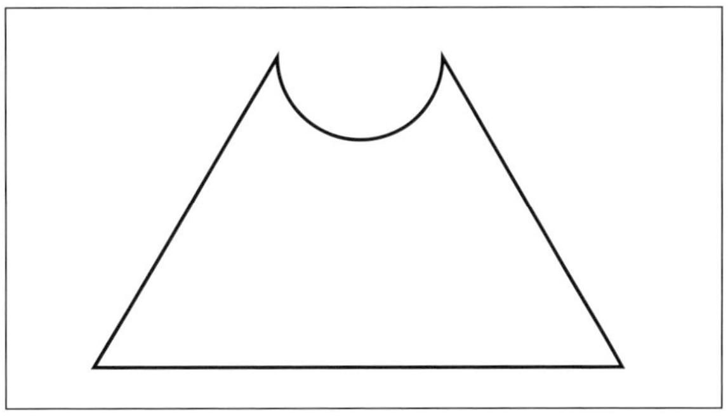

The Winston method.

Rods built in this manner became lighter and faster and, using one in 1934, Marvin Hedge set a new distance-casting record of 147 feet.

Another hollowing process was developed at the same time by Edwin Powell. His method was to remove the inner side of each bamboo strip down to the power fibers and glue a strip of cedar wood to the remaining layer of fibers. Then, he gave his strips their triangular shape, and, finally, removed a uniform thickness from the inner apex. The idea also included leaving cross-ridges at certain intervals, and at each of these locations Powell's rods were reinforced with an intermediate wrap.

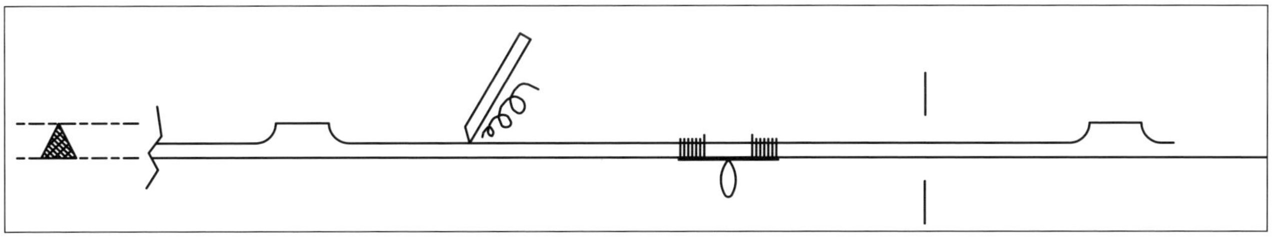

The Powell method.

To Mill or Plane?

Particularly in the early years, most rods were planed by hand, but public demand soon called for large quantities of rods, and to survive the competition, rod-makers needed new manufacturing methods. Quite a variety of machines emerged, all intended to shape the bamboo strips more quickly, and for the most part, more precisely. The objective was to make the process of copying a rod more reliable, or in other words, to produce larger numbers within the same series -- and quickly. Mostly, these machines were designed with two cutters oriented at an included angle of 60°. The idea was to shape the bamboo strips to their final taper in a single pass. Some of the old machines are still used today for rod-building.

Thomas Dorsey with the milling machine he designed and built.

Several machines also reside in museums, and can be admired as technical masterpieces of design and construction.

A complex mechanism: The milling machine from the Norwegian company, Hørgård, as displayed in the Hunting and Fishing Museum in Elverum, Norway.

In earlier years, both the design and the operation of these machines were held secret, and during factory visits, one often saw a sign saying: "Sorry -- No Entrance" applied to the workrooms occupied by the mills (or bevellers).

One of the most famous machines (still working today, I believe) was developed about 1908 by Loman Hawes, a nephew of Hiram Leonard. Its two, small sawblades were designed to cut at a 60° angle to each other, and the bamboo strip was simply pushed through. In one pass, the strip had a perfect taper.

More common, however, are milling-machines with a 60° cutter-head, intended to pass over the stationary, bamboo strip.

The 60-degree angles for shaping splines are clearly seen within the milling cutters..

The precise taper is produced by the shape of the form on which the bamboo strip rests, and today, anyone can buy such a machine. A small company in the USA, called, "Golden Witch," deals in rod-building tools, materials and accessories, and until recently, sold these machines.
Simple, basic forms for hand-planed strips were known long before rod-makers developed machinery, although these were mostly used by cabinet makers.

A modern milling machine, as could be purchased from "Golden Witch" in America.

Bamboo strips were also glued to metal forms, then shaped into their triangular cross-section with sandpaper or with a plane. One can argue about the aesthetics of this method, but it was actually used and is mentioned as one, possible method in Herter's *Rod-Building Manual.*

Popular rod grips, such as those used by the author.

Discussions about the proper grip for a rod are as old as the development of the fishing rod itself. The quarrel has not yet ended, and if recorded in all its facets, would fill an entire book. Length, diameter, and shape have varied over time as greatly as have the techniques and form of casting. Of course, the nature of the "home-waters" where rod-builders lived also had its influence. In any case, although many early rods had much shorter and smaller grips than would commonly be seen today, it hardly seems possible that fishermen 100 years ago would have had hands that much smaller than ours.

Most grips were developed for some particular casting style, while others have been oriented more towards the anatomy of the hand. Still others simply follow the design of the rod. All have their justifications!

Personally, I have difficulty with the discussion only when someone makes a rule out of a particular grip shape and denigrates all those who don't follow the rule. In this, I make no exception even for the notorious Charles Ritz, who found just one, single, grip shape acceptable -- the one appearing on Pezon & Michel's rods.

Many rod grips are based on the "cigar" shape used by Samuel Phillippe.

Various modifications of this grip are seen on the rods from Leonard, Payne, Hardy, Sharpe, Divine, Edwards, Orvis, Cross, Heddon, Young and others.

The "full-Wells" style was introduced by Henry Wells during the late Nineteenth Century, and appeared on rods built by Winston, Powell, and Phillipson, as well as on some rods from Hardy. The "half-Wells" grip also became popular on many rods -- those built by Hardy, Young, Dickerson, Heddon, South Bend and several others.

There have been repeated attempts to establish "anatomically" shaped grips, some with cut-outs for thumb and fingers formed in the cork, others being fashioned with slots or wood inlays for ease of holding. None of these shapes lasted, however, and all disappeared relatively quickly.

In Germany

"The fly rod remains the casting equipment offering the finest sport; the requirements for a fly rod are, therefore, justly demanding. It would almost be foolish to believe that any ordinary fishing rod could be appropriate for fly fishing. Fly fishing is, essentially, nothing without a rod made especially for this sport. Using other rods, it would be nearly impossible to make a single, decent cast; one could, at best, fish in ponds and waterfalls with a fly. In a word, a bad fly rod brings more trouble than pleasure. Of course, moderate trouble, and especially in the outdoors, is presumed to be healthy for those of phlegmatic nature, or with poor blood circulation. Despite that, I would not wish to recommend poor fishing gear, for in today's active life, both anglers and other persons can readily find other opportunities to bring their blood to boil."

"A good, single-handed fly rod should not weigh over 10 5/8 or, at most, 12 5/16 ounces, and not be longer than 10 feet 8 inches...."

From H. Stork, Munich, *On Fishing Rods*, AFZ of June 15, 1900.

In terms of international recognition, the history of German, split-cane rods is probably of little importance. Initially, only a few rods were made directly in Germany and many companies imported blanks from England or America, finished them, and attached their own logo. In many cases, it's impossible to determine with certainty if a rod actually was produced by the company or if it came from elsewhere.

The first producers of German fishing tackle appeared in the southern areas because this is where one finds the greatest number of trout-fishing streams. In the Nineteenth Century, fishing was mostly a privilege of the nobility, or at least, of the upper classes. Nearly all waters were in private hands, and fishing by the average citizen was not allowed. In Munich (Bavaria, which joined the German Empire in 1871), a small center of fishing-gear products developed, but for many years, merely imitated English and American equipment.

The first reference to split-bamboo rods in German literature can be dated to 1875. Max von dem Borne states on page 12 of his *Illustrated Handbook of Angling*:

"Finally, the jungle or Chinese cane should be mentioned. It can be as big around as a man. The thickest hollow pieces are split into thin strips, smoothed, and then form the full, striped-looking pieces in the rod tip.

"The strength of this cane -- the true bamboo -- is in its skin. One cuts it, therefore, along the length and makes rods out of the epidermis in such a clean and delicate fashion that a solid, round piece is formed.

"These are the most expensive and prized rods in America. Andrew Clerk of New York makes such split-bamboo rods, which are about 35-40 percent lighter than equally thick rods built from other materials...."

The original edition of the 1875 book, Handbook of Angling, which first introduced split-cane rods to Germany.

The second, revised edition, containing a description of split-cane rod construction.

The Noble Tradition Began

Max von dem Borne came from nobility and owned a manor, but because of his publications on angling and fish-rearing, he became known in Germany as a sport-fisherman. Internationally, however, he was a highly-respected fisheries scientist, playing a significant role in the widespread stocking of rainbow and brook trout in Germany. He even tried to introduce the American large and smallmouth bass.

He stayed in touch constantly with fellow American and English fishermen and scientists, and it was probably through these colleagues that von dem Borne became aware of split-cane rods. In any case, he was the first in Germany to become enthusiastic about these new rods and to recognize their new possibilities for lighter fishing equipment. In his book, *Illustrated Handbook of Angling*, von dem Borne describes all the wood types then commonly used for rod-building (citing their advantages and disadvantages), but he assigned the greatest importance to split-cane -- astonishingly farsighted for 1875. Germany is obligated to him for "discovering" bamboo rods and for bringing their potential to the attention of the public. In his 1882 *Pocket Book of Angling*, von dem Borne writes:

"East Indian bamboo provides the material used in the recently and extremely popular split-bamboo rods; it is sawn into strips and they are glued together. The first rod of this type was made by Samuel Philippi *[sic]* in Easton, Pennsylvania in 1848. These rods are mostly used in North America and the best-known makers are H. L. Leonard, earlier in Bangor, now in Central Valley, Orange County, and Abbey & Imbrie, 48 Maiden Lane, New York..."

His various involvements with American rod companies were probably also responsible for the first German production of split-bamboo rods. At the time, he was in close contact with the well-known German tackle maker, Heinrich Hildebrand in Munich, and we can assume that Hildebrand's methods for constructing bamboo rods first came to Germany through von dem Borne. The "Clerk" company mentioned above produced no rods itself, but exported rods built by various American makers worldwide. Presumably, this would have been the source of von dem Borne's building instructions.

The first bamboo rod built in Germany is documented in the records of Heinrich Hildebrand (which lists the dates for all new orders), and there, we learn of a split-cane fly rod having been sold to a Mr. Wieland in 1882 for a price of 60 Marks.

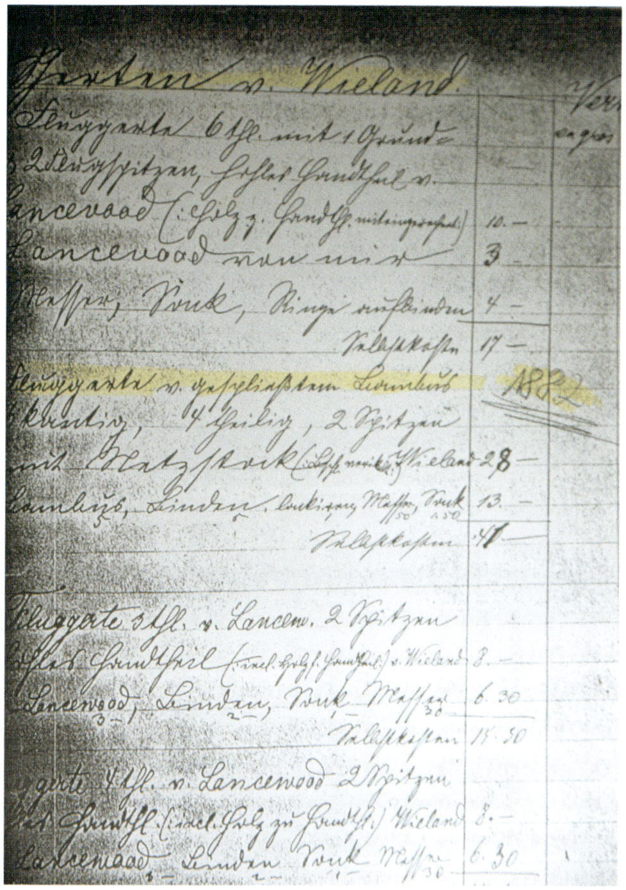

The first split-bamboo rod produced in Germany was probably built in 1882 and sold for 60 Marks -- an astonishing sum of money for the time.

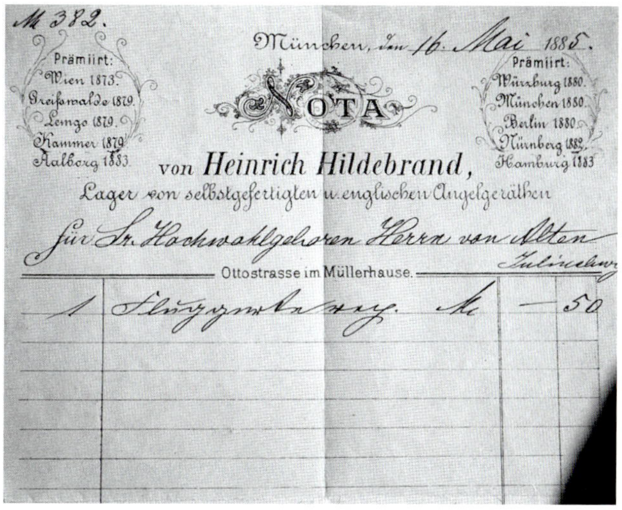
M 382.
München, den 16. Mai 1885.
Prämiirt: Wien 1873. Greifswalde 1879. Lemgo 1879. Hammer 1879. Aalborg 1883.
Prämiirt: Würzburg 1880. München 1880. Berlin 1880. Nürnberg 1882. Hamburg 1883.
NOTA
von Heinrich Hildebrand,
Lager von selbstgefertigten u. englischen Angelgeräthen
für Sr. Hochwohlgeboren Herrn von Alten
Ottostrasse im Müllerhause.

An original invoice from Heinrich Hildebrand, Munich.

Jakob Wieland was a master lathe-operator who made angling equipment for the Hildebrand company. In 1882, he successfully turned to machine-made, split-bamboo rods, and took over the Hildebrand company shortly after the turn of the century.

Another early proponent of bamboo was Dr. Karl Heinz (1850-1925). As the old master of German sport-fishing, he was important to development of fishing gear in South Germany with his many "incidental" inventions.

It's wonderful that such rarities remain: An early catalog of the Wieland company in Munich.

PREIS-COURANT

von

Heinr. Hildebrand

MÜNCHEN

Ottostrasse Müllerhaus.

LAGER

von selbstgefertigten und englischen

Angelfischerei-Geräthschaften.

Gegründet 1843.

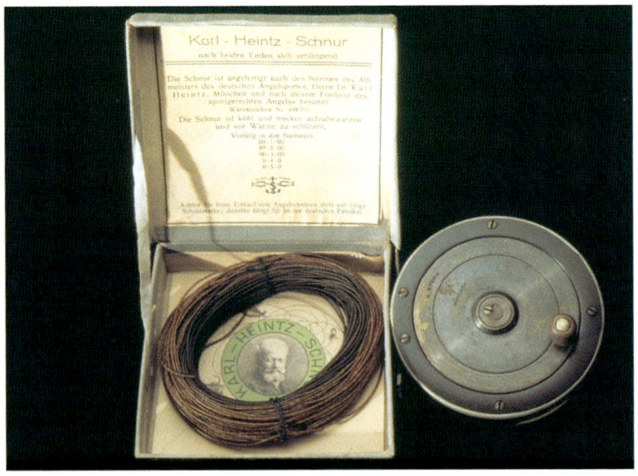

A double-taper, silk line from Dr. Karl Heintz, together with a rare and nearly contemporaneous reel by Storch of Munich.

The „Preis-Courant" the Fa. Heinrich Hildebrand.

Some examples are the famous "Heintz spoon," the "kingfisher fly," "the celluloid spinner," and Hardy's "crocodile spinner." In 1904, Heintz founded a Munich sport fishing club, called "The Split-Cane," still in existence today. His 10 1/2-foot, two-handed, bamboo, spin/casting rod was designed for distance-casting (later made as a series by Jakob Wieland), and remains a legend today.

It seems certain that split-bamboo rods became generally known in Germany by about 1900, at the latest, although this wouldn't suggest much about how widely the rods may have been used. The price for a bamboo rod was immensely high. Considering the average income in 1900, a split-bamboo fly rod would cost more than a month's salary, but this was also the case in England and America! Of all the types of rods, made of whatever exotic woods, those built from bamboo have always been the most expensive throughout the world. For this reason, it's likely that only the very rich used split-cane rods, and in comparison to wood, only a small number was being produced. Hence, we can be grateful for any equipment preserved from those early times. We can be grateful, too, that later developments in the manufacture of bamboo rods made them much more cost-effective than 100 years ago.

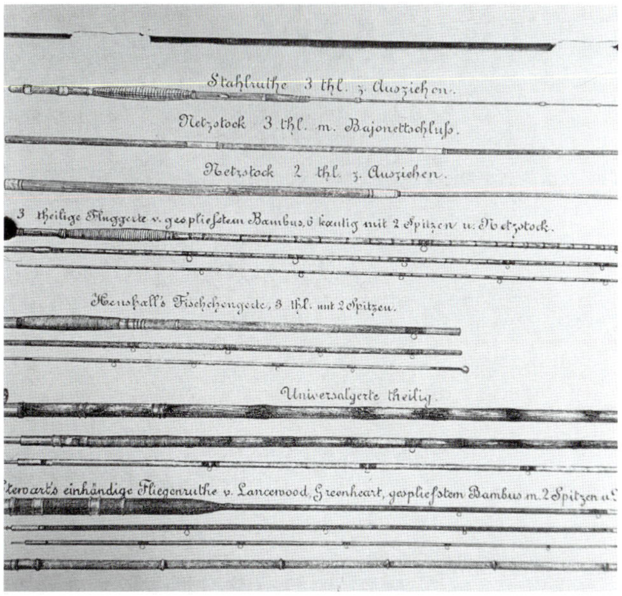

A description of available German and English rods, ca. 1900.

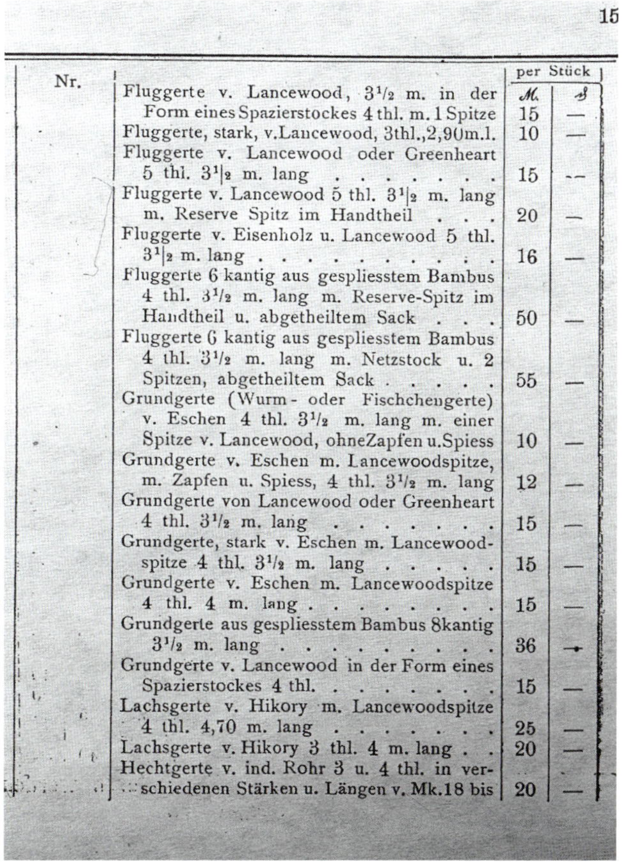

15

Nr.		per Stück M.	₰
	Fluggerte v. Lancewood, 3 1/2 m. in der Form eines Spazierstockes 4 thl. m. 1 Spitze	15	—
	Fluggerte, stark, v. Lancewood, 3thl., 2,90m.l.	10	—
	Fluggerte v. Lancewood oder Greenheart 5 thl. 3 1/2 m. lang	15	—
	Fluggerte v. Lancewood 5 thl. 3 1/2 m. lang m. Reserve Spitz im Handtheil . . .	20	—
	Fluggerte v. Eisenholz u. Lancewood 5 thl. 3 1/2 m. lang	16	—
	Fluggerte 6 kantig aus gespliesstem Bambus 4 thl. 3 1/2 m. lang m. Reserve-Spitz im Handtheil u. abgetheiltem Sack . . .	50	—
	Fluggerte 6 kantig aus gespliesstem Bambus 4 thl. 3 1/2 m. lang m. Netzstock u. 2 Spitzen, abgetheiltem Sack	55	—
	Grundgerte (Wurm- oder Fischchengerte) v. Eschen 4 thl. 3 1/2 m. lang m. einer Spitze v. Lancewood, ohneZapfen u.Spiess	10	—
	Grundgerte v. Eschen m. Lancewoodspitze, m. Zapfen u. Spiess, 4 thl. 3 1/2 m. lang	12	—
	Grundgerte von Lancewood oder Greenheart 4 thl. 3 1/2 m. lang	15	—
	Grundgerte, stark v. Eschen m. Lancewoodspitze 4 thl. 3 1/2 m. lang	15	—
	Grundgerte v. Eschen m. Lancewoodspitze 4 thl. 4 m. lang	15	—
	Grundgerte aus gespliesstem Bambus 8kantig 3 1/2 m. lang	36	—
	Grundgerte v. Lancewood in der Form eines Spazierstockes 4 thl.	15	—
	Lachsgerte v. Hikory m. Lancewoodspitze 4 thl. 4,70 m. lang	25	—
	Lachsgerte v. Hikory 3 thl. 4 m. lang . .	20	—
	Hechtgerte v. ind. Rohr 3 u. 4 thl. in verschiedenen Stärken u. Längen v. Mk.18 bis	20	—

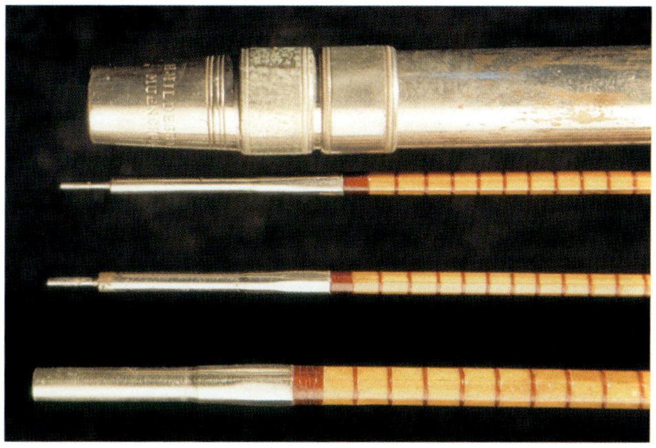

A very well-preserved Hildebrand rod with closely-spaced intermediate wraps and pin ferrules.

The price list from a Hildebrand catalog shows a split-bamboo rod cost at least 50 Marks, a price that only the very wealthy could afford.

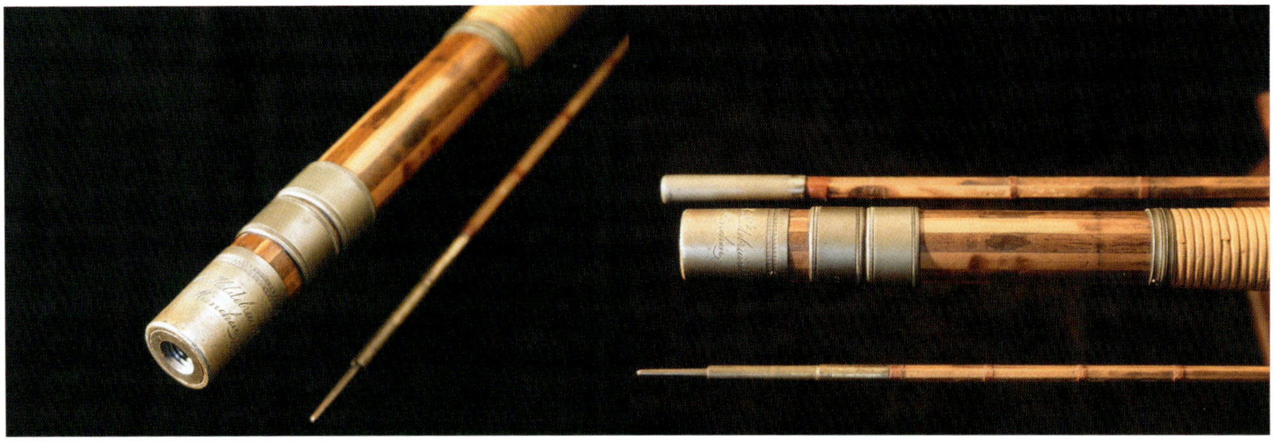

A Hildebrand rod with rattan grip. Notice how clearly the rod splines continue through the reelseat.

Detail photos show the similarity of Hildebrand and Leonard rods from about 1910. It is possible that Leonard built the rods, then to be marketed under Hildebrand's name in Germany.

The Hildebrand…

…and the Leonard.

Munich was considered to be the capital of German sport-fishing in the Nineteenth Century, and in 1856, yet another maker opened his business in this Bavarian capital. The H. Stork Fishing Equipment company (with its stork trademark) began by producing fine equipment, and continued to operate into the 1980s.

The Stork company existed between 1856 and the 1980s.

An early Stork catalog. The mustache and hat identify the fisherman as Bavarian.

From the catalog. Apparently, the H. Stork company obtained its bamboo from Japan.

Bamboo storage within the H. Stork company of Munich.

An early catalog from the company depicts its workshops -- showing a room for building split-bamboo rods adjacent to the area where rods were made of traditional woods. In addition to the detailed descriptions of rod-making, it's interesting to note that this catalog contains the first mention of "Tonkin" cane in Germany.

Rod-building at Stork, ca. 1910.

"Suitable woods for making rods are mostly ash, lancewood, greenheart, hickory, and others, while hazelnut has almost disappeared as a rod-building material because of its weight and great tendency to warp."

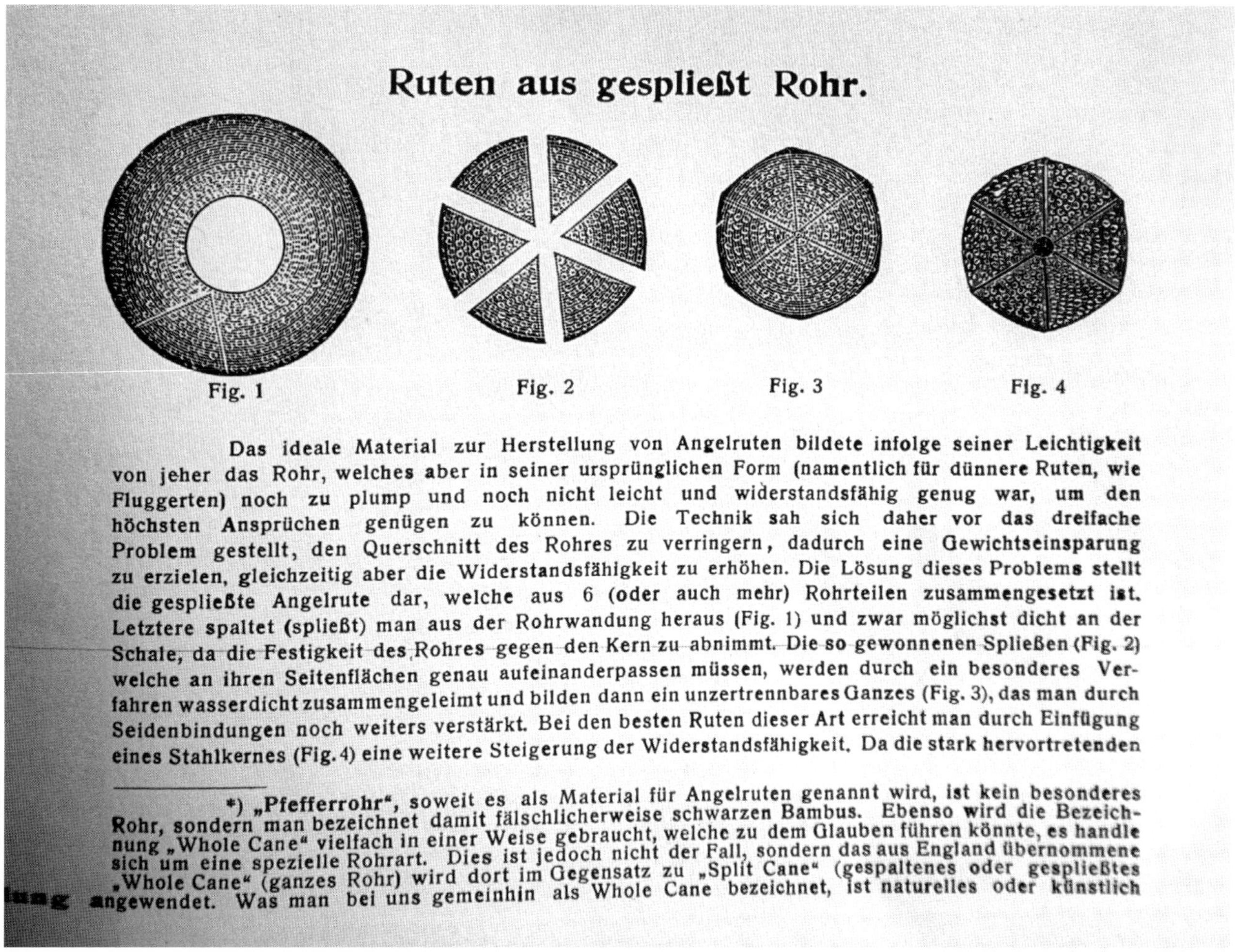

Ruten aus gesplieẞt Rohr.

Fig. 1 Fig. 2 Fig. 3 Fig. 4

Das ideale Material zur Herstellung von Angelruten bildete infolge seiner Leichtigkeit von jeher das Rohr, welches aber in seiner ursprünglichen Form (namentlich für dünnere Ruten, wie Fluggerten) noch zu plump und noch nicht leicht und widerstandsfähig genug war, um den höchsten Ansprüchen genügen zu können. Die Technik sah sich daher vor das dreifache Problem gestellt, den Querschnitt des Rohres zu verringern, dadurch eine Gewichtseinsparung zu erzielen, gleichzeitig aber die Widerstandsfähigkeit zu erhöhen. Die Lösung dieses Problems stellt die gesplieẞte Angelrute dar, welche aus 6 (oder auch mehr) Rohrteilen zusammengesetzt ist. Letztere spaltet (spließt) man aus der Rohrwandung heraus (Fig. 1) und zwar möglichst dicht an der Schale, da die Festigkeit des Rohres gegen den Kern zu abnimmt. Die so gewonnenen Spließen (Fig. 2) welche an ihren Seitenflächen genau aufeinanderpassen müssen, werden durch ein besonderes Verfahren wasserdicht zusammengeleimt und bilden dann ein unzertrennbares Ganzes (Fig. 3), das man durch Seidenbindungen noch weiters verstärkt. Bei den besten Ruten dieser Art erreicht man durch Einfügung eines Stahlkernes (Fig. 4) eine weitere Steigerung der Widerstandsfähigkeit. Da die stark hervortretenden

*) „Pfefferrohr", soweit es als Material für Angelruten genannt wird, ist kein besonderes Rohr, sondern man bezeichnet damit fälschlicherweise schwarzen Bambus. Ebenso wird die Bezeichnung „Whole Cane" vielfach in einer Weise gebraucht, welche zu dem Glauben führen könnte, es handle sich um eine spezielle Rohrart. Dies ist jedoch nicht der Fall, sondern das aus England übernommene „Whole Cane" (ganzes Rohr) wird dort im Gegensatz zu „Split Cane" (gespaltenes oder gesplieẞtes angewendet. Was man bei uns gemeinhin als Whole Cane bezeichnet, ist naturelles oder künstlich

This 1911 catalog explains why split-cane rods are superior.

"The cane types which come into consideration are marsh cane, bamboo (yellow or black), Tonkin cane, Indian or jungle cane, and some related species of bamboo such as Jambis, etc. "Pepper" cane, when referred to as a material for fishing rods, is not a special type of cane. It is an incorrect designation for black bamboo. Also the term "whole cane" is often used in a way that could lead one to believe that this is some special kind of cane. This is, nevertheless, not the case, rather the term "whole cane", which came from England, is used there in contrast to "split cane" in order to provide a distinction. What is here commonly called whole cane is natural or artificially spotted Tonkin bamboo."

It seems evident that Stork's production was strongly influenced by the large English companies.

"In the best rods of this type, the insertion of a steel core achieves…a further increase in durability."

The procedure employing a steel core, as already mentioned, was invented in England. Just as had been true for Hildebrand, rods from England and American were available through Stork.

It's likely that early German rod-makers were influenced by English and American examples, for although many early German rods carried German labels, they probably were not built locally.

A Stork rod and rod-bag logo from ca. 1950.

A wonderful poster from Stork. The action of the rod shown appears to extend into the grip.

A well-preserved Stork rod and a very rare Stork reel.

The single, most serious competitor in these early years was the Company for Hardware, Sporting Goods, and Fishing Tackle, established by Oskar and Fritz Ziegenspeck in 1875, Berlin. This company continued after 1902 under the name German Fishing Tackle Manufacturer (Deutsche Angelgeräte Manufaktur, or "D. A. M."). Fritz Ziegenspeck was the technically-capable and imaginative entrepreneur who formed the F. Ziegenspeck company in 1898, thus converting his former side-line interest into a full range of fishing tackle. In 1902, however, increased demand and sales required a restructuring of their production, and the new name, D. A. M., showed this change. In 1909, the businessman, Otto Kunze, joined the firm and developed business contacts throughout the world, while Fritz Ziegenspeck left the company for reasons of age. As sole owner, Otto Kunze led the company successfully through the difficult times of the First World War, and together with his son, Hellmuth Kunze, expanded the company in following years.

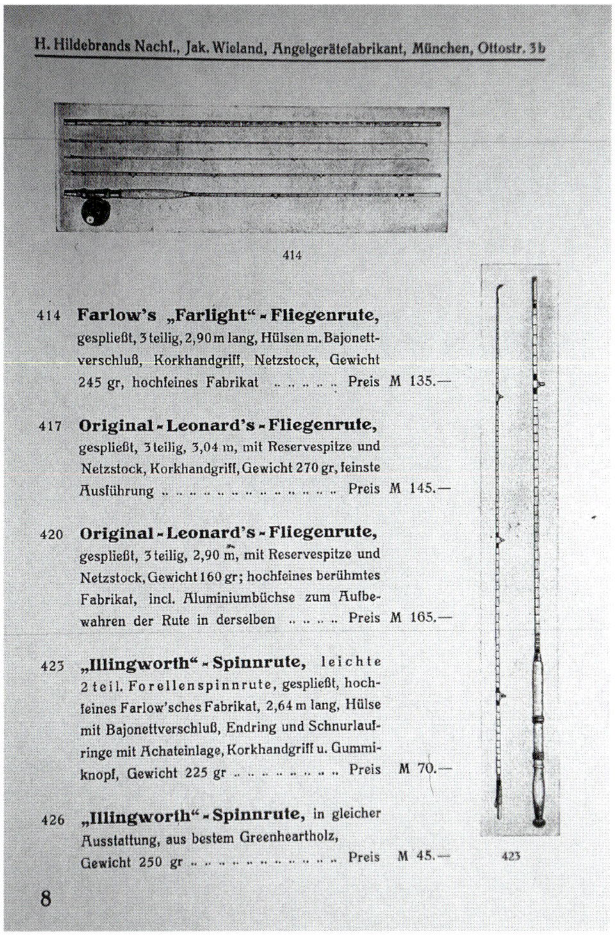
H. Hildebrands Nachf., Jak. Wieland, Angelgerätefabrikant, München, Ottostr. 3b

414

414 **Farlow's „Farlight" - Fliegenrute,** gespließt, 3 teilig, 2,90 m lang, Hülsen m. Bajonettverschluß, Korkhandgriff, Netzstock, Gewicht 245 gr, hochfeines Fabrikat .... Preis M 135.—

417 **Original - Leonard's - Fliegenrute,** gespließt, 3 teilig, 3,04 m, mit Reservespitze und Netzstock, Korkhandgriff, Gewicht 270 gr, feinste Ausführung .... Preis M 145.—

420 **Original - Leonard's - Fliegenrute,** gespließt, 3 teilig, 2,90 m, mit Reservespitze und Netzstock, Gewicht 160 gr; hochfeines berühmtes Fabrikat, incl. Aluminiumbüchse zum Aufbewahren der Rute in derselben .... Preis M 165.—

423 **„Illingworth" - Spinnrute,** leichte 2 teil. Forellenspinnrute, gespließt, hochfeines Farlow'sches Fabrikat, 2,64 m lang, Hülse mit Bajonettverschluß, Endring und Schnurlaufringe mit Achateinlage, Korkhandgriff u. Gummiknopf, Gewicht 225 gr .... Preis M 70.—

426 **„Illingworth" - Spinnrute,** in gleicher Ausstattung, aus bestem Greenheartholz, Gewicht 250 gr .... Preis M 45.—

423

8

In addition to its own products, Hildebrand in Munich also sold English and American rods. Notice the prices!

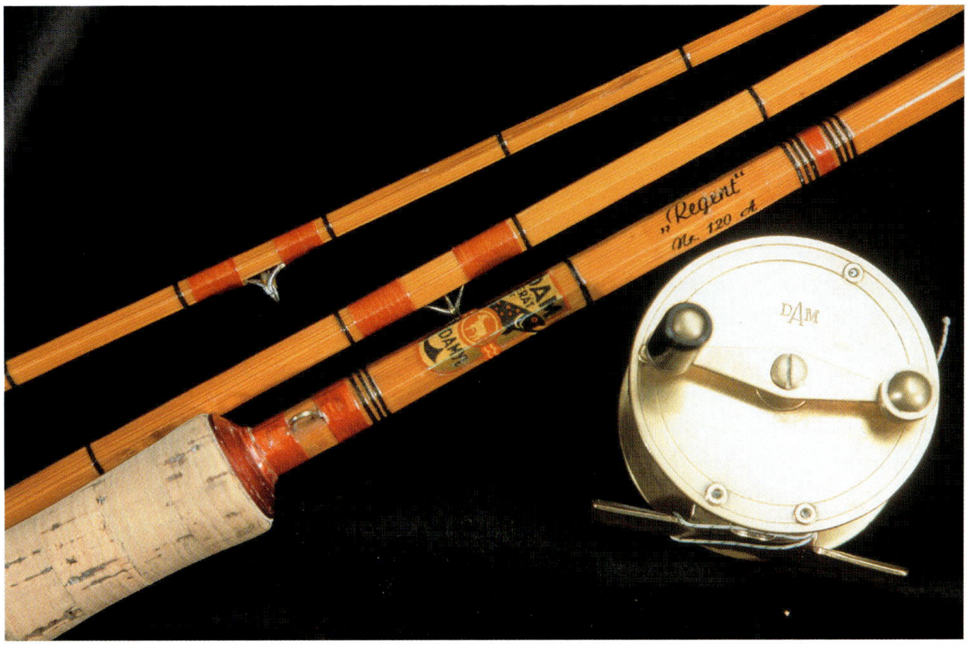

D. A. M. Regent rod and reel from about 1958.

D. A. M. produced split-bamboo rods after 1913. In addition to various patents for locking ferrules, an astonishing patent was registered in 1929 under the number "D.R.P/ 483301." This so-called "Tonkinola" patent described to the world the very first procedure for impregnating bamboo rods. By contrast, Wes Jordan's similar discovery for Orvis was not patented until 1946.

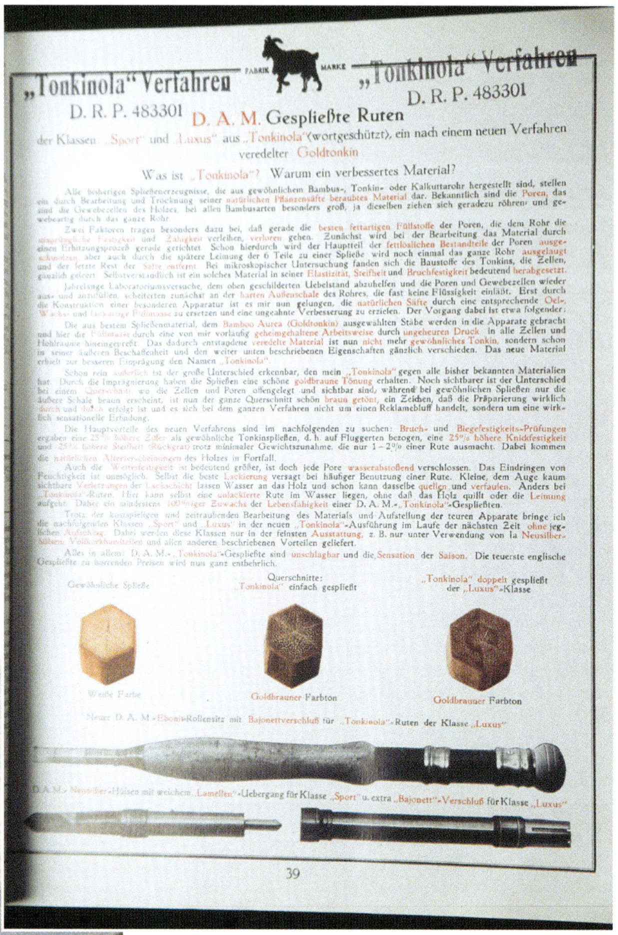

„Tonkinola" Verfahren D. R. P. 483301 — FABRIK MARKE — „Tonkinola" Verfahren D. R. P. 483301

D. A. M. Gesplieβte Ruten

der Klassen „Sport" und „Luxus" aus „Tonkinola" (wortgeschützt), ein nach einem neuen Verfahren veredelter Goldtonkin

Was ist „Tonkinola"? Warum ein verbessertes Material?

Alle bisherigen Spließenerzeugnisse, die aus gewöhnlichem Bambus-, Tonkin- oder Kalkuttarohr hergestellt sind, stellen ein durch Bearbeitung und Trocknung seiner natürlichen Pflanzensäfte beraubtes Material dar. Bekanntlich sind die Poren, das sind die Gewebezellen des Holzes, bei allen Bambusarten besonders groß, ja dieselben ziehen sich geradezu röhren- und gewebeartig durch das ganze Rohr.

Zwei Faktoren tragen besonders dazu bei, daß gerade die besten fettartigen Füllstoffe der Poren, die dem Rohr die ursprüngliche Festigkeit und Zähigkeit verleihen, verloren gehen. Zunächst wird bei der Bearbeitung das Material durch einen Erhitzungsprozeß gerade gerichtet. Schon hierdurch wird der Hauptteil der fettlöslichen Bestandteile der Poren ausgeschmolzen, aber auch durch die spätere Leimung der 6 Teile zu einer Spließe wird noch einmal das ganze Rohr ausgelaugt und der letzte Rest der Säfte entfernt. Bei mikroskopischer Untersuchung fanden sich die Baustoffe des Tonkins, die Zellen, gänzlich geleert. Selbstverständlich ist ein solches Material in seiner Elastizität, Steifheit und Bruchfestigkeit bedeutend herabgesetzt.

Jahrelange Laboratoriumsversuche, dem oben geschilderten Uebelstand abzuhelfen und die Poren und Gewebezellen wieder aus- und anzufüllen, scheiterten zunächst an der harten Außenschale des Rohres, die fast keine Flüssigkeit einläßt. Erst durch die Konstruktion einer besonderen Apparatur ist es mir nun gelungen, die natürlichen Säfte durch eine entsprechende Oel-, Wachs- und lackartige Füllmasse zu ersetzen und eine ungeahnte Verbesserung zu erzielen. Der Vorgang dabei ist etwa folgender:

Die aus bestem Spließenmaterial, dem Bamboo Aurea (Goldtonkin) ausgewählten Stäbe werden in die Apparate gebracht und hier die Füllmasse durch eine von mir vorläufig geheimgehaltene Arbeitsweise durch ungeheuren Druck in alle Zellen und Hohlräume hineingepreßt. Das dadurch entstandene veredelte Material ist nun nicht mehr gewöhnliches Tonkin, sondern schon in seiner äußeren Beschaffenheit und den weiter unten beschriebenen Eigenschaften gänzlich verschieden. Das neue Material erhielt zur besseren Einprägung den Namen „Tonkinola".

Schon rein äußerlich ist der große Unterschied erkennbar, den mein „Tonkinola" gegen alle bisher bekannten Materialien hat. Durch die Imprägnierung haben die Spließen eine schöne goldbraune Tönung erhalten. Noch sichtbarer ist der Unterschied bei einem Querschnitt, wo die Zellen und Poren offengelegt und sichtbar sind, während bei gewöhnlichen Spließen nur die äußere Schale braun erscheint, ist nun der ganze Querschnitt schön braun getönt, ein Zeichen, daß die Präparierung wirklich durch und durch erfolgt ist und es sich bei dem ganzen Verfahren nicht um einen Reklamebluff handelt, sondern um eine wirklich sensationelle Erfindung.

Die Hauptvorteile des neuen Verfahrens sind im nachfolgenden zu suchen: Bruch- und Biegefestigkeits-Prüfungen ergaben eine 25% höhere Zähigkeit als gewöhnliche Tonkinspließen, d. h. auf Fluggerten bezogen, eine 25% höhere Knickfestigkeit und 25% höhere Steifheit (Rückgrat) trotz minimaler Gewichtszunahme, die nur 1–2% einer Rute ausmacht. Dabei kommen die natürlichen Alterserscheinungen des Holzes in Fortfall.

Auch die Wetterfestigkeit ist bedeutend größer, ist doch jede Pore wasserabstoßend verschlossen. Das Eindringen von Feuchtigkeit ist unmöglich. Selbst die beste Lackierung versagt bei häufiger Benutzung einer Rute. Kleine, dem Auge kaum sichtbare Verletzungen der Lackschicht lassen Wasser an das Holz und schon kann dasselbe quellen und verfaulen. Anders bei „Tonkinola"-Ruten. Hier kann selbst eine unlackierte Rute im Wasser liegen, ohne daß das Holz quillt oder die Leimung aufgeht. Daher ein mindestens 100%iger Zuwachs der Lebensfähigkeit einer D. A. M.-„Tonkinola"-Gesplieβten.

Trotz der kostspieligen und zeitraubenden Bearbeitung des Materials und Aufstellung der teuren Apparate bringe ich die nachfolgenden Klassen „Sport" und „Luxus" in der neuen „Tonkinola"-Ausführung im Laufe der nächsten Zeit ohne jeglichen Aufschlag. Dabei werden diese Klassen nur in der feinsten Ausstattung, z. B. nur unter Verwendung von Ia Neusilberhülsen, Vollkorkhandteilen und allen anderen beschriebenen Vorteilen geliefert.

Alles in allem: D. A. M.-„Tonkinola"-Gesplieβte sind unschlagbar und die Sensation der Saison. Die teuerste englische Gesplieβte zu horrenden Preisen wird nun ganz entbehrlich.

Querschnitte:

Gewöhnliche Spließe — Weiße Farbe

„Tonkinola" einfach gesplieβt — Goldbrauner Farbton

„Tonkinola" doppelt gesplieβt der „Luxus"-Klasse — Goldbrauner Farbton

Neuer D. A. M.-Ebonit-Rollensitz mit Bajonettverschluß für „Tonkinola"-Ruten der Klasse „Luxus"

D. A. M.-Neusilber-Hülsen mit weichem „Lamellen"-Uebergang für Klasse „Sport" u. extra „Bajonett"-Verschluß für Klasse „Luxus"

39

Apparently, the process of impregnating fishing rods was developed in Germany as early as 1929.

The logo of D. A. M. was always a billy-goat.

"All previous split-cane products made from normal bamboo (Tonkin bamboo, or Calcutta cane) represent material which has been robbed of natural plant juices through processing and drying. It is well-known that the pores, that is, the cells of the wood, are very large in all bamboo types, and that they extend almost tube- and fabric-like through the entire cane.

An older D. A. M. catalog. Notice the nice salmon fly.

DEUTSCHE ANGELGERÄTE-MANUFAKTUR FRITZ ZIEGENSPECK, BERLIN SW.

Direkter Import von Bambus-Angelruten.

Lagerbestand in der Saison über 100000 Stück.

Die von Konkurrenzseite beliebte Anpreisung: „**Keine rohe Exportware**" und „Nicht zu verwechseln mit der auf den Markt kommenden ordinären Ware in Originalballen" ist nur auf Marktschreierei zurückzuführen und wird nur auf Nichtkenner des Bambus-Angelruten-Geschäfts die beabsichtigte Wirkung ausüben.

Ich versichere, dass kein Einkäufer, wo solcher auch domiziliert sein mag, in der Lage ist, eine bessere Qualität zu führen, **als ich sie anbiete**, denn meine Ware ist **unter Garantie erstklassig** und nichts Besseres davon auf dem Markte.

es Bild stellt den **fünften Teil** einer **Bambus-Angelruten-Sendung** dar, welche soeben **direkt aus** pan eingetroffen. Die ganze **für mich bestimmte** Ladung repräsentierte das respektable Gewicht von **35000 Kilo** und die Zahl von **ca. 80000 Angelruten** von 8—30 Fuss Länge, leider konnte dieselbe aber infolge der Frequenz in der Strasse **nicht komplett** im Bilde wiedergegeben werden.

D. A. M., too, obtained bamboo from Japan.

"Two factors, in particular, lead to the loss of the best fatty, pore-filling materials which give the cane its original strength and toughness. In initial processing, the material is straightened by heating. At this point, most of the fat-soluble parts of the pores are already melted out. Then, during the gluing of the 6 pieces into a blank, all the cane is once again sucked dry and the last remnants of juice removed. Microscopic inspection shows the construction material of the Tonkin bamboo, the cells, to be completely empty. It is obvious that such a material has greatly reduced elasticity, stiffness, and durability.

"Years of laboratory tests -- aimed at improving the above-described conditions by filling pores and tissue cells -- failed initially because of the hard outer shell of the cane which allows almost no penetration of fluid. Only by constructing a special apparatus have I been able to replace the natural juices with a corresponding oil, wax, and varnish-like filler, and to produce unimaginable improvements. The process is approximately as follows:

"Selected strips of the best material, 'Bamboo Aurea' (Gold Tonkin), are put into the apparatus and the filler, in a process I am initially keeping secret, is forced by enormous pressure into all of the cells and hollow spaces....

"While normal cane strips show brown in the outer shell, now the total cross-section is tinted brown, an indication that the preparation fully penetrated, and that the total process is not an advertising gimmick, but a truly sensational discovery. The primary advantages of this new process are shown by the following: tests of breakage and bending show values 25% higher than normal Tonkin strips. That means, for fly rods, 25% higher breaking-strength and 25% greater stiffness (backbone), despite minimal weight increase, which is only 1-2% per rod....

"Also, weatherproofing is considerably greater because each pore is water-repellently sealed. The penetration of moisture is not possible....

"All in all: D.A.M. - 'Tonkinola' split-cane rods are unbeatable, and are the sensation of the season. The most expensive English split-cane rods, at horrible prices now, become completely unnecessary."

Despite these largely non-scientific descriptions and claims, the basic ideas for the process are correctly presented. Nevertheless, the advantages could not have been "the sensation of the season" because, even with their low prices, these rods were not sold for very long .

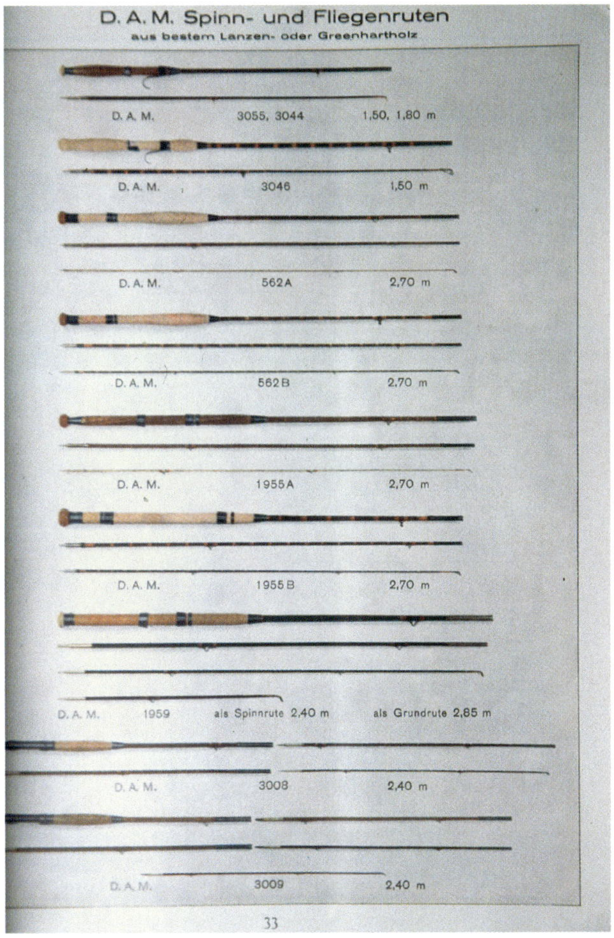

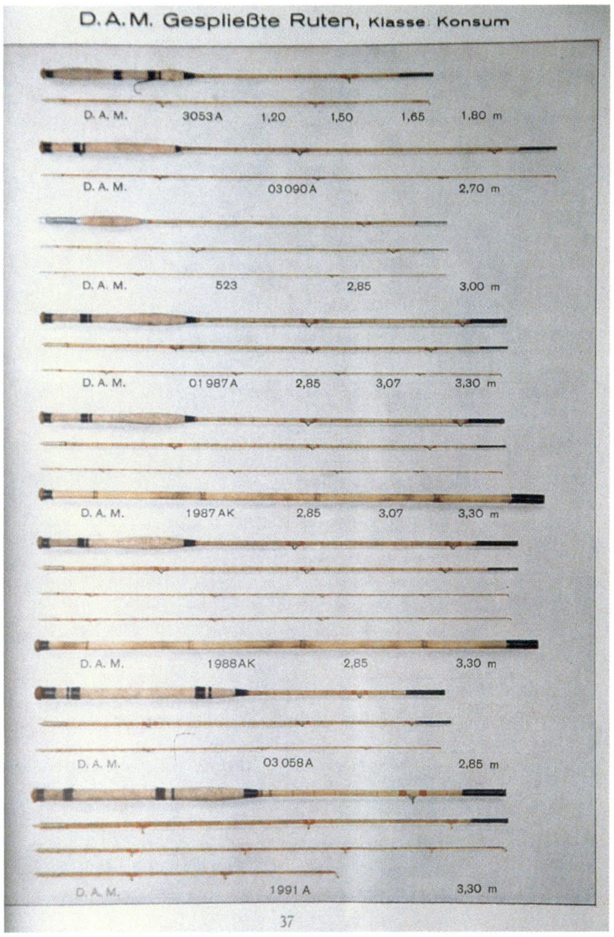

Just as did other companies, D. A. M. offered both wooden and split-bamboo rods.

The company was, in many ways, ahead of other companies in terms of advertising. One publicity stunt was spawned because of an inadequate supply of trucks. Elephants from the Hagenbeck Circus were used to move the Japanese bamboo directly to Kurassier Street in Berlin. In 1937, the company published their *Pocket Catalog for Everyone*.

One of the last split-bamboo rods built by D. A. M. The billy-goat always remained somewhere in the logo.

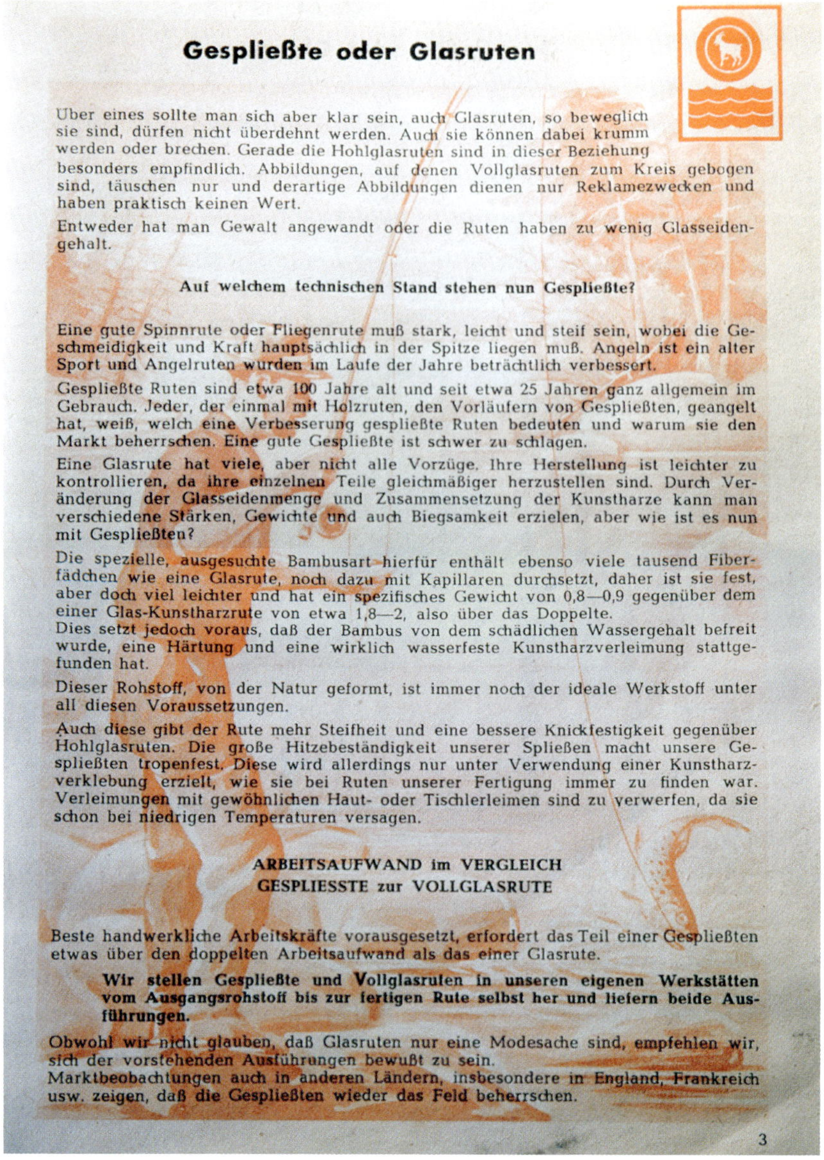

Gespließte oder Glasruten

Über eines sollte man sich aber klar sein, auch Glasruten, so beweglich sie sind, dürfen nicht überdehnt werden. Auch sie können dabei krumm werden oder brechen. Gerade die Hohlglasruten sind in dieser Beziehung besonders empfindlich. Abbildungen, auf denen Vollglasruten zum Kreis gebogen sind, täuschen nur und derartige Abbildungen dienen nur Reklamezwecken und haben praktisch keinen Wert.

Entweder hat man Gewalt angewandt oder die Ruten haben zu wenig Glasseidengehalt.

Auf welchem technischen Stand stehen nun Gespließte?

Eine gute Spinnrute oder Fliegenrute muß stark, leicht und steif sein, wobei die Geschmeidigkeit und Kraft hauptsächlich in der Spitze liegen muß. Angeln ist ein alter Sport und Angelruten wurden im Laufe der Jahre beträchtlich verbessert.

Gespließte Ruten sind etwa 100 Jahre alt und seit etwa 25 Jahren ganz allgemein im Gebrauch. Jeder, der einmal mit Holzruten, den Vorläufern von Gespließten, geangelt hat, weiß, welch eine Verbesserung gespließte Ruten bedeuten und warum sie den Markt beherrschen. Eine gute Gespließte ist schwer zu schlagen.

Eine Glasrute hat viele, aber nicht alle Vorzüge. Ihre Herstellung ist leichter zu kontrollieren, da ihre einzelnen Teile gleichmäßiger herzustellen sind. Durch Veränderung der Glasseidenmenge und Zusammensetzung der Kunstharze kann man verschiedene Stärken, Gewichte und auch Biegsamkeit erzielen, aber wie ist es nun mit Gespließten?

Die spezielle, ausgesuchte Bambusart hierfür enthält ebenso viele tausend Fiberfädchen wie eine Glasrute, noch dazu mit Kapillaren durchsetzt, daher ist sie fest, aber doch viel leichter und hat ein spezifisches Gewicht von 0,8—0,9 gegenüber dem einer Glas-Kunstharzrute von etwa 1,8—2, also über das Doppelte.
Dies setzt jedoch voraus, daß der Bambus von dem schädlichen Wassergehalt befreit wurde, eine Härtung und eine wirklich wasserfeste Kunstharzverleimung stattgefunden hat.

Dieser Rohstoff, von der Natur geformt, ist immer noch der ideale Werkstoff unter all diesen Voraussetzungen.

Auch diese gibt der Rute mehr Steifheit und eine bessere Knickfestigkeit gegenüber Hohlglasruten. Die große Hitzebeständigkeit unserer Spließen macht unsere Gespließten tropenfest. Diese wird allerdings nur unter Verwendung einer Kunstharzverklebung erzielt, wie sie bei Ruten unserer Fertigung immer zu finden war. Verleimungen mit gewöhnlichen Haut- oder Tischlerleimen sind zu verwerfen, da sie schon bei niedrigen Temperaturen versagen.

ARBEITSAUFWAND im VERGLEICH
GESPLIESSTE zur VOLLGLASRUTE

Beste handwerkliche Arbeitskräfte vorausgesetzt, erfordert das Teil einer Gespließten etwas über den doppelten Arbeitsaufwand als das einer Glasrute.

Wir stellen Gespließte und Vollglasruten in unseren eigenen Werkstätten vom Ausgangsrohstoff bis zur fertigen Rute selbst her und liefern beide Ausführungen.

Obwohl wir nicht glauben, daß Glasruten nur eine Modesache sind, empfehlen wir, sich der vorstehenden Ausführungen bewußt zu sein.
Marktbeobachtungen auch in anderen Ländern, insbesondere in England, Frankreich usw. zeigen, daß die Gespließten wieder das Feld beherrschen.

3

D. A. M. came under pressure as well, with the appearance of tubular glass rods.

D. A. M. developed the first German spinning reel (the "Quick"), and similarly, put the first fully-synthetic, German line (the "Damyl") on the market. In the late 1930's, demand for their products increased so much that a subsidiary was established in Hollfeld, Upper Franconia, although the company was later moved to Gunzenhausen. Hollfeld was a small fishing center in Franconia with an attractive little marketplace. Here, the Wiesent flowed -- one of the few chalk-streams in Germany -- and the area became well-known both for its excellent fishing and for the many famous anglers who made it their stopping-point for trout and grayling. After D. A. M. moved its factory from Hollfeld, the empty facility was taken over by the Bavaria fishing tackle company. This firm prospered under the leadership of M. Bischoff (later succeeded by Willi Rodler), and still trades in fishing tackle and accessories under the name, Expert. It was there, in 1980, that I personally observed the work of the last, professional, female fly-tyer in Germany.

Cover and an inner page from a Bavaria catalog of the 1960s.

The women were paid according to the number of flies tied, but if a hook were to break in the process, the fly was thrown into a special container so it could be counted later against her pay.

Heinz Weiland, a well-known casting master in the 1960s, led Bavaria's fly-fishing school, and was also responsible for training the tackle-store owners who were customers of Bavaria. Unfortunately, many of these merchants were not as interested in the training as they were in the local varieties of beer -- all in close proximity and readily available for tasting in the many, traditional, Franconian restaurants.

On the morning of his final training day (never an easy one for Weiland, due to his disinterested, "expert" merchants), he would reach into the container of broken flies and stuff a bunch of them in his pocket. At the end of the course, when the merchants asked which fly patterns were best, Heinz threw 30 or so of his pocketed flies onto the water saying, "And now gentlemen, you must carefully watch which pattern is taken by the trout. You must simply 'chum.'" Some even believed him.

By the 1930s, as many as 350 people worked at D. A. M., but a later expansion phase was interrupted by the Second World War, and in 1945, the factory in Berlin was almost completely destroyed. Otto Kunze died in 1943, and his son, Hellmuth, began rebuilding after the war -- in 1955, opening new factory headquarters in Gunzenhausen, where they remain to this day.

A smaller company, specializing only in rods, was owned by Bonifaz Wieland (not to be confused with Jakob Wieland of Hildebrand). In a 1930 advertisement, his company declared that Bonifaz Wieland to be "the first German-certified split-bamboo Master." Indeed, this was quite an accomplishment, considering the strict testing procedures leading to a "Master" at that time in Germany.

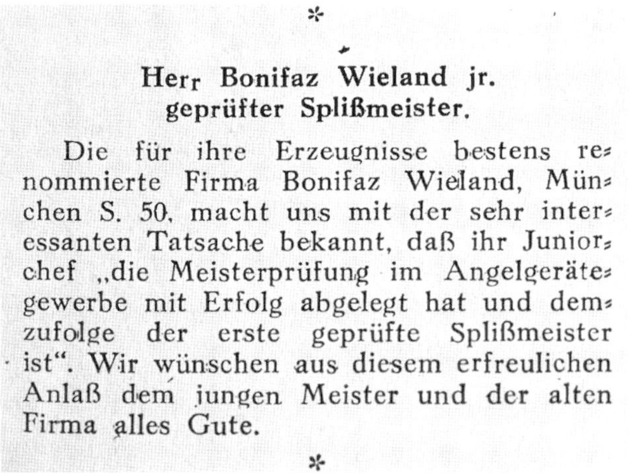

Herr Bonifaz Wieland jr.
geprüfter Splißmeister.

Die für ihre Erzeugnisse bestens renommierte Firma Bonifaz Wieland, München S. 50, macht uns mit der sehr interessanten Tatsache bekannt, daß ihr Juniorchef „die Meisterprüfung im Angelgerätegewerbe mit Erfolg abgelegt hat und demzufolge der erste geprüfte Splißmeister ist". Wir wünschen aus diesem erfreulichen Anlaß dem jungen Meister und der alten Firma alles Gute.

Unique: A notice of successfully completing an examination leading to the "Master's Certificate" in split-cane rod-building.

The catalog from Bonifaz Wieland, not to be confused with Jakob Wieland of Hildebrand.

A wonderfully preserved "huchen" (Danube salmon) rod from Bonifaz Wieland. The reels are from the Hildebrand-Wieland company in Munich.

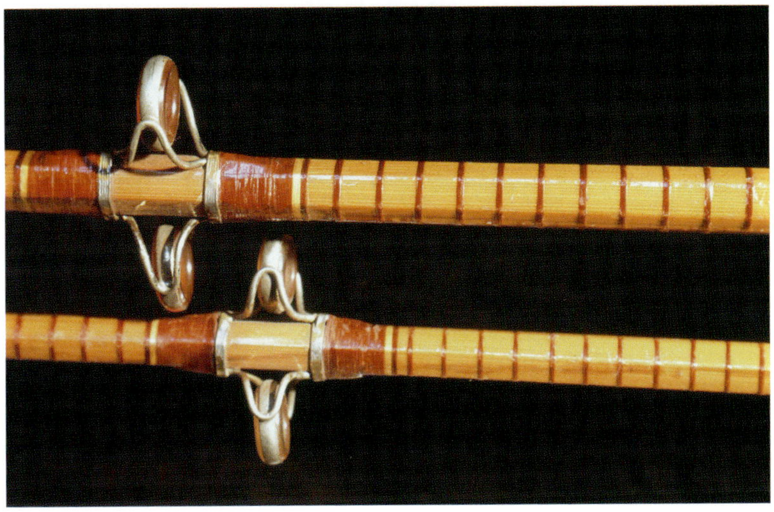

The unusual double-guides of this rod had a specific purpose: Fishing for huchen in winter often led to frozen guides, but this rod could simply be turned over for the angler to continue fishing.

Courageous Color

Yet another company, Noris, opened in Nuremburg in 1925, and came to be known for particularly well-made rods. Guide wrappings were meticulously fashioned, and intermediate wraps were much more closely-spaced than on other rods.

New and more colorful silks were used for the wrappings, and some models were finished with a colored varnish rather than with the usual clear.

Later, Noris entered a joint venture with Shakespeare, soon to be called Noris-Shakespeare. As far as is known, this company existed in Germany into the 1980s.

In summary, only three German companies had begun building split-bamboo fly rods prior to the First World War, with Noris joining these after 1925. An inspection of the many rod lengths and weights displayed in catalogs, indicates that nearly all rods (notwithstanding certain innovations, inventions or other exceptions) were 8 feet and longer. From our present point of view, these were also quite clumsy and tip-heavy. Unfortunately, throughout the period of German, split-bamboo, rod production, these latter features remained.

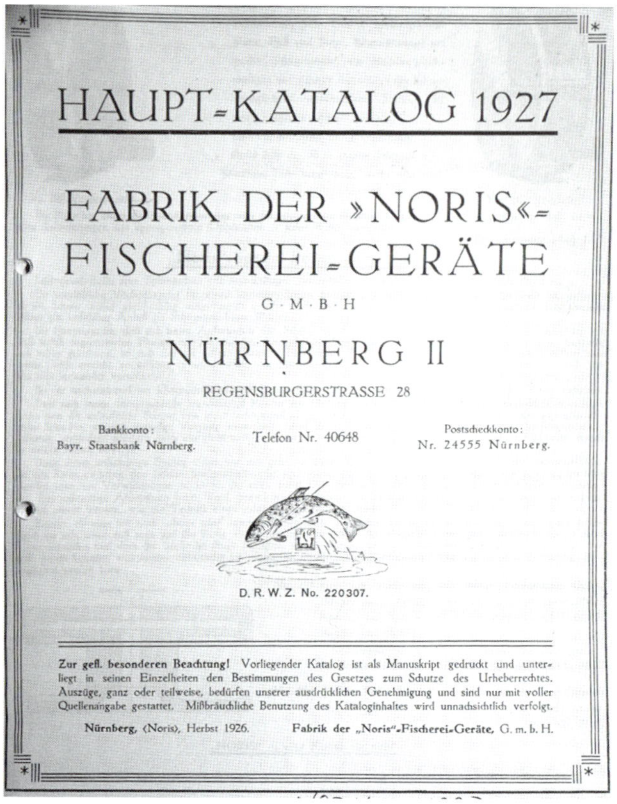
HAUPT-KATALOG 1927

FABRIK DER »NORIS«-
FISCHEREI-GERÄTE
G·M·B·H

NÜRNBERG II

REGENSBURGERSTRASSE 28

Bankkonto:
Bayr. Staatsbank Nürnberg.

Telefon Nr. 40648

Postscheckkonto:
Nr. 24555 Nürnberg.

D. R. W. Z. No. 220307.

Zur gefl. besonderen Beachtung! Vorliegender Katalog ist als Manuskript gedruckt und unterliegt in seinen Einzelheiten den Bestimmungen des Gesetzes zum Schutze des Urheberrechtes. Auszüge, ganz oder teilweise, bedürfen unserer ausdrücklichen Genehmigung und sind nur mit voller Quellenangabe gestattet. Mißbräuchliche Benutzung des Kataloginhaltes wird unnachsichtlich verfolgt.

Nürnberg, (Noris), Herbst 1926. **Fabrik der „Noris"-Fischerei-Geräte**, G. m. b. H.

The Noris catalog of 1927.

110

111

A black-lacquered, Noris rod. The color choices were surprisingly progressive, considering the rod was built around 1930.

A Noris "220" with generous decorative wraps.

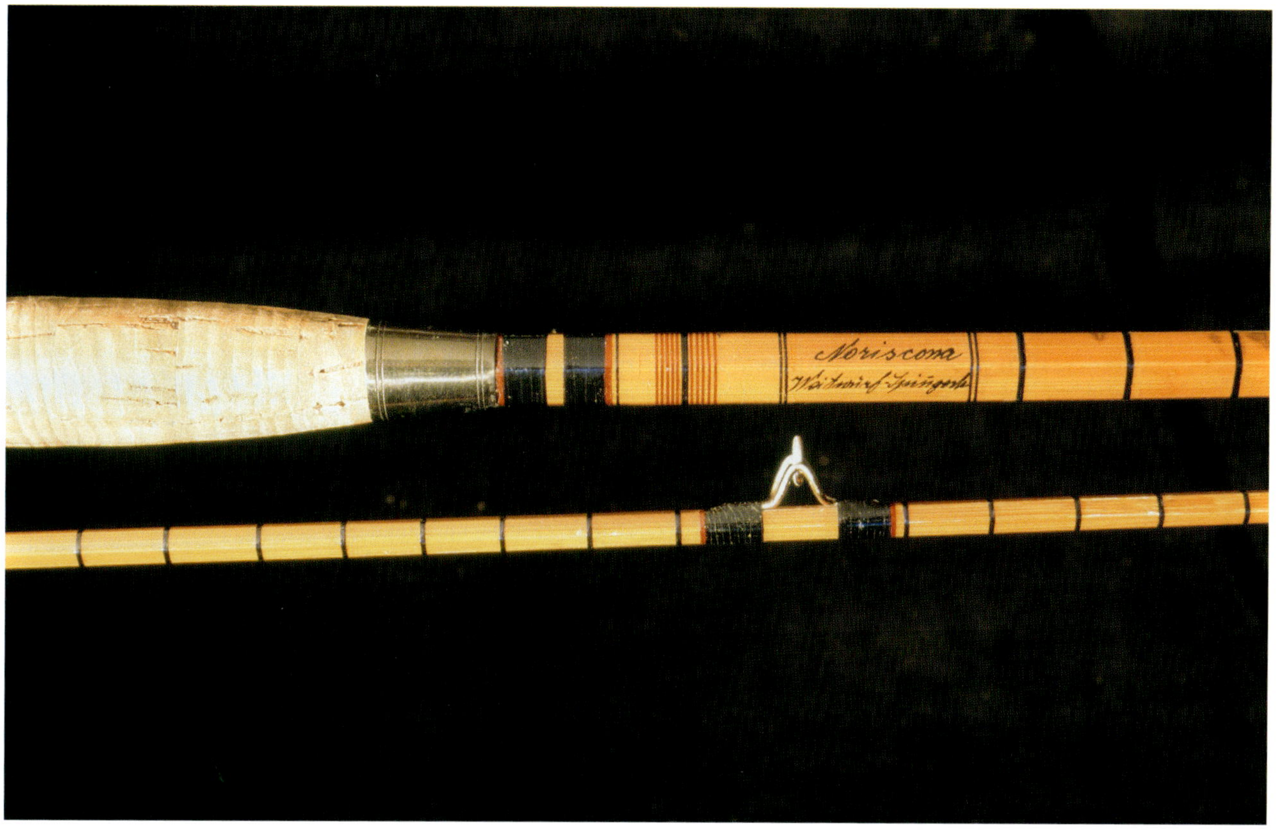

The "Noriscona" with dark-blue wraps is a distance-casting, spin/casting rod of the Dr. Karl Heintz type.

Plagiarized

The only German-language book on bamboo rod-building I've been able to find, appeared in 1958 -- *Tinkering Book for Sportfishermen* (Eugen Hager and Hellmut Lorenz, published by Albert Müller Verlag). Here, we find a description of a most peculiar method for building a split-cane rod:

"Wrapped around the split-bamboo rod is a generous garland of legend and secrecy which is still being woven. If it were all true, then surely we would not be offered so many unsatisfactory rods over a store's counter. The making of a split-cane rod is anything but a secret, highly scientific process. It was developed from A to Z by trial and error methods (and how much error!), but overall, has produced few easily-understood rules, and these still await scientific confirmation. Building a split-bamboo rod is fully within the range of possibilities and abilities of any amateur who works precisely and carefully."

The instructions on the following 16 pages would have driven many an amateur to despair. Anyone able to build a rod according to these methods would be a true craftsman and should be very proud of himself. First, the outside of each bamboo strip needed to be glued to a so-called "former." Then, everything was wrapped with thread and set aside to dry for several days. After drying, a plane was used on all three sides to produce the desired triangular cross-section. The three flats of the former were shaped to produce the rod's final taper, so only one taper could be produced with each former -- and finally, everything had to be heated in order to remove the planed strip. A more complicated method would hardly be possible

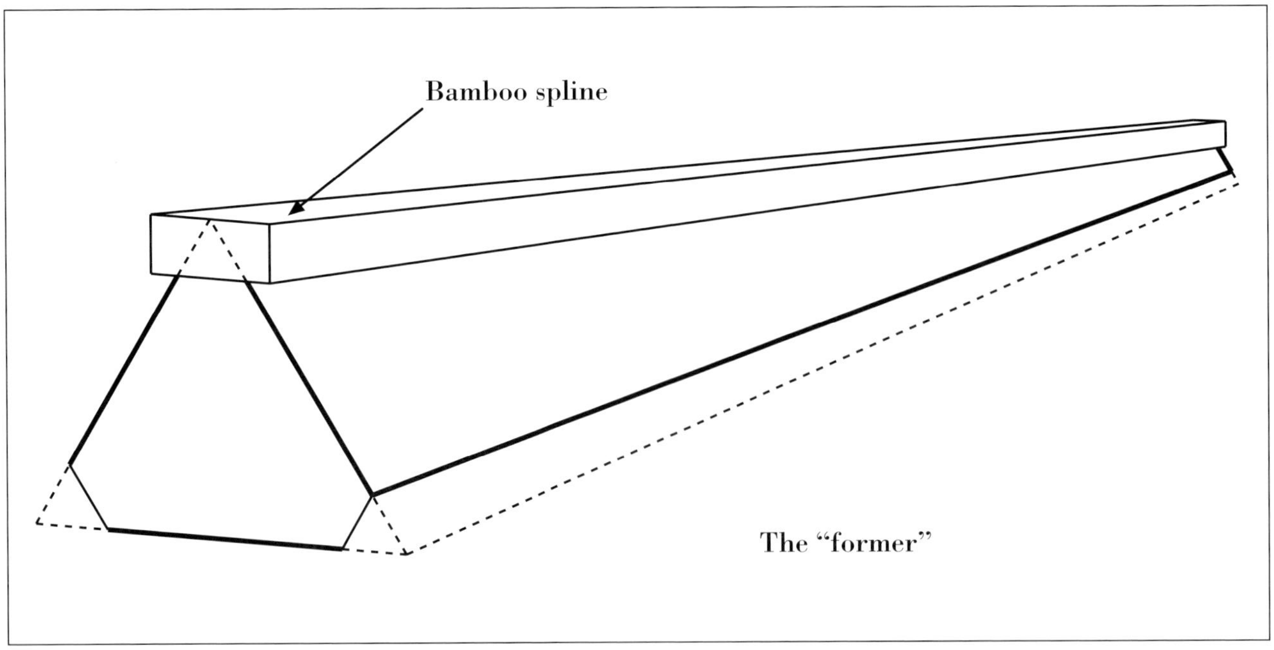

The following remarks from the end of this book are barely comprehensible -- at best, mistaken and narrow-minded:

"We are aware that in the USA a slotted board (planing form) is used instead of a former. This board is of aluminum or steel and has several slots with various angles into which the raw strips are laid, one after the other, to be planed. They do not need to be glued, only planed. The slotted board does not allow working to such fine tolerances as does the former. The board is hardly something we can produce ourselves, but it would not pay to obtain one from the USA since the Americans all have an embarrassing preference for "tip-action" -- in casting rods as well -- and the grooves are always formed with these shapes. We know, however, that the tip action does not give satisfactory results for casting rods. Despite this, we wanted to mention the method."

In their references, the two authors even mention Dr. George Parker Holden's book, *The Idyl of the Split-Bamboo*. Simple-to-make planing forms are thoroughly described in this wonderful book!

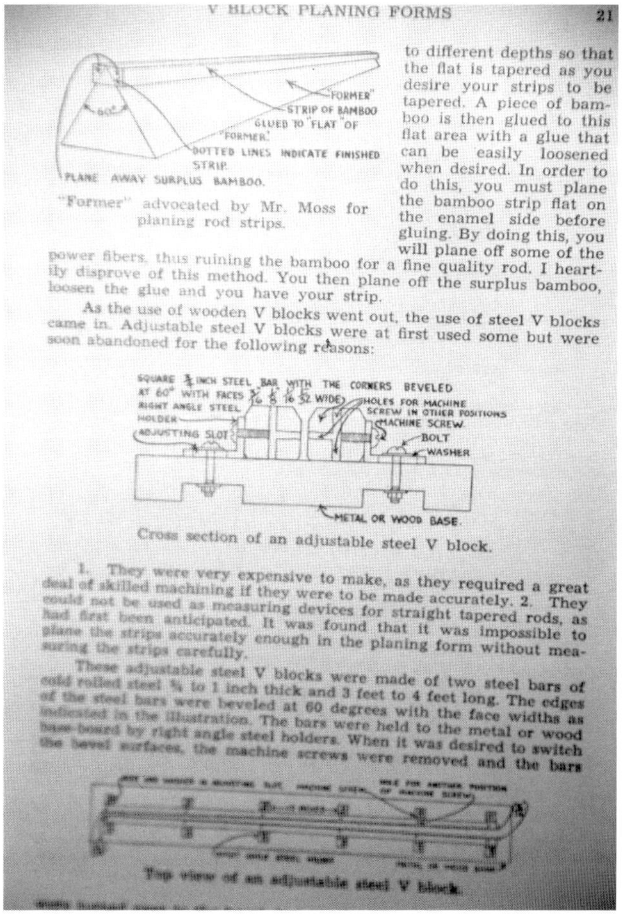
V BLOCK PLANING FORMS 21

"Former" advocated by Mr. Moss for planing rod strips.

to different depths so that the flat is tapered as you desire your strips to be tapered. A piece of bamboo is then glued to this flat area with a glue that can be easily loosened when desired. In order to do this, you must plane the bamboo strip flat on the enamel side before gluing. By doing this, you will plane off some of the power fibers, thus ruining the bamboo for a fine quality rod. I heartily disprove of this method. You then plane off the surplus bamboo, loosen the glue and you have your strip.

As the use of wooden V blocks went out, the use of steel V blocks came in. Adjustable steel V blocks were at first used some but were soon abandoned for the following reasons:

Cross section of an adjustable steel V block.

1. They were very expensive to make, as they required a great deal of skilled machining if they were to be made accurately. 2. They could not be used as measuring devices for straight tapered rods, as had first been anticipated. It was found that it was impossible to plane the strips accurately enough in the planing form without measuring the strips carefully.

These adjustable steel V blocks were made of two steel bars of cold rolled steel ¾ to 1 inch thick and 3 feet to 4 feet long. The edges of the steel bars were beveled at 60 degrees with the face widths as indicated in the illustration. The bars were held to the metal or wood base-board by right angle steel holders. When it was desired to switch the bevel surfaces, the machine screws were removed and the bars

Top view of an adjustable steel V block.

The former and the planing form in Herter's book.Only the former remained in Hager-Lorenz's book.

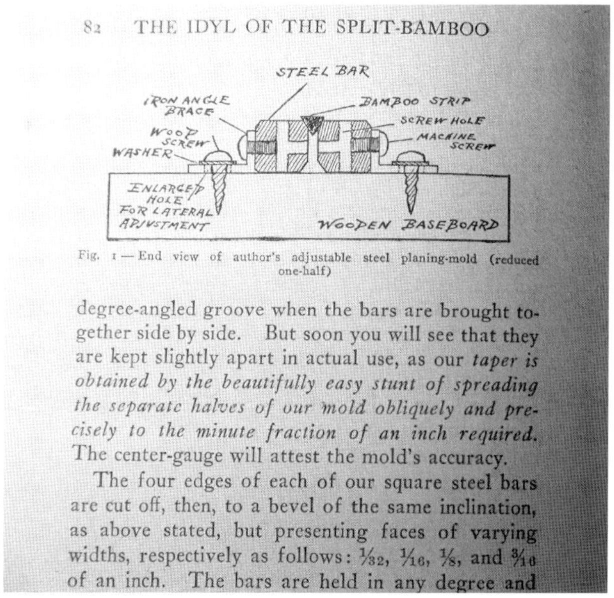
82 THE IDYL OF THE SPLIT-BAMBOO

Fig. 1 — End view of author's adjustable steel planing-mold (reduced one-half)

degree-angled groove when the bars are brought together side by side. But soon you will see that they are kept slightly apart in actual use, as our *taper is obtained by the beautifully easy stunt of spreading the separate halves of our mold obliquely and precisely to the minute fraction of an inch required.* The center-gauge will attest the mold's accuracy.

The four edges of each of our square steel bars are cut off, then, to a bevel of the same inclination, as above stated, but presenting faces of varying widths, respectively as follows: 1/32, 1/16, 1/8, and 3/16 of an inch. The bars are held in any degree and

Drawing of a simple planing form from Dr. George Parker Holden's book, The Idyl of the Split Bamboo

Finally, two fold-outs are supplied at the end of the book, giving information for several rod tapers. Surprisingly, even the possibility for hollow construction is mentioned in this book:

"Without greatly influencing the action of a rod, we can reduce its weight by removing the inner side of the strip until only a 1/10 inch of the outer wall remains. At the ferrules, and at regular intervals, one leaves transverse ridges to assure stability. Or, instead of leaving ridges, strips can be made by gluing light balsawood to their backs -- or the rod can be built with a solid balsa core."

What is not mentioned, however, is that much of this chapter is simply plagiarized!

Richard Walker's 1952 book, *Rod-Building for Amateurs*, was published in England by Belfield and Bushell, Ltd. Included within Walker's text are several drawings, all copied by Hager and Lorenz, but without indicating their origin. These two, German "authors" offer nothing in this chapter beyond a summation of already-published material. Even the tapers at the end are copies -- merely converted into metric units. Very likely, the two German authors never built a rod according to their own instructions, and the innocent reader would have been defrauded. I find it regrettable that the only German-language book on rod-building was simply copied from another author, and I only hope there wouldn't have been many enthusiasts attempting to follow this book's instructions.

I was even more surprised, however, when I held an original edition of George Leonard Herter's *Rod-
114 Building Manual and Manufacturer's Guide* (1949) in my hands. After going through a number of
115 pages, I was taken aback, for the same drawings appearing in Richard Walker's book (and the same method describing the "former") appear in Herter's book. One might conclude that Walker copied from Herter, but Herter cites G. Lawton Moss, another British author, as the source for the "former." Some of Walker's illustrations are drawn to the same scale as Herter's, while others are slightly different. Herter's book was published in 1949, Walker's three years later, and Hager and Lorenz's, an additional six years later.

Herter mentioned rod-building with a "former" only incidentally, as just one among many methods for producing a rod, but his point was to demonstrate the variety of planing forms. Apparently, these may have been too complex for Richard Walker, while Hager and Lorenz would have been unfamiliar with Herter's book. Even more discouraging for me is that many statements from Hager and Lorenz's book continue to be mentioned even today, leading to misconceptions about split-bamboo rods.

Another Development

Prior to reunification, many fishermen also enjoyed the "other" part of Germany -- that is, the GDR, also called East Germany. If the 1960 GDR catalog for angling and sporting goods can be taken seriously, its expectation was that fishing should proceed "in the genial spirit" of socialism. The introduction says:

"The German Angler's Club, as all other sports clubs in the GDR, has the duty of providing rest and recreation for the broadest levels of the working population, thereby, strongly contributing to the elevation of the people's health.

"The German Angler's Club sees the enlightenment of its members as its educational duty -- to love and to be faithful to our worker and farmer strength, and to be ready to defend our socialistic accomplishments. Thanks to the generous support through the party of the working class and the government of the GDR...the mass-organization of sport fishermen has been established politically, ideologically and organizationally, fulfilling its duties, particularly, in the development of group and performance-sports."

An East German, fishing tackle catalog from 1960.

Because very little equipment from the west was available in the GDR, rods and reels were produced by what were called "Businesses of the People." Many Tonkin rods continued to be produced and fished in the 1960s and 1970s.

A well-known GDR company, called Kuckuck, built split-bamboo rods and began in 1950 with Fritz Kuckuck and his father. The company obtained its material from Vietnam, but, because Fritz Kuckuck participated in competitive casting, he knew well how the rods should be constructed. By 1955, the company had 35 employees and produced up to 200 rods per week! Unfortunately, however, business dropped rapidly with the development of fiberglass rods. After the Berlin Wall was built, Kuckuck was sent to prison for treason, and upon his release he worked as a miner until the end of the GDR. Today, he heads a small fishing shop in the vicinity of Leipzig.

It wouldn't be accurate to assume that the quality of split-bamboo rods coming from the GDR was poorer than that of western rods, but fishing accessories (such as fly-lines and monofilament) never equaled the standards of western products.

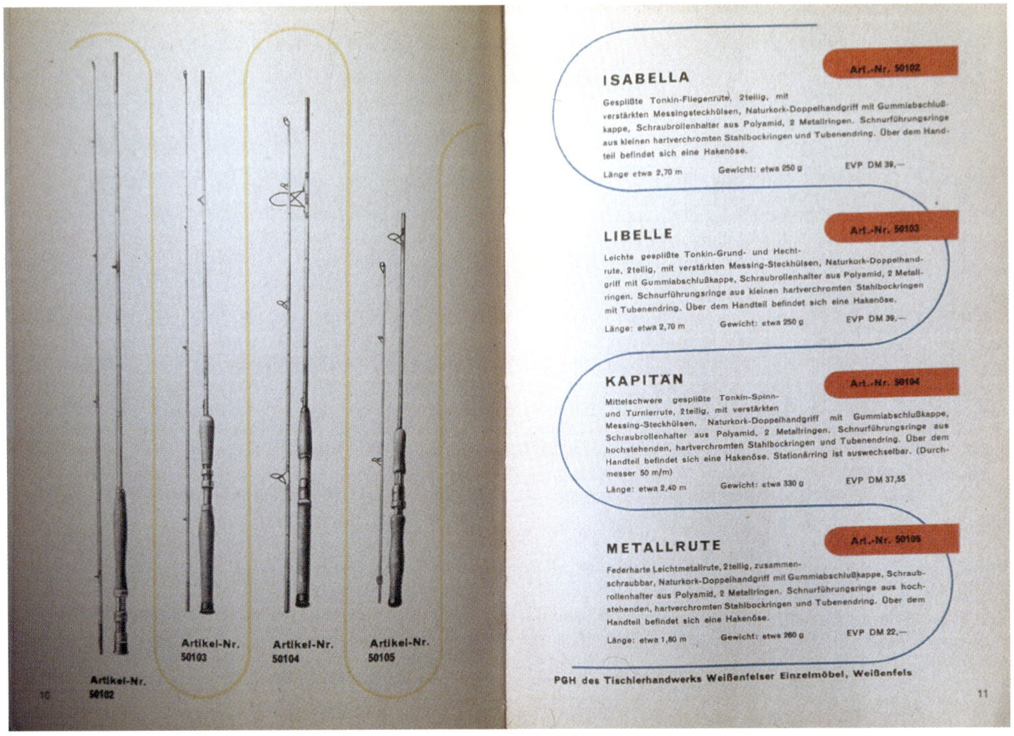

Rods produced in the former East Germany had names like "Isabella" or "Captain." The quality of these rods was quite acceptable.

A Belaco and a Libelle reel, together with a medal from an East German angling championship.

Much of the fishing equipment produced in the GDR was designed for competitive casting, for this was thought to be an important way to gain honor for the socialistic society. The focus was on winning as many competitions as possible, thus demonstrating the superiority of this "country of workers and farmers." In 1961, a world casting-championship was held in the Heinz-Steyer Stadium in Dresden (GDR), and in the women's competition, nearly all events were won by contestants from the GDR. This was not the case for the men, however, particularly in fly-casting, which was won by a gentleman from Switzerland.

A Leska fishing line and the logo of the Kuckuk company. The English and French inscriptions on the line's label are surprising.

Fritz Schreck, from the land of high mountains, was a world-champion caster several times over, and built all his own, bamboo casting equipment. For a number of years, his rods carried the Kingfisher logo and were regarded as among the best in all of Europe. Schreck designed nearly all his tapers himself -- using the old trial-and-error methods, as he himself said. Being innovative, he also discovered a new process to harden his bamboo strips, using a system of infrared radiation.

Some of his hexagonal rods were constructed of as many as 36 strips, and to obtain the highest possible speed for competition, he used only the outer layer of power fibers. Several, thin layers of these were glued together to make up the separate strips, then machined and planed to their final tapers. Even today, Schreck says it was always important to split by hand rather than to saw strips from the culm, finding fault with Pezon et Michel rods because their cane had been sawn. When Charles Ritz visited him one day, he told Ritz about this criticism, later saying: "The only rod builder I had contact with was Charles Ritz. I discussed technical details of building split-cane rods with him. Interestingly enough, we had very similar views."

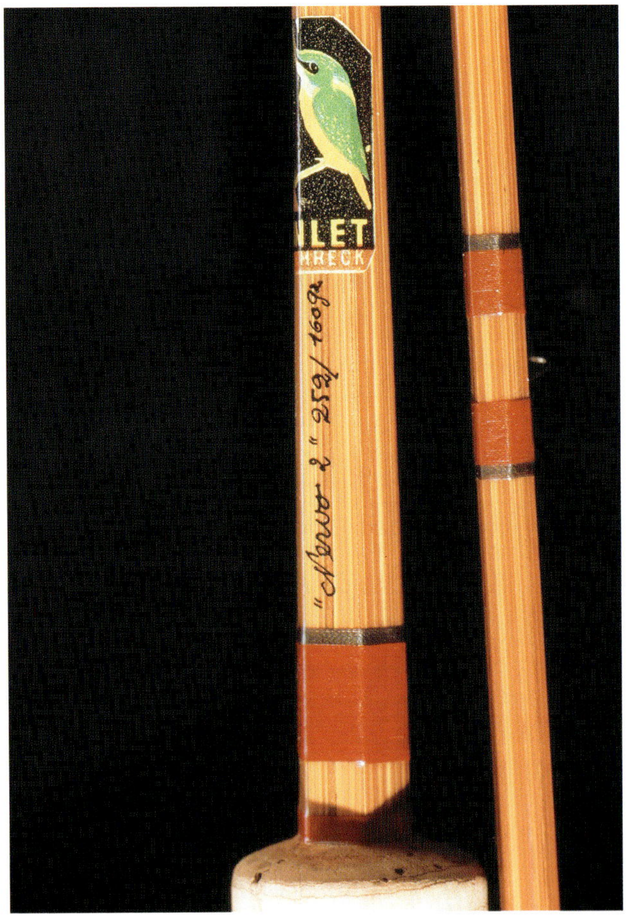

A Schreck rod, clearly showing the many laminated segments of each spline. This is a hexagonal rod, consisting almost entirely of power fibers.

Detail photo showing the power fibers.

The "Inlet" logo of Fritz Schreck.

In the meantime, another rod builder had made a name for himself in Austria. Walter Brunner began his career in 1963, and, soon, his "Brunner – Austria – Fliegenruten" ("Fliegenruten" translates as fly rods) became highly touted along the streams. In his catalog he writes of earlier days:

"One day in 1949, I arrived at my favorite spot on the Enns, and observed a man fishing in a very peculiar way. He had no bobber on his line and no worm on the hook. Attached to his leader was a little, black, artificial fly, and he was catching grayling with it. That fascinated me, but because he was obviously a gentleman, I had to build up enough courage to talk to him. He had come from England and was visiting a count in the vicinity of Enns. He was very friendly and explained to me that his rod was a split-bamboo fly rod. It was the first time I had heard of this, but my decision was made. I would build something like that for myself. I obtained a copy of an old book, *Borne Flies*, which offered a picture of the cross-section of a split-cane fishing rod, and stated that only Tonkin cane was suitable for such a rod. Beginning at once, I began to experiment, working half-through the nights – in addition to my job as a cabinetmaker. Over the years, I was able to produce some usable fly rods and I only fished with dry flies. In those years, however, fly-fishing was unknown in our area... My greatest wish was to have plenty of time for my rods, not just at night, but throughout the day. Consequently, I decided in 1963 to quit my profession as cabinetmaker. 'Brunner – Austria – Fliegenruten' was born."

Since that time, Walter Brunner's rods have always been considered among the finest in Europe. His cooperation with Hans Gebetsroither, with whom he didn't always agree in the matter of rod-action, influenced many of his earlier rod designs, while later models were influenced by Charles Ritz and other master fly-fishermen in the 1960s and '70s.

Sadly, Walter Brunner passed away in January of 2007, but throughout his career he always built rods using methods he developed himself – splitting the bamboo with hammer and knife, straightening the nodes perfectly, and then machining the strips with equipment of his own design.

Brunner is owed a huge debt of gratitude for helping the split-bamboo rod survive an era when society seemed to be jumping on everything new and innovative. Despite the new and "better" materials, Brunner continued to build his rods in the traditional way and remained true to bamboo. For this, his many customers throughout the world remain thankful. When I first began as a maker, I owned a "Brunner" and admired its fabulous quality. Soon, and without his knowing it, he became my rod-making mentor in all matters of craftsmanship.

A Brunner rod from 1993, produced on the occasion of the company's 30th *anniversary.*

Left to right: Hans Gebetsroither, Charles Ritz, and the young Walter Brunner.

When I called Brunner to make an appointment and discuss his work, he said, " I've worked through the entire winter. Please do me a favor and call me far enough in advance before the visit. I'd like to have the chance, finally, to go fishing again." Fishing was always his favorite activity, and anyone lucky enough to have joined him on the stream, would confirm that he was an excellent caster, an outstanding fly-fisherman, and beyond that, a gentleman.

Rolf Baginski and Walter Brunner in front of Brunner's shop in Steyr, Austria, 2003.

A Test

When we met at the agreed-upon time, Walter Brunner was standing in front of the door to his shop. We were invited inside in a friendly fashion, but before the shoptalk began, he said, "Mr. Baginski, first I want to see one of your rods, and then I have another request. I want to see you cast!" The rods were taken out of my car and, at once, we were in front of Brunner's shop, comparing tapers and rods while casting. Apparently, I passed his "test" because the master then gave me a complete tour of his workshop, including his method of machining splines, his binding apparatus, and much more. The time flew by, particularly while he told me about the good old days with Hans Gebetsroither -- how he determined what the "proper" taper of a rod should be and what length was "correct." Brunner added at last, "It was not always easy with Hans Gebetsroither."

Understandably, after the death of Gebetsroither, Brunner developed a new series of rods to incorporate new tapers. I was particularly impressed by a barely 6-foot-long rod for a 2-weight line. A wonderful piece -- I could cast nearly the complete line with this rod, and without problem! The finish-work on Brunner's new series became much finer than before, and was characterized by selected burlwood and polished nickel-silver.

When I asked about the famous people he had fished with over the years, Brunner told me this story:
"Hans Gebetsroither came by with Charles Ritz, and we went down to the river to fish for grayling. I used a dry fly, had the right patterns, and caught fish after fish. After a short time, Hans came up behind me, tapped me on the shoulder, and said, 'Stop it now. We have an important guest here who'd also like to catch something.'"
When I asked about the casting abilities of Charles Ritz, Brunner answered diplomatically, but with a little smile; "Not so bad."

Stylistically, much changed on Brunner's rods over the years. The relatively small and short grip, the simple black windings, and the all-cork sliding-ring reelseat are retained only in the "Wildwater" series. Listed in his latest catalog, are:

"Wildwater" Series

Cheri 190cm = 6 feet 3 inches (5 weight)
Gebetsroither super 200cm = 6 feet 7 inches (5-6 weight)
Gebetsroither 212 cm = 6 feet 11.5 inches (5-6 weight)
H.R. Hebeisen 190 cm = 6 feet 3 inches (5 weight)

This series was developed in cooperation with Hans Gebetsroither and built with sections of un-equal length -- shorter butts and longer tip-sections. In his catalog, Brunner states that perfect timing and mastery of one's casting technique are necessary to use these rods.

"Salza" Series

Salza 190 cm = 6 feet 3 inches (4 weight)
Salza 210 cm = 6 feet 11 inches (4-5 weight)
Salza 3-teilig 210 cm = 6 feet 11 inches (4-5 weight)
Salza 3-teilig 230 cm = 7 feet 6.6 inches (4-5 weight)
Salza 230 cm = 7 feet 6.6 inches (5-6 weight)
Salza sensitiv 230 cm = 7 feet 6.6 inches (4-5 weight)

122 These rods are described as somewhat softer, but with sufficient power in reserve for distance-casting.
123 Additional features are the fine wood reel-seats and the very best cork.

"Pielach" Series

Pielach 215 cm = 7 feet 6.6 inches (4-5 weight)
Pielach 230 cm = 7 feet 0.6 inches (4-5 weight)

This softer rod type is described as being for fishing dry flies with fine tippets.

For the finest fishing, Brunner's catalog offers his "Amabile" series in lengths of 6 feet 11 inches (3-4 weight) and 7 feet 2.6 inches (4 weight), in addition to his "Thymalli," which is 7 feet 10.5 inches (4-5 weight).

In the Far North

In Norway, the Høgård company built good, utility rods for daily fishing, well-suited to Norwegian fishing conditions. These were quite heavy rods, but they lasted a lifetime. Even today, fishermen with Høgård rods are frequently encountered on the rivers of northern Scandinavia. Rods, reels, and machines from the company's former days are on display in the Norwegian "Hunting and Fishing Museum" in Elverum. Høgård closed its doors in the 1980s when customers simply wanted to fish with the new and lighter graphite rods.

By the beginning of the 1980s, most of the large companies either had stopped building bamboo rods or had disappeared altogether, as it simply was not possible for bamboo to remain competitive. Newer, synthetic materials had taken the industry over, but, inevitably, many rod-makers carried on in small, one-man shops. The "Fly Fair" in Holland is a very large, fly-fishing convention with international participation, and continues to take place every two years. By the end of the 1970s, and after the bamboo rod-building virus had infected me, Holland's Fly Fair was the place to meet other European makers and to compare techniques and products.

Hørgård rods and reels in the museum.

The machine used to bind splines together in Hørgård's factory.

In contrast to the American rod-builders (already publishing newsletters with discussions of building techniques and tips), the work-ethic among European makers continued in strict secrecy. With few exceptions, no help could be expected from colleagues. Each produced his own luck or stewed in his own juice, and often, that's what the rods looked like. One of the great exceptions (relative to sharing experience) was the father of Dutch rod-building, Piet Veugelers, who passed away much too early. Not only did many Dutchmen receive good advice from him, but I too, was able to profit from his experience, and several of his tricks-of-the-trade will be found in the later chapter on construction methods. Below, I refer to several rod-builders in Europe with whom I remain in close contact. There are, of course, many others who surely make good rods, but who aren't mentioned here. I hope they can forgive my omitting them.

The Dutchman, Leen Huisman (today, best-known worldwide for his fabulous titanium reels), also taught me a great deal, never scrimping on his humorous remarks. To him, I owe thanks for my first steps in a rod-builder's life, and I often think of what I learned from him (not all of it correct). Happily, when Leen visited me recently, I was able to show him a number of my own developments -- proud to be able to give back some of what he once gave me.

European rod-builders at the 1988 Fly Fair in Holland. Standing, from the left: Gerrit Glezer of G&G, Piet Veugelers, Tom Moran, Ids Schukken, Stefan Pauli, Rolf Baginski, Leen Huisman, and Mike Brooks. Front, from the left: Günter Henseler, BSH Splitcane, Ger Vroomen of G&G, and P. J. Budde. Photo by Axel Blindow.

Over the following years, we shared a lot of laughter, and when time allows, we also fish together, compare rods and exchange tapers. The two of us (but particularly amusing for Leen) can't escape from one story:

Somehow, we met each other at one of the first Fly Fairs in Hattem, near Zwolle, Holland ("we," being Lars Østergaard from Denmark, Leen Huisman and Ids Schukken from Holland, and myself from Germany). It was impossible to resist Lars' many enticing stories, but his information about sea-run, brown trout in Denmark seemed unbelievable. You could catch them from the beach, and do it with a fly rod! Still somewhat unconvinced, we discussed Lars' tall tales around the table in the evenings, but secretly, each of us thought, "Maybe I'll just take a little drive up there sometime to try it out." Back in 1986, fishing of this sort was still rather unknown and our skepticism was great. But, within a couple weeks following the show in Holland, I just couldn't stand it anymore, so I called Lars and arranged to give these Danish, sea-run browns a shot. In short, my trip was a success, and shortly after, I called Leen in Holland to confirm Lars' stories. Over the following years, I drove to Denmark several times and frequently had great luck, but it always seems to take a little longer for my Dutch friends to make their decisions. First, of course, every detail required thorough discussion, and each connected expense had to be evaluated with great care. Nevertheless, one fall, Lars informed me that, "The Dutchmen are coming for a week of fishing. It took them long enough...!"
Fishing for sea-run trout is as much a mental test as anything else. You must believe in it, otherwise the idea of your tiny fly searching such an enormous expanse of water will drive you to despair.

Without success, my Dutch friends had already tried their luck, and when I met them on the beach, they were in a correspondingly foul mood. "No fish here! Don't even bother to unpack your equipment," was their comment. Lars winked at me and said, "Oh well, if you don't try, it becomes even more difficult!" We'd developed an odd form of humor -- a little hard, perhaps, for others to take. Anyway, we spaced ourselves about 15 yards apart and I stripped some line off my reel. I was lengthening the stroke for my first cast, but dropped the fly in the water about 10 yards behind me. When I began my forward cast, I felt a little resistance -- which turned out to be a large trout. Immediately, Lars came over, took out his tape measure, then, turning in the direction of our Dutch friends, he yelled "Hey, 18 inches! Congratulations!"

Dutch swearing can be amusing!
In the evening we discussed the "catch," and seeing a grin from Lars, I ventured, "Oh well, you just need to know how to fish!" The laughter from Leen and Ids seemed a little forced.
The next year, we all met again in Denmark, but once again, their lack of success made the mood nasty when I appeared on the beach. I don't know what devil made me say, "So, let's see how big the fish are here."
On my third cast, I caught a 20-inch fish, chuckling as I watched my Dutch friends turn away to avoid congratulating me. I'm very certain there would've been no dinner together had Leen and Ids not caught their own fish later that day! But, of course, I was to be paid back for my arrogance. The next year, I got to hold the landing net for my friends from Holland while being treated to some very rude and uncalled-for remarks about "knowing how to fish."

Leen Huisman with one of his outstanding 2-handed rods.

In Holland, Ger Vroomen and Gerrit Gleser became known early-on for their nodeless, G&G rods and their perfect finish. In the 1980s, their tapers and workmanship set new standards, and these rods became leaders of the European style. Unfortunately, because of a very bad accident Ger suffered a few years ago, only a few G&G rods now come onto the market.

With good-natured teasing, some makers maintain that the only reason it was Dutchmen who perfected the technique of nodeless rods (this method, briefly described by Garrison) was simply because there's almost no waste in the construction process, and they could get their full value by pressing an entire culm of bamboo into service. But, no matter, their nodeless rods reveal the latest innovations coming from Europe.

Two exquisite G&G rods with unusual reelseats. In the lower rod, continuous rod splines form the hexagonal grip - also reflected in both the reelseat and its sliding ring. The ferrules have been engraved.

Bjarne Fries of Denmark (living today in Randers), turned his hobby into a profession as early as 1983. Bjarne studied classical guitar for 2 years, but like so many others, is self-taught as a rod-builder. He finds it important to produce rods entirely by hand, without help from machines. Fries developed all his tapers himself, and his present-day series are the result of extensive research into rod-action. "I avoid everything unnecessary -- that is, extra weight. Relative to length and line weight, my rods are among the lightest on the market, worldwide." In 1998-1999, he developed a ferrule built entirely of bamboo and fully integrated into the rod. "This connection is characterized by its very low weight, and in comparison to a traditional nickel-silver ferrule, barely influences the action at all."

Bjarne Fries planing.

By the time I began to build rods, Tom Moran, from England, had already become known for turning out work of the finest sort. When I first visited the Dutch Fly Fair and saw his rods, I found his tapers and finish to be so perfect that I doubted I'd ever be able to measure up to his standards. Later, Moran went to the USA for several years to work at Thomas & Thomas -- the contact, I believe, being established at one of the Dutch shows.

Udo Hildebrand, from Germany, also began rod-making during these years, and wrote several articles about the process in various, specialty magazines. Udo is an absolute perfectionist when it comes to the action of his rods, blurting, "What use is the most beautiful rod, if it doesn't cast right!?" After I was infected with the rod-building virus, I called Udo to ask if he could spare me a culm of Tonkin bamboo. He did it! Today, he concentrates mostly on antique, fishing-tackle auctions (see the chapter on collecting), but I'm certain he will also continue to build a few excellent rods.

Udo Hildebrandt, one of the first in Germany to resume traditional rod-building.

Gunter Hensler is yet another of my professional colleagues in Germany. Ever since he began his career in 1980, we've remained in constant contact and enjoyed an exchange of ideas.

It is largely due to Hensler's perfection and his relentless search for new methods that German rods have achieved the international recognition they enjoy today. Personally, it's very satisfying to see so much activity in Germany, and to know that bamboo rod-building continues. Despite the endless, new versions of graphite, split-bamboo will never again be dismissed from fly-fishing, for new makers continue to emerge, carrying the split-cane rod and its tradition into future generations. I think it was Udo Hildebrand who said, a short time ago: "Split-bamboo rods swing, graphite rods, at best, nod."

A Henseler rod with the typical "H" symbol.

Günter Henseler in front of his workshop. He doesn't offer rods of a specific type, but builds only to customers' preferences.

Bamboo can grow to great height. The stems in this grove are about 45 feet tall and have diameters exceeding 4 inches. Unfortunately, Tonkin bamboo does not grow this large.

Arundinaria Amabilis

*"Science recognizes over 1500 species of bamboo.
Only one species, commercially known as
'Tonkin' bamboo, is suited
for building first-class rods."*

Arundinaria amabilis, a grass to love.
This stuff-of-dreams has a name, *Arundinaria amabilis* (the lovely grass), and is the single species of bamboo suitable for making first-class rods.

Bamboo belongs to the grass family, but I remember being quite disappointed when that fact became clear to me after several years of building fly rods. The raw material which I handled so proudly was not a precious wood (which I had thought until then), but a grass. Now, you can mow grass and feed animals with it, but who would feel pride in fishing with grass? Even so, my consternation departed with time, and I consoled myself in knowing that, indeed, grasses are some of the most important plants on earth.
Actually, this type of grass is one of the world's most impressive. More than 500 species grow in China alone, but those numbers only represent a third of all of the world's known varieties.

Science recognizes over 1500 species of bamboo.

The history of rod-building has shown that only one species is suited for building the finest rods, *Arundinaria amabilis*, commercially known as "Tonkin" bamboo. This preference clearly reflects the unusual properties of the plant, for it's the only species of bamboo whose fiber content constitutes 53 percent of its total bulk, and this explains its stiffness and strength.

A cross-section of a cane, clearly showing individual fibers. The outermost "power fibers" of Arundinaria amabilis are responsible for its great strength.

The fibers along the outside are known as "power fibers," and are of critical importance for rod-building. Extremely flexible and tough, they give the rod a large measure of its strength. As we will see later, it's of great importance that these outer fibers not be disturbed during the construction process.

Tonkin bamboo grows relatively straight, and the distance between growth nodes increases as we look upward from the plant roots. Nodal spacing can exceed 20 inches in the uppermost parts of the plant.

Arundinaria amabilis grows to 40 feet, but reaches its full height within only five to eight weeks -- the stem attaining a diameter of nearly 3 inches near its base. The process of ripening and hardening will then require another three to six years.

In addition to the density of the power fibers and wall-thickness, rod-builders appreciate yet another important property of this species: Heat the bamboo, and it becomes plastic enough to be bent in nearly any direction.

Heat makes Tonkin cane plastic and bendable.

Was I ever proud...! After several weeks of trying, I finally succeeded in my attempt to locate some bamboo for rod-building. Other rod-builders didn't want to sell their bamboo, but I really needed this "stuff" so I could begin. I had almost given up because, at the time, I didn't have the money to travel to England. (I heard it was possible to buy Tonkin bamboo there, somewhere in the vicinity of Liverpool.) And I didn't want to go to Belgium because my Dutch, rod-building friends warned me that the quality of material there was uncertain.

Then, one frustrating evening, and after a second glass of wine, my girlfriend pointed out that perhaps I was something less than mentally bright, suggesting that I simply pick up the telephone book and take a gander in the Yellow Pages. She also said that, when she'd been in town, she saw a store-window using bamboo as decoration, sagely observing that the store must have obtained it somewhere!

I imagine I looked a little sheepish when I read the entry, "Rattan, Woven Cane, Bamboo, and Garden Material." She was laughing at me, but that didn't stop me from giving her a big kiss. The next day I called the company, explained what I was looking for, and was connected to the company manager. He answered with, "Please tell me why you want Tonkin bamboo." We agreed that I should come by to discuss the matter with him in person.

But, when I accounted for all my needs and showed him a bamboo rod, he asked the question I had not expected: "How many pieces are you thinking of?" I went pale and mumbled, "Well, 50 pieces or so," which produced a long laugh.

I'm sure he felt sorry for me, but he explained that this material is only traded in units of more than a 1000 pieces. I went pale again, but as I was leaving, he said maybe he could make an exception by adding something like 300 pieces to an existing order. As I left his office, I was told that Tonkin bamboo is sold in China under the names "Tsing Li" or "Tea-Stick Bamboo."

I left that store in absolute delight. I had ordered enough Tonkin bamboo for hundreds of rods -- and this, in my own city.

Tonkin culms, in bundles of 25. Often, pieces of lower quality need to be culled from the lot!

Dr. Floyd Alonzo McClure was the first to devote years of study to this species of bamboo. When he finally determined that Tonkin is very different from other bamboo species, he decided to give his discovery its own name, *Arundinaria amabilis*. The precise recognition of the species was first published in 1931, although by this time, rods had been built of Tonkin bamboo for well over 30 years. No doubt (just as for me when I began), rod-builders in those early years weren't interested in the source or the name of this wonderful material, but cared only about its unique properties -- and that the cane was available!

Later interviews showed that McClure (who died in 1970) was not a fisherman, but in the final sentence of the first part of his 1931 paper in *The Lingnan Science Journal*, he wrote:

"The quality of the stems of this plant fit it admirably for many uses, among which is the manufacture of split-bamboo fishing rods, which appears to be its chief use abroad."

Appearing in the second section is this sentence: "Western people find this bamboo ideally adapted to the manufacture of the highest quality split-bamboo fishing rods."

The difficulty McClure faced in establishing the species was that not only did bamboo's roots, stem, leaves, and seeds need to be studied, but also its blossoms. But, depending upon the species, the intervals between flowering can range anywhere between 3 to 120 years. In 1928, McClure had the good fortune to be in China during flowering, and was thus able to carry out his species determination. A further flowering was reported in 1963, indicating a 35-year cycle for this new species. I describe this so carefully because bamboo plants (often an entire grove) completely die upon flowering, and it can take several years before new bamboo re-grows. Potentially, a complete nightmare for the rod-builder.

The cross-hatched rectangle shows the Hauiji growing area.

136

137

It was Luis Mardin who followed McClure's footsteps to the source area in China, and in his wonderful book, *The Angler's Bamboo*, Marden describes where and how Tea-Stick Bamboo grows. The "Lovely Grass" for building rods is cultivated in the province of Kwangtung -- or more precisely, in a half-circle, about 45 miles across, high in the hills along the Sui River and near the town of Waitsap, Huaiji (perhaps 140 miles northeast of Canton).

During his trip, Luis Marden investigated the area and spoke with the growers.

Tonkin bamboo grows best in warm, moist regions and at altitudes of about 1500 feet. The region around Waitsup has an average temperature of 21° C (70° F), which, in the coldest month of January, falls to 11° C (52° F), and the average rainfall is 65 to 70 inches per year. Several attempts have been made to cultivate *Arundinaria amabilis* in other parts of the world, but, while successful, all have yielded unsatisfactory results for the rod-maker.

The average annual harvest in China is about 66,000 tons, and is done by hand. The stems are cut just above the ground with a large knife and the culms are then brought to the banks of the Sui River.

Workers use sharp knives to cut the canes just above the ground.

After harvesting, the canes are bundled and, later, tied together to form rafts.

Before the canes arrive at the processor, they're dried over a period of time on the river banks.

There, they're gathered into large bundles which, in turn, are tied into gigantic rafts to be transported down the river to a sandy beach near the harbor. These rafts are up to 260 feet long and steered by only two people using long poles. At the beach, the canes (still green-colored but scrubbed clean with water and sand), are set upright to dry for eight-to-ten days. The scrubbing and the sun give the cane its characteristic, straw-yellow color. But it should not rain during this drying period, so the best harvest time is from October to February. After drying, the cane is loaded onto ships and brought to factories in the city of Fatshan. There, if necessary, the culms are straightened by hand, using heat.

Over a container of glowing coals, the cane is rapidly and continuously turned (to avoid burning) until it's hot enough to be bent straight over a wooden rack. Culms that measure 2 to 2 3/4 inch in diameter and are suitable for rod-building, are wrapped and shipped in bundles of 25 pieces.

Canes will be straightened and trimmed in a work-room.

This worker is sitting on a bamboo stool: Tonkin bamboo is also used to make furniture.

Tea Stick Bamboo is sent all around the world, with the thinner canes used in gardens or fields to support beans, tomatoes, or flowers. Tonkin sticks are also used in vineyards, and the Scandinavians use them to make snow fences, ski poles and walking sticks. In China itself, the thicker canes are used to build many kinds of furniture.

Packed as shown, bamboo reaches the entire world - including, of course, the many rod-makers.

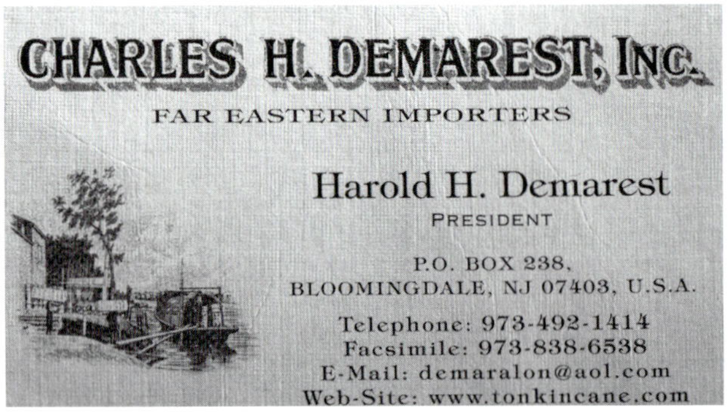

The company's business card.

Bamboo rod-builders around the world owe a word of thanks to Charles H. Demarest of New York. Even prior to 1900, his company was importing Chinese, Tonkin bamboo to the USA and rest of the Western World. An invoice, dating back to 1897 remains in the company records and documents -- an order of Tonkin cane intended for rod-building. Charles' son, Harold H. Demarest, continues the business today, and the company remains an excellent source for rod-building bamboo. I had the chance to meet Mr. Demarest on the occasion of a 2002 show in New York. Upon looking at my rods, his first question was, "Do you want to buy first-class Tonkin from me?"

Harold H. Demarest, President of the famous company, and his wife in New York, 2002.

For almost 100 years, split-cane rods had been produced from bamboo grown in India, known commercially as "Calcutta Cane." The species grows wild in the provinces of Assam and Chittagong and has the scientific name *Gigantochloa macrostachia*. This bamboo grows with much thinner walls than does Tonkin, but up until 1900 or so, Calcutta Cane (often with its burned-in patterns) was considered the ideal material for rods of any kind.

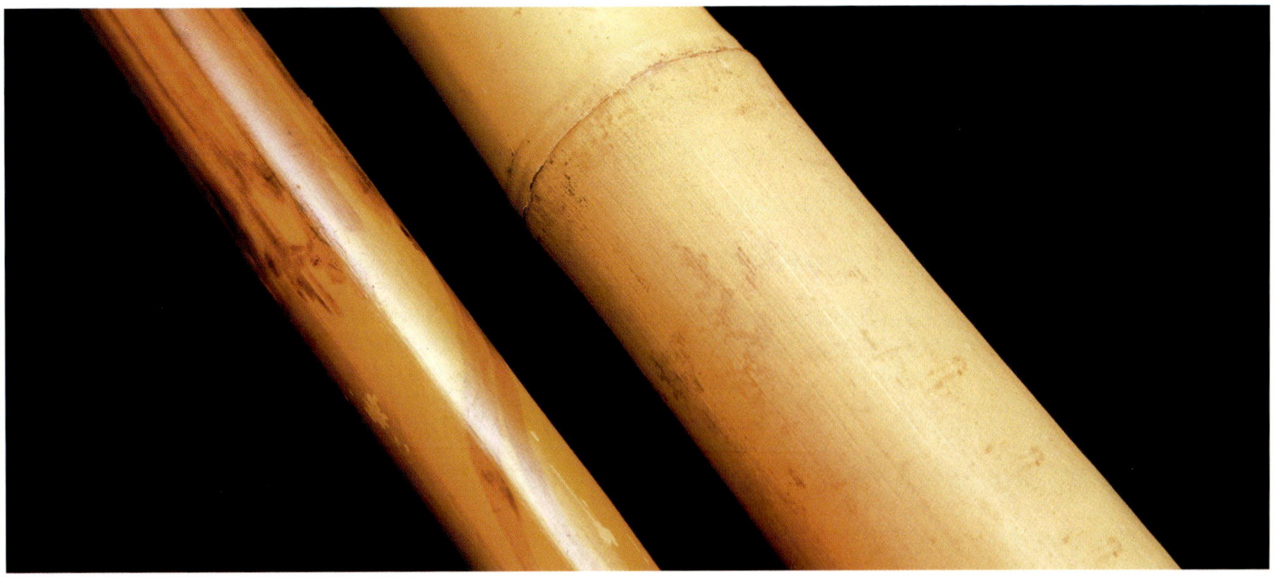

Calcutta bamboo on the left and Tonkin on the right.

According to an unconfirmed story, Tonkin was first used to fasten down carpets on stairs and in rooms. The bamboo was split and the resulting strips would be screwed down along the carpet edges.

One day, a strip of Tonkin bamboo came loose from a stair and tripped a man -- who just happened to be employed as rod-builder by a well-known American company. When the gentleman discovered what had tripped him, he angrily tore out the entire piece of bamboo, looked at it carefully, and immediately recognized the difference between this "new" species and his usual raw material.

Whether or not this man ripped up the remaining carpet strips to build a rod from Tonkin is unknown -- indeed, as is the veracity of the story itself. It's certain, however, that the first rods built from *Arundinaria amabilis* began to arrive on the market before 1900. During a long period of transition, rods made of Calcutta Cane continued to be sold in dealers' catalogs, but the "lovely grass" ultimately prevailed. In some flea markets today, it's still possible to find cheap, mass-market rods from Japan -- built from Indian or Japanese bamboo in the years between 1950 and 1965.

A rod-builder at the source of his dreams - even though this bamboo is not Tonkin.

The three most common planes for rod-building: The Stanley #4 bench plane, together with the 60 ½ and 9 ½ block planes.

Tools

*"You can make
many of the tools needed
for rod-building."*

How the shavings fall depends on how you plane....
Clearly, planing is necessary to build a split-bamboo rod, but the quality of the rod produced only partly depends on the quality of tools used.

1. The Plane

Planes of very high quality (as well as their blades, or "irons") are essential for good work, but only metal planes are suitable for building split-bamboo rods. These can be adjusted with precision, and with modest care, will provide service for many decades. Unfortunately, good tools are expensive, but one should not scrimp here, because high-quality tools make high-quality work much easier.

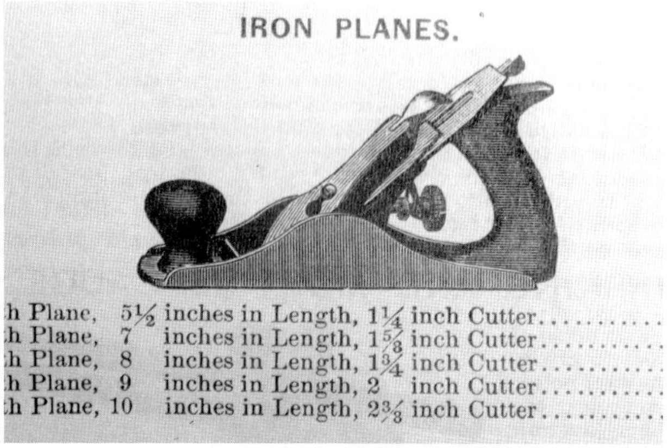

A bench plane from the 1879 Stanley catalog. Its construction remains almost the same today.

144

145

Augustus and Timothy Stanley founded the A. Stanley & Company in 1854 in New Britain, Connecticut. In a few short years, this company became a world-leader in the production of woodworking tools. In 1869, they bought Bailey, Chany & Co. of Boston, Massachusetts. This latter company had long been recognized for its specialized planes and plane irons, but beginning in the year of Stanley's purchase, all products bore the Stanley name. In subsequent years, nearly every metal plane (manufactured by any company) was based in form and function on the Stanley models. This remains true even today, and ever since their introduction, very little has changed in construction.

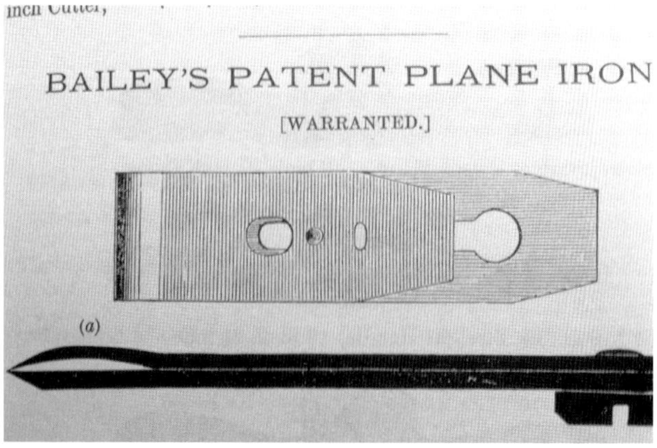

Even the manner of holding the iron in the plane is unchanged.

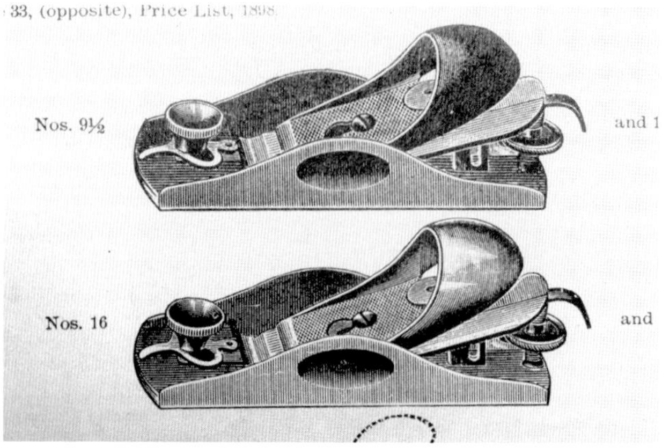

Today's block planes are held to the same high standards.

For rod-making, two different models of planes should be considered:.
1. The "smoothing," or bench plane
2. The "block" plane.

The Bench Plane
In nearly all bench planes, the blade is fixed at a 45° angle to the sole, and should be sharpened at an angle between 25° and 30°. The construction of the plane ensures that its cutting angle will always be at 45°. In truth, this type of plane is primarily for coarse work, but I agree with many colleagues that they work well even when final-planing the strips. Still, well-sharpened blades and precise adjustments are necessary. Because of their weight, bench planes lie nicely on a planing form (or cane strip), and can be controlled easily. Most rod-makers choose the #3 or #4 sizes from well-known manufacturers like Stanley, Record, Anant, Kunz, Clifton, and Lie-Nielson. Least expensive, are those planes from the Indian company, Anant, although they're almost perfect copies of the Stanley. These, together with Stanley, Record, and Kunz planes form the "middle-class" of metal planes. If choosing these brands, however, some preliminary tuning will be necessary to achieve optimal results.

A modern Stanley bench plane.

An inexpensive alternative made by the Anant company of India.

If you want to realize the benefit of their fine adjustments, it's usually necessary to hone the sole perfectly flat. This is readily done by gluing a piece of wet-or-dry sandpaper (twice as long as the sole of the plane, and, initially, 100 grit) to a piece of plate glass, then rubbing the sole of the plane (naturally, with its blade removed) over the sandpaper. This procedure is repeated with ever-finer paper until 320-grit is reached, and the sole will be perfectly prepared. Your final results will be obvious when fine scratches from the sandpaper are evenly distributed over the entire surface of the plane's sole). It's also important to realize that the blades, as supplied, are usually simple, tool steel and quickly become dull. Better blades are made from high-speed steel. These are much more difficult to sharpen, but well worth the effort.

Ron Hock, in the USA, produces high-quality plane blades. In describing his irons, he says:

"The three qualities that most affect the selection of steel for hand-tool application are edge-holding, sharpenability, and corrosion-resistance. For metallurgical reasons, you can only have two of the three…in woodworking, corrosion-resistance is the least important of the three, and prefer[able is] an edge that is easily sharpened and long lasting. A steel's carbon content determines its ability to harden with heat treatment. That hardness determines a tool's ability to hold a sharp cutting edge under abrasive pressure. Generally, the harder the metal the better its edge holding, but it will be more brittle. …. So a balance must be struck to decide how hard a blade should be. 'Tool Steel' refers to a class of steels that are metallurgically very 'clean' and fall within strict limits for alloy proportions. Vanadium, tungsten, and molybdenum are often added to tool steels to make the steel resist annealing (softening) when used in "high-speed" (high heat) applications. Chromium is added in very large quantities for corrosion resistance ('stainless'). … Correctly heat-treated, tools made from high-speed, stainless, and "chrome-vanadium" steels may hold an edge well in woodworking applications, but, due to the large, hard carbide particles that form during hardening, they are difficult to sharpen and cannot be honed as sharply as a blade of plain high-carbon steel. Our choice of High-Carbon Tool-Steel (.95% Carbon) offers the finest, sharpest edge possible. Its chromium and vanadium additions amount to only 1/2% each allowing quick, clean honing with traditional techniques. High-carbon steel holds and takes an edge better than anything else."

From my own experience, I can only agree. An additional advantage is that the irons made from high-quality, fine-grained, high-carbon steel are 17% thicker and help enormously to lessen the "chatter" when planing. Chatter can be reduced still further by using a heavy chip-breaker, also made by Ron Hock. Recently, his company began offering "A2 Cryo" steel blades, presently regarded as the best of the best. I could have saved a lot of time had I known, earlier, of Ron Hock's products.

Nevertheless, it's indeed possible to purchase a relatively inexpensive plane, tune it, and outfit it with an excellent blade and chip-breaker. At once, you'll have greatly raised the potential of the tool!

In all cases, I would recommend buying several blades, because it's irritating to have to stop and re-sharpen your blade while in the midst of planing a strip. Having two or three perfectly sharp blades at the ready will provide a comfort-factor, and you'll be more likely to change an iron before pushing it to the "limit." A dull plane iron can ruin a cane strip because it tears the bamboo easily!

Without question, the finest products are manufactured by Lie-Nielsen Toolworks, Inc. (founded in 1981) in the USA.

Block plane from Lie-Nielsen.

Block plane with its iron removed.

The range of planes offered by this company is extensive and leaves nothing to be desired. Many models are suitable for working on bamboo rods and come in cast iron or bronze with wooden handles. You'll quickly recognize the advantage of wood when blisters on your hands (from a plastic handle) prevent you from going into the workshop for a couple days. The beauty of these planes practically brings tears to the eyes of every fan of fine tools. Unfortunately, so does the price. Nevertheless, one should consider that they last a lifetime; their construction is perfect; and their irons/blades are thicker (about 3.5 mm) than usual and made from a very long-lasting, special steel. I recommend these planes to any who can afford them.

The sole of this plane has a shallow, milled groove that keeps the iron from contacting the planing form.

The Clifton plane - a very fine tool.

Another wonderful tool (the Mercedes of planes for me) is produced by the English, Clifton company.
It has a thick, hand-forged, high-carbon, steel blade and a two-piece chip-breaker.

A Clifton plane with its iron removed. The chip-breaker consists of two parts, and the iron is hand-forged.

A Lie-Nielsen block plane with a bedding angle of 12°.

Block Planes

This "workhorse" in the stable of planes is much different from a bench plane. It's constructed differently, is smaller and lighter, has multiple uses, and is designed to cut the finest shavings. Two models are suited for rod-building: the "60 1/2" low-angle plane with its blade bedded at an angle of 12° to 13° (depending on manufacturer), and the "9 1/2" standard-angle plane with its blade bedded at an angle of 20° to 21° (again, depending on manufacturer). The designations, "60 1/2" and "9 1/2", come from the Stanley originals. Both planes allow for their cutting-angle to be changed by varying the sharpening angle. In contrast to the bench plane, the blade of a block plane lies with its sharpened side facing upward in the plane bed. The result is that the fixed angle of the plane bed + the sharpening angle of the blade = the cutting angle.

Example: Low-angle plane with a 12° bedding angle + a sharpening angle of 30° = Cutting angle of 42°.

Usually, planes are manufactured with a sharpening angle of 20° or 25°, but I often re-shape the blade of a block plane to an angle of 30°. It's a good idea to hone only its leading edge to the final angle, as this makes re-sharpening much easier. Most block planes have an adjustable mouth.

The mouth of a plane should be adjustable.

The mouth allows you to set, exactly, the space through which the shavings pass, and should always be positioned for the narrowest gap possible. Block planes can be obtained from Anant, Stanley, Record, Kunz, and Lie-Nielsen. In addition, two versions from Veritas (Canada and the USA) are now available in Germany. These can be adjusted with precision; they lie perfectly in the hand, and they're delivered with top-notch blades. I put them in the "premium" class.

My recommendation is that, if one intends to build only one or two rods, a single plane would be adequate. Preferably, these would be either a #4 bench plane or a "9 1/2" block plane. However, if the plan is to build large numbers of rods, three planes should be purchased, including the #4 bench plane and the "9 1/2" and "60 1/2" block planes.

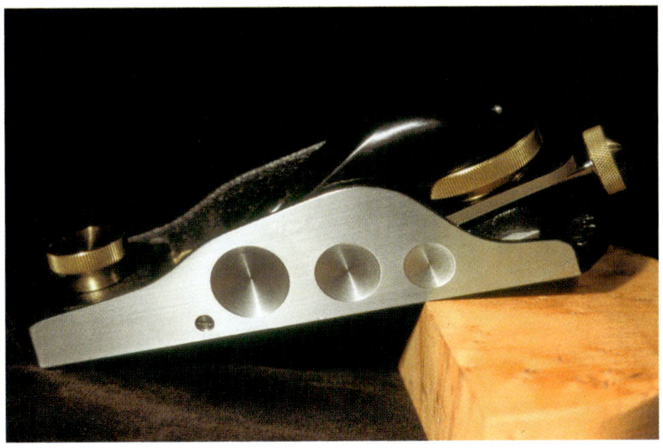

This modern block plane from Veritas fits the hand nicely.

Sharpening

Even the best plane is useless if its iron is dull. A dull blade can lead to unpleasant injuries because it can snag all-too-easily in the bamboo and suddenly pull the strip through the "retaining" hand. The result will be a deep cut. When I was still a beginner, the fingers of my left hand were usually decorated with a variety of band-aids. Plane blades should be sharp enough to cut paper.

Correct sharpening begins by using a grinder to produce the correct cutting-angle, but the only suitable grinders are those whose wheel turns slowly in water. If one uses a regular, high-speed grinder, the steel will overheat and the valuable plane iron will be ruined. The Swedish company, Tormek, produces machines perfectly suited for sharpening plane blades, but if you consider buying this device, plan on a couple days of "vacation" too. Your experience will surely be like mine. Once my plane irons were well-sharpened and a number of bamboo strips were finished, it occurred to me that many other items in my home also needed to be sharpened. Tormek's large selection of attachments allows one to sharpen tools of every type, and ever since, the edges of my kitchen knives and scissors have become much too keen. The guide that comes with the machine is necessary, and care should be taken to clamp the blade parallel to the grinding wheel. Sharpening is accomplished by taking careful, back-and-forth passes with only slight pressure. Finally, to avoid digging into your planing form, the iron's outer corners should be dressed with a gentle radius .

This guide on this grinder ensures sharpening at the correct angle.

After producing the proper angle on a sharpening machine, you still need to hone the blade on a series of finer bench stones (and using a different a guide). But before proceeding, the tiny burr on the backside of the blade must be smoothed-off. Sharpening machines that include a leather belt or disk are very good for this, and the leather belt, in particular, provides perfect stropping at the conclusion of honing.

Of course, the angle can be ground entirely by hand -- it just takes longer. I know some colleagues who take special pride in sharpening all their plane irons by hand. They love their various sharpening stones, and even maintain that there's something mystical about the slow, hand-sharpening process.

A wide variety of stones is available, and each rod-maker I know swears by "his" stone. Most stones are immersed in water before use, and the sharpening process is wet, while others must be saturated with oil. "Combination" stones of more than one grit are also available, and I can recommend them. A good choice would be one with 1000-grit on one side and 6000-grit on the other.

The more perfectly the iron is sharpened, the easier the planing goes.

A simple sharpening guide serves well enough to approximate the correct angle.

A precision guide provides the exact angle for hand-sharpening.

Jig for setting the correct angle.

Measuring Tools

A simple, flexible, dressmaker's tape (purchased at any sewing or crafts store) can be used to mark the width of your strips directly on the bamboo culm.

A dial-indicator depth-gauge, fitted with a 60° point, is needed to set the planing form. These gauges have an adjustment screw, used to establish its "zero-point" when placed on the planing form. For this, the gauge will be mounted in a small block of metal (ground absolutely flat on its bottom). The depth gauge can be purchased from a machinist's supplier, while the metal piece can be made in one's shop. The complete assembly can also be purchased from suppliers who cater to rod-builders (see Appendix).

Either a vernier or a dial caliper (for convenience, I use a digital model), or a micrometer will be necessary to ensure that the cane strips have been planed to their exact dimensions.

A depth gauge, fitted with a 60° point, measures the planing form precisely at each adjusting screw.

Splitting Tools

A dull knife is adequate for splitting the bamboo, but it should have a heavy blade because it will be driven into the culm with a wooden mallet. The blade should be at least 4 inches long. A slightly sharpened screwdriver is also useful. In difficult splits that want to veer off-course, the screwdriver can be driven into the bamboo from its outside surface, again using a simple wooden mallet.

Simple splitting tools.

Files

One will need both a fine- and a medium-cut wood file, with blades at least 8 inches long and 1 1/8 inches wide. A brass brush (or "file card") is needed to clean the files.

Sharpening Stones

If a power-grinder is used, the grinding wheel must be suitable for the type of metal being worked. A simple, scissors sharpening-stone can be mounted in a drill for tapering the feet on snake-guides.

Abrasives

Sandpaper (intended for wood) will be needed in grits of 60, 100, 180, and 220. Wet-or-dry sandpaper (600, 800, 1000, and 1200 grits) is used to prepare the ferrules. Final polishing of the finished blank will be done with 000 and/or 0000 steel wool.

Simple tools serve well: A heat gun, flat files and a straight chisel are available in most hardware stores.

Night Fishing

What, me afraid? Never! And while fishing? Impossible!

I was once again in Denmark to visit a good friend (let's call him Ole) and fish for sea-run browns. It was almost the end of June, and Ole, who knows the area well, explained that at night, the trout come close to shore near one of his favorite spots -- an area backed-up by a high bluff. Everything was arranged, so we drove off as twilight was setting, parked in a thick stand of beech trees, and walked the rest of the way to the beach by failing light. Getting down the bluff in the half-light was something else again, but when we arrived at the bottom, the Baltic Sea was black and mirror-smooth in front of us. The moon was nearly full and it illuminated what looked like exaggerated skeletons -- beech trees, eroded from the bluff by winter storms, had become stripped and bleached by the salt water.

After climbing over these branchy obstacles, Ole declared that we had reached the right spot. A breeze was at our backs and we had to wade out about 50 yards to reach water of adequate depth. Everything lay completely still, and only the occasional cry of a seagull echoed eerily off the bluff behind us. Truth to be told, I felt reassured to hear the clicking of Ole's reel only about 30 yards away from me. I began to strip line from my reel and prepared to cast toward a silver band the moon was making on the water. Short motions at first, while the knot to my leader went through the tip-top with a "click-click." Cast again. Then, a short distance away...a distinct splash. "Ah-ha, some fish seem to be near us." Cast again, and with expectations high, strip in the line -- nothing! An owl joined the seagull, and I began to wonder a little if night fishing was really all that much fun.

Suddenly, I noticed some sort of motion in the water in front of me. What the devil was that? A porpoising, sea-run brown? My next cast was exactly in that direction. Nothing!

I froze when, about 10 yards ahead of me, something very large broke the surface, then disappeared again. Timidly, the following conversation evolved (or, as much of it as I can remember, for though I was waist-deep in the cool, dark, Baltic water, I began to sweat profusely). "Hey, Ole!" "Yeah?" "Something very big is swimming in front of me." "What is it?" "No idea, can you come over here?" Pause….. Suddenly, a strange noise -- like a deep cough -- directly behind me. I turned around, but I couldn't recognize anything against the bluff -- only little waves came toward me. Pure panic set in and I was ready to believe anything. This must have been obvious from my voice because I heard Ole quickly move closer, "What's going on?" Now there was a splash very close to my right and I saw something large and black swimming before it dove again. Again, that very strange noise! Now Ole was beside me and whispered, "I saw it, too." We stood almost back-to-back, watching the surface of the water around us. Suddenly, a big bow-wave spread rapidly...then, the cute head of a seal appeared in the silvery light, exchanged looks with us, and disappeared back into the water. A couple seconds later (that seemed like minutes to me), Ole volunteered, "Oh well...guess we don't need to fish here anymore."

Measuring is important. Check repeatedly to assure that proper dimensions are being maintained.

In the workshop

156

157

"Bamboo means that you can make something yourself. Anyone can build a split-cane rod, but good tools are necessary"

The Way to Long Success

It takes quite a bit of time to gather what you need to build your own rod. But, don't worry, everything will work out. Just don't get impatient. The good news is, you can make just about everything yourself.

Before you read further, let me warn you: It's possible you may undergo some peculiar changes. Your house or apartment will be carefully inspected, storage areas measured, shops selling hardware and building materials take on a new meaning, and, from time-to-time, newspaper ads for real estate may come in for intensive study.

You phone old acquaintances you've not seen for a long time: "You still work at the same place where … uhh … well, I need to get something from you."

The following instructions for building a bamboo rod offer only one among several possibilities, but throughout, I've concentrated on describing simple tools and methods.

Bamboo culms need to be evaluated carefully before you begin splitting, but unfortunately, the external surfaces don't always determine how good the bamboo may be. The most important criterion for building a good rod is a sufficiently thick layer of power fibers. Tonkin culms are usually sold in twelve-foot lengths, but the layer of power fiber in the lower part (where growth-rings, or nodes, are relatively close together) is thicker than in its upper part. If you were to saw through a culm very close to a node, the power fibers are always extremely thick and it's not possible to determine the quality of the cane at these locations. It's best to cut through the cane at a mid-point between nodes, or at least four inches from a node, to evaluate the power fibers.

Unfortunately, some culms have such a thin layer of fibers that they may as well be discarded immediately to avoid unnecessary work. Even with the most careful attention, it's not possible to build an acceptable rod from such a culm. The action will be much too soft, and the rod will take a set even with moderate loads.

I separate my material into three categories: useless bamboo for the fireplace, usable material with average fiber density for butt sections, and material with greater fiber density for middle and tip sections. If you have a good supply of bamboo, you should choose a piece from the middle part of the culm. Here, the fiber density is usually well-balanced and the nodes are more widely spaced -- meaning less work.

Two bamboo bundles. The best culms still need to be identified.

Sawing across a culm reveals the fibers clearly. This culm shows only a moderately-thick band of fibers.

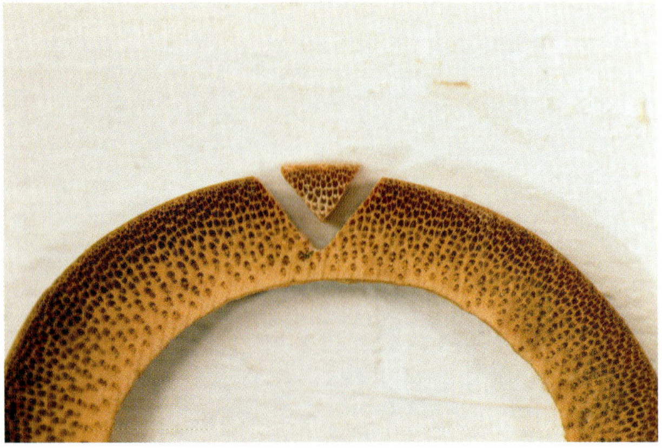

The dream of every rod-maker: A perfectly developed layer of power fibers.

Quality is Foremost

The appearance of the surface of a culm should not be the basis for selection. Many canes have water-spots or dark areas which, in part, remain visible in the finished rod. On the other hand, cosmetic blemishes alone shouldn't cause you to reject a culm, for it would be much better to build a rod that casts well and has cosmetic flaws, than to build a visually-perfect rod from a culm containing an insufficient layer of power fibers! It is necessary to watch for holes in the bamboo, however, since most of these will indicate insect damage and may render the culm unusable.

The upper culm shows some small dark spots and stripes caused by water and insects. The lower culm has a perfect surface.

A leaf scar on a culm is not a problem. Only one strip needs to be discarded after splitting, leaving the remainder of the culm usable.

Another technique for evaluating the quality of the bamboo is a breakage test. You take a piece of bamboo about 5/16 inches wide by 8 inches long and break it in the middle. The quality of individual power fibers can be seen in the break, and you can quickly determine if the quality is adequate. Poor material breaks easily, showing only a few long fibers, and the break itself will be localized. A strip of suitable material, however, breaks slowly and over a wider area, showing many, long fibers that spring out, dense and brittle. Be careful: You can easily hurt yourself on the splayed-out fibers.

Break-test: To be sure of the results, two strips are broken. High quality strips are seen on the left, revealing broadly-splintered fibers. The strips in the middle and on the right are of lower quality.

Upon receiving a bamboo culm, a so-called "check-split" needs to be made in the lower end of the cane. This is necessary because stresses in the bamboo increase as the cane continues to dry, and without a pre-determined starting point, a culm could split, haphazardly in several places at once, leaving you with a great deal of unusable material. Normally, if you extend that split just beyond the second growth node, the culm will continue to open from that point onward as it dries out. The check-split is easy to make, using only a wooden mallet and a heavy knife.

This is how a good bamboo strip breaks.

A mallet and simple knife are used to begin a "check-split" at the thick end of the culm.

Nobody told me! How are you supposed to transport 12 bales of cane, all holding 25 pieces, and with each monster piece being 12 feet long? Each bale weighs over 100 pounds and measures more than 20 inches in diameter!

Naively, I drove to the harbor in my old, diesel Mercedes, with only a roof-rack mounted on top. My Tonkin bamboo had arrived! With papers in hand, I asked my way to the warehouse, and stared in disbelief at an enormously long pile of cane lying in front of me. How in the world could I manage that? "I'll loan you a trailer," was the warehouse man's helpful comment. But that really wasn't the problem. I suddenly realized that I could never get this quantity in my apartment, and I really did want to be able to move from one room to the other without needing to become a contortionist. My friend in the country had a barn. Called him -- "Okay," he says. So I borrowed the trailer, and after three hours, only two bales (50 culms) remained in the trailer. See, I wanted to unpack all those culms at once, hold each one in my hands, sort through, and...well... everything. In those days, I was living, essentially, in an attic. An attic was good, though, because I remember reading in our rod-building literature that bamboo is best stored high in a house or building. Heat rises, and warmth is good for seasoning the culms -- they dry better and lose their remaining moisture quickly.

But, the problem was how to transport my 50 culms up a newly-renovated stairwell without ruining the walls. And how do you explain to the landlord what you're doing, and why!?

All books about building split-cane rods say that you should use only aged bamboo, but what does "aged" mean – weeks, months, or years?
It's been reported that some companies used only 20-year-old material, as if this would explain why their rods are so good. From my point of view, that's nonsense. As already described in the chapter on history, most companies never maintained large stocks of bamboo. And, in America, where one couldn't get bamboo from China during the Embargo, many makers simply had to accept whatever they could find. Storage capacities of the various companies (at least the ones I visited) were not nearly large enough to hold a 20-year supply, especially considering the several thousand culms needed for each year's production. Because of costs, most firms couldn't afford to have that much capital tied up in "dead inventory." I believe that, even at the height of their success, most companies dried their bamboo for only one or two years, and if no other bamboo were available, "fresh" culms were probably used. Additionally, we might consider the amount of time needed to transport the bamboo to any destination. Six-to-ten months could easily stretch between harvest and delivery. I have many culms that have aged 20 years, and I sometimes use one, but in all honesty, I can't distinguish a difference between these and the ones that have aged only two years. One also needs to consider the wall-thickness of bamboo. To build musical instruments, the old saying is still valid, "The grandfather buys and stores the wood for his grandson." But, these materials are a true wood, mostly cut into planks two-or-more inches thick. Storage, in this case, needs to extend over several years because moisture escapes hardwood only very slowly.

Tonkin bamboo has, at best, a wall thickness of only 5/16 of an inch! Moreover, the properties of wood cannot be compared to those of a grass – which is what bamboo is. Also, the rod-maker's technique of heat-treating (or "tempering") will drive the water out of the bamboo's pores and remove any remnant moisture.
My experience is that, even when stored for a 15 year period, bamboo will still contain considerable moisture. This is readily seen by applying a flame to a culm before working with it. When the flame is brought close to the end of the cane, the remnant moisture appears as a white foam bubbling from power fibers at the end-cut.
It's important that bamboo be stored dry and indoors, but some moisture will always remain, and this must be extracted through the hardening process. My suggestion is to store the material 6 to 12 months in a warm, dry place before working with it.

But the "remnant moisture" in bamboo can cause problems of another kind! Let's say we had quite a warm summer and fall was very beautiful, but now it is wintertime and the heat is running full-blast. My bamboo culms are resting nice and clean in a corner of my "attic," each prepared with an initial check-split, and my bed located right next to them. But nobody told me what was going to happen. After a couple days in the dry, heated air, the culms began to split open. And how! It was around four o'clock, early on that first morning, when some of the culms began to crack apart – blasting off like rounds of ammo. My girlfriend and I shot straight up in bed! We'd drift back to sleep, but after the third one fired its volley, I really couldn't hold it against her when she went packing back to her own apartment for a little peace and quiet. This went on for three or four weeks....

I'm often asked, "How many rods can you make from a single culm?" My answer is indirect, "That all depends...," because the real answer to the question is between none and (if stretched to absurdity) maybe seven. Too many factors are involved to wager a guess – the length of the culm, its quality and type, and the length of rod desired, and, and, and....
A novice rod builder will, with some skill, produce about two rods from one culm. There are other makers, however, who use every little piece from a culm because they build nodeless rods. They really do!

Splitting Bamboo
After sawing-off to the necessary length (more about that later), one uses a hammer and knife to split the culm into two halves. Hand-splitting is the single acceptable way to produce a good rod, because only in this manner will the split follow the natural path of the bamboo fibers. This means that no fibers will be damaged or cross-cut, as would happen if the cane were sawn.

The culm is split with a mallet and knife.

The "node-dams" on the inside of the culm are removed cleanly with a mallet and straight chisel.

The inner node-dams are now visible, and these must be removed cleanly with a hammer and straight chisel. Care must be taken not to cut into the material too deeply, because the culm could split at this location.

This work should be done with care in order to simplify later steps.

Don't Hammer Through the Nodes

Now, the individual strips or splines will be split from the half-culm, and as an approximate guide, the desired width of each spline is first marked on the bamboo. I use the following widths for the bamboo strips:

Butt Section = 5/16 - 1/2 inch
Middle Section = 1/4 - 13/32 inch
Tip Section = 3/16 - 5/16 inch

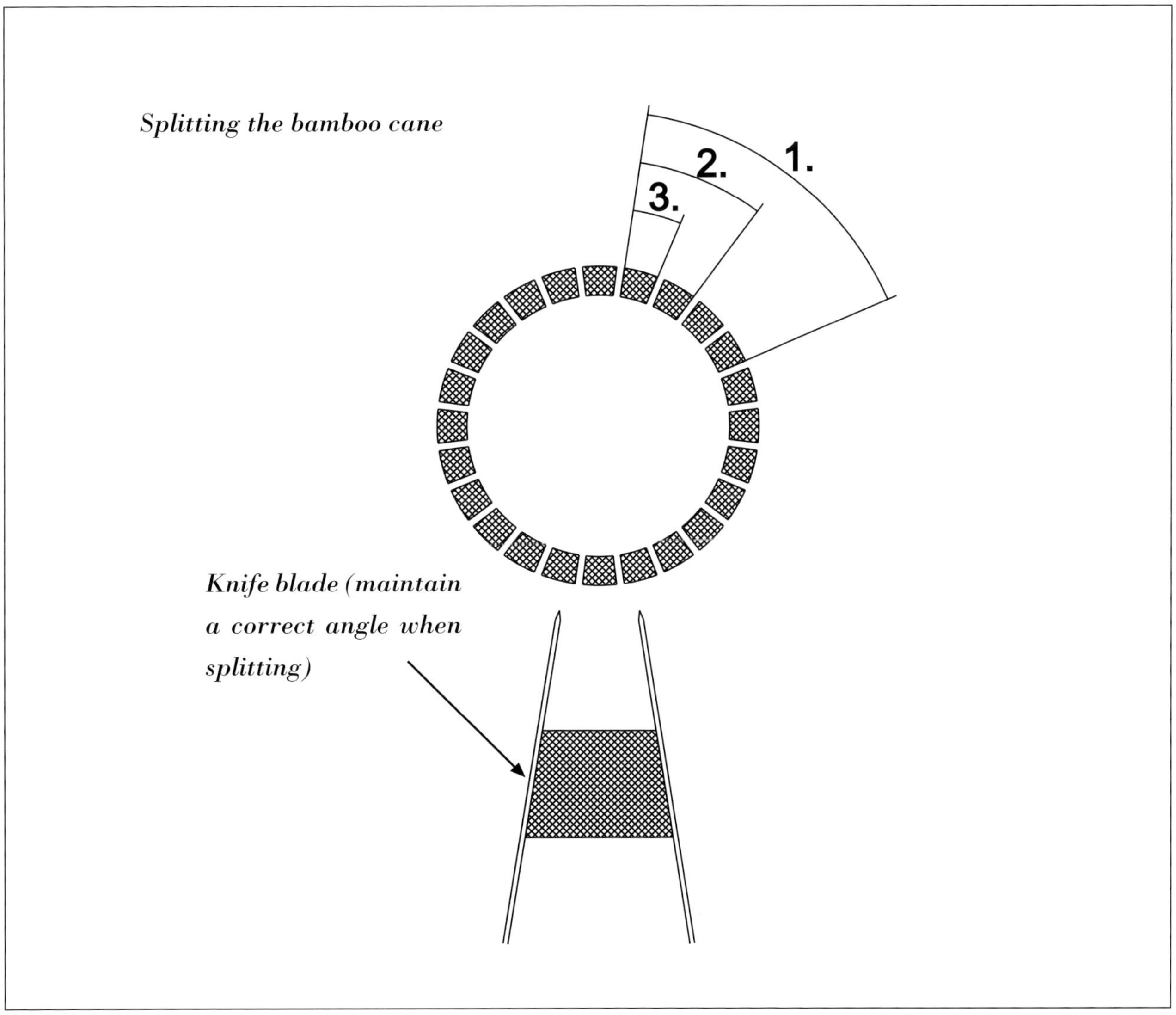

The strips would be somewhat wider, of course, for a salmon rod.
If you're inexperienced, the width should be a little more generous because splits can "jump" across the fibers. Practice is necessary to push the opening left or right to obtain parallel strips from the culm.

A dull knife is held in the vise. A "starter" split at one end divides the strip in half, then it's pushed slowly against the knife.

There are various methods to guide the bamboo, but one very simple method is to fasten a heavy, dull knife (pointed upward) in a vise. Make an initial or "starter" split at one end of the large strip (using another knife and a quick hammer-blow), then "thread" this split onto the upright knife in the vise. Slowly push the section forward, working the split down the culm, but take care, as the split jumps very easily at nodes! The initial split must be made cleanly for satisfactory results.

When pushing, be careful to keep the bamboo square to the knife, maintaining as rectangular a cross-section as possible. The slower the bamboo is pushed, the better one can observe whether the split is running straight. If a split begins to migrate away from its ideal line, pressure from an opposing direction will bring the split back to its correct path.

A useful trick is to split "doubles." First, mark a piece that would be twice the desired, final width, and then split. The resulting strip will then be divided exactly down its middle, and we end up with two perfect widths. This method makes it much easier to obtain strips of equal and parallel widths.

In this way, six strips for each rod section are split-out and laid next to each other on a work surface.

Offsetting Is a Must

Offsetting the Nodes

Within a bamboo strip, nodes are the toughest areas and, therefore, also the most troublesome. For this reason, the nodes in each strip must be offset (or "staggered") relative to adjacent strips, otherwise all nodes would be located together and produce a predetermined stress-point.

There are various possibilities for offsetting nodes in the splines. The simplest is shown in Drawing 1.

Possibilities for offsetting the nodes.

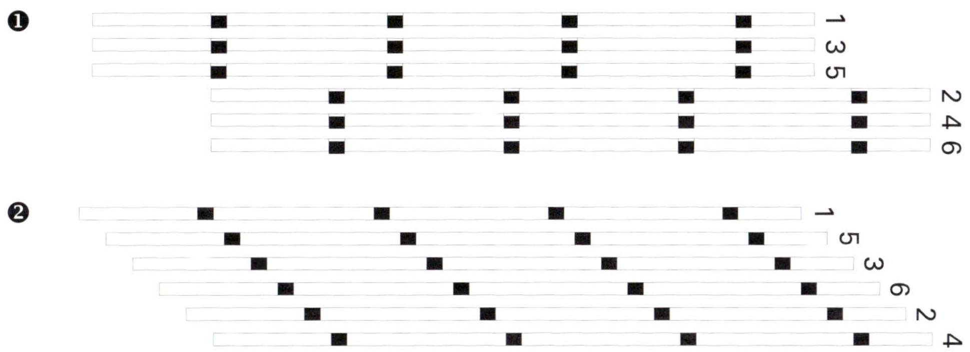

Method 1

The distance between the nodes should be at least four-to-six inches.
Maintaining this offset, the strips are cut simultaneously to a common length.
In determining the proper working-length for each strip, one must include both the effect of node-staggering and the corresponding, final cut-off. For the simple offset, the formula is:
Pre-offset length = Rod-section length + 4 to 6 inches + 7/8 inch extra

A simple method for offsetting the nodes. Every second spline is shifted.

This extra allowance will be necessary after completion, when the blank is cut squarely to length. A butt section of forty-seven inches, therefore, requires strips 52 to 54 inches long.

Method 2 is the so-called "Garrison" method, which distributes the nodes in a more-or-less spiral pattern along the blank. First, each strip is numbered in order by marking lines across the strips as, "I" through "III III." The strips are then laid on a work surface in the sequence, 1/5/3/6/2/4, each then being offset from its neighbor about 1 3/4 inches.

Using the "Garrison" method, each spline is marked from 1 to 6. The strips are then laid out in a sequence of 1-5-3-6-2-4 with their nodes offset. These splines have been flamed.

The splines are cut to an identical length, then, for optimal node distribution, they're rearranged in the original sequence of 1-2-3-4-5-6.

Maintaining this offset, all the strips are then cut to a common length. Lastly, the strips are reassembled in the sequence, 1/2/3/4/5/6, with all nodes perfectly distributed around the blank, and no area showing adjacent nodes. The Garrison method gives the following formula for strip length:

Pre-offset length = Rod-section length + (5 x 1 3/4 inches) + 7/8 inch extra
= Rod-section length + 8 3/4 inches + 7/8 inch extra

In this example, the length of each split strip should be slightly more than 56 inches to obtain a desired rod section of 47 inches.
From the earlier chapter on history, we recall that many of the most important developments took place in America and England, and because of this, international rod-building measurements are given in units of inches and feet. For the convenience of my European readers, however, one inch equals 2.54 cm, and one foot is 12 inches – exactly 30.48 cm. Because so many tapers and lengths also appear in inches and feet, I use these units here as well.

At the other end, the splines are sawed at the marks.

Following, is an example for calculating the length of a strip for a 7-foot 6-inch (90-inch), two-piece rod:
Each final section will be 45 inches long. For the Garrison offset, the initial strips should have a length of 45 + 8 3/4 + 7/8 = 54 5/8 inches when they are first split from the culm. The application of Method 1 is managed similarly.

There are, of course, other methods for offsetting the nodes, but I don't consider them very useful. Personally, I prefer the Garrison method, as it's the most reliable way to obtain an orderly distribution of nodes in the rod blank.

It's absolutely necessary (even following offsetting) to avoid locating a node close to the rod's tip or near the ferrule of a butt-section. Because of casting stresses, these areas are more vulnerable to breakage than any other area in the entire rod.

The final location of nodes needs to be taken into account when first cutting the bamboo culm to length. A basic rule is: No node should be present within 3 inches from the ends of either a butt or a tip-section – similarly true for rods of three or more pieces. When sawing the bamboo to its initial, required length, you must be sure that the upper part of each bamboo strip (the uppermost parts of each strip) is kept node-free.

For this reason, the rod builder wants to use bamboo with the longest possible distance between nodes.

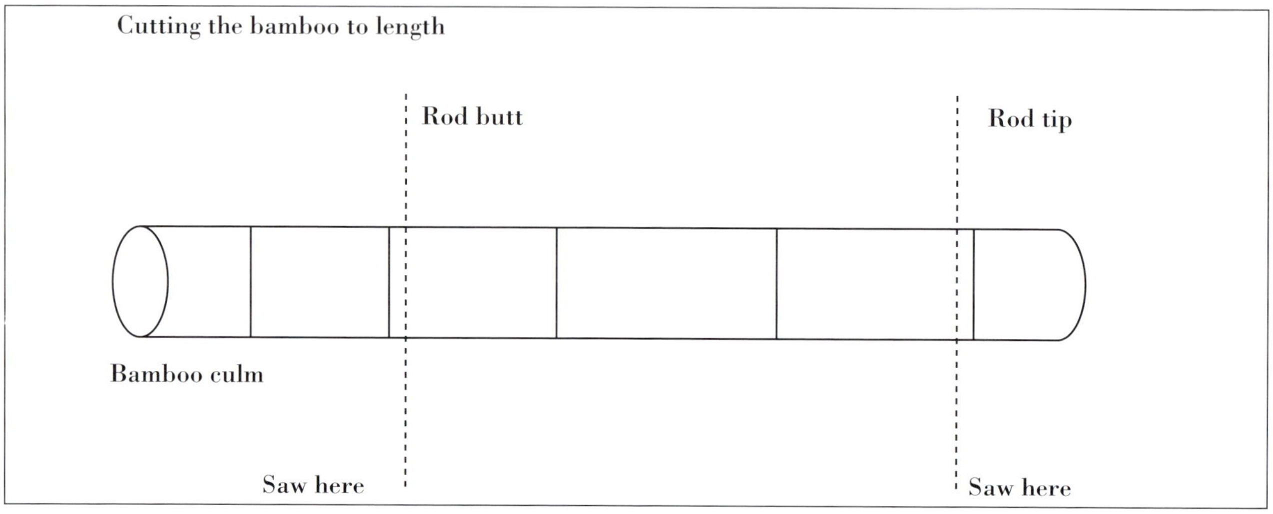

Caution! Bamboo has very sharp corners and can produce very dangerous splinters, so always wear appropriate gloves to avoid injury when working with this material. A good first-aid kit should always be in easy reach – and I speak from painful experience. I found a special kind of glove to be highly protective. These are sold in my local nurseries as "rose gloves," and their high resistance to penetration provides excellent protection against injuries.

Good gloves are absolutely necessary to protect your hands from bamboo's sharp edges and splinters.

If everything has gone well, we now have, lying before us on the workbench, six, numbered, bamboo strips (splines). Before going further, however, these need to be straightened – but even preceding this, all the nodes must be prepared. The first step is to use a medium file and carefully remove the outer "lips" on each node.

Most of the unworked strips are crooked.

Splines are most frequently crooked through the nodes.

A file is used, quickly removing the "lips" from each node.

A node after filing.

Tonkin Can Be Bent

Tonkin has the wonderful property of becoming "plastic" when subjected to heat, and can be reshaped by making a bend in just about any direction. After the cane cools, the strip retains its new shape.

Heat makes Tonkin cane pliable.

A heat gun with fine adjustments will maintain an optimum temperature, and in the next step, the nodes will be heated for the straightening process. At all cost, we want to avoid damaging the outer fibers through over-heating, so the nodes must be pressed flat quickly and while still very hot – accomplished with ease in a vise with smooth jaws.

A hot-air gun is used to heat the spline.

The hot spline is place in the vise.

Pressure is applied by carefully closing the vise.

A bamboo strip will almost always be crooked in the nodal areas, and practice is necessary to straighten these spots properly. Caution! Bamboo must not be heated to the point of charring, and be sure to wear gloves.

When straightening the nodes, you should be careful not to overstress the area, for if you do, the fibers will break with a little "crack" and the strip becomes useless.

After a node is straightened lengthwise, it must be pressed flat. Vise-jaws must be soft and smooth, preferably covered with plastic or aluminum. I outfitted my vise with aluminum jaws, cut from right-angle, extruded aluminum. These were simply glued to the existing jaws.

When flattening, the vise should be tightened very carefully, otherwise the bamboo will break, crush, or develop cracks.

The vise presses out and straightens the nodes.

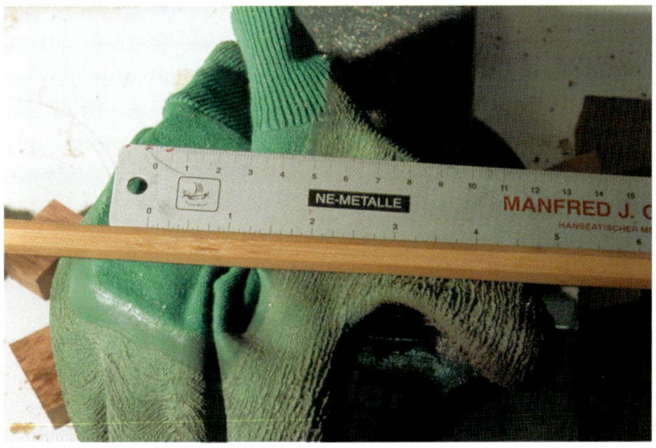

This node was filed too much. The "damage" to the spline's surface is about 1 ½ inches long.

The vise-jaws are covered by soft aluminum.

The care needed for this next step cannot be emphasized strongly enough, but care requires a lot of time. For your efforts, the finished rod will reveal nodes whose fibers enter and leave in a straight line. This is a sign of a good, handmade rod, and demonstrates skill and craftsmanship. Most commercial, rod manufacturers (whose requirements for high-production render proper node preparation unfeasible) simply hold the nodes against a belt sander and grind them flat. This process creates visible node damage, and is easily recognized by the wide breadth of fibers exposed on either side of the node – sometimes, leaving a scar on the bamboo more than an inch in length. Since we know that nodes are easily broken, as little material as possible should be removed from their surface.

After straightening and flattening a node, it should be carefully filed with a fine file until no surface elevation can be discerned. Following this, the remainder of the strip must be heated and straightened in the same fashion.

At the end of the process, it should be possible to lay each strip flat on the workbench. They should all be straight, both horizontally and vertically – a requirement for the accuracy of all further work.

This spline is straightened nicely and ready for the next step.

This is what a properly straightened node looks like in a finished rod. The fibers run straight into and out of the node.

The First Triangle

Now, we've fulfilled all the preliminaries and are ready to convert the splines into their triangular shape. We do this in two steps, first coarsely, and then ever more finely. Cutting the initial angle into the strip requires both a "roughing form" and a bench plane (see section on plane types).

You can either buy a roughing form (see Appendix: Planing Forms) or you can easily make one yourself. This latter would be a so-called "parallel form" (without taper), and can be made from two, hardwood or metal bars joined with screw-fasteners, each bar having an angle beveled along its inner edge.

If you don't want to go to that effort, you can ask any good carpenter to rout the required angles. He may well have suitable hardwood boards, and could drill holes for the adjustment screws at the same time. It's also possible to make these forms from aluminum.

Roughing form for producing the initial, triangular cross-section
(a simple form, made of wood)

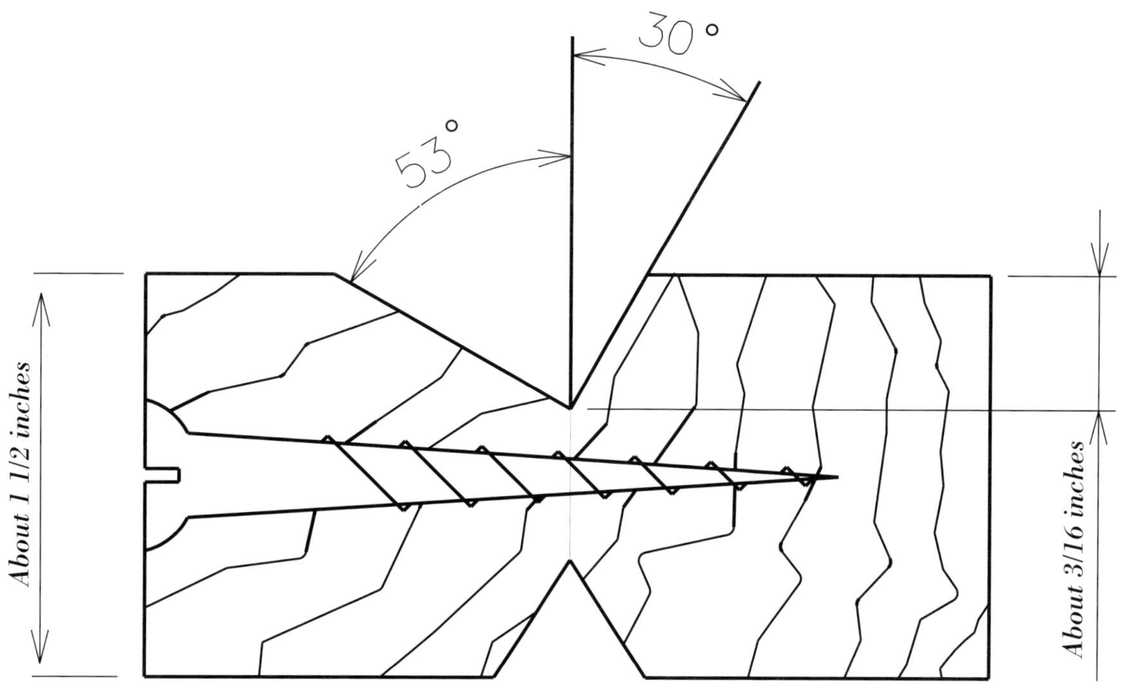

Now, the strip is placed in the roughing form, with one hand holding the strip at its rear, while planing the first side. Begin by pressing the strip into the groove, but be careful not to plane along the enamel (outer) side of the strip because, for now, this surface must remain untouched.
After the first passes with the plane, flip the strip in place, and plane the opposite side until you have attained three angles, each of sixty-degrees. The amount of material to be removed from the spline depends, of course, on the type of rod being built. A light trout rod, for instance, can be planed much thinner at this stage than a salmon rod, and a tip section can be planed thinner than a butt. A good rule-of-thumb to consider at this stage is that a spline should be planed to about twice its finished dimensions.
The plane's blade (or "iron") will dull in rather short order, particularly if the plane isn't held straight, and this will be indicated by its jerking motion during cutting. Be sure to re-sharpen the blade frequently – it saves a lot of work. Try to move the plane parallel to the form, cutting only thin shavings at first, and always wear a glove on the hand that holds the bamboo strip in the form.

Another way to produce the rough triangle is grinding or sanding. This requires a rather powerful motor with a 60°, slotted disk attached to it. Sandpaper is then simply glued into the slot. Lastly, some method for dust extraction will be essential.

First, the spline is planed to a triangle in the roughing form.

A washing machine motor with a sanding wheel attached to the shaft.

The motor should turn at a minimum of 2000 rpm: Then, simply pull the bamboo strip through the sandpaper slot to produce the 60° angle. This method saves a great deal of time, but it's most useful when building several rods at once. Noise, safety considerations, and a firmly mounted motor are factors, but so is the inevitable mess.

The sanding wheel has a 60° slot cut into its edge, with sandpaper glued into the slot.

Sixty-degree, milling cutters are available, but I recommend against using them for two reasons: First, they can be very dangerous to use, and secondly; they become dull very soon, and re-sharpening is expensive.

A 60° milling-head for metal. Used improperly, this tool is dangerous.

Binding the Splines

The six splines, which now have their rough angles cut, need to be bound together in preparation for hardening (or "oven-tempering"). Various methods and possibilities are available in preparation for this step.

The simplest way is to lay a strip of tape on a work surface (sticky-side-up), and then press each spline onto it, retaining the sequence from one-to-six. The splines can be rolled together easily at this point, and tied at one end with sturdy, cotton thread. The thread is then wound very tightly from one end to the other, then back again, and fixed with a double knot. This process creates a criss-crossed binding, and holds the raw blank together. For the occasional rod-builder, this is fully adequate, even if it's a little awkward for long sections.

Much more elegant, is the simple binding-machine described in Garrison's book. It's robust and easy to operate. Such a binder does take some time to build, but it can also be purchased as a finished product in the USA.

When operating binding machines, there's the danger that splines can twist under the pressure of the thread, so one must always check that the tension is adjusted correctly. If twisting appears after binding, and cannot be removed by hand-torquing the blank in an opposite direction, the thread must be removed and the entire process repeated.

A large pulley with attached hand-crank is mounted on one side of a piece of angle iron. The drive belt (shown as heavy white cord) is placed around the large pulley, then the four smaller ones.

Tension is applied to the drive belt by hanging a weight from its lowest course (shown on this somewhat different machine).

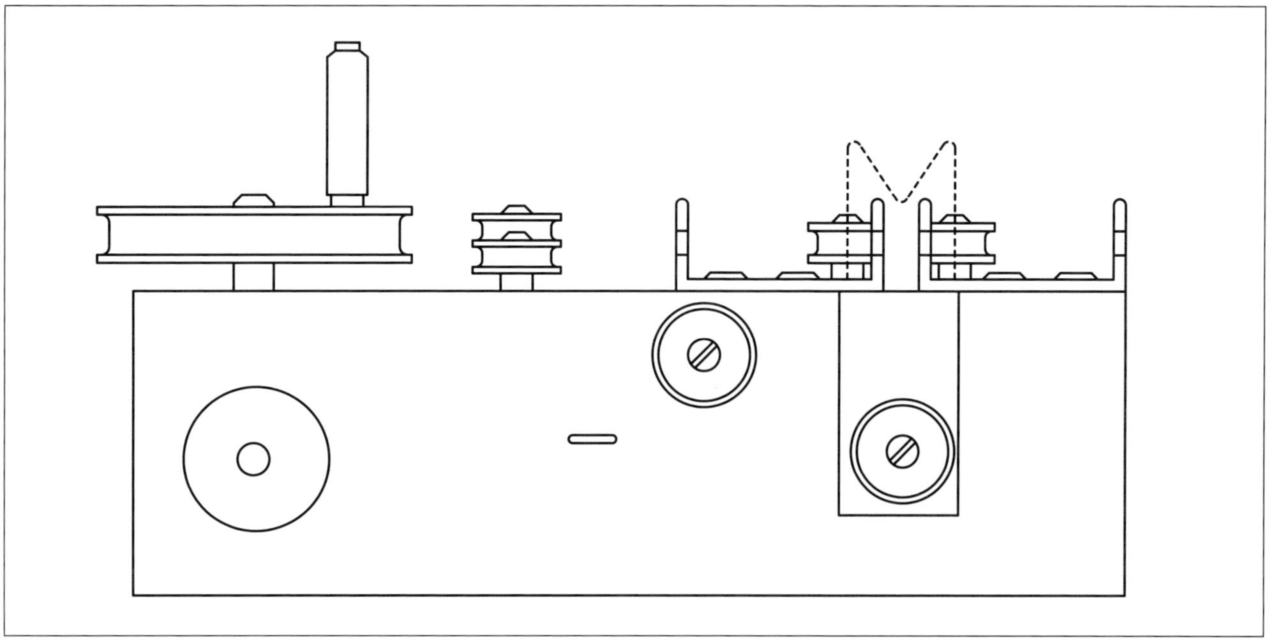

Garrison binding machine (top view)

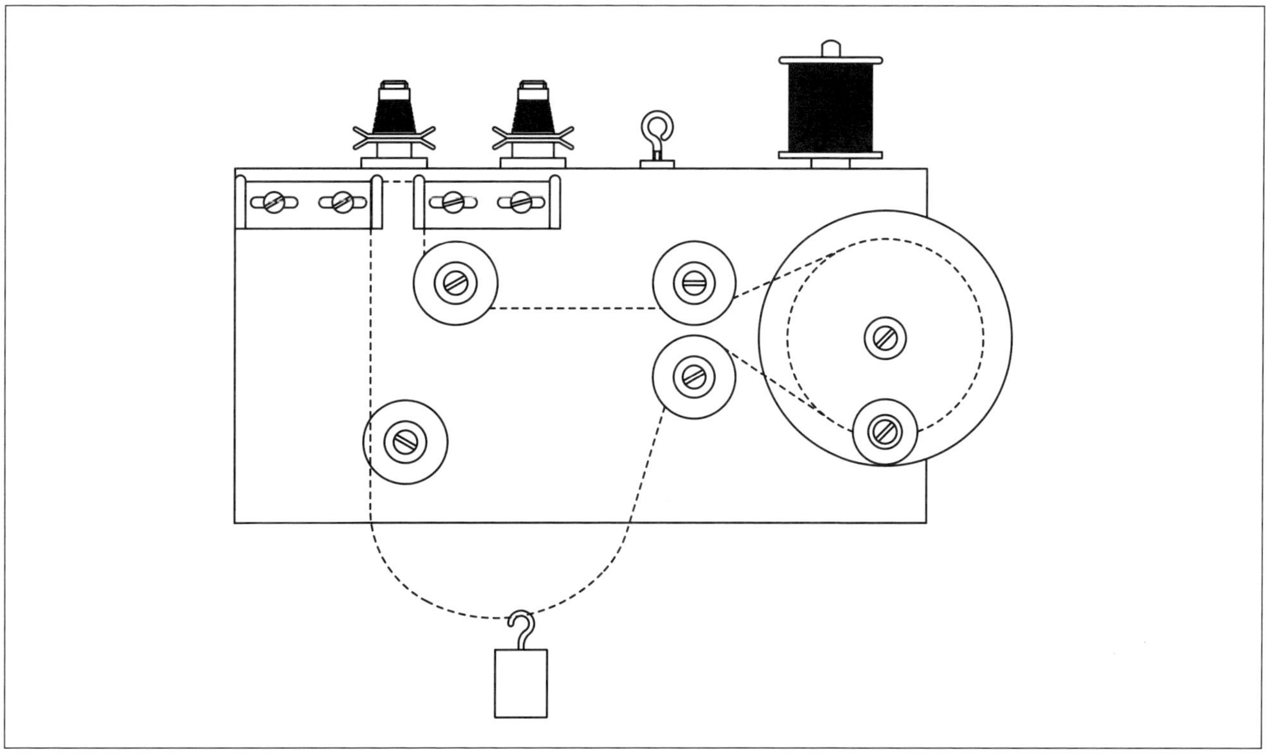

Garrison binding machine (side view)

The drive belt wraps twice around the six splines, holding them together in their proper sequence. Binding thread is fed from above, brought under and through the drive belt and locked in place. It's then tied securely at the end of the splines.

The binding thread passes through a tensioner before reaching the splines. When the crank is turned, the drive belt moves the section forward at a uniform rate and guides the binding thread progressively around the splines.

Upon reaching the end of the section, the binding thread is tied off. Then the section is removed and placed in the binding machine for a second pass. Binding thread is attached once again, but the crank will be turned in the opposite direction to counter-wrap this second thread.

Now the six splines are bound together with crossed threads and ready for hardening.

A New Idea

At this point, I want to suggest a very simple alternative. I received the basic idea years ago from Piet Veugelers, a Dutch rod builder who, unfortunately, died most prematurely. His binding process employs a plastic pipe with a continuous, longitudinal, open slot. Curtain rods are fitted over each edge of the slot to prevent the thread from catching on the plastic pipe.

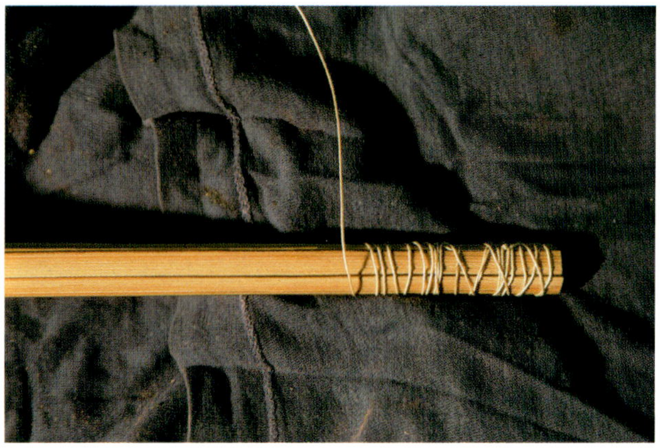

Splines are tied together with the binding thread and placed in a motorized chuck, set to turn slowly. Then, slide the tube over the splines with its opening facing upwards.

First, the six splines are tied together at their ends. Then, one end is chucked to a drive motor, set to turn very slowly. It's important for the binding thread to feed from the top of its spool.
Slide the pipe over the splines with the slot facing upwards and with the thread coming up through the slot. It's also useful to support the pipe at the end opposite the drive motor.

A bearing supports the opposite, un-chucked end of the splines.

Now, we turn the motor on to rotate the rod section, guiding the binding thread by hand and moving it back-and-forth along the slot. The hand also serves as the "tensioning device," and with a little practice, this becomes a fine method to bind the splines. The splines can be prevented from twisting by using heavier tension in the forward direction, and somewhat lower tension in the return direction.

The machine is turned on and the thread is tensioned and distributed back-and-forth along the section by hand.

Careful! Hold the pipe securely while binding.

No matter what binding method is used, the thread must be wrapped very tightly around the blank, and no spline should become twisted, relative to another. This can be checked by placing the blank on a flat work surface. Make certain that both ends of the uppermost spline lie flush and parallel to the underlying surface.

The pipe is removed and the splines are tightly bound.

The wound thread holds the raw splines together very tightly.

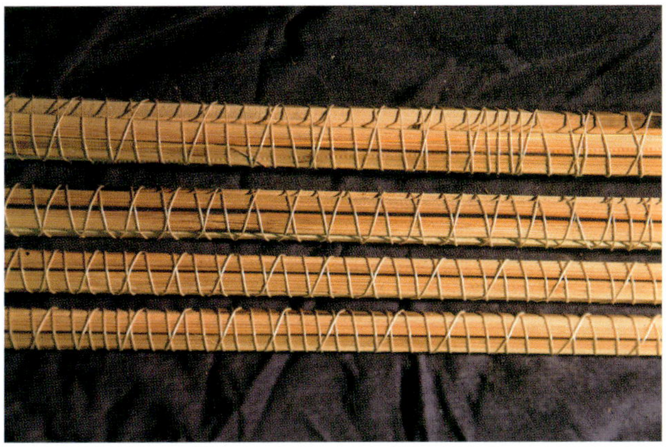

A rod in preparation: The butt, mid- and two tip-sections are now ready for hardening.

This method also works well to bind the tapered and finished splines after gluing.

The Right Time

Brrrr…! It was so cold that our fingers were stiff and almost numb, and the rising, northwest wind gave a preview of the days to come. Despite our best efforts and all the ground we covered, we had no strikes. It was the end of February, but the day had begun with such promise.... In the morning, the temperature was about 4° F and the water glass-clear. Then, in the afternoon, a little sun even broke through. Casting was great and our thoughts were filled with visions of those big fish that had to be near at this time of year. And they were! In the early morning we could see rising trout just out of reach, but would they move closer to shore? Cast followed cast, but no takers. This was simply one of the typical days of coastal fishing, and now it was turning very cold. Slowly, we began to realize that a warm stove and some hot tea would be the best way to end the day. My Danish friend, Ole, stripped-in his fly, and thinking of our cozy cabin, gave the command, "That's all!"

The thought of a little warmth was not a bad one, but I made one more cast so I could wind my line back onto its reel smoothly. I turned around and headed toward the beach, dragging line and fly behind me, then…snagged! Swearing, I went back toward the fly… and the snag moved. After some strong tugs, three wads of seaweed and a small cod came to the surface. Oh well, off the hook. After offering sage advice to grow much bigger, I released the fish. Now, my line was back on the reel, but far from orderly, so I made another cast and slowly wound the line in cleanly and…strike! What now? Three or four yards of line were pulled off the reel and then everything went quiet and still. After pumping the rod and a lot of resistance, a three-pound cod came up and I thought, "This can't be an accident."

Another cast, this one less than 30 feet, and the next fish was hooked – taking several yards of line from the reel before it sat solidly on the bottom. This time all I brought to the surface was a bunch of seaweed. Next cast; bang! This fish was well-hooked, so I gave it no chance. I brought it up quickly and decided it would contribute nicely to our dinner. Next cast – hookup – and again a nice fight. In the meantime, it had become completely dark, but, truly, every cast produced a fish. Of course, by now, Ole was also back in the water, and his rod, too, was constantly bent. Then, after 30 minutes everything was over, the cold seemed to have dissipated, and we called it a day. As we walked in silence along the beach toward our cabin (each with a nice cod hanging from a finger) I thought, "Fishing for 'sea-run browns' can really be great."

The Hardening

As already mentioned, even well-aged bamboo contains excess moisture, and if this isn't driven out with heat, one ends up with a very soft rod. Worse, upon casting, it will begin to take a permanent set.

There are two basic ways of heating and hardening the bamboo.

1. As a complete culm or a section of culm,
2. As individually prepared and bound splines.

Normally, one chooses the second method, although Tom Dorsey (of Thomas & Thomas) once told me that strips can be split more easily from a culm that's been hardened as a whole.

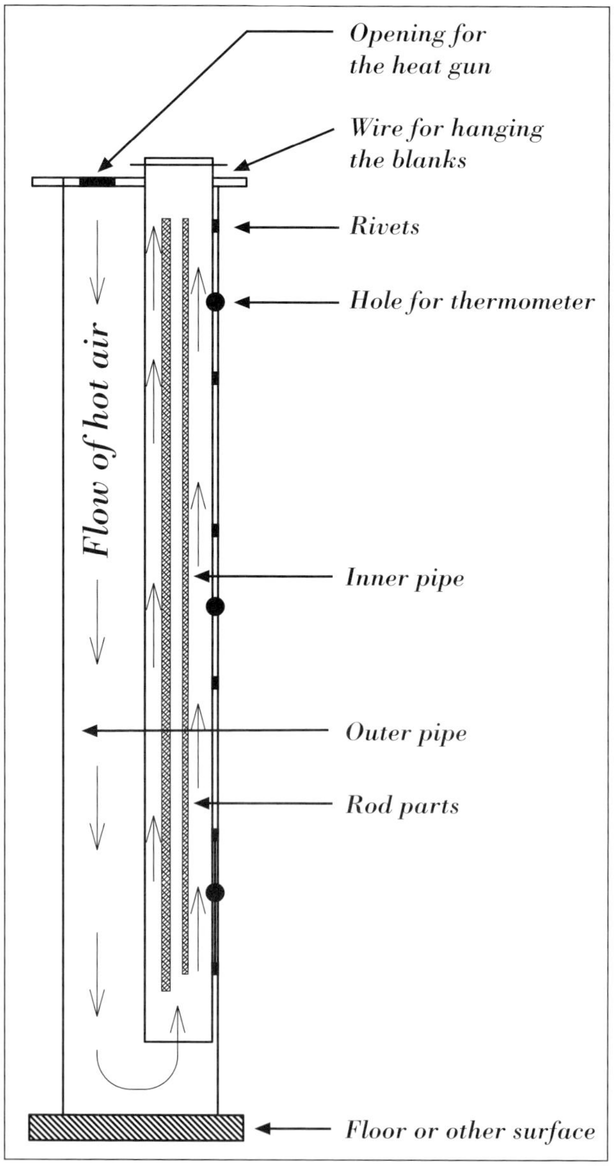

Some rod-builders harden their bamboo out-of-doors, using a large, open flame or a propane burner. This method surely yields satisfactory results, but requires a great deal of experience.

Once, when I asked a rod-building friend why he built only nodeless rods, I heard a long list of explanations, but found only his last one important, "...I can temper the short pieces easily in my microwave oven."

There are many types of ovens, and you can build one quite easily yourself. The necessary materials can be found in most building-materials or hardware stores.

A particularly effective type of oven was described several years ago in the specialty, rod-building newsletter, "The Planing Form." I built this oven for myself and am very satisfied with it.

Oven for hardening bamboo.

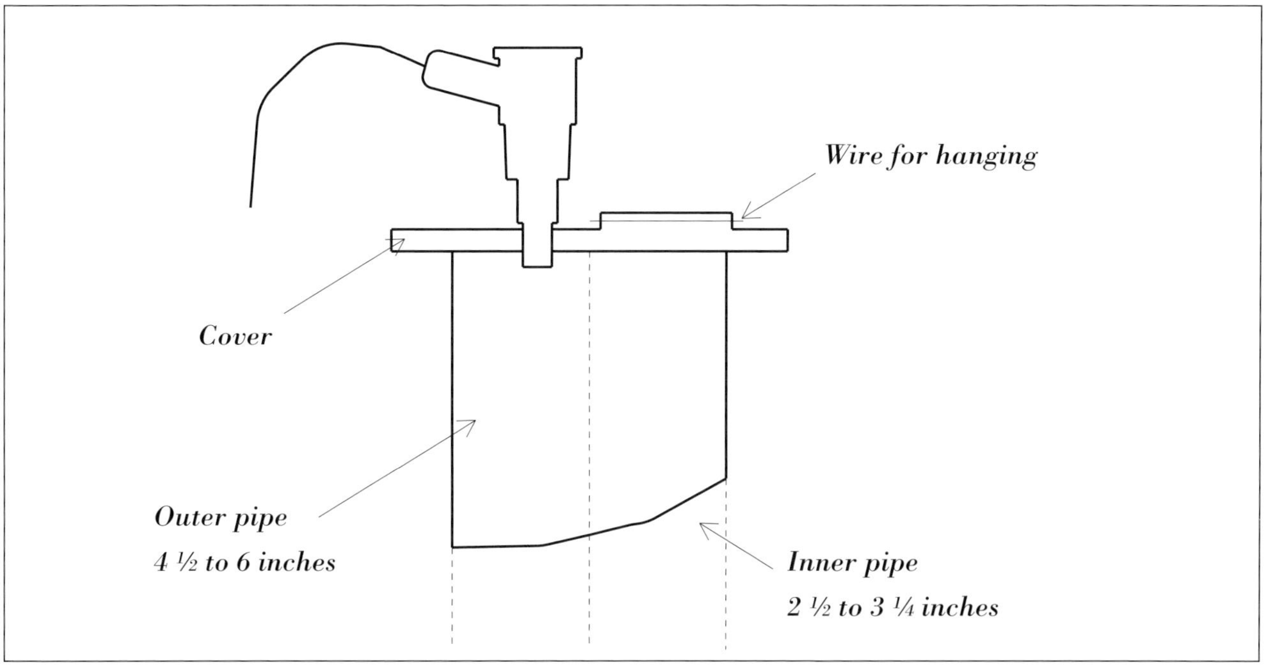

The principle of this oven relies on a large pipe, with a smaller pipe fastened inside. Then, a hot-air gun directs heat down through the larger pipe, exiting up and out through the smaller pipe (see drawing).

Metal ducts of different diameters are suitable, and the small pipe can be fastened in place with simple pop-rivets. Standard flue or duct-caps will close off the device at its bottom and top. The upper cap, however, needs to have holes cut to accept both the nozzle of the hot-air gun and the smaller pipe. The oven is completed by drilling two (or, better, three) small holes for thermometers – at the bottom, middle and top. In order to heat-treat strips for the longest desired rod, the pipes should not be shorter than about 63 inches. In operation, the untreated blanks will be hung from the top of the smaller pipe, and for this, a wire needs to be fastened at the upper edge of the smaller pipe (see drawing). The base-cap must be sturdy, but removable, so if a rod section should accidentally fall to the bottom, it can be retrieved readily (after the oven cools!). When the oven is first turned on, a higher temperature will be established at the bottom of the smaller pipe, but in a only few moments this temperature distributes uniformly through the entire unit.

The advantages of this oven are very clear for me:

1. The rod parts hang freely and without contacting support-areas that could become too hot,
2. The rod parts are fully surrounded by hot air,
3. The temperature can be controlled perfectly,
4. The working temperature is quickly achieved,
5. Moisture content can be determined by holding a small mirror over the air-exit, as any remaining moisture will fog the mirror.

Caution! Never touch the pipe while hot air is circulating. Wait at least thirty minutes for it to cool.

High Temperatures

I really don't want to add to the endless discussion about the "correct" temperature and time needed for hardening, but a good average with my oven is about 30 to 40 minutes, at a temperature of about 170° C (or about 340° F). Both the action and the color of a rod will be influenced by the time and temperature. With higher temperatures (caution! the bamboo can begin to burn at temperatures above 185° C, or 365° F), the rod will be faster, but also more brittle and more likely to break. With temperatures too low, the rod will be softer and may contain remnant moisture. With varying temperatures, the color of the cane can vary from honey-colored to a deep brown.

A darkly "baked" rod.

Suitable thermometers can be found in stores carrying laboratory or electronic equipment.
As soon as the heat-treatment is finished, moisture from ambient humidity will begin to reenter the bamboo. It doesn't matter if the blank is in the workshop or on a radiator, it will draw in moisture! For this reason, the final planing and gluing should be done relatively quickly, no later than the day after hardening. Upon gluing, however, the blank is protected, and can be stored for awhile before subsequent work.
Relative humidity is naturally dependent on season and geographic location. I once met an American rod builder who told me enthusiastically that he had recently moved to Texas. In response to my question, "why," he answered, "Because the relative humidity in Texas is perfect. I can build much better rods there!" I think sometimes we take things a little too far.
After the raw blanks have been laid or hung in the oven, heated and hardened, the next step in our work is to begin final planing.

After heat-treating, you'll notice that the binding thread, which was once wrapped tightly, is now loose, and the simple explanation is that the bamboo has shrunk because of the lost moisture.

The Planing Form

You must decide whether to invest $800 to $900 to buy a planing form, or spend about $250 for materials and make the form yourself – not to mention about 40 to 50 hours of work.

Particularly for beginners, I recommend considering buying a completed form. The quality is superb, and you can begin planing the moment it arrives. I know from my own experience how impatient I was to build my first rod.

Those who choose the second path should have experience in metalworking and a number of tools at hand. If tools need to be purchased, it wouldn't pay to make your own form, and it's better to buy one. I don't subscribe to the well-meant suggestion, found in some books, that one can make a form from hardwood or aluminum – unless you really only want to build three or four rods in your lifetime.

Such forms cannot stand up to heavy or repeated use, and I find that the time invested in making one is too great. As to the expensive and long-lasting forms, after building your own first rod, you'll have plenty of friends asking if you couldn't just make one for them, too!

A planing form using single screws to make adjustments. Each screw has two, different threads.

This planing form uses two screws: One pushes and the other pulls.

The process for building a form is summarized here, but is only an overview of the most important steps. Those who wish to follow this path can download precise plans and instructions from the Internet (a few appropriate sites are listed in the Appendix).

Top view of a planing form
The adjustment screw has two different threads.
Pushing and pulling occur simultaneously.

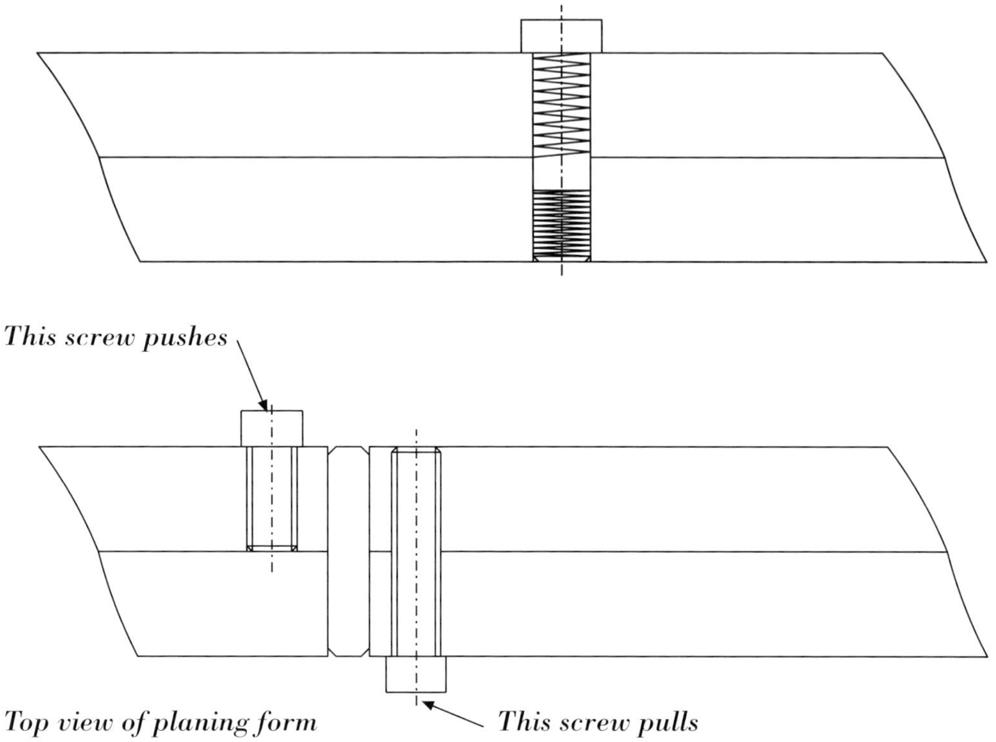

First, you need a length of cold-rolled steel, measuring 1 x 2 x 61 inches. Other types of steel are available, but these are likely to have internal stresses and will surely warp .

The steel should be cut longitudinally into two, equal 1 x 1 x 61 inch halves, and must be done by the steel supplier. You can also start with two pieces of steel this size.

In the next step, the two inner surfaces must be ground absolutely flat. Then, the two halves will be clamped together, precisely flush and parallel, and all outer surfaces will be worked to identical dimensions with files and sandpaper. To maintain these dimensions during the process, repeated measurements must be taken. Then, three (or, better, four) holes are drilled crossways through the two pieces, and retaining rods are placed through the holes to keep the two pieces flush and parallel. The holes should have a diameter of about 3/16 of an inch.
In the next step, it's necessary to decide what type of adjustment screws will be used.

There are two basic types – the first being a single screw that simultaneously opens and closes the form. This is achieved by incorporating both left and right-hand threads on the screw's shaft – one each, formed at opposite ends.

The second type requires two screws to be mounted at each station setting. One screw pulls the bars of the form together, while the second pushes them apart.

Adjustment of the form to prepare for cutting the 60° angle

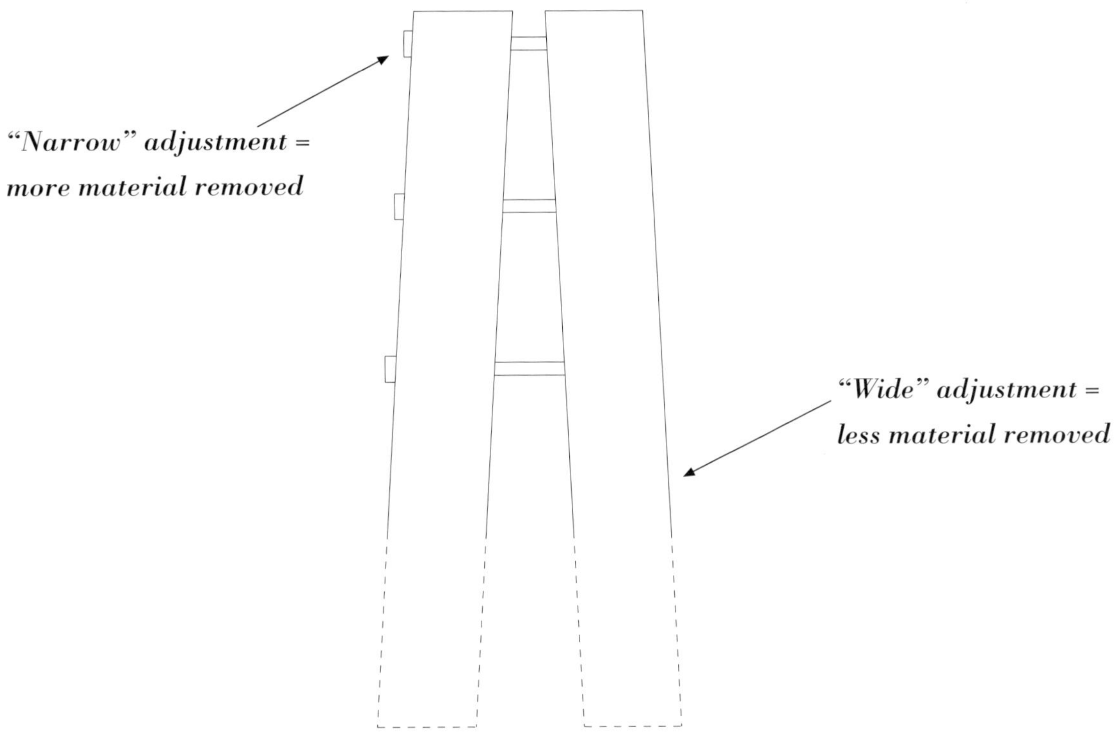

If you decide on the first type, horizontal holes are drilled through both bars, 5 inches apart, and will be tapped for their threads in the next step. For the second type, two such holes must be drilled, each set located at a 5-inch interval. The 5-inch spacing is advisable because almost all internationally-known tapers are given in these increments.
After threads are tapped in all the holes, the screws are inserted and the work of cutting in the inner, 60° angle begins.

Two tools are necessary for this. One is a dial-indicator depth-gauge, fitted with a 60° point (which will also be used later to set the form to your desired taper). The second tool is homemade, and consists of a wooden block with a 60° triangular file glued to it.

At this point, the adjusting screws are used to open the form – one end will be separated only slightly, and the other end opened rather wider. If the form has an overall length of 60 inches, the depth of the "V-groove" on the butt-section side should taper conically from 0.177 inches to 0.047 inches. For the tip-section side, the V-groove should taper from 0.087 inches to 0.012 inches.

A piece of a triangular file is glued into a block of wood. This simple tool produces a planing form.

The file device is used to cut the 60° angle from one end to the other, but this process will take considerable time and the angle must be checked constantly with the depth gauge. The correct depth will have been reached when the wooden block touches down along the top of the form. In this, it's absolutely essential to keep the file-block exactly parallel to the form.

The tool files a 60° angle in the form.

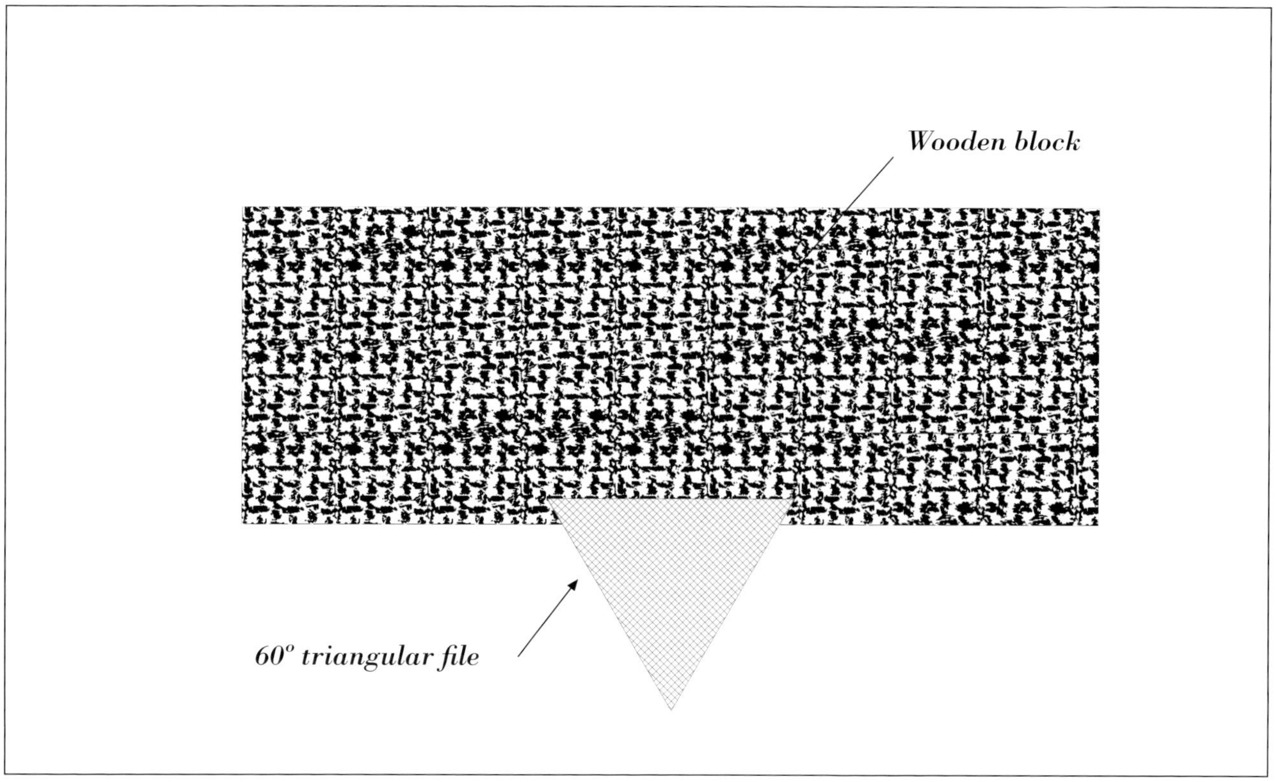

Tool for cutting the angle into the steel form

Measuring errors will occur because the tip of the depth-gauge does not meet with a solid surface at the bottom of the groove.

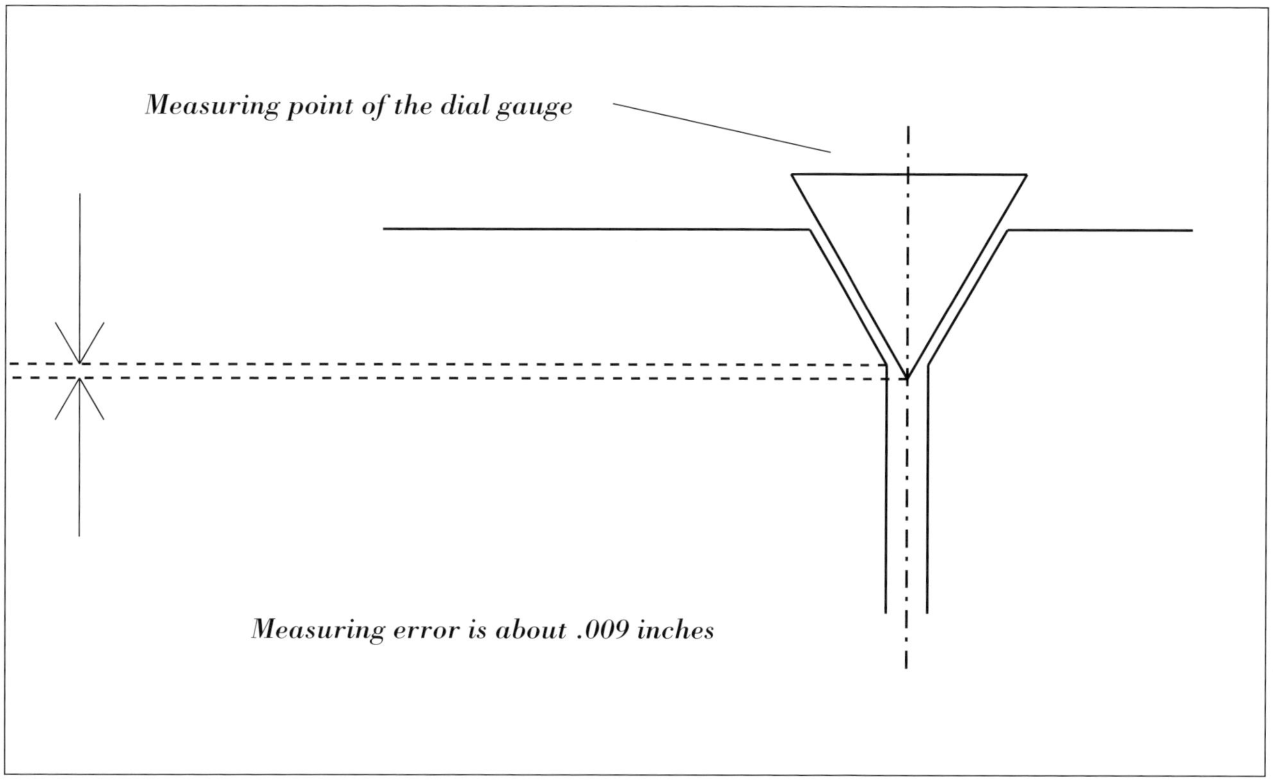

One side of the form will be adjusted to accommodate strips for the butt sections, while the opposite side will be used to prepare narrower strips for mid- and tip sections. This means that, once we've filed the V-groove on one side, the form will be turned over and a second, different groove will be filed into the other side. To finish the filed surfaces of these grooves, they must be smoothed with sandpaper and a honed with a stone.

The work must be done with care to avoid irregularities, so it's important to use the depth-gauge and to check your work constantly!

When planing splines, one always moves the plane from the thicker to the thinner end. For this reason, you must file the form's V-grooves with the adjustment screws on the side that's convenient for you to reach. This usually means that the wide ends of the two grooves will be on opposite ends of the form. It can be a little tiresome if the adjustment screws are located on the front face of the form for butt-section splines, but on the back face for the tip-section splines.

Preparation for Final Work on The Splines

The depth gauge is used for adjusting the planing form to the precise taper one wants. All adjustments should be checked at least twice because it's very common that adjusting one screw will change the adjustment of others! In addition, you should consider that the depth-gauge will have its own measuring "error" of about 0.009 inches. This occurs because when the 60° point in placed within the groove, its tip doesn't actually reach a solid surface for its "reading." Instead, the point only registers its depth by contacting the beveled sides of the groove. Therefore, the taper, as it is charted, should be reduced about 0.009 inches.

In order to correct for this error, after the form is adjusted to a desired taper and the corresponding measurements are recorded, a test spline is planed flush to the surface of the form until no more material can be removed. Next, using a micrometer or vernier caliper, you measure the spline at each of the taper's control-points. The resulting variation from your initial settings will represent the measuring error. The tip of the gauge's measuring point must be undamaged, otherwise all measurements become unreliable. Always have an extra point on hand, and when appropriate, make comparative measurements. Now, the binding thread is unwrapped from the prepared splines. Carefully inspect each spline to see if they are straight, twisted, or if the nodes have raised up again. The latter often happens upon hardening, and such nodes must be treated once again to obtain an absolutely flat outer surface.

A dial gauge with a 60° point is used to measure the form's settings at each of the adjusting screw(s).

The screws set the form along its length, as needed, and each adjustment is read off the dial gauge.

When all splines have been inspected, it's time to remove the outermost layer ("enamel") from the bamboo. This can be done by placing the spline enamel-side-up in the form and simply using a cabinet scraper or a scraper plane .

A Lie Nielsen scraper. A simple blade scraper is just as efficient in removing the outer layer of "enamel."

Great care should be taken when drawing the scraper over the enamel surface – we want to avoid removing too much material.

This procedure may not be pleasant for those of a "delicate" nature, because it makes a scraping sound that can send chills up and down your spine. When the fine, white lines of the underlying fibers begin to show, you know you have removed enough material. Before beginning the planing phase, lay each spline in the form to see if the strips are truly straight – first with their outer-side facing right, and then left. If this check shows any irregularities, the spline must be re-straightened or trimmed, for failing to do so may cause the finished rod to show significant glue-lines.

Should a node not be perfectly straight or flat, one's planing may remove too much material at this location, and the result will show up later as a wide, glue line.

All six splines are now prepared, and we're ready for our final steps.

When nodes are poorly prepared, glue-lines often show up in the finished rod.

All a Matter of Adjustment

The Final Taper

We begin the last phase with a finely-adjusted plane, working the two, inner sides of each bamboo strip down to the final taper by continuously flipping our spline from one side to the other. One hand is used to secure the spline in the form. (Wear a glove on that hand. If the plane's blade should dig or catch in the cane, the entire spline will jump forward in the groove, producing deep cuts in your holding hand. The wise maker will always ensure that bandage material is readily available in the workshop.)

The more finely we set the plane's cut, the better! After three or four passes on one side, the spline is flipped and the other side planed. Plane shavings should always be thin, even upon beginning. There's no point in trying to cut thicker shavings, as this only risks compromising the 60° angle. Constantly check the angle being planed at several positions along the bamboo strip.

If you have removed too much material from one side, immediately turn the spline and plane the other side until the angle of the apex is again correct.

Final dimensions are approached carefully in the planing stage.

The accuracy of the 60° angle should be checked regularly during planing.

It's essential that we maintain the 60° angle, so the plane must be held absolutely parallel to the form. Tilt the plane to one side or the other, and the angle of the cut will have changed immediately.

A little trick, particularly helpful for beginners, is to place a mirror at the end of the planing form toward which you're working. Looking at the reflection, you can observe the level of your plane, and if necessary, correct its position.

It's a good idea to keep a few remnant pieces of cane handy (set aside during the earlier splitting stage), for you may need some "spare parts" if something goes wrong later on. This is important because replacement splines should always come from the same culm and have the same nodal spacing.

In the book on Everett Garrison, we read that he carried the matter even further.

As an absolute perfectionist, Garrison would split the required strips from a culm and then store the remainder, marked with the customer's name. In this manner, if a repair or new tip section were needed, he could use the same material and the repaired rod would retain exactly the same action.

Today's rod-builders hold a variety of opinions on this issue. Some makers I know, purposely mix splines from different culms to be sure of having a "balanced" action, arguing that bamboo culms are not the same all around their circumference. Various factors, such as wind, rain, and sun, may affect one side of a culm differently from the others, and these natural conditions often influence how the culm will grow. In truth, sometimes wall-thickness varies a good deal within a single culm. Despite these observations, I make all splines for a rod from the same culm.

The closer the strip comes to the form while planing, the thinner we adjust the cut. A bench plane can be used upon beginning to taper because this tool's greater weight is easier to guide. Later, however, it's time to change to the smaller block plane, set to take shavings thinner than paper – so thin you can see through them.

When our planing begins to approach the metal form, the last strokes should be made very carefully and with less downward pressure. If sufficiently sharp, a plane's blade can even shave metal from the form, and when your plane digs into steel, you'll discover why it makes little sense to fabricate the form from any other material.

When no more bamboo can be removed from the strip's planed surface, your goal has been reached. The spline is finished and the next step can be taken.

As soon as the plane begins to tear the bamboo, leave irregular edges or remove chips, the plane blade must be sharpened immediately. Absolute sharpness is required, but particularly near the end of the process when the spine is becomes almost flush with the form. Nothing is more frustrating than having your blade tear the bamboo just when you're nearly finished, and all your work goes for nothing. If that does occur, however, the damaged spline should be replaced immediately. There's no point in ignoring the mistake because you'll surely see it in the finished rod and regret that you did not take that extra bit of effort when there was time.

Sharp Iron

When I first began to build, I bought several planes to make the work more efficient. Sharpening always goes better when dealing with several blades at once, and knowing that you always have a few sharp irons ready, you rarely need to interrupt the planing. Depending on the quality of the blades, it's sometimes possible to complete a rod from beginning to end without significant interruptions. This accelerates the work process and is more satisfying.

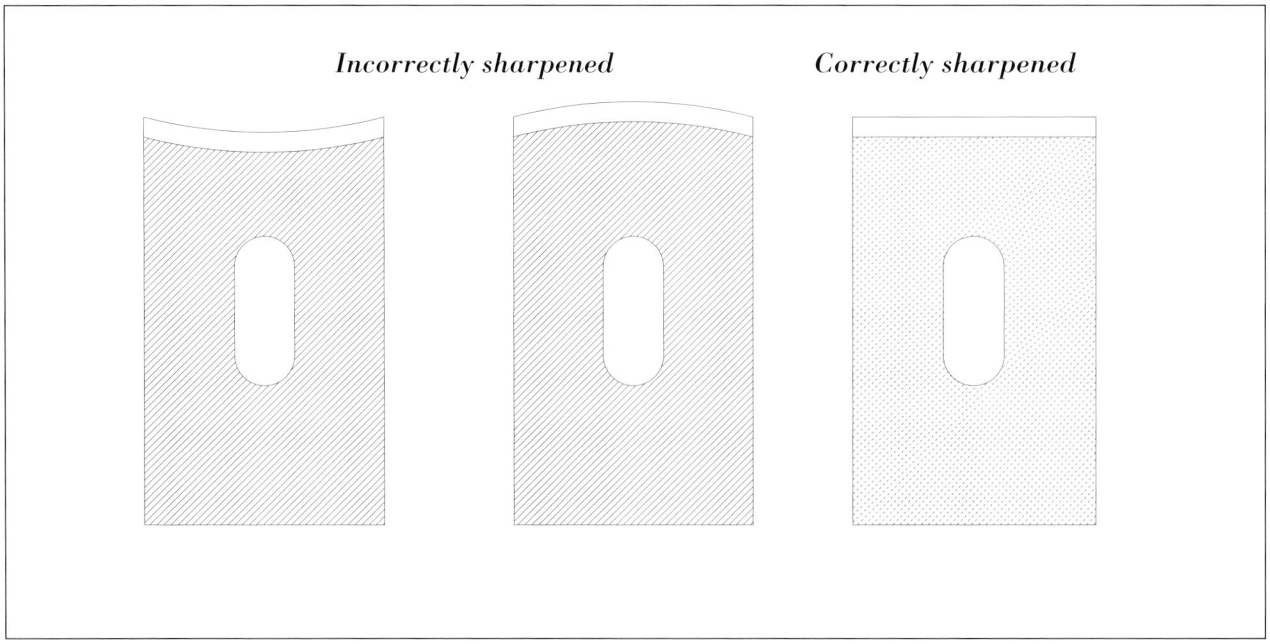

When a spline is finished, it should be marked and measured at each of its control points – all finished splines being measured at precisely these same locations. In addition, it's advisable to check all splines for perfect triangularity by running a center gauge along the full length of their cross-sections. If you have worked accurately, the variations in measurements should range no more than 0.0008 inches to 0.0016 inches.

Still a little to go.

Most beginning makers will shy away from working on the tip-section of a rod. Just the thought of planing a spline down to a thickness of perhaps 0.0275 inches is shocking. Nevertheless, I find the tip-section of a rod much easier to plane than the butt. For one thing, tip-section splines usually require more material to be removed and frequent flipping, so the danger of losing the apex angle is reduced. Secondly, however, because the surface being worked on is relatively smaller, very little effort is necessary to move the plane. Tip sections require much less energy to accomplish the work, so I always begin with the butt in order to have enough "reserve power" for the easier tips.

Final dimensions are reached when the plane can no longer remove material.

Dust and Dirt Are Never Helpful

After all splines for the rod have been finished, lay them on your work surface, inner-apex-up. Then, using fine sandpaper, "break" this inner corner, using long strokes and moving from the thicker ends to the thinner.

This sanding will improve glue distribution through the center-most areas of the blank.

Now, in preparation for the next step, all dust must be removed meticulously.

Six fully-planed splines are laid on their "backs" on a work surface. The uppermost edges (the corners pointing to the inside of the finished blank) are then "broken" with sandpaper.

After sanding, the slightly flattened corners help to distribute glue more uniformly inside the blank.

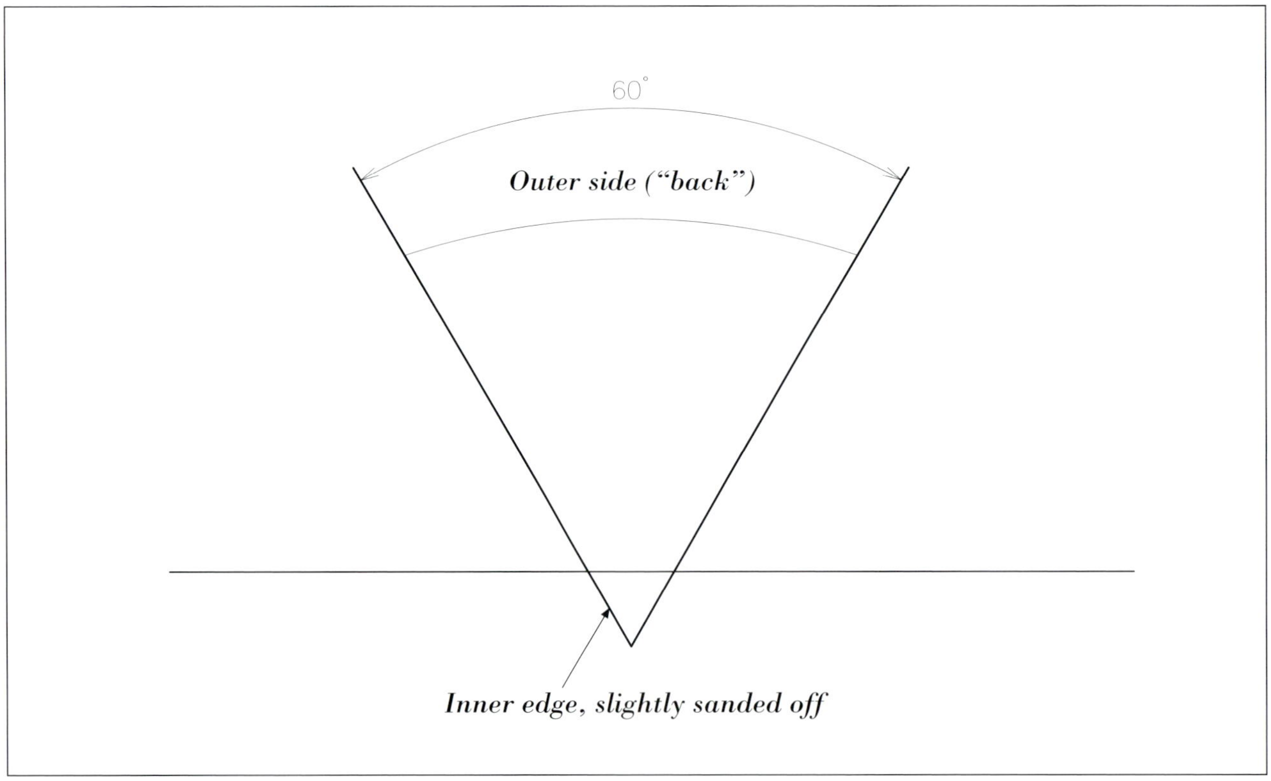

Gluing

One piece of equipment is essential to rod-building, but I have left it out – a good vacuum cleaner! Before gluing, the work bench and all surrounding areas must be absolutely clean. Nothing is worse at the last moment, than to find grains of dust (or, horrors, pieces of shavings) in the glue. It might be possible to overcome very tiny particles when gluing a butt-section, but these will inevitably lead to catastrophe in a tip-section!

Accurate gluing requires an absolutely flat working surface. A thick sheet of glass is well-suited (also, because it can be cleaned easily). To keep the glue off the work surface, I recommend covering an appropriate area with plastic, tape or something similar. After gluing, this tape can be removed and thrown away without much mess.

I just can't endure all those stupid remarks any longer! Each time, I swear to myself that I won't put up with them again. But what else can you expect when you're standing at the supermarket checkout with fifty, "special offer" toothbrushes in your basket? "You trying to set a world record for tooth-brushing?" – just one of the more friendly remarks I get.

Glues

Over the years, I've experimented with various kinds of glue, and can recommend two types. One is "Resorcinol," commonly used for applying veneer in furniture-making, and consisting of a liquid resin and a powdered hardener. Its set-up time allows plenty of opportunity to correct mistakes, and the product is available in many hardware and woodworking stores.

The disadvantage of resorcinol glue, however, is the deep-red (to dark-brown) color of the resin. The finished rod will reveal dark stripes in its glue-lines, and cause even the tiniest mistakes show up badly. An additional concern is that resorcinol has a very short shelf life and must be stored in a cool place.

Epoxy glues (in Europe, "Uhu Endfest 300," for example) are a good alternative. They're easy to buy, even in small quantities, have a longer working-time, and achieve bonding strengths that rod-builders could only dream of 40 years ago. The bond of an epoxy glue can be further enhanced if the blank is heat-cured after the glue has set. Epoxies will harden glass-clear, and are highly resistant to moisture of any kind.

No matter what glue you use, good ventilation in the workroom is necessary.

Glue is best applied with a "hard-bristle" toothbrush. First, lay a strip of masking tape on the work surface, sticky-side-up. Each spline is then pressed onto the tape with its enamel side down, and in the proper order – that is, from 1 to 6. The tape should be long enough for its two ends to be picked up easily after spreading the glue.

A toothbrush is used to spread glue on the splines.

Once the spines are spaced together closely, and lying flat on the tape, glue is spread from the thicker end to the thinner. Not too much glue should be applied, but it's especially important to check that plenty has been spread along the splines' outer edges.

To protect your hands (most glues are quite aggressive), be sure to wear thin, single-use gloves. These should allow adequate sensitivity in your fingers.

Now, pick up the ends of the tape and roll the splines together. These can be held with one hand while the tape is removed with the other. Then, replace the tape with a few turns of binding thread, and rotate the splines in your hands one more time to check that their sequence is correct. This is your last chance to do so!

Various types of thread for binding and gluing.

An Attempt

It had rained for weeks – pouring, unendingly, by the buckets-full. Fishing was next-to-impossible. Farmers were unhappy this June because they couldn't mow their fields – those beautiful, flowering fields along a small stream in the Franconian hills. Then, suddenly one morning, without transition, the weather turned nice. The mist disappeared and the blue sky looked as if it had never contained a cloud.

It was the weekend, and the valley stretched peaceful and empty, in front of me. The change in the weather had come so fast that everyone remained home, apparently in disbelief that the day would remain sunny. Some, inner voice had whispered: "Drive there, and you will fish!" So, I had the entire stretch to myself.

This morning, the insect world, freed from the long days of rain, had already become active. It was as if every bug needed to prove it had survived the rain. Everywhere, something buzzed, hummed, flew or crawled. Iridescent beetles sat on the flower stems; mayflies emerged almost in swarms; great dragonflies hovered motionless in the air…only the fish seemed to notice nothing.

High, off-color water flowed through a bend in the stream, down a small chute, and disappeared from view around the next bend. Not one rise to suggest that trout and grayling had taken notice of the awakening life….

I stood for a number of minutes in the shade of an old willow tree, whose overhanging branches gave good cover. The pool was still, and nothing moved on the water's surface. But, because I had no desire to fish beneath with a nymph, I simply waited and enjoyed the quiet beauty around me.

My attention drifted off to the beautifully-flowered field, but was suddenly drawn back to the water by a subtle splash. Again, the tiny splash, but without any sign of a rise on the water's surface.

I stared at the water in front of me, for the sound didn't seem to come from far. Sure enough, not 6 yards away, along the opposite bank, I could now see the source. Appearing between some overhanging alder branches and a tendril of waterweed, swinging back and forth in the current, I spied some small ripples. These seemed to be related to the barely audible splashes, so I concentrated on this spot and the water flowing past it. A rock, just below the surface and about 20 inches upstream, was guiding the flow into a seam near the bank. Newly-emerged mayflies, struggling to escape from the surface tension, were being carried into this seam, only to disappear with the now-familiar little splash. Selecting a matching fly was no problem, but what about the presentation? I knew a poorly thought-out cast would cause the fly to drag and would surely put the fish down, and I was well aware of how shy the fish in this stream are. An upstream, angular cast was out of the question. Perhaps a slack-line pitch, or a parachute cast? None of these possibilities seemed suitable. Briefly, I considered putting this fish into the category "can't reach it – so forget about it." Then, I had an idea. Why not take a risk for once! Carefully, I inspected the opposite bank and, yes, there was a possibility. I stripped line out quietly and cast my floating emerger about a yard in front of the fish…precisely onto the opposite bank. Putting a little tension on the line and hoping that the fly wouldn't snag, I tugged. It worked! The fly dropped into the water just in front of the fish and floated perfectly down the seam. Without suspicion, the fish took the fly and began a run. Following a nice fight, I unhooked a wonderful rainbow and released it, unharmed.

That Which Belongs Together, Comes Together

The binding thread for gluing should be very strong, but as thin as possible so the strips' alignment can be seen during the work. With thick thread, it's not possible to see if a strip may have twisted in the process. Blended, cotton thread serves well, or the kind of thread used by shoe repairmen. The binding thread is then wound around the blank with considerable tension. You may apply by hand, use a binding machine, or employ my simple method with the blank chucked in a drill. Using the latter technique, maintain good tension with your fingers, guide the string back and forth, up and down the blank, then tie-off securely at the end.

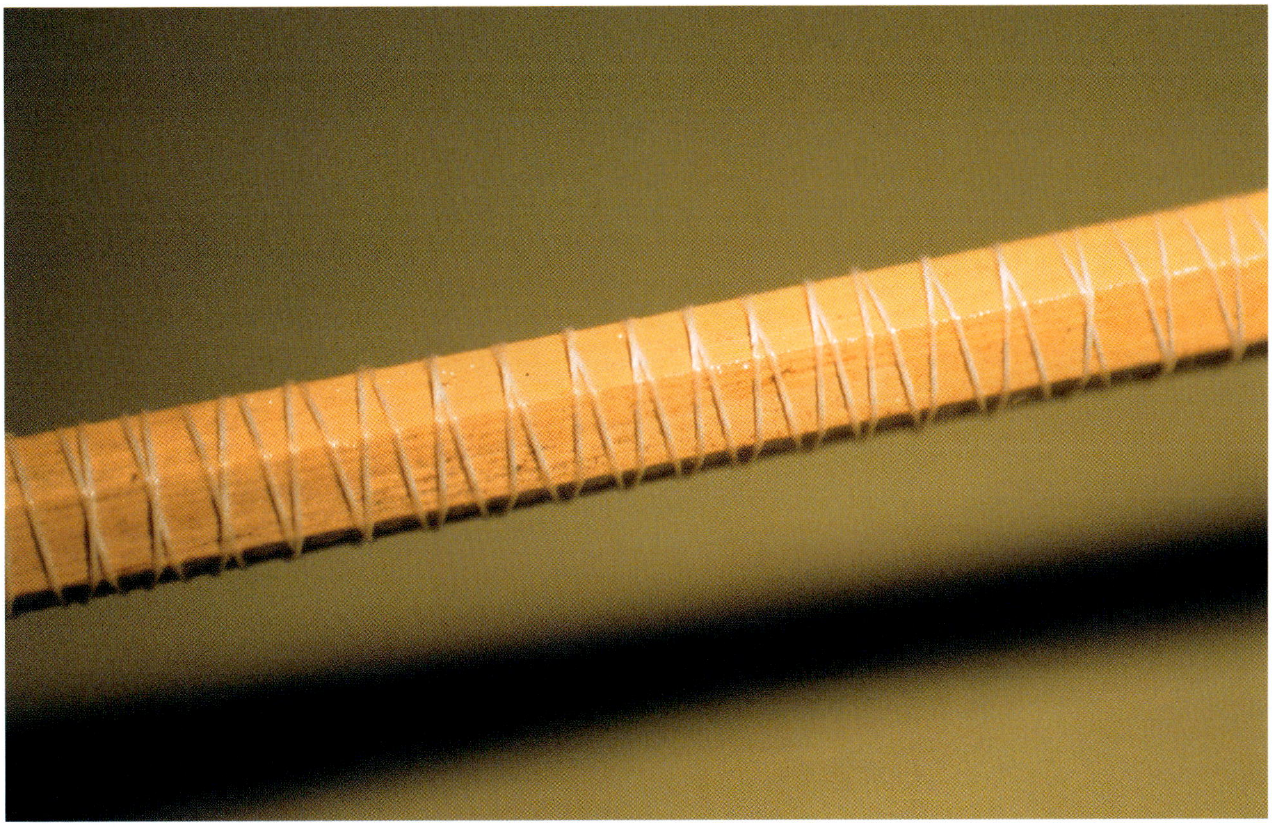

After gluing: Everything fits and no glue line is visible.

The extra glue that squeegees out of the joints needs to be removed with care. Lastly, using both hands, roll the blank back and forth on your work surface to straighten any bends or sweeps. Sight down the flats, looking for possible twists, and if present, remove them by applying torque to the blank, twisting in the opposite direction.

When you're sure that everything is straight, tie a loop around one end and hang the finished piece in a drying cabinet, where it will remain until the glue is fully set.

You can easily make a drying cabinet yourself. The only important considerations are that it must close tightly and that it should have two, lightbulb sockets installed at its bottom. The lights need to maintain an operating temperature between 85° and 100° F. My cabinet was purchased from a well-known Swedish furniture company and has glass in its door (although this certainly isn't necessary), so I only needed to add the light sockets and install hooks at the top to hang my blanks. A drying cabinet is necessary, however, for it will also be used later to dry rod sections after applying the finish. A perfect little touch might be to install a connection for a vacuum cleaner – then, from time to time, you can "purge" the drying cabinet of dust particles.

The bamboo strips are so well-protected by the glue, that further steps in the work can wait as long as days or weeks.

A home-made drying cabinet: Light bulbs provide an increase in operating temperature.

Finish: Step 1

Now, our work will begin to convert the homely pieces lying in front of us into a real fly rod. First, remove the binding thread. Gloves are useful for this step as well, because, often, tiny glue fragments are produced when removing the thread, and these can cut like pieces of glass.

For me, the most pleasant (but also the most anxious) moment in rod-building comes when I remove the binding thread after gluing and drying.

This is the moment when one discovers if all the previous work has paid off. Under bright light, I inspect every glue joint, hoping to find no mistakes – and, in particular, no wide glue lines. If all seems well, then I know the coming work will be a pleasure, because everything that remains is aimed only at bringing a perfectly-glued rod to its full beauty.

The binding thread can be removed after drying. The sections of the blank are now quite unsightly.

First, lay the rod section on a flat work surface – once again, to see if any twists are present. Then, sight along the blank from its thicker end to see if there are any bends. Both conditions are common. The affected areas must be heated with the hot-air gun and straightened with counter-bending or twisting. The heat-level must not be so high that the glue will soften, however, so it's important to study the manufacturer's instructions carefully!

Now, the excess glue must be removed from the blank, using sandpaper of increasingly fine grits. Start with 80 grit, go to 120, and end with 220 paper.

As might be expected, sanding must be done slowly and carefully to avoid contacting the delicate corners and rounding them. It is best to use a solid sanding block and to maintain parallel sanding motion. Although very little material will be removed, the surface of the blank, at first, will look like a series of little mountains which, grit-by-grit, becomes ever flatter until the last passes with 000 or 0000 steel wool reveal a gentle shine.

When this step is finished, the blank is sawed to its final length with a very fine-toothed saw. Either a coping saw or a fine-toothed Japanese saw works best to prevent fibers from being torn up and ruining the rod.

A good way to protect the cane against the saw jumping out of its cut is to wrap a piece of tape around the blank, just behind the cut-off mark. Turn the rod section while sawing, cutting each side in turn, carefully toward the center.
When the blank is completed, remove all remaining dust by wiping it down with a slightly moistened cloth, and then dry.

Six tips after removing glue-remnants and polishing. These have already been ferruled.

Finish: Step 2

Dip-finishing is best for protecting the rod. Of course, a finish can be applied by brush, but your results are not likely to achieve the quality of a dipped finish. No matter what method you choose, however, finish must be applied to the entire blank (including its ends) to protect against moisture penetration. Particularly important, are the areas under the grip and at the ends where ferrules will be mounted – even though these areas wouldn't seem vulnerable in the completed rod. Whether you apply one or several coats depends upon the thickness or consistency of the finish used. One might say, "Apply as thinly as possible, but only as thick as necessary!" It's important to realize that the finish adds a great amount of weight to the rod, especially in its tip area. A thickly-applied varnish will alter the rod's action, causing it to feel slower and softer than intended.

In deciding which finish might be best, one needs to depend on the manufacturer's specifications. When fully cured, however, the varnish should be non-chipping, flexible, and (most particularly) UV resistant. My experience is that the best finishes are those that are recommended for wooden stair-treads.

Before sawing a hole in the ceiling to obtain enough space for your dip-finishing equipment, you should have a good idea how many rods you're likely to build. If only a few, you may decide to use a brush because a hole in the ceiling isn't worth the hassle. But stairwells, or places under stairs, may provide enough height for dipping equipment.

You should not let too much time pass between polishing the blank and applying the finish. Bamboo can absorb moisture through its unsealed, outer surfaces, so it's best to varnish immediately after removing excess glue. A finish will give the bamboo a protective layer and greatly retard later moisture penetration, although, to the best of my knowledge, there's no finish that can absolutely prevent absorption of ambient humidity. The ends of the blank are of particular importance, and these should be sealed with varnish immediately.

The end of a blank should be sealed soon after it's completed.

The construction of a dipping-machine presents no problems, except perhaps, for obtaining an electric motor that turns at very low rpm. You need a pipe of the appropriate length (63 inches is enough for almost all rod sizes) which is closed at its bottom, but with a removable, threaded cap at its top. The pipe should be between 2 and 4 inches in diameter, then mounted vertically in a location having a total, free height of at least10 ½ feet. Fasten a screw-eye directly above the center of the pipe, and locate the electric motor to the right or left of that. Now prepare an 11 ½-foot “dipping cord” by attaching a weight of about 2 to 4 ounces to one end, while at its other, a clamp for gripping the rod blank. Wrap the dipping cord twice around the shaft of the motor and pass the clamp through the screw-eye so that it’s just above the top of the pipe. When you turn the motor on, the weight will pull the cord slowly upwards and over the motor shaft. The blank needs to rise very slowly out of the finish, so, depending on its size, the weight attached to your cord will need to be selected accordingly.
Now you just need to fill the pipe with the finish of your choice, and you can begin.

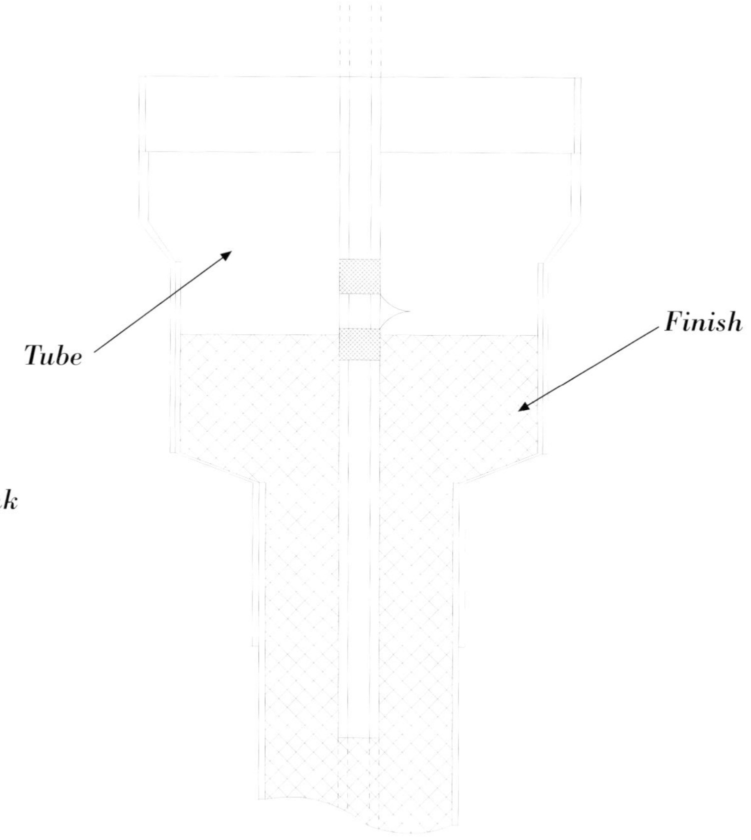

Dip-finishing tank

You’ll need to inquire about motors from someone who’s knowledgeable. I scavenged my motor from an old rotisserie, but others, such as those for opening garage doors, can also be used. It’s important to consider that the withdrawal speed will be regulated with counterweights, causing the rod to be drawn very slowly from the varnish reservoir (about 2 to 4 inches per minute). Blanks can be held with wood or plastic clothes-pins, with a loop of string attached. The loop will be used later to hang the pieces in the drying cabinet.

Applying finish can be very frustrating, particularly in late summer. Small insects are flying around everywhere and you can be certain that one will be magically attracted to your freshly varnished rod, and will end up stuck to it. The only solution is to let the rod dry, scrape the finish off the rod and start all over...

The drying cabinet will be put to use immediately after applying the first coat of finish. Depending upon the varnish used, drying time will be between 6 and 12 hours, but the cabinet should first be wiped out with a damp cloth to eliminate any dust. After all your careful work, it's very frustrating to discover that grains of dust, hair, or lint have settled on the finish.

Ferrules

Before mounting the ferrules, we must measure the diameter of our blank at its end to determine which size to use.

Proper selection of the ferrule's inside diameter will ensure that only a minimum of material need be removed from the blank. Ferrule stations are easily broken when casting a rod, and these areas must not be weakened.

Nickel-silver ferrules are best for split-cane rods.

The inner depth of the ferrule must now be measured, and that length marked on the blank. Then, the rod section is chucked into a motor (wrap tape on the area within the chuck to avoid scratching the surface). Carefully sand the end protruding from the chuck until the ferrule can be pushed snugly onto the blank. In no case should too much material be removed because, after the ferrule is glued in place, the rod section will not fit securely against the ferrule's inner walls .

If you do accidentally remove too much material, that spot must be wrapped with a thread (or a piece of masking tape) to assure a tight fit once again.

The ferrule should slide onto the blank without a great deal of pressure, but neither must it have any free play. The serrated tabs should extend about 1/16 to 1/8 of an inch beyond the sanded-down area.

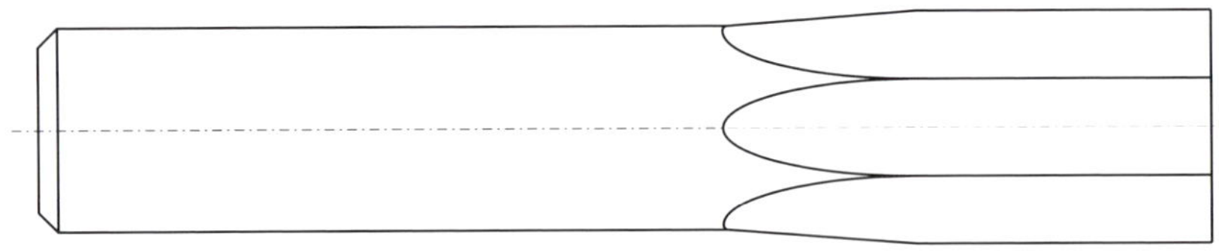

Sanded-down end of the blank

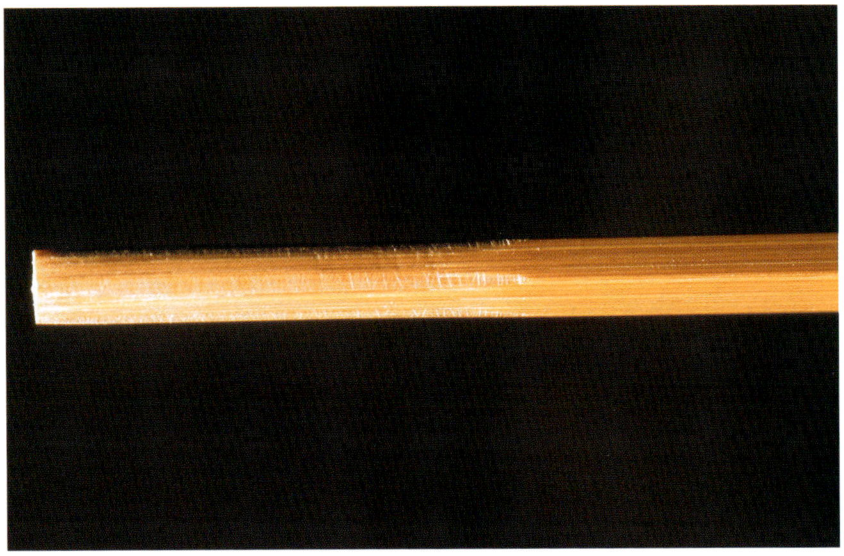

The blank is sanded with coarse sandpaper to fit the ferrule.

The Tension Rises

Some books give strict advice not to sand the blank's ferrule-station at all, warning that this could create a predetermined break-point. This advice, of course, is nonsense because the tapered area will be made sturdy by the serrated tabs that extend beyond the sanded-down area. Nothing can break within the metal ferrule, while a too-large ferrule, fitted over an un-sanded blank, only produces a heavy and unsightly lump in the rod.

Now, the glue is put into the ferrule and the ferrule slowly pushed onto the blank. Extra glue will squeeze out and should be wiped up immediately with a rag. Now, position the ferrule tabs on the flats of the hexagon, checking that the ferrule aligns properly with the rod section. If you bend the tabs slightly inward before gluing, you can avoid the need to wrap with thread (holding them in position while the glue sets), for the tabs will already be lying tightly on the blank.

For this photo, the ferrule was darkened and the tabs pointed. Slight force is used to slide the ferrule onto the blank.

The ferrule's tabs extend over the sanded part of the blank, and the tab points are aligned with the blank's corners.

Most commercially-available ferrules are sold with over-dimensioned, mating surfaces (that is, not pre-fitted), and they cannot be pushed together until the male "slide" is lapped or sanded to fit. This can be a tedious process and may take more than an hour because of the very fine sandpaper that must be used (at least 800 grit and finer). For this reason, I recommend fitting the ferrules before gluing them.

Fitting is done by securing the male part of the ferrule in a motorized chuck. Set the motor to turn at medium-to-slow rpm, and carefully remove material with a strip of sandpaper. Alternatives to sandpaper would be the so-called "extra-fine" files, such as those from Swiss Grobet. These are available in various sizes from companies specializing in rod-building tools (Golden Witch, for example).

Sometimes ferrule parts are difficult to separate during lapping. A simple tool for freeing them can be made from two pieces of wood, connected by a leather hinge. The several holes grip a variety of ferrule sizes securely.

For lapping or preparing the tabs, ferrule sections are pushed onto an appropriately-sized wooden dowel, held in a drill chuck.

Coming to the End

Check frequently and repeatedly to see if the female is beginning to fit over the male slide, but stop lapping as soon as the female part can be pressed onto the male a small fraction of an inch. If you remove more material, the ferrule will quickly become useless. Continue the final lapping by hand until the two parts can be pushed together, but only within about one-eighth-of-an-inch of the full depth.

This remaining space is left as a "reserve" because the ferrule slides will undergo a little wear over time.

After the glue sets, some rod-builders put the blank and ferrule back in the chuck, then sand or file the ferrule's tabs down to a very thin edge to effect as gentle a transition from metal-to-bamboo as possible. The idea is to try to prevent the crack in the wraps that often develops, exactly at this transition. The area is wrapped and covered by finish, of course, but the flexing motion of casting causes the bamboo to "work," while the metal ferrule does not. My experience is that you can work the tabs down as much as you like, but the crack still forms!

Cork Grips

For a precious, split-bamboo rod, you should fashion an appropriately attractive grip yourself. The reason is simple. You simply cannot buy really good, completed grips. There are a few exceptions, but these will have correspondingly exceptional prices. Only your own selection of individual cork rings will provide a first-class grip – one that retains a smooth, fine-pored surface for years.

A second reason for making your own grip relates to the size of the hole in their centers. Seldom is it possible to file the existing hole on a purchased, pre-glued grip so that it fits your blank without any play. First-class cork rings are costly, but you should not save money here. What pleasure can come from looking at the finest rod when the first thing you see is a poor grip?

A piece of cork-oak bark. The best quality comes from the innermost layer next to the tree's wood.

One good, and one very bad cork ring. The ring on the left was cut from the inner bark, while the right-hand ring was cut from outer areas.

A useful tool for gluing cork rings.

After selecting suitable cork rings, each must be drilled for a properly sized hole and pushed onto the blank. Slide the first ring over the ferrule and down to the mark you've made, indicating the length of the reelseat. Due to the taper, hole sizes will need to be a little larger as they approach the reelseat. Push the rings on, piece by piece, until the necessary length of the grip is reached. Each ring should fit snugly on the blank, as well as to the other rings.

Another technique is to make a jig for gluing the cork rings. Use a simple aluminum tube, a threaded rod, two pieces of wood, and two wing-nuts. Cork rings are pushed onto the aluminum tube in the same sequence as if one were fitting them directly on the blank. Glue is applied, then the rod, wing-nuts, and pieces of wood are used to clamp the rings together for drying. A waterproof, light-colored, wood glue is best suited for this procedure.

After the glue has set, the unfinished grip can remain on the aluminum tube while you turn the cork to shape. It's better, however, to prepare a second tube that holds the cork more securely (shown in the photo).

The grip can be shaped to its final form by placing one end of the tube in a lathe or drill-chuck (set to high rpm), while supporting the other with a live-center of some sort. The grip's basic shape is produced with 80 grit sandpaper, followed by grits of 100 and 220. Stop frequently and wrap your hand around the cork until you're satisfied you have a comfortable grip. While sanding, a vacuum hose should be positioned as closely as possible to the cork.

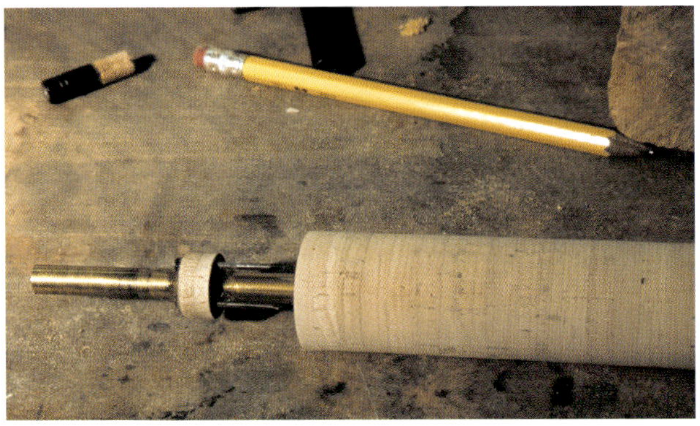

A wooden ring with three, exposed nails is glued to a metal tube. For shaping the grip, the cork rings are pushed over the tube and against the nails, then the tube is mounted in a drill-chuck.

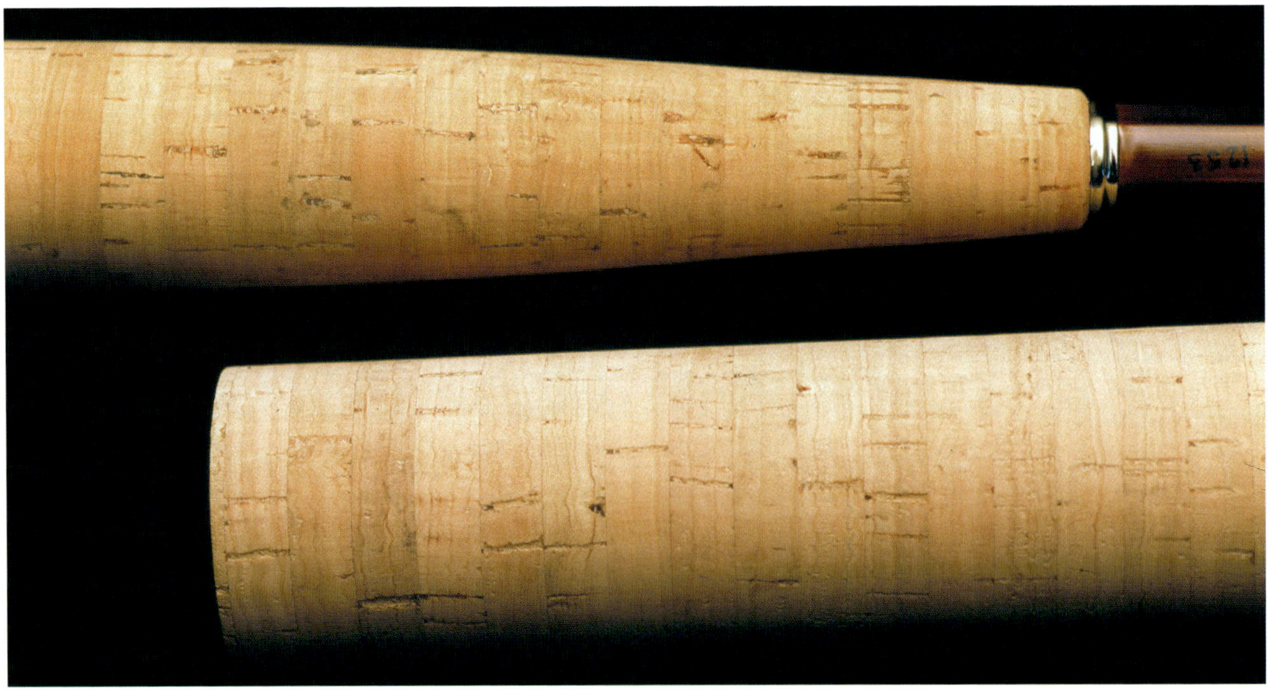

Top: shaped cork grip.
Bottom: cork grip before shaping.

When the grip is finished, it can be removed from the tube quite easily. Use a rattail file to remove any remnants of glue from the hole. Carefully push the grip into position on the blank, avoiding damage to the rod's finish, and check for play. Then glue it in place and immediately wipe off any extra glue. A so-called "winding check" can be glued in front of the cork to make a more attractive transition from cork-to-blank.

It's easier to assemble the grip, reelseat, and winding check if corresponding areas on the blank are turned round. A lathe is necessary for this work.

How to get the perfect fit for a winding check directly on the blank .

Most winding checks are made of nickel silver, and are available from rod-building suppliers in various diameters. Unfortunately, these are only sold round, but can be formed into a hexagon with a tapered, hexagonal punch or an allen wrench. The allen wrench may need to be tapered appropriately.

Reelseats

In one's hunt for a beautiful piece of burl wood, you can plan on adventure.

One day, I dropped in on some rod-building friends and was astonished to find them with a big saw, cutting down a pear tree in their front yard. Once it was down, they began working at the roots with a tractor, leaving an enormous hole after tying a large chain to the root-ball and ripping it out of the earth. I stood there in awe, while my friends ran excitedly around the root-ball, commenting on its size. But they never answered my inquiry as to whether the tree might have been sick.
Later that evening, I discovered they'd cut the tree down only to make reelseats from the root burls.

Many types of wood are suitable for a reelseat. For me, the beauty of wood grain is important, because the reelseat (as with first-class cork) represents the "face" of a rod and is an important factor in the total composition. Of course, you can buy excellent finished reelseats, but the very beautiful ones also have a very beautiful price! In any case, it seems to me that if you can build a rod, you can make a reelseat insert.

Reelseat inserts: "Still-life," showing various woods.

I've had good luck working with olivewood root-burl, gum-juniper root-burl, amboyna, or briar. If these woods are well-aged, they can be turned easily. Attaining the correct color is perhaps a minor issue, but the color of the wood should match the rod blank and wraps. Of course, this is a matter of taste, but as a little hint, I'll tell you that some of the best, natural stains for wood can be found in pipeshops. First, the selected piece of wood is sawed to approximate size to form a blank, usually about 4" x 1" x 1". The center points of the block's ends are found by drawing diagonals from corner to corner. Drill shallow holes at these centers.

The center of the wood is marked and can now be drilled.

The reelseat is drilled and turned with a lathe.

The blank is mounted in a lathe with its center-points fixed in the blank's shallow holes. Then the wood is turned to the desired diameter – usually, about 5/8 to11/16 of an inch. The center hole will now be bored to a diameter corresponding to end of the rod's butt.
Using a special router bit (prepared by a tool-sharpening shop), a mortise can be shaped along the insert to accept the reel's foot.
You can also purchase a "fingernail" router bit, ready-made, and sources are listed in the Appendix.

The depth of the mortise will depend on the thickness of the reel's foot. It's not supposed to be the case, but unfortunately, almost every reel manufacturer uses a different "standard" for the proportions of their reel feet, and even reels in the same series can have different feet. Consequently, you should take a little time to determine an average depth for your mortise.

You can leave the reelseat round if you use a pocketed butt-cap. Garrison used such reelseats and caps.

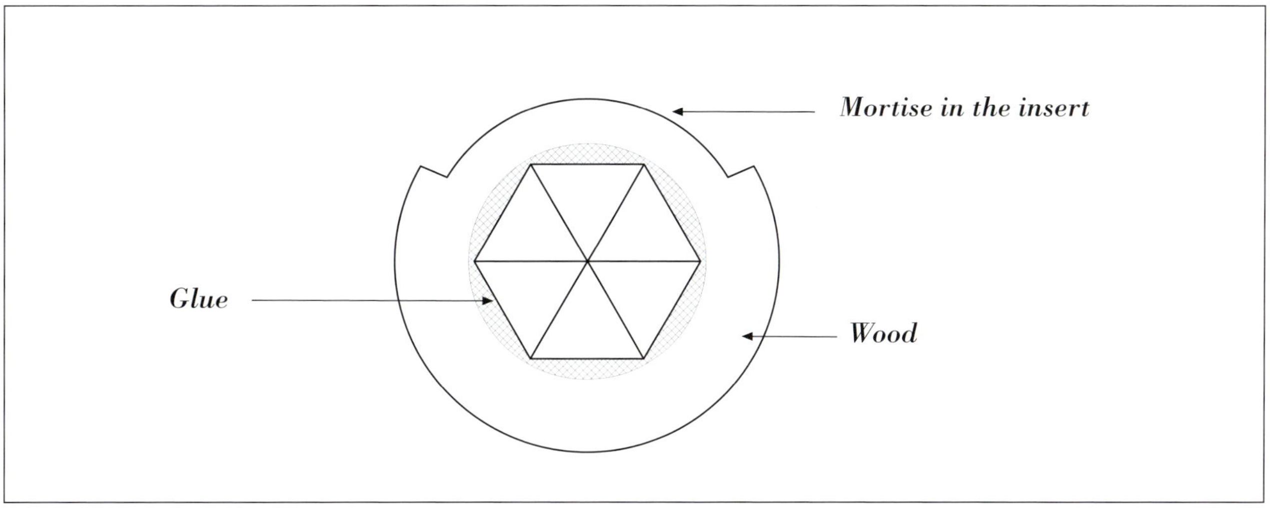

Cross-section of mounted reelseat

Two different "fingernail" bits for routing a mortise in the reelseat insert.

A pocketed end-cap on a Garrison rod.

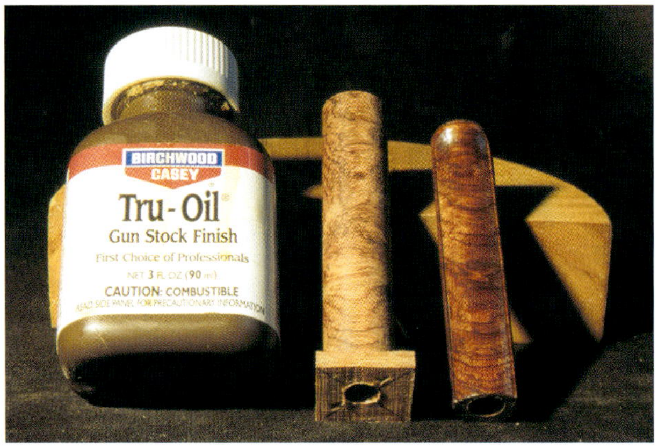

A reelseat in raw form, and oiled.

Finally, the unfinished reelseat must be polished, but first, you need to decide if your wood is to be protected by an oil or a surface finish. A finish that forms a surface film is the simplest to apply, but you should consider that such surfaces scratch easily and can become unsightly after long use.

For an oil-finish insert, turn the wood to a diameter about 1/16 of an inch larger than final measurement, drill it out, and immerse it for about a week in a good wood-finishing oil (such as the oil used for wooden boat decks). After the wood is saturated, remove it from the oil, let it dry for several days, and begin the final shaping. This process is a little more trouble, but you can be sure that such an insert will last for many years and will keep its natural beauty. If the surface becomes dull after time, apply a little wood-finishing oil with a rag, polish, and the insert will look like new again.

The transition between the reelseat and the cork grip is a matter of personal taste, but most makers use a metal or wooden ring for this decoration. Slide the butt-cap and sliding ring into place, and secure the butt-cap with a two-component glue.
Caution: The reelseat should not be glued in place until after the location of the guides is known. That is, it's necessary to determine, first, which of the six splines will receive the guides – then to align the mortised insert accordingly.
Of course, it's possible to use a simple cork reelseat – particularly to save weight – and this would be assembled and shaped in the same way as the grip.

On this rod, a nickel-silver ring forms the transition between the grip and the reelseat.

A Reward

Assembly
Now, comes the exciting moment when one assembles the rod for the first time. If you have worked carefully, you may be able to sight lengthwise down from the grip and see that the sections are aligned. On first assembly, however, this is usually not the case. Simply disconnect the ferrule, rotate the tip-section by one spline (or "flat"), and join the tip and butt ferrules once again. Often, there's just one position where the two sections will find their best alignment, but if no satisfactory position can be found, the rod will need to be straightened before proceeding further.
A heat-gun is used to warm the crooked areas as much as possible, but without burning the finish or softening the glue. A rule-of-thumb is that you should be able to hold the heated spot momentarily, without burning your fingers. When the area is hot enough, carefully counter-bend in the appropriate direction – a process that's repeated until the entire rod is straightened.
Now, lay the assembled blank on your left, index finger, and support the rod horizontally by placing the right, index finger a little more than 3 feet closer to the tip.

When you rotate the rod from one of its surfaces to another, it will always come to rest on one, particular "flat," for even though the rod is hexagonal, it will always have a spine. You should do this test several times to be sure that you're truly locating the same "flat" with each attempt. When you've made your final determination, the guides will be mounted either on this spline or on the one diametrically opposed. If this rule is not obeyed, the rod will not cast straight, as the casting energy will be deflected, instead, along the natural path of least resistance. You can test rods constructed of other materials as well, to see if their guides are properly placed. Many graphite rods, for instance, will have their guides positioned only to give the rod its straightest appearance! So too, many bamboo rods – and not excepting even very expensive models – fail to have their guides placed along the ideal flat. No wonder people are perplexed when their leaders refuse to drop, straight-out, on the water....
Now that you know which splines ("flats") should receive the guides, the reelseat finally can be glued on.

Something that really bothers me (and it does deserve to be pointed out) is that everyone who takes a split-bamboo rod in his or her hand, will sight down its length to check that it's truly straight. On the other hand, even without checking, people always assume that a graphite rod will be straight. But if you turn these rods with their guides facing to one side, and then sight along the shaft, you'll find that about fifty-percent of graphite rods are considerably less than straight.

Selecting the Guides
Manufacturers offer the rod-builder an endless palette of guides, of every type and for every rod. They all have their own purposes and advantages, but fortunately, the selection suitable for split-bamboo rods is limited.

Except for the stripping guide and tip-tops, simple snake guides should be the first choice, and the reasons extend beyond tradition and appearance. They're light in weight, sturdy, and, when well-fastened to the rod, they serve for decades. It's important, too, that these guides be perfectly hard-chromed. In recent years, snake guides have appeared on the market coated in a variety of shades and tones, and I, too, once yielded to the temptation to try the different colors. I found, however, that after a few months of use, the fly line nearly always wore the coating away on the inside of the guides.
Before wrapping, all guide feet must ground down so that when the thread is applied, no transition can be seen between the blank and the foot.
Guide feet can be ground by mounting a soft, grinding-stone in a drill. A simple scissors sharpening-stone would make a suitable grinding-stone, and can be purchased easily and inexpensively. But, take care! If the drill turns too fast, the guide will get hot and you can burn both the metal and your fingers.

The first guide, just up from the fly rod's grip, is called the stripping guide, and is very important. Other than the tip-top, it's the stripping guide that receives the greatest stress. When single- or double-hauling, the hand holding the fly line will pull the line through the stripper nearly at a right angle, so only guides of the finest quality should be used.

The guide feet must be ground perfectly to shape.

Precise grinding is particularly important for the stripping guide feet.

A selection of stripping guides for the split-bamboo rod: On the left, showing a tungsten-carbide inlay; in the center, an agate inlay; and, on the right, a simple hard-chromed guide.

Traditional stripping guides with an agate inlay framed in nickel silver, provide a wonderful, nostalgic appearance. These guides are also made with synthetic inlays, called "Agatine." But, despite their beauty, both types have a disadvantage; they're not unbreakable and can easily shatter.

Best, are stripping guides with a tungsten-carbide inlay. These are all but unbreakable, while still being very "classic" in design. A simple, hard-chromed, stripping guide is also serviceable and has the additional advantage of costing only a fraction of the other types. The advice for tip-tops would be the same, but it's also important to check tip-tops carefully to be sure of flawless brazing between the guide and the tube.

Guide Spacing

I suggest the following for spacing the guides:

Distance from guide-to-guide in inches -- two-piece rods

T = tip-top, S = Stripping guide

Guide	6ft	6 1/2ft	7ft	7 1/2ft	8ft
T	Tip	Tip	Tip	Tip	Tip
1	3.54	3.35	3.74	3.54	3.54
2	4.53	4.33	3.94	3.94	3.94
3	6.30	5.12	5.51	5.12	5.12
4	7.48	5.90	6.89	6.30	6.30
5	8.27	6.69	7.87	7.07	7.07
6	8.66	7.68	8.86	7.87	7.48
7		9.06	9.06	8.66	8.07
8				9.06	8.27
9					9.45
S	9.84	10.63	11.22	11.42	10.24

222
223

Distance from guide-to-guide in inches -- three-piece rods

T = tip-top, S = Stripping guide

	6 ft	6 1/2 ft	7 ft	7 1/2 ft	8 ft	8 1/2 ft	10 ft
T	Tip	Tip	Tip	Tip	Tip	Tip	Tip
1	3.54	3.94	3.94	3.54	3.94	3.94	5.12
2	3.94	4.33	4.53	3.94	4.53	4.53	6.30
3	5.12	5.12	5.90	5.51	5.51	5.51	6.89
4	6.30	6.30	7.28	5.90	6.10	6.10	7.87
5	6.50	7.48	8.07	6.30	6.69	6.89	8.27
6	6.69	8.07	8.46	6.69	7.48	7.68	8.66
7	8.27	9.06	9.84	7.48	7.87	8.07	9.45
8				8.66	8.66	8.66	10.24
9				9.06	9.84	10.24	11.02
S	9.45	9.84	10.43	11.02	10.63	10.63	11.81

The ten-foot rod is a two-handed model, and its grip length, including reel seat is 20 1/2 inches. (See the "Seatrout" taper.)

I've noticed that many rods locate the first guide too far from the tip-top. Under high stress, this condition can quickly cause the tip to take a set (becoming permanently crooked), or even break. To avoid either of these problems, I often use an extra guide even if it increases the weight at the tip.

Wrapping

I hope the reader will excuse a possible excess of detail as I describe the process of applying wraps, but our current literature contains little helpful information on winding-threads and their application. Unfortunately, I constantly see split-bamboo rods that "sport" indescribably poor work in their wrappings. This only diminishes the value of the total product, and that's just a shame. A "perfect" finish is particularly important for split-bamboo rods, but why invest all that work in building and finishing your rod, only to see your beautifully-colored bamboo disfigured by ugly, gap-filled, guide wrappings? Ultimately, you want to fish your rod for many years, but just consider how irritated you'll be each time you look at those carelessly wrapped guides and ferrules.

Silk Time

Nylon or Silk

You must decide whether you want to wrap with nylon or pure, silk thread. This isn't a question of cost, because both products are about the same price. Still, each material has advantages and disadvantages.

Nylon wrapping threads are easy to work with and will produce good results. They do not break easily, will not "fuzz-up" upon application, and a wide range of colors and weights is available. Weight "A" is standard for nylon thread and is used by nearly all rod-building companies, while the thinner, "00" weight should be used for lighter-weight rods. The disadvantage of nylon thread is the appearance of its finish.

Top-quality nylon wrapping thread.

The color will change greatly! The moment varnish is applied, a bright orange becomes medium brown, and a dark red becomes almost black. The only "cure" for this is to apply a color-fixative over the wrappings. There are also some commercially-available nylon threads with "pre-fixed" colors. The disadvantage of color-fixatives, however, is that they prevent varnish from penetrating into the thread. The windings only become coated with the fixative, not impregnated, and not bonded to the cane beneath. Additionally, if you don't work with great care, water can penetrate the windings (later to reveal water-spots on the cane), and within a few months, the windings will begin to disintegrate from the inside. Overall, it's best simply to avoid using a color-fixative. Instead, prepare a number of test-wraps, using different colors of threads and varnishes to see what the final colors will be. Be certain to allow your sample windings to dry completely, because, while the initial effect will be a good deal darker than the thread's original color, when dry, these shade will lighten somewhat. Then decide on the color. Pure silk is perfectly suited for windings on a split-bamboo rod.

Split-cane rods call for wraps of the best English silk.

You should take care to buy three-filament, spun thread, as this is much stronger than the less expensive, two-filament thread. In comparison to nylon, silk is much more difficult to handle. Silk will break under too much tension, and some practice is needed to learn how to deal with this. Additionally, because silk is usually thinner than nylon thread, greater numbers of turns are necessary to wrap a guide. A further disadvantage of this natural fiber is that it can absorb and hold a great deal of water. So, take care, because any moisture that's not thoroughly evaporated will cause your wraps to show ugly, light-colored spots after the varnish is applied. For this reason, completed wrappings must be heated prior to receiving their first coat of finish, and the hot-air gun is perfect. On the positive side, the absorbent character of silk also soaks-up the varnish, bonds this to the cane, and seals the guide's feet completely. Depending on the color, a correctly applied finish will transform silk into an elegant, translucent wrap which lies flat and endures for decades.

If you use white silk, as I do on nearly all of my rods, the color disappears completely and the winding will appear to be transparent.

White, silk thread is wrapped over the foot of a snake guide.

The transition from ferrule to blank is wrapped as well.

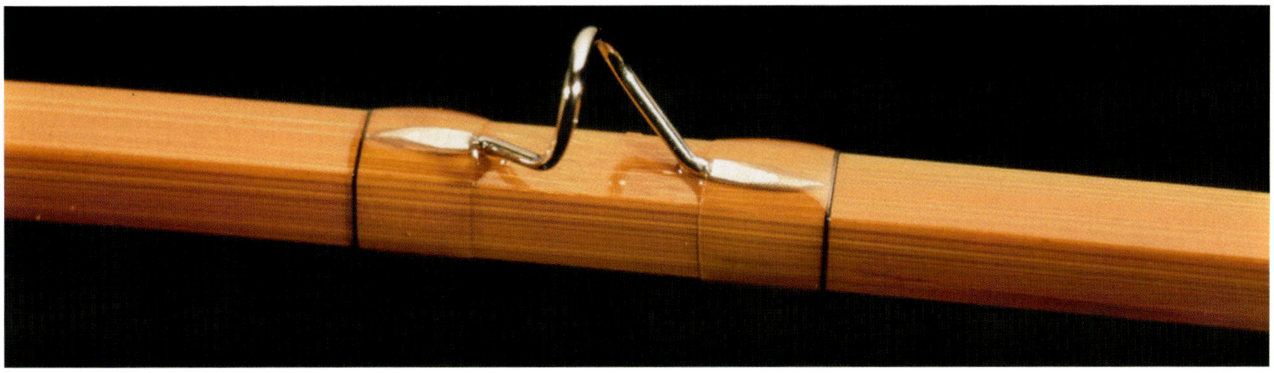

White silk after applying the finish.

When a finish is applied, white silk loses its color and becomes transparent.

As with nylon thread, one should make test-wraps with various colors of silk to choose among the resulting shades. Very good results can be achieved with Pearsall's "Gossamer Pure Silk," which is made in England. Actually, this thread is meant for fly-tying, and according to the manufacturer, has been made in the same way for the last 150 years.
At this point, I want to tell a little secret – namely, how I achieve transparency in my wrappings. To obtain this effect, it's absolutely necessary to use a colorless, natural-oil varnish for the initial coat. After heating the thread, apply this first coat, but be prepared to wait before continuing, for it's very slow to dry. Pure, oil-based varnish is not easy to find nowadays, but I've found that certain, two-component epoxy coatings also penetrate well, achieving the same result.

A wrapping that's been heated (along with the cane beneath) has the additional advantage of causing the varnish to become more fluid. In turn, this allows every micro air-pocket within the fibers to be filled. In order to avoid trapping air in this process, it's important to apply the finish from the outer tip of each guide foot, and work toward the center. Following the initial coat, the number of subsequent applications will depend on whether epoxy or polyurethane is used to build the final surface. Either way, allow each coat to cure thoroughly and shave-off any surface irregularities with a razor blade before applying the next coat. For epoxy, usually one coat is sufficient, but the rod must be rotated in a horizontal position for at least three-to-four hours. If one uses thin applications of polyurethane, the rod can simply be placed horizontally in a warm place (such as near a radiator). Polyurethane will require a minimum of three additional coats, but be certain to follow the manufacturer's directions for drying time!

In action: The greatest pleasure comes from playing a fish with a split-cane rod.

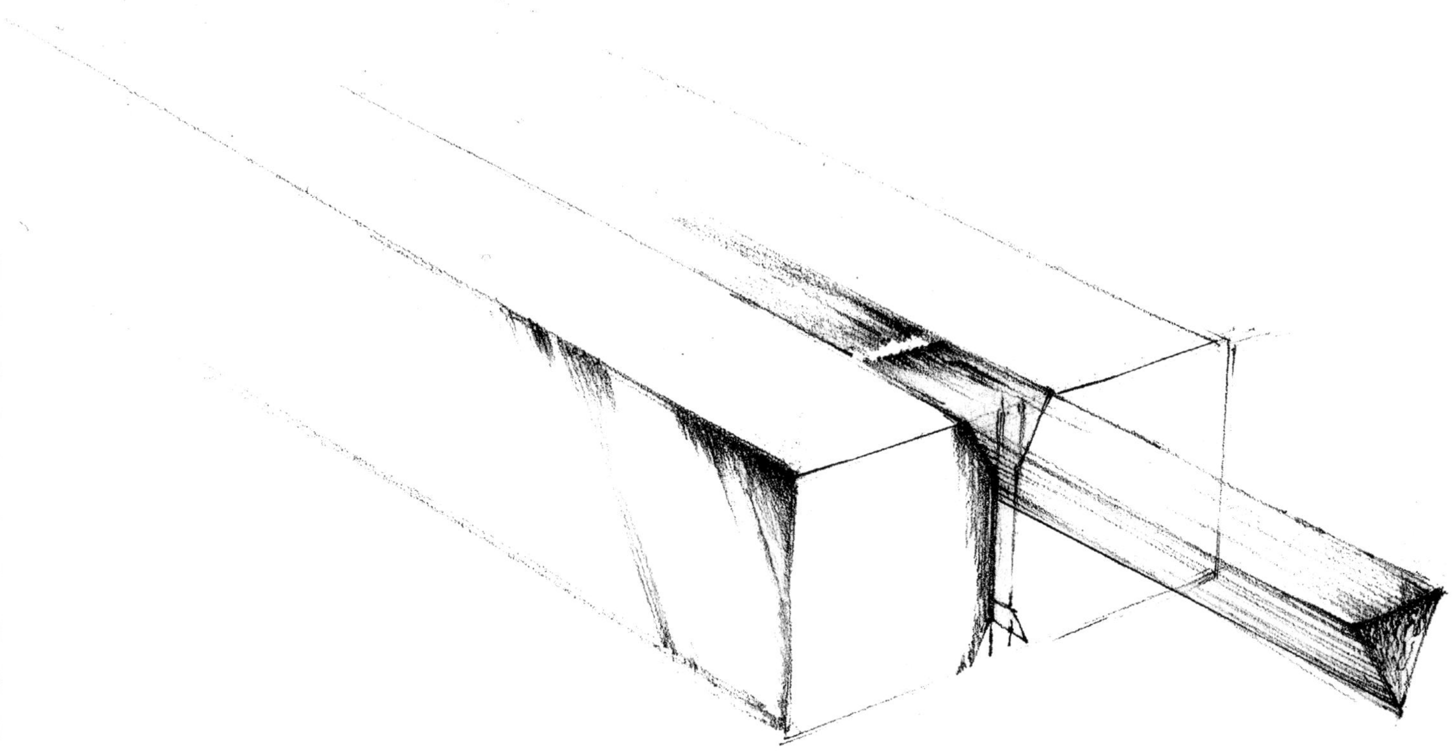

The adjustments of the planing form should be checked often. Adjusting one screw will commonly change the settings of others

Tapers

"There are computer programs for calculating proper tapers for particular rods. Unfortunately, a computer can't fish."

Taper

Most books dealing with the subject of rod-making present complex instructions to calculate "correct" tapers. Unfortunately, most of these procedures can be followed only by mathematicians or engineers. For this reason, I'll dispense with theory and suggest, instead, a computer program in the Appendix, one that's readily available for downloading from the Internet. That said, I also want to warn against considering computer-calculated tapers to be "correct." A computer cannot go fishing!

Points of View

Too many variables need to be considered to arrive at a truly good rod by formula alone. Variations in the quality of bamboo, alone, quickly devolve all calculations into pure theory. I prefer to keep my advice in the form of suggestions, meant to be used only as working guides. For this reason, I've asked a selection of rod-builders to assist me in this book by offering a few of their own tapers. Here, particularly, I want to express my gratitude for their contributions.

If you build according to these tapers, you can decide for yourself whether or not they please you. The results will become apparent only when you're on the water and casting a line of proper weight. Only then, can you can decide for yourself if certain areas in the blank have too much or too little power – or, indeed, if the rod works well for your style of casting. You can be sure that the tapers presented here are effective for any ordinary use, and because they've been developed through long experience, each deserves serious consideration.

New and better glues have allowed rod-builders to produce finer and finer tapers over the last twenty years, but Tonkin cane has limits of its own, and if tips should become too delicate they can easily take a set when stressed. Rods for 3- and 2-weight lines, especially, are not easily designed, and very delicate taper curves must be used.

A number of years ago, it became clear to me that the action of a rod is greatly affected by the weight of the guides, and particularly those near the tip. Even an additional hundredth of an ounce can change certain rods nearly a full line-weight. The short "Brunner" rods built from the 1970s to the 1990s had very heavy tungsten-carbide tip-tops. When I asked Walter Brunner about these rods, he replied, "With those tapers, the additional weight did not matter; but with finer rods, you cannot do that." His remark caused me to realize that one can actually "depress" the line-weight of a rod by using heavy tip-tops with similarly heavy wraps and finish. A rod initially intended for a 5-weight line might be reduced to a 4-weight. In practice, however, this works only to a limited extent, because the heavier rod also becomes more "whippy" when casting a 4-weight line. So, I thought a bit more, and over time, tried something else.

I built an experimental rod, designing thicker areas through the entire tip section, while keeping the butt section relatively "thin" (see Baginski Taper, 7 feet, 2-piece, 3-weight). The result was convincing. The flex curve turned out to be very balanced and, due to the total weight of the tip section, the rod easily cast its 3-weight line. Moreover, a tip built like this will not take a set as easily as a finer version. No computer would "spit out" or accept such a taper. So, you can see that there is still much room for experimentation.

Many tapers develop by accident. Apparently, I was not yet awake one morning as I began to set my planing form for a 7 1/2-foot, 5-weight rod. My depth-gauge had gone out of adjustment, and when the rod was finished, I discovered to my dismay that it was 0.008 inches too thick along its entire length. Despite that, I mounted the ferrules, eager to see if the rod could be used with a 7 or 8-weight line. When "loaded," its flexing-action looked good, and it suddenly dawned on me how I could use this rod – it seemed perfectly suited for a spin/caster.

A beautiful sea-run brown caught on a light spinning/casting rod. (Photo by Lars Østergaard Jensen)

I often travel up to the Baltic Sea to fish for sea-run browns, but it always bothered me that I couldn't use a fly rod to cast against the strong, onshore winds. At some point, I overcame my resistance and tried a spin/casting rod. Nearly all commercially-available, light spin/casters are built to cast lures weighing between 1/2 and 1 ounce – meaning that the spinners or spoons will be 4 to 5 inches long. But the wet-flies used for "sea-runs" are lighter and only about an inch long. These weight- and size-differences eventually motivated me to develop a bamboo rod for casting smaller lures; those weighing between 1/8 and 1/4 ounce. On the very day I mounted spin/casting guides and an appropriate grip on my "mistake rod" and tried casting, my first light, spin/casting rod was born – catching large numbers of sea-run browns ever after (see Baginski Taper, 2-piece, 7 1/2 foot spinning/casting rod). On one occasion, when fishing with my Danish friend, Lars, I put the rod into his hands, and after trying a couple of casts, he said: "You don't really want to have this back, do you?" For me, that's the highest praise any rod builder can receive.

The "classic" tapers, as listed, are reliable, but with some explanation. Many tapers had to be derived from completed rods, already varnished, but the thickness of a finish can only be estimated. Only experience can help. Additionally, where a wrap or a ferrule was in the way of my measurements, an estimate was necessary.

You can't begin to imagine the looks on collectors' faces when you pull out a relatively sharp-edged, dial caliper from your pocket and begin to measure a classic rod. Absolute terror alternates with bewildered and helpless staring! The only reassurance is a quiet discussion, perhaps longer than half an hour; and sometimes even that doesn't help!

If you read a taper's numbers carefully, you often notice that certain butt sections show a sudden "jump" near the grip area. This usually indicates that the taper is beginning to form a "swelled-butt," causing this rod's effective flexing-action to stop about 4 to 6 inches in front of the grip. Cast a rod with a swelled-butt, and its action will "work" only down to this point.

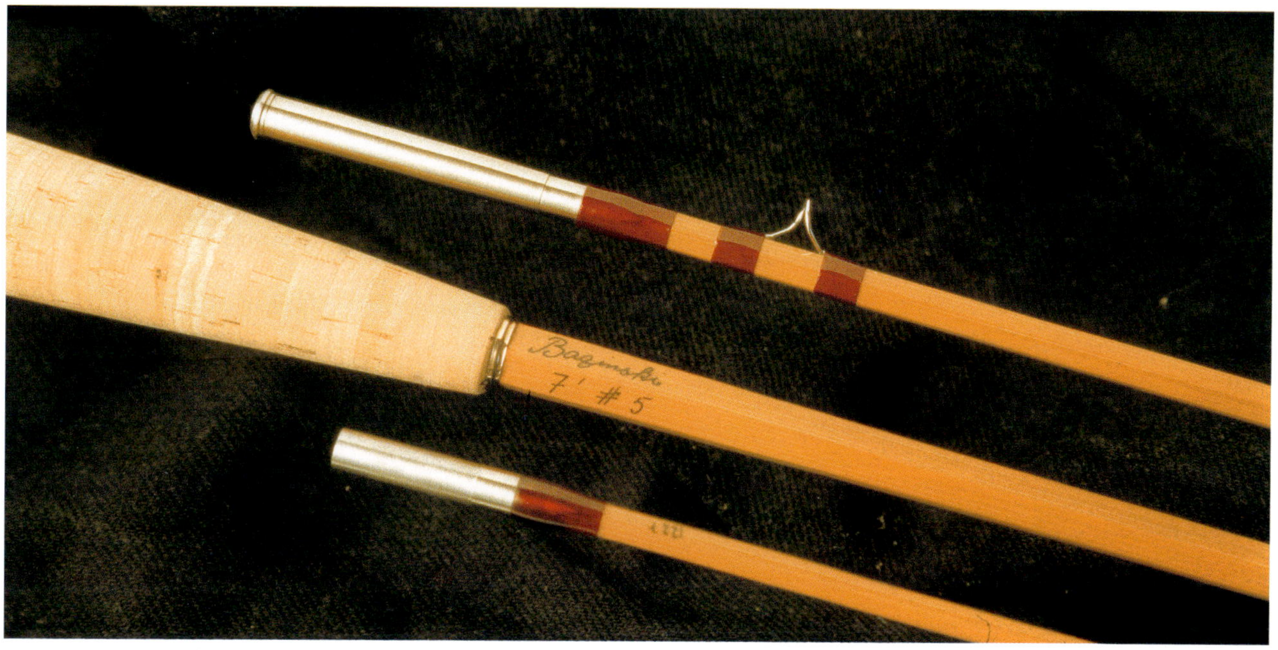

This blank increases in diameter just in front of the grip, forming a "swelled butt."

It appears that many early rod-builders used this swell in front of the grip only to effect a nice, visual transition into the grip. Despite that, the tradition continues, particularly among American rod-builders, and is still seen on many modern rods. But the effect is not only decorative, because a swelled-butt makes good sense for stronger tapers. When casting longer rods with heavier line weights, any action that flexes into the grip can be disturbing, even an encumbrance. Here, the swell makes sense and improves the action of the rod. On the other hand, lighter rods may be more desirable when their flexing extends well into the grip – I know some fishermen who treasure this "full flavor."

The rod-builder who wants to build a swelled-butt may have problems adjusting his planing form, as only brute force will open the bars wide enough to produce the desired increase in dimension.
Special forms, already tapered to produce the swelled-butt, are available from rod-building suppliers.
When adjusting the form, the values given in the following table must be halved, as these tapers indicate a finished rod's total diameter.

Baginski 2-piece, 8 feet, 4-weight

inch	butt section inch	butt section mm	tip section inch	tip section mm
0	.199	5.05	.065	1.65
5	.210	5.33	.072	1.82
10	.222	5.63	.087	2.20
15	.230	5.84	.102	2.59
20	.238	6.04	.115	2.92
25	.248	6.29	.129	3.27
30	.258	6.55	.142	3.60
35	.260	6.60	.158	4.01
40	.265	6.73	.173	4.39
45	.265	6.73	.187	4.75
48	.265	6.73	.199	5.05

Baginski 2-piece, 7 feet 6 inches; 5-weight

inch	butt section inch	butt section mm	tip section inch	tip section mm
0	.218	5.53	.068	1.72
5	.231	5.86	.093	2.36
10	.239	6.07	.119	3.02
15	.247	6.27	.136	3.45
20	.262	6.65	.149	3.78
25	.280	7.11	.163	4.14
30	.295	7.49	.181	4.59
35	.298	7.56	.198	5.02
40	.300	7.62	.212	5.38
45	.300	7.62	.218	5.53

Baginski 2-piece, 6 feet; 4-weight

inch	butt section inch	butt section mm	tip section inch	tip section mm
0	.166	4.21	.070	1.77
5	.173	4.39	.073	1.85
10	.181	4.59	.076	1.93
15	.192	4.87	.097	2.46
20	.206	5.23	.119	3.02
25	.214	5.43	.137	3.48
30	.228	5.79	.150	3.81
35	.228	5.79	.166	4.21
36	.228	5.79	.166	4.21

Baginski 2-piece, 6 feet 6 inches; 3-weight

inch	butt section inch	butt section mm	tip section inch	tip section mm
0	.170	4.31	.070	1.77
5	.184	4.67	.080	2.03
10	.198	5.02	.088	2.23
15	.212	5.38	.105	2.66
20	.226	5.74	.120	3.04
25	.239	6.07	.133	3.37
30	.241	6.12	.147	3.73
35	.241	6.12	.159	4.03
39	.241	6.12	.170	4.31

Baginski 2-piece, 7 feet; 4-weight

inch	butt section inch	butt section mm	tip section inch	tip section mm
0	.184	4.67	.066	1.68
5	.205	5.20	.070	1.77
10	.213	5.41	.081	2.05
15	.219	5.56	.102	2.59
20	.243	6.17	.123	3.12
25	.258	6.55	.137	3.48
30	.270	6.85	.153	3.88
35	.298	7.56	.166	4.21
40	.300	7.62	.182	4.62
42	.300	7.62	.184	4.67

Baginski 2-piece, 8 feet; 5-weight

inch	butt section inch	butt section mm	tip section inch	tip section mm
0	.214	5.43	.072	1.82
5	.228	5.79	.081	2.05
10	.238	6.04	.100	2.54
15	.246	6.24	.114	2.89
20	.254	6.45	.127	3.22
25	.265	6.73	.143	3.63
30	.274	6.96	.154	3.91
35	.278	7.06	.172	4.36
40	.280	7.11	.189	4.80
45	.282	7.16	.204	5.18
48	.282	7.16	.214	5.43

Baginski 3-piece, 7 feet; 4-weight

inch	tip section inch	tip section mm	middle sec. inch	middle sec. mm	butt section inch	butt section mm
0	.070	1.77	.150	3.81	.245	6.22
5	.075	1.90	.168	4.26	.264	6.70
10	.083	2.10	.188	4.77	.280	7.11
15	.104	2.64	.210	5.33	.295	7.49
20	.125	3.17	.220	5.58	.310	7.87
25	.138	3.50	.225	5.71	.315	8.00
28	.150	3.81	.245	6.22	.315	8.00

Baginski 3-piece, 7 feet 6 inches; 5-weight

inch	tip section inch	tip section mm	middle sec. inch	middle sec. mm	butt section inch	butt section mm
0	.070	1.77	.155	3.93	.238	6.04
5	.080	2.03	.173	4.39	.248	6.30
10	.093	2.36	.195	4.95	.260	6.60
15	.115	2.92	.208	5.28	.272	6.90
20	.134	3.40	.217	5.51	.281	7.13
25	.145	3.68	.226	5.74	.285	7.24
30	.155	3.93	.238	6.04	.285	7.24

Baginski 3-piece, 8 feet; 5-weight

inch	tip section inch	tip section mm	middle sec. inch	middle sec. mm	butt section inch	butt section mm
0	.072	1.82	.165	4.19	.256	6.50
5	.082	2.08	.179	4.54	.262	6.65
10	.100	2.54	.195	4.95	.270	6.85
15	.112	2.84	.210	5.33	.280	7.11
20	.126	3.20	.225	5.71	.286	7.26
25	.144	3.65	.236	5.99	.288	7.31
30	.155	3.93	.244	6.19	.288	7.31
32	.165	4.19	.256	6.50	.288	7.31

Baginski 3-piece, 7 feet 6 inches; 4/5-weight

inch	tip section	tip section	middle sec.	middle sec.	butt section	butt section
	inch	mm		mm	inch	mm
0	.070	1.78	inch	3.90	.229	5.84
5	.077	1.98	.153	4.28	.257	6.54
10	.090	2.30	.168	4.60	.261	6.64
15	.101	2.58	.181	5.30	.324	8.24
20	.126	3.22	.208	5.64	.334	8.50
25	.141	3.60	.222	5.74	.334	8.50
28	.153	3.90	.225	5.84	.334	8.50
			.229			

Baginski 3-piece, 7 feet 6 inches; 5/6-weight

inch	tip section	tip section	middle sec.	middle sec.	butt section	butt sectionl
	inch	mm	inch	mm	inch	mm
0	.081	2.06	.170	4.32	.259	6.60
5	.092	2.34	.191	4.86	.279	7.10
10	.118	3.00	.207	5.26	.297	7.56
15	.127	3.25	.235	5.98	.309	7.86
20	.140	3.56	.238	6.06	.374	9.50
25	.155	3.96	.248	6.30	.374	9.50
30	.170	4.32	.259	6.60	.374	9.50

Baginski 3-piece, 8 feet; 4-weight

inch	tip section	tip section	middle sec.	middle sec.	butt section	butt section
	inch	mm	inch	mm	inch	mm
0	.070	1.80	.161	4.10	.252	6.42
5	.078	2.00	.185	4.72	.265	6.74
10	.098	2.50	.109	4.84	.273	6.94
15	.103	2.64	.200	5.08	.277	7.04
20	.118	3.00	.223	5.68	.314	8.00
25	.138	3.52	.236	6.00	.374	9.50
30	.154	3.92	.248	6.30	.374	9.50
32	.161	4.10	.252	6.42	.374	9.50

Baginski 2-piece spin/casting rod, 7 feet 6 inches, 0.2-0.4 ounces:
grip, 12.2 inches long; very light guides

inch	butt section inch	butt section mm	tip section inch	tip section mm
0	.224	5.70	082	2.10
5	.252	6.42	.093	2.38
10	.272	6.92	.121	3.08
15	.288	7.34	.138	3.52
20	.299	7.60	.155	3.94
25	.307	7.80	.166	4.24
30	.322	8.20	.174	4.44
35	.362	9.20	.193	4.92
40	.362	9.20	.206	5.24
45	.362	9.20	.224	5.70

Baginski 2-piece spin/casting rod, 6 feet 6 inches, 0.2-0.4 ounces:
grip, 11.4 inches long; light guides

inch	butt section inch	butt section mm	tip section inch	tip section mm
0	.211	5.38	.078	2.00
5	.214	5.44	.101	2.58
10	.231	5.88	.116	2.96
15	.236	6.00	.129	3.30
20	.244	6.20	.151	3.84
25	.292	7.42	.172	4.38
30	.392	9.98	.185	4.72
35	.392	9.98	.196	4.98
39	.392	9.98	.211	5.38

236
237

Baginski 2-piece spin/casting rod, 8 feet, 0.4-0.6 ounces:
grip, 19.3 inches long; standard guides

inch	butt section inch	butt section mm	tip section inch	tip section mm
0	.303	7.70	.130	3.32
5	.309	7.85	.140	3.56
10	.312	7.95	.166	4.22
15	.320	8.15	.188	4.80
20	.326	8.30	.205	5.22
25	.334	8.50	.225	5.72
30	.338	8.60	.240	6.10
35	.354	9.00	.255	6.50
40	.354	9.00	.281	7.15
45	.354	9.00	.299	7.60
48	.354	9.00	.303	7.70

Baginski 3-piece salmon rod, 12 feet; 10-weight

inch	tip section inch	tip section mm	middle sec. inch	middle sec. mm	butt section inch	butt section mm
0	.125	3.20	.318	8.10	.448	11.40
5	.133	3.40	.334	8.50	.472	12.00
10	.165	4.20	.354	9.00	.484	12.30
15	.188	4.80	.362	9.20	.488	12.40
20	.204	5.20	.377	9.60	.496	12.60
25	.220	5.60	.393	10.00	.507	12.90
30	.248	6.30	.401	10.20	.519	13.20
35	.259	6.60	.409	10.40	.527	13.40
40	.275	7.00	.417	10.60	.527	13.40
45	.295	7.50	.433	11.00	.527	13.40
50	.318	8.10	.448	11.40	.527	13.40

Baginski 3-piece salmon rod, 10 feet; 8-weight

inch	tip section inch	tip section mm	middle sec. inch	middle sec. mm	butt section inch	butt section mm
0	.097	2.48	.212	5.40	.338	8.60
5	.111	2.82	.237	6.02	.355	9.04
10	.129	3.28	.259	6.58	.371	9.44
15	.145	3.70	.274	6.98	.394	10.02
20	.162	4.14	.284	7.22	.448	11.40
25	.177	4.50	.292	7.42	.448	11.40
30	.189	4.82	.305	7.76	.448	11.40
35	.198	5.03	.318	8.10	.448	11.40
40	.212	5.40	.338	8.60	.448	11.40

238

239

Salmon, Salmon!

1

Our excitement grew even in the dead of winter.

After the third beer at our monthly fly-fishing get-together, we just couldn't resist the enticements of one of our friends any longer, so we arrived at a decision. This fellow was an experienced salmon-fisher who maintained quite a number of private contacts, and had paid his dues, long-since, on the more famous salmon waters. Because his fishing travels often led to Norway, he ventured a proposal that evening: "If you want, we could fish the last 14 days of the season on the upper Gaulfossen." Now, my friend and I had already heard quite a bit about those big salmon on the Gaula, but licenses for the more exclusive stretches were completely beyond our financial range. Our colleague's offer was substantial too, but we thought we could manage it somehow – actually, in comparison with other packages we knew, his price could even be considered cheap.

At the time, we had only theoretical knowledge of salmon fishing, so in the following months, we met to discuss fly patterns, fishing tactics, and gear. Our friend often explained, "Salmon fishing builds character," teasing us with tall stories to build our dreams through the following weeks.

Our 20-hour drive was interrupted only once, when Swedish Customs tore our car apart and fined us heavily for the excessive alcohol we were carrying (intended for introducing ourselves to new friends and celebrating our catch), so we arrived thoroughly exhausted. We managed only two hours of disturbed, half-sleep just outside Oslo, and that didn't help much.

What a tableau we saw! Three guys in bathing suits, lying in hammocks on the deck, just enjoying the sun. Lazily, they said hello. No doubt, the looks on our faces suggested that some sort of explanation was expected. It came indirectly, while we were setting up our tent between the forest and the shoreline, and in the hot sun.

Eating ice cream seemed appropriate because the sun was shining and temperatures had been high for more than a week. But the water was too low and too warm – no fish in the river and not one caught in the last 14 days. What a disappointment after a 20 hour-drive and months of anticipation! But "Salmon fishing builds character," we reminded ourselves. So, we unpacked and set everything up at the campsite. Then, despite fishing conditions, we dragged out all the new and expensive salmon gear, if only to get our more experienced colleagues to confirm that we novices had spent our money well. All was inspected with "oohs, aahs and hmmms..." and found to be alright. "I'm going to do some practice casting," said my friend, Werner, and 'midst amused, sideways glances, he went down the opposite bank. What happened next, sounds so unlikely – but I swear to this day, I have six people to confirm the story!

With half-closed and exhausted eyes, I watched as Werner stripped out line, put something red and quite large on his leader, and with some false-casting, put the fly upstream in the Gaula. My eyes must have fallen fully closed, because I remember being startled to consciousness by Werner's yell, "I have one!!!" Five, full-grown men jumped up, shot down to the water's edge, and after staring in disbelief, began running in all directions. Suggestions...well, commands...barked through the warm air: "Rod up!" "Give him line!" "Reel-in your line!" "Run after him!" "Give him line!" "Reel it in!" "Run after him!" "Now!" "Take your time!" On later reflection, I think we were more excited than Werner, but after about 15 minutes, the first estimates of the fish's weight were wagered – probably only between 5 and 9 pounds. Then, a final tug...and Werner was left sitting on his backside. Gone, lost, over with – the line flowing in great curves on its way downstream.

A profound disappointment spread and the line was reeled in. Werner's fly was still on, but what was this!? The hook was absolutely straight. Disbelief spread as quickly as the disappointment, and expressed in non-printable commentary. Had Werner fished with plain old streamer hooks? "Yes," he said sheepishly, "but how was I supposed to know…" The disgust of everyone standing around hung like a heavy cloud in the air. "What an idiot!" was the most complimentary thing we heard. Salmon fishing, after all, "builds character." Nevertheless, we all suddenly found ourselves in a great rush to pull our gear together. This was against all odds (warm sunshine, low water, water temperature of 68° F), but what could you do, the fish were in! In the meantime, Werner, with head hanging, moved a little farther along and continued to fish his "pass" (we learned during the winter that each person fished a pass, followed by the next fisherman).

Words can't express what we thought when Werner's rod again bent in a strong curve. Quickly, it all began again, but with an important difference. A half hour later, Werner filled our glasses to toast his 12-pound salmon, now hanging from a tree. That was the first and the last fish caught during our first week.

Salmon, Salmon!

2

The weather was changing. During the morning, we were still squeezing our bottles of suntan lotion, but a few hours later, the temperature fell to 45° F, clouds of drizzle blew-in over the water, and the bank opposite us was nearly invisible. For the companions during our first, sunny days, everyday-life back at work had begun, but for the rest of us, normal salmon fishing began. The water rose, the temperature approached an optimum, and we were convinced that schools of grilse and salmon would soon begin their trip upstream. They'd make their way through the fast water of the Gaulfossen, then spend several hours in "our pool" as they gathered strength for further migration. Day after day, night after night, we three fished our passes without a single fish showing itself. The days were just endurable, but at night there was a bit of cursing upon hearing, "Your pass!" Our only relief came with the 2-to-3 hour break we took early each morning, grateful for the chance to drive to a truckstop on the main road for a hot shower and a warm breakfast. All pleasure can flee when a week of drizzle leaves even the best clothing damp and cold – and when your stolen hours of sleep are spent trying to forget your chattering teeth.

Only one thing made our runny noses bearable: They had to come sometime… the salmon. Each day, we built a large fire at the upper end of the pool – both for warmth and to keep off the mosquitoes that emerged towards morning. But it was also needed to avoid missing out in case some errant fish – newly arrived in our pool and confused – should show itself. Smelling of smoke and frustrated, we occupied our nights with stories, coffee, and cigarettes – alternated with fishing. I wasn't the only one whose language grew foul during those long hours: "I'll never go #^$?&%#^ salmon fishing again!!" particularly when I thought how pleasant the brief pursuit of grayling or trout might be under these conditions.

The words "true salmon-fishing weather," seemed most cynical, and I think I would've given up, had not a loud splashing torn me out of my lethargy one morning. Finally! Energized and motivated, we fished our passes – but again, without success. Nevertheless, we were in a little better mood as we drove to our truckstop, and were actually (surprise again!) in a hurry to return to the water we'd been whipping for days without success. Salmon fever! The second pass was nearly complete when, suddenly, a silver torpedo shot out of the water and Rüdiger's reel began to produce that wonderful scream. We felt electrified – this monster-fish had showed itself. We all grew nervous and tense, but thanks to our superb bank-side advice, the first runs were handled without a problem... until a very soft "pop" and the fly flew out of the water. Hook broken! The quality of the swearing was both profound and admirable, but I'd best not repeat it here. No matter what, our waiting was over. There were salmon in the river!

At the lowest end of the pool lies a boulder, directly blocking a fast section of water – which, depending on the flow, either gurgled or roared with ferocity on its way to the fjord. This boulder is like a reef off the coast, and causes a large bulge of water to form. Just to its left, a reverse-hydraulic is created (called "the wave"), and this offers an ideal resting place for fish as they arrive in the pool. With great anticipation and concentration, we let our flies drift time and again over this spot. But, we were warned: If you hook a fish here, the chances of landing it are maybe one-in-four. The current below is strong, and you could only pray that your hooked fish wouldn't turn and run down through the 350 yards of fast water to the next pool downstream. Oh, the poor tackle! The question always arose: What tippet should we choose for this spot? Because you had to make every effort to keep a fish from turning downstream, the tippet needed to be as heavy as possible. On the other hand, if the fish succeeded in turning anyway, and the tippet were to hold, then practically everything is lost – or, at least the entire fly line. It's a debate between conscience and mettle.

Many wonderful salmon have gone forfeit at this precise spot where our friend had now hooked into a fish weighing more than 20 pounds. After seeing him lose his first good fish to a broken hook, I wished Rüdiger luck. I watched him wobble a bit (the rod bent to its limit) in his attempt to move the fish out of the danger zone, slowly walking backwards. We tried to reassure him because anyone who's had such a fish hammer his line knows it's helpful to calm down and drop the adrenaline level a few points. For about 10 minutes, the battle could have turned either way, then the fish showed briefly at the surface, and we all thought it was gone. But suddenly it began a dash upstream – a moment of shock, because of the slack line. Then...breathe again...still on! After another 10 minutes, the fish lay on the bank. We all gathered 'round to congratulate the proud fisherman (estimating his prize to weigh-in around 24 pounds), and we knew our waiting had paid off. The congratulatory schnapps rolled slowly and sweetly down our throats.

There were still two days remaining and we had each caught a fish – not always the case, as so many salmon fishermen will confirm from toughened experience. Despite all the hardships (particularly for us beginners), we enjoyed a fabulous introduction to this business of salmon fishing. But, regardless of our success, some of us had not yet paid all their dues. The next day, I hooked a strong fish. The line fairly ripped off my reel, yard after yard of backing disappearing downstream, but then my fish jumped directly opposite my position, near the far bank. At first, I didn't realize it was my fish – my line still pointed directly downstream. Apparently, the fish had returned in a wide circle, costing him a great deal of strength. After 15 minutes and truly wobbly knees, my salmon was ready. We had learned how to grab these fish by the root of their tails and lift them out of the water, but it still remains like a slow-motion film for me: Werner jumped into the water, gripped and lifted the fish, and a let out a cry of joy. I put my rod down and Werner did the same with the fish…which, with two, quick flops, disappeared back into the water. It's useless to describe how I felt…I just went into the forest to be alone.

Günter Henseler, 2-piece, 8 feet; 4-weight
Germany

cm	butt section inch	butt section mm	tip section inch	tip section mm
0	.204	5.20	.071	1.82
5	.211	5.38	.083	2.13
10	.226	5.76	.103	2.64
15	.238	6.07	.122	3.10
20	.252	6.42	.135	3.45
25	.265	6.75	.148	3.78
30	.279	7.11	.161	4.11
35	.295	7.50	.174	4.44
40	.309	7.85	.187	4.75
45	.309	7.85	.200	5.08
48	.309	7.85	.204	5.20

244

245

Günter Henseler, 2-piece, 7 feet 2 inches; 4-weight
Germany (Adjust the form at 12 cm intervals!)

cm	butt section inch	butt section mm	tip section inch	tip section mm
0	.195	4.97	.064	1.64
12	.214	5.44	.077	1.97
24	.223	5.67	.094	2.39
36	.236	6.00	.109	2.78
48	.252	6.42	.130	3.31
60	.254	6.47	.139	3.55
72	.296	6.85	.155	3.94
84	.334	8.50	.166	4.22
96	.334	8.50	.177	4.51
108	.334	8.50	.195	4.97

Hildebrandt, 2-piece, 240 cm; 5/6-weight; type "Elv"
Germany

inch	butt section inch	butt section mm	tip section inch	tip section mm
0	.208	5.30	.074	1.88
5	.214	5.44	.085	2.16
10	.228	5.80	.106	2.70
15	.240	6.12	.124	3.16
20	.254	6.46	.137	3.50
25	.266	6.78	.151	3.86
30	.281	7.14	.164	4.18
35	.296	7.52	.177	4.50
40	.314	8.00	.188	4.80
45	.314	8.00	.202	5.14
48	.314	8.00	.208	5.30

Hildebrandt, 2-piece, 200 cm; 3/4-weight; type "Rio Segre"
Germany

inch	butt section inch	butt section mm	tip section inch	tip section mm
0	.167	4.26	.062	1.58
5	.181	4.60	.070	1.78
10	.192	4.90	.089	2.28
15	.205	5.22	.105	2.68
20	.216	5.50	.119	3.04
25	.240	6.10	.131	3.34
30	.248	6.30	.144	3.66
35	.248	6.30	.155	3.96
40	.248	6.30	.167	4.26

G&G Rodbuilders, 2-piece, 205 cm; 5-weight
Holland (Adjust the form at 10 cm intervals!)

cm	butt section inch	butt section mm	tip section inch	tip section mm
0	.198	5.05	.070	1.80
10	.212	5.40	.078	2.00
20	.220	5.60	.096	2.45
30	.230	5.85	.112	2.85
40	.246	6.25	.124	3.15
50	.260	6.60	.135	3.45
60	.275	7.00	.147	3.75
70	.278	7.30	.159	4.05
80	.299	7.60	.171	4.35
90	.307	7.80	.185	4.70
100	.314	8.00	.192	4.90
102,5	.314	8.00	.197	5.00

G&G Rodbuilders, 2-piece, 240 cm; 3/4-weight
Holland (Adjust the form at 10 cm intervals!)

cm	butt section inch	butt section mm	tip section inch	tip section mm
0	.188	4.80	.066	1.70
10	.200	5.10	.074	1.90
20	.212	5.40	.086	2.20
30	.224	5.70	.094	2.40
40	.236	6.00	.106	2.70
50	.248	6.30	.118	3.00
60	.259	6.60	.129	3.30
70	.267	6.80	.137	3.50
80	.279	7.10	.149	3.80
90	.291	7.40	.161	4.10
100	.299	7.60	.173	4.40
110	.307	7.80	.185	4.70
120	.314	8.00	.188	4.80

Brunner, 2-piece; type "Traun," 228 cm; 6-weight (uneven length sections) Austria

inch	butt section inch	butt section mm	tip section inch	tip section mm
0	.256	6.50	.083	2.13
5	.260	6.60	.104	2.65
10	.277	7.05	.124	3.15
15	.295	7.50	.138	3.51
20	.303	7.70	.165	4.20
25	.318	8.08	.178	4.53
30	.334	8.50	.194	4.95
35	.334	8.50	.207	5.28
40	.334	8.50/37,6	.220	5.60
45			.236	6.00
50			.246	6.25
52			.252	6.40/52.6

Brunner, 2-piece; type "Gebetsroither Super," 200 cm; 5-weight (uneven length sections) Austria

inch	butt section inch	butt section mm	tip section inch	tip section mm
0	.236	6.00	.082	2.10
5	.247	6.28	.108	2.75
10	.258	6.55	.126	3.20
15	.278	7.10	.143	3.65
20	.295	7.50	.157	4.00
25	.303	7.70	.176	4.48
30	.303	7.70/31	.189	4.81
35			.198	5.05
40			.216	5.50
45			.230	5.85
48			.236	6.00/48,6

Garrison 201E, 2-piece, 7 feet Classic taper

inch	butt section inch	butt section mm	tip section inch	tip section mm
0	.183	4.64	.063	1.60
5	.189	4.82	.079	2.00
10	.203	5.16	.099	2.51
15	.215	5.46	.114	2.89
20	.228	5.79	.128	3.25
25	.241	6.12	.141	3.58
30	.254	6.45	.153	3.88
35	.282	7.16	.165	4.19
40	.290	7.36	.177	4.50
42	.290	7.36	.183	4.64

Leonard 50, 2-piece, 8 feet; 6-weight

inch	butt section inch	butt section mm	tip section inch	tip section mm
0	.196	4.98	.067	1.70
5	.202	5.13	.097	2.46
10	.215	5.46	.112	2.84
15	.226	5.74	.127	3.22
20	.242	6.14	.132	3.35
25	.258	6.55	.147	3.73
30	.267	6.78	.159	4.03
35	.280	7.11	.170	4.31
40	.290	7.36	.177	4.49
45	.305	7.74	.190	4.82
48	.320	8.12	.196	4.98

Orvis "Battenkill" 2-piece, 7 feet 6 inches

inch	butt section inch	butt section mm	tip section inch	tip section mm
0	.197	5.00	.082	2.08
5	.220	5.88	.099	2.51
10	.235	5.97	.116	2.94
15	.249	6.32	.129	3.27
20	.270	6.85	.141	3.58
25	.282	7.16	.153	3.88
30	.293	7.44	.161	4.08
35	.306	7.77	.174	4.41
40	.319	8.10	.188	4.77
45	.333	8.45	.197	5.00

Paul Young, 2-piece, 7 feet 6 inches; 4/5-weight Classic taper

inch	butt section inch	butt section mm	tip section inch	tip section mm
0	.218	5.53	.066	1.67
5	.224	5.68	.090	2.28
10	.230	5.84	.106	2.69
15	.244	6.19	.116	2.92
20	.250	6.35	.132	3.35
25	.264	6.70	.142	3.60
30	.274	6.96	.158	4.01
35	.278	7.06	.184	4.67
40	.284	7.21	.202	5.13
45	.288	7.31	.218	5.53

Dickerson, 2-piece, 8 feet; 6-weight

inch	butt section inch	butt section mm	tip section inch	tip section mm
0	.226	5.74	.071	1.80
5	.232	5.89	.080	2.03
10	.250	6.35	.096	2.43
15	.266	6.75	.115	2.92
20	.276	7.01	.135	3.42
25	.292	7.41	.150	3.81
30	.310	7.87	.164	4.16
35	.322	8.17	.176	4.47
40	.354	8.99	.190	4.82
45	.369	9.37	.202	5.13
48	.369	9.37	.216	5.48

Phillipson, 2-piece, 7 feet 6 inches; 4-weight

inch	butt section inch	butt section mm	tip section inch	tip section mm
0	.190	4.82	.066	1.67
5	.204	5.18	.086	2.18
10	.230	5.84	.100	2.54
15	.252	6.40	.114	2.89
20	.268	6.80	.130	3.30
25	.282	7.16	.140	3.55
30	.292	7.41	.150	3.81
35	.338	8.58	.164	4.16
40	.338	8.58	.174	4.41
45	.338	8.58	.190	4.82

Garrison 206, 7 feet 6 inches, 2-piece Classic taper

inch	butt section inch	butt section mm	tip section inch	tip section mm
0	.194	4.92	.063	1.60
5	.206	5.23	.087	1.98
10	.220	5.58	.100	2.54
15	.233	5.91	.117	2.97
20	.247	6.27	.131	3.32
25	.260	6.60	.144	3.65
30	.275	6.98	.156	3.96
35	.306	7.77	.168	4.26
40	.312	7.92	.181	4.60
45	.317	8.05	.194	4.92

Leonard 38, 7 feet, 2-piece; 4-weight

inch	butt section inch	butt section mm	tip section inch	tip section mm
0	.169	4.29	.064	1.62
5	.181	4.60	.080	2.03
10	.198	5.02	.092	2.33
15	.212	5.38	.105	2.66
20	.223	5.66	.118	2.99
25	.235	5.97	.130	3.30
30	.250	6.35	.140	3.55
35	.272	6.90	.148	3.75
40	.290	7.36	.156	3.96
42	.300	7.62	.169	4.29

Orvis "Midge", 7 feet 6 inches, 2-piece

inch	butt section inch	butt section mm	tip section inch	tip section mm
0	.189	4.80	.075	1.90
5	.200	5.08	.095	2.41
10	.221	5.61	.108	2.74
15	.235	5.97	.121	3.07
20	.247	6.27	.132	3.35
25	.260	6.60	.142	3.60
30	.280	7.11	.154	3.91
35	.295	7.49	.161	4.09
40	.310	7.87	.168	4.26
45	.325	8.25	.189	4.80

Dickerson, 2-piece, 7 feet; 4 -weight Classic taper

inch	butt section inch	butt section mm	tip section inch	tip section mm
0	.189	4.80	.061	1.55
5	.195	4.95	.065	1.65
10	.202	5.13	.081	2.05
15	.211	5.35	.094	2.38
20	.227	5.76	.111	2.81
25	.240	6.09	.125	3.17
30	.253	6.42	.139	3.53
35	.305	7.74	.154	3.91
40	.321	8.15	.163	4.14
42	.321	8.15	.175	4.45

Payne, 2-piece, 7 feet; 3/4-weight

inch	butt section inch	butt section mm	tip section inch	tip section mm
0	.161	4.09	.056	1.42
5	.163	4.14	.062	1.57
10	.175	4.44	.074	1.88
15	.189	4.80	.087	2.20
20	.204	5.18	.102	2.59
25	.221	5.61	.117	2.97
30	.232	5.89	.133	3.37
35	.297	7.54	.139	3.53
40	.305	7.74	.154	3.91
42	.305	7.74	.157	3.98

Hardy "Phantom", 2-piece, 8 feet; 5-weight

inch	butt section inch	butt section mm	tip section inch	tip section mm
0	.215	5.46	.078	1.98
5	.227	5.76	.093	2.36
10	.245	6.22	.109	2.76
15	.262	6.65	.126	3.20
20	.273	6.93	.143	3.63
25	.289	7.34	.155	3.93
30	.305	7.74	.168	4.26
35	.320	8.12	.184	4.67
40	.333	8.45	.197	5.00
45	.348	8.84	.209	5.30
48	.364	9.24	.215	5.46

Granger, 7 feet 6 inches, 3-piece; 4-weight

inch	tip section inch	tip section mm	middle section inch	middle section mm	butt section inch	butt section mm
0	.060	1.52	.158	4.01	.244	6.19
5	.076	1.93	.172	4.36	.250	6.35
10	.092	2.33	.186	4.72	.260	6.60
15	.110	2.79	.198	5.02	.272	6.90
20	.122	3.10	.208	5.28	.316	8.02
25	.136	3.45	.211	5.35	.321	8.15
30	.142	3.60	.224	5.69	.321	8.15

Granger, 8 feet, 3-piece; 5-weight

inch	tip section inch	tip section mm	middle section inch	middle section mm	butt section inch	butt section mm
0	.072	1.82	.164	4.16	.242	6.14
5	.074	1.87	.168	4.26	.246	6.24
10	.090	2.28	.186	4.72	.258	6.55
15	.110	2.79	.196	4.97	.276	7.01
20	.124	3.14	.208	5.28	.291	7.39
25	.138	3.50	.218	5.53	.346	8.78
30	.148	3.76	.228	5.79	.351	8.91
32	.152	3.86	.236	5.99	.356	9.04

Fred Devine, 7 feet 6 inches, 3-piece; 3/4-weight

inch	tip section inch	tip section mm	middle section inch	middle section mm	butt section inch	butt section mm
0	.060	1.52	.158	4.01	.226	5.74
5	.080	2.03	.164	4.16	.240	6.09
10	.098	2.48	.178	4.52	.261	6.62
15	.112	2.84	.184	4.67	.276	7.01
20	.124	3.14	.199	5.05	.284	7.21
25	.136	3.45	.211	5.36	.286	7.26
30	.148	3.76	.226	5.74	.291	7.39

Payne, 8 feet, 3-piece; 5-weight Classic taper

inch	tip section inch	tip section mm	middle section inch	middle section mm	butt section inch	butt section mm
0	.062	1.57	.168	4.26	.252	6.40
5	.067	1.70	.174	4.41	.256	6.50
10	.088	2.23	.188	4.77	.268	6.80
15	.107	2.71	.200	5.08	.282	7.16
20	.119	3.02	.213	5.41	.302	7.67
25	.131	3.32	.224	5.69	.354	8.99
30	.142	3.60	.234	5.94	.354	8.99
32	.154	3.91	.240	6.09	.354	8.99

Gillum, 8 feet 6 inches, 3-piece; 6/7-weight

inch	tip section inch	tip section mm	middle section inch	middle section mm	butt section	butt section mm
0	.068	1.72	.188	4.77	inch	7.31
5	.082	2.08	.196	4.98	.288	7.54
10	.098	2.49	.208	5.28	.297	7.84
15	.112	2.84	.226	5.74	.309	8.23
20	.130	3.30	.242	6.14	.324	8.63
25	.142	3.60	.254	6.45	.340	9.70
30	.164	4.16	.270	6.85	.382	9.80
35	.174	4.42	.276	7.01	.386	9.80
					.386	

Heddon, 8 feet, 3-piece; 5/6-weight

inch	tip section inch	tip section mm	middle section inch	middle section mm	butt section inch	butt section mm
0	.066	1.67	.166	4.21	.248	6.29
5	.074	1.88	.170	4.31	.256	6.50
10	.088	2.23	.184	4.67	.268	6.80
15	.102	2.59	.202	5.08	.282	7.16
20	.118	2.99	.216	5.33	.290	7.36
25	.128	3.25	.226	5.74	.371	9.42
30	.142	3.60	.240	6.09	.371	9.42
32	.156	3.96	.246	6.24	.371	9.42

Fishing tackle requires little care. Follow just a few recommendations, and rods and reels will last a lifetime.

Fishing and care

"Split-cane rods are remarkably sturdy.
Some have remained in use for more
than 80 years."

Quite Robust

Split bamboo rods are extremely robust, much more so than one would think. Nevertheless, when fishing, handling or storing them, a few considerations will contribute to continued enjoyment of these rods.

In conversations, even with other fishermen, I hear prejudices against split-bamboo rods, but the complaints all sound as if they originated from publications in the 1950s – and they are all quite incorrect.
Most typically, I hear, "I'd love to fish with a bamboo rod, but they're so fragile."
Sometimes, when giving one of my public lectures, I start with a demonstration. I throw the butt-section of a bamboo rod on the floor and jump up and down on it with both feet. When the shock of the audience dies down, I pass the mistreated rod section around to be checked for damage. Invariably, the audience registers surprise upon seeing that the rod has suffered very little, and it delights me when folks finally recognize split-bamboo's durability. At the end of my lectures, I ask (a little mischievously) if someone in the audience would loan me their graphite rod for the same test. To date, I've not had a single volunteer. Today's split-bamboo rods are at least as durable as graphite rods!

By following only a few rules, the owner of a bamboo rod can enjoy 20 to 30 years of pleasure from a wonderful fishing instrument.

Because of their solid construction, bamboo rods are unlikely to break. Even a weighted nymph banging against the tip, usually only damages the finish. Such chips should be repaired as soon as possible, however, and usually all that's needed is a little touch-up with a brush. This must be taken care of because, otherwise, moisture will begin to penetrate the unprotected area, soon damaging the bamboo.

Occasionally, I'll build a rod section that doesn't work out for me, and I use these pieces for demonstrations – asking someone from the audience to come up and break one of my "mistakes" in two. Amusingly, even strong men start to sweat before breaking a butt section. Less strength is necessary for a tip, of course, but the person's arms often become crossed before the piece breaks. When you witness this, even a couple times, you'll begin to appreciate the durability of your rods, and also gain confidence in how you play a fish. Upon hook-up, I recently heard a bamboo-convert saying, "I'm not giving him an inch!"

I'm often asked how best to store a bamboo rod – folks always hear that the rod should be hung. Of course, this is always fine, but you can also store them in a rod-stand. Rod-stands, in several basic models, can be built quickly and easily, as shown here. Only your imagination limits further developments.

Corner Rod Holder

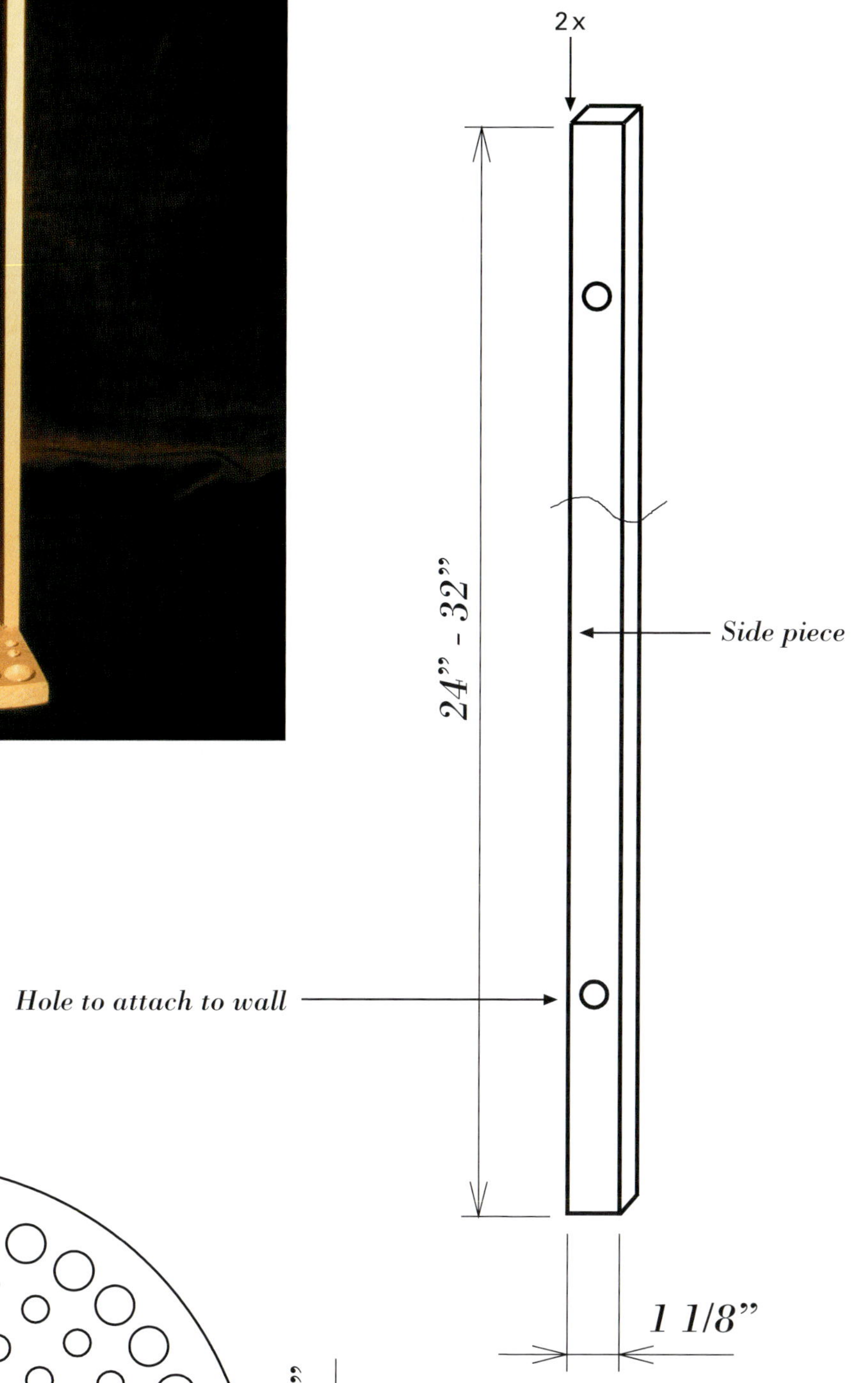

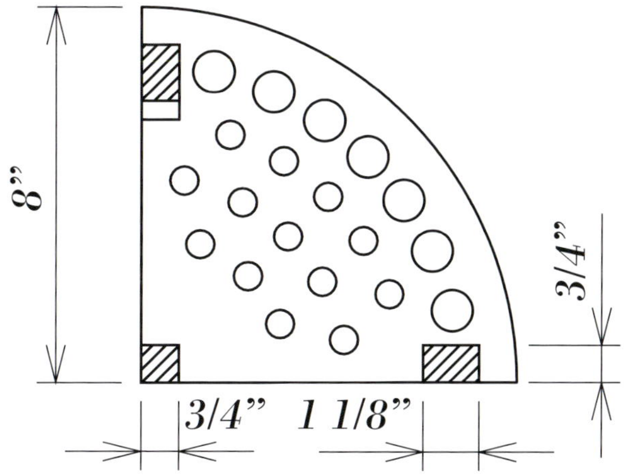

Hole diameters: 7/8" and 5/8"

Hanging/Standing Version

258

259 *Elegant rod holder.*

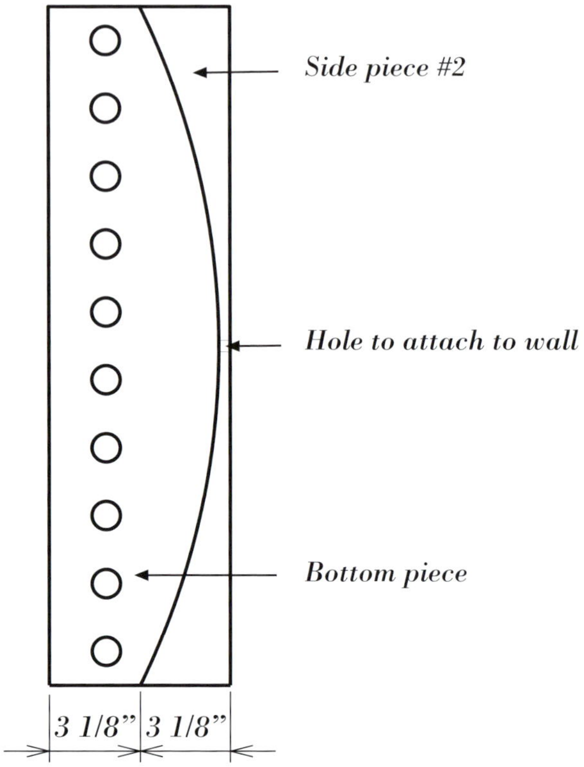

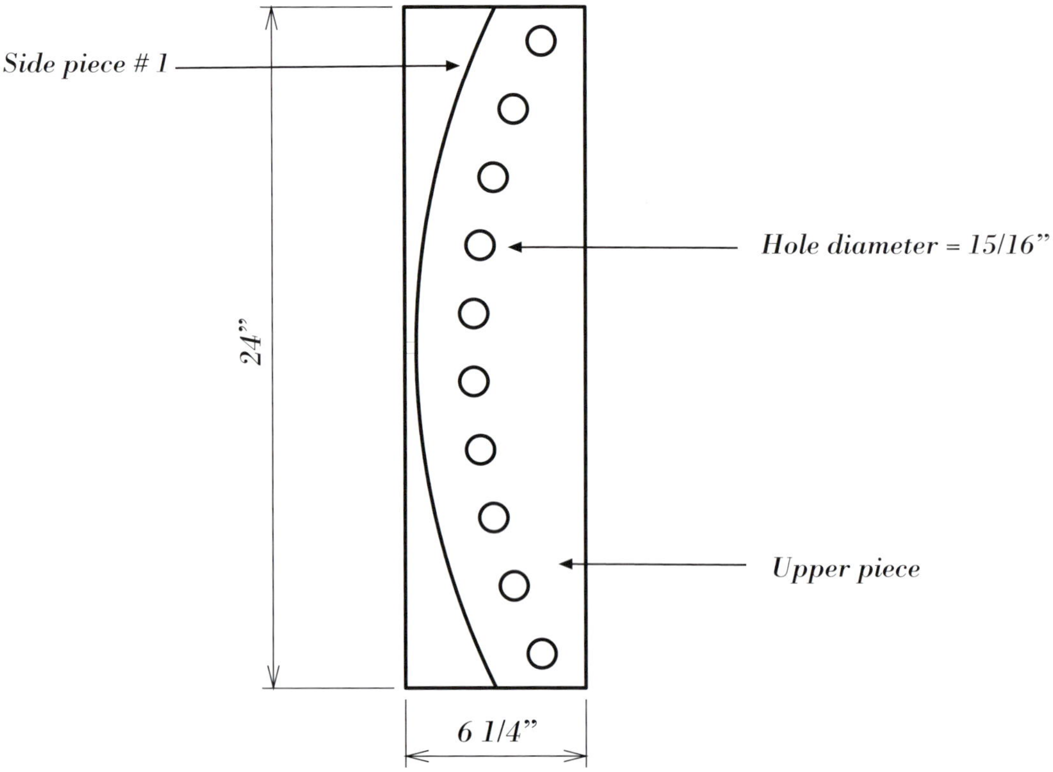

If you leave your rod sections assembled, the ferrules may become oxidized and jammed, and they may not want to come apart again. In this case, only a second person can help. You stand facing one another, each of you grasping a butt section with one hand and a tip section with the other. Then, at the same time, both people pull the rod steadily and strongly apart. A small piece of rubber (cut from a bicycle inner-tube) will prevent your hands from slipping along the blank.

It's most important that you avoid twisting the sections – either when seating the ferrule parts, or when pulling them apart. Always move the ferrule slide straight in and straight out. The following rule applies:
Put the rod together; put your hands together.
Pull the rod apart; place your hands apart.

This means, when aligning the two ferrule parts for assembly, keep your hands close together. But when pulling the sections apart, it's important to avoid the risk of kinking at the ferrule, so separate your hands on each section as far as possible.
A ferrule plug should be used to keep dirt out of the ferrule.

To make a ferrule plug, turn a small piece of wood on the lathe (equal to the outer diameter of the ferrule) and then drill a small hole partially into one end. Insert a short piece of threaded rod into this hole and glue the rod in place. Next, punch out a small piece of cork and drill this with a similar-sized hole. Now, simply glue the cork onto the exposed, threaded rod. When the assembly dries, use 220-grit sandpaper to reduce the cork and match it to the inner-diameter of your ferrule.

A lot of fuss is required to produce these small plugs, but they're very important. Be warned, however! They have the peculiar habit of becoming invisible while fishing. That is, you've just lost them! After years of intensive field research and study, I recently discovered how to resolve the puzzling disappearance of ferrule plugs. When you put your waders on, stick the ferrule plugs in your street shoes. Then, when you've finished fishing, simply put your shoes on again. At once, the plugs re-appear. Remarkable! But it really works.

No split-bamboo rod is built to lift a fish out of the water.
Overloading can occur if the rod is held at an improper angle while playing a fish. Particular care should be taken to avoid too great an angle between the rod and the surface of the water. Never point your tip high. When held incorrectly over a period of time, the tip section becomes over-stressed and causes a permanent bend or "set." Especially when playing a large and heavy fish, it's good practice to turn the rod occasionally on its "back." That is, rotate the rod in your hand so the reel and guides face upward: The tip will now bend in a direction opposite to its guides.

260

261

Walter Brunner shows how to hold a split-cane rod when playing larger fish: The rod tip must not be over-stressed. Photo: Thomas Wölfle.

I can think of only one other method to ruin your prized possession: Don't bother to dry it off after fishing! Just go ahead and stuff the rod, wet, into its bag. Then, put the wet rod and its sack into your tube, screw the lid on, and keep it in your warm house for a few days. Success is guaranteed! This technique also works well for other types of rods.

On the other hand, if you want to enjoy your rod for a long time, dry it well, and store it dry. It's only a matter of choice whether you hang it in its bag or keep it in an open rod-case. Either way, you don't have to go as far as one of my American friends who keeps his rods nicely lined up in the bathroom. It's a mystery, but he claims that, overall, this is the driest room in his house, adding, "no thief would think to look for my valuable rods in the bathroom."

Many rod-cases have drawbacks. They're not ventilated and they're often black. Leave your rod in such a case (locked in the trunk of your car with the sun beating down), and it can be subjected to temperatures exceeding 140° F. This will damage any rod.

If you'd like to do something special for your prized piece, you might wipe your rod occasionally with a dab of ordinary furniture polish on a rag. Further care is not necessary.

I think much of the folklore about fragility comes from the days when split-bamboo rods were built with fish glue – and varnish, too, was anything but durable. Today, however, nearly all the glues we use can endure great stress, and some glues are even stronger than the material they hold together. And, as to varnish, some of the new products are so tough, a rod can even withstand banging on rocks.

Fifteen Ways to Leave Your Lover – or Fifteen Good Ways to Break Your Rod

After years of painful tests, carried out through personal experience, I can assure you that, from the very start, the only way to protect your rod is never to use it! Immediately after purchasing your rod, you should store it in its bag and tube in a protected place at home – preferably, lying horizontally in a controlled climate.

Think about it. The moment you unpack your rod, the world becomes dangerous – very dangerous. Just ask your friends and colleagues. The question of a broken rod always ends in silence. Apparently no one, truly no one, has ever broken his precious bamboo rod. Still, through the silence, tears may well-up in the eyes of one fisherman or the other, and upon departing from one friend, I'm sure I actually heard sobbing.

In what follows, I'll be strictly scientific as I rank the various methods of destruction, working in order of the most common occurrences. This hasn't always been easy, and I don't suppose I've included all possible permutations. For this reason, I devised separate categories for each scenario, followed by particular descriptions for the most dangerous and common methods.

"Done for"

On the Water

1. The simplest way, especially while releasing a fish, is to place your rod flat on the ground next to you – or just behind – and then take a little step to the side or back. (Yields a simple "crack," perhaps muffled a little by the grass.)

2. Also easily accomplished, carry the rod proudly with its tip in front of you. Here, there are two possible variations:
   a. You poke the searching rod tip against some carefully-positioned obstacle (fenceposts work particularly well), or;
   b. You stumble across a twig (or flounder in your clumsy waders) and fall forward without letting go of the rod. (Long "craaaackkkk".)

Arrival and Departure

The automobile, always a reliable stronghold of delights, offers almost limitless possibilities. Here are the most important:

3. The rod (fully-assembled, either at the beginning or the end of a windy day of fishing) is leaned against the outer corner of your open car door. A little puff of wind does the trick nicely.... (A brief "scritch" sound.)

4. The trunk lid is also happy to oblige. First, we fish until dark (yet again), then the rod is taken apart and laid lengthwise in the trunk. Because we're in a hurry (maybe the hotel restaurant is still open!), we slam the trunk shut. (One hears only the trunk – guillotined pieces of bamboo wafting, silently, to the ground.)

5. Even better: In order to take off wet clothes (of course, it rained half the day), put your rod on the car's roof, forget it is there (ummm, nice and toasty inside...), then wonder what made that "clunk" while backing up. Finally, you simply drive over the rod. (Here, one hears no sound because the engine is running. But as an added bonus, there's every chance you may have been fortunate enough to flatten your favorite reel.)

Changing Location

6. By comparison to the others, this next possibility is almost exotic. Since we're usually too lazy to walk to our next fishing spot, we drive the car. It's a form of efficiency, really, and the same explanation justifies leaving the rod assembled. So, we open the sunroof, put the rod (or several rods, since we're all friends here) on the rear, parcel shelf – their tips pointing upward and through the sunroof. If you lack a sunroof, a rolled-down front window works just as nicely. Next, we want to find a dandy, low-hanging branch! (Depending on your speed, this produces either a brief "chuck" or a long and tiresome scraping sound.) In insider circles, this method is also known as the "four-in-one."

7. Let's return to simple fishing. The fly snags somewhere on a rock or a plant in the water, but we need to recover it without jeopardizing our inventory of a thousand flies, stashed in various boxes in our vest. So, we try to free the fly with several, smart, upward yanks on the rod. (Less dramatic, often we hear only a puzzling "creak," sounding almost like "spliiiitt" coming from near a ferrule.)

8. As all rod-makers will agree, when they hear: "I dunno…all of a sudden, the tip just broke off during my back-cast!" this translates into English as: "I was casting a heavily-weighted nymph (tied with a gold bead, and lead wire), but my tailing-loop didn't quite make it past the rod and smacked the tip a few inches below its top." (Smooth break, slight "tick," no real sound – a true mystery!)

For me, one of the most wonderful ways to produce the inimitable sound of shattering bamboo is devised during the back-cast (it's best to use the double-haul for the benefit of those observers a few yards off). Here's the deal. Catch your fly on a bush behind you, and then begin your forward cast – giving it the Full Monty with your hardiest haul! (The sound will depend on the rod's type and length, but often gets your attention.)

9. Other well-established possibilities arrive on those occasions when your leader wraps itself around the tip of your rod. Whatever you do, don't rest the butt and reel on the ground (they could get dirty); or, if standing in the river, don't put the butt under water (it could get wet!). Instead, try to untangle the leader with just one hand, while using the other to grab the rod near its tip. Then hold the rod as horizontally as possible. (Strong, simple "crack".)

The Boat

10. A boat offers nearly as many possibilities as does your car for sending a rod to the great Rod-Recycling-Center in the sky. I will, therefore, limit myself. One should (and particularly with small boats) thoroughly fasten all rods across the tops of the seats to avoid being scratched, then put your first foot into that rocking boat....

11. A variation with our boat-and-rod techniques calls for an outboard motor. For trolling, we'll need a strongly-set drag, then we want to catch the line in the propeller, and in mere fractions of a second, we can turn any rod into chop-sticks. (Alas, the outboard will be loud and could rob us of our audio-effect.)

Home Sweet Home

12. Here are some tips for preparing to return home. When packing everything together, first throw the rod in the car trunk (if possible, neither in its sack, nor certainly, in the rod tube). Then, throw all other equipment on top. (This produces a sound you just can't make out.)

13. If you return home on foot, leave the rod assembled, if possible, and enter your lodging using as many doors as possible. (See number 3.)

14. The most elegant method has been saved for last. This technique takes place far from the water and the many splendid opportunities offered-up by Mother Nature – namely, in your living room. Good fishing-friends are visiting; it's February; stories are told around the fire during the off-season – and then, out comes the Christmas present! It's been unpacked and assembled, but it's still virginal. The rod is admired, its fantastic action praised. Then, after several drinks, you must pass it around to one and all, asking each to demonstrate its flexing with élan. Then, from nowhere, comes the corner of that bookshelf....

15. And your version...?

266

267

Collecting historical equipment can provide a lot of pleasure, but one needs to determine, beforehand, the true value of a particular piece.

Collecting

"In many cases, the value of an old split-bamboo rod will be over-estimated!"

Hunters and Collectors

Some folks buy everything that looks like bamboo; others hunt for decades to find a particular rod, while still another clan collects only information about rods. There are many ways to treasure our split-cane rods.

To be perfectly clear at the outset, it won't be easy to find the rod that Ernest Hemingway fished. But who knows – sometimes one comes across an unusual rod, exchanges a little money, and the proud, new owner discovers only later that he stumbled onto a treasure.

For those who might like to collect split-bamboo rods, a few suggestions may help the unsuspecting enthusiast to avoid what I did many years ago. I used to be one of those guys that bought anything looking like bamboo, only to learn later that much of it was only the cheap, mass-produced stuff made in Japan during the 1960s.

Before beginning to collect rods, you need to consider whether the valued item is only to be admired or if you actually want to fish with it. Indeed, many old rods are beautiful objects that fill us with nostalgia, but many are actually unsuited for fishing and really belong on the wall or in a showcase.

Although most of these old rods may be relatively inexpensive, only the collector's resources can determine how much a particular piece of fishing history is worth. Such rods, nowadays, will cost between $60 and $150, but most of these will have taken a considerable "set" in their tip sections (having been "fished out"), and many will be over 50 years old.

Old rods, still suitable for fishing, actually can be found rather easily, but these are often in lengths and actions that were popular 50 to 60 years ago. Typically, they'll be 9 or 10-foot "monsters," with average weights of a pound and more, and built for 5- and 6-weight lines, no longer serving today's needs. When casting these rods, you need to brace yourself sturdily to prevent being ripped to the rear on your back-cast.

Split-bamboo rods in lengths between 7 and 8 feet are in much greater demand, and unfortunately, are correspondingly expensive. Certain Hardy rods in excellent condition (for example the "CC de France" or "Marvel" models) may cost the collector anything from $1200 to $1800.

The most desirable examples, built by the most famous American rod-makers, can cost as much as $13,000 if in perfect condition. At the same time, a Leonard rod from the 1960s that's still in good condition will be well worth its price of $2500, and likely to enjoy increased value over the coming years. Choosing to fish with such equipment might seem to border on elitism or snobbery, yet I know a number of people who use their fine, bamboo rods regularly and are, in no way, snobs.

The average collector will want to know the basic criteria for purchasing. You should begin by evaluating the rod's general appearance, its apparent physical condition, and with particular attention to the following questions:

1. What is the condition of its finish?
2. Does the rod exist in its original length, or is a tip-section a little shorter than the butt? The latter usually indicates a broken tip, fitted with a new tip-top.
3. Is the hardware in good condition; can a reel be securely fastened?
4. What's the condition of the ferrules (can they be put together, or, as in most cases, are they worn and loose)?
5. Are all guides present?
6. What is the condition of the wrappings?
7. Is the grip still in good condition, or was it reshaped at some point?

In most cases, at least two or three of these questions will result in negative answers, and if so, the rod may no longer suitable for fishing. These rods belong on the wall or in a display case, unless you're willing to invest a lot of time or money for a thorough renovation – usually, not worth the effort. I'm often asked about restoring a rod, but in 90% of the cases, I recommend against doing so because of the costs involved. Consider the effort. Usually, the guides must be removed and the finish stripped. Then, the rod needs to be totally re-done with new guides, wrappings and varnish. In addition, it's not unusual that new ferrules and a new grip may also be necessary, and the list grows.

A notable exception to this warning, however, can be the truly historical piece. The earlier chapter on the history of rod-making should be of help as a modest introduction to collectable equipment. It can be a great pleasure to trace the history and origins of one's rod, for in most cases, it's possible to discover the date and the maker (or company) who produced it. Doing so, often involves a good bit of research, and you'll need to become well-informed to make the necessary comparisons.

Important identifying features are:

- Rod inscriptions
- Serial numbers on the rod or hardware
- Trademarks or emblems on the rod
- Special wrapping
- Particular types of ferrules or reelseat hardware
- Grip shape.

One of the simplest ways to become informed is to familiarize yourself with some of the dealers who sell such tackle and publish catalogs on a regular basis. A few of those to be included in this group, are:

1. Udo Hildebrand, Bremer Str. 26A, D-34385 Bad Karlshafen, Germany
2. Len Codella, 2201 South Carnegie Drive, Inverness, Florida 34450, USA
3. Carmine Lisella, 4 Kolka Lane, New City, New York 10956, USA.

Studying their catalogs will give a good overview of the range of rods on the market, and at what prices. At once, you'll encounter terms describing a rod's condition. These have become more-or-less standardized, and are used to determine the price-range for that model. Depending on condition, a good and useable rod can cost between $250 and $1700. A few of the more important and internationally-common terms are:

"New" = New, never used
"As new" = As good as new, probably unused
"Mint" = Essentially un-fished, little indication of use
"Excellent" = Very good condition with some indications of use
"Very Good" = Indications of use, but good general condition
"Good" = Used and shows it, still okay
"Needs cleaning" = Needs overhauling
"Needs refinishing" = Must be restored
"Refinished" = Has been restored.

Of course, you can expect every dealer to exercise a little "freedom" in applying these descriptions, but, should the buyer not agree with the rod's condition, good dealers always have a return policy. Below, is a compilation of the rods and rod-makers most frequently collected, and most likely to remain fishable. The historical examples (80-to-100 years old, or more) reflect strictly collectors' prices – always determined on the basis of the rod's rarity and its condition. An example, here, would be the rods made by the German companies, "Hildebrand" and "Storck" (Munich). So few rods from these companies remain in existence that it's impossible to establish even an approximate price.

Most manufacturers marketed a variety of models over the years, and for this reason, the following lists are not complete. The indicated prices are shown at the upper end of each rod's range, and have been extracted from auction results and catalogs – as well as from 2001-2004 price-lists offered by the better dealers in Germany, England, and the USA. Price variations can depend upon the country. A rod from Hardy, for example, will often cost less in the USA than in Europe, and correspondingly, American rods are sometimes less expensive in Europe. As is the case for so many other collectors' items, rod prices, too, fluctuate and are dependent on exchange-rates and the general state of the economy.

In addition to bamboo rods, collectors also regard antique reels and catalogs to be highly desirable.

Well-Known rod-builders

- Allcock & Co., Ltd.
- Brunner Austria
- Cross Rod Co.
- Deutsche Angelgeräte Manufaktur DAM
- Fred Devine Rod Co.
- Lyle L. Dickerson
- Edwards & Son Rod Co.
- Farlow & Co., Ltd.
- Fosters of Ashburne
- Everett Garrison
- Harold Steel Gillum
- Goodwin Granger Rod Co.
- Hardy Brothers Ltd.
- Heddon Rod Co.
- H.L. Leonard Rod Co.
- Noris Nürnberg
- Orvis Co., Inc.
- Jim Payne
- Pezon & Michel
- Phillipson Rod Co.
- E.C. Powell
- Sharps of Aberdeen
- South Bend Bait Co.
- F.E. Thomas Bangor
- Thomas & Thomas
- R.L. Winston Rod Co.
- Wright & McGill Rod. Co
- Paul Young

Allcock & Co., Ltd.

Model	Length	Pieces	Line Weight	Notes	Price US $
Londsdale	**9 ft**	**3/2**	**5**		**54**
Medina	**8 ft**	**2/1**			**600**
The Imperial Standard	**14 ft**	**3/2**			**252**

Brunner Austria

Model	Length	Pieces	Line Weight	Notes	Price US $
Austria	**230 cm**	**2/1**	**7/8**	**7 ft 6 1/2in**	**300**
Cherie	**185 cm**	**2/2**	**5/6**	**6 ft 1 in**	**780**
Gebetsroither Super	**200 cm**	**2/1**	**5/6**	**6 ft 7 in**	**630**
Orbigo	**245 cm**	**2/1**	**5/6**	**8 ft 1/2 in**	**480**
Pielach	**230 cm**	**2/1**	**4/5**	**7 ft 6 1/2 in**	**540**
Salza	**190cm**	**2/1**	**4**	**6 ft 3 in**	**540**
Traun	**228 cm**	**2/1**	**5/6**	**7 ft 6 in**	**420**
WB- Spezial	**175 cm**	**2/1**	**4/5**	**5 ft 9 in**	**480**

Deutsche Angelgeräte Manufaktur D. A. M.

D. A. M. marketed a large and wide range of rods during its long history. Those that are neither rare nor very old sell for $50-$180, depending on condition.

Fred Devin Rod Co.

Model	Length	Pieces	Line Weight	Notes	Price US $
Rainbow	8 ft 6 in	3/2	5		750

Lyle L. Dickerson

Model	Length	Pieces	Line Weight	Notes	Price US $
561710 RB	7 ft 6 in	3/2			4020
7012	7 ft	2/1	4		8280
7012	7 ft	2/2			7860
7012 E	7 ft	2/2	4/5		3720
7612	7 ft 6 in	2/2			2760
8012 - 5X	8 ft	2/2			3720
8013	8 ft	2/2			3720
8013-48	8 ft	2/2			4320
801510 D	8 ft	3/2			1620
861711	8 ft 6 in	3/2	5		3000
861711	8 ft 6 in	3/2			2700
961913 - 47	9 ft 6 in	3/2	Salmon		1140

Edwards & Son Rod Co.

Model	Length	Pieces	Line Weight	Notes	Price US $
Quadrate	7 ft 6 in	2/2	5	4-sided	2160
Quadrate	8 ft	2/2	6	4-sided	2040
Special	8 ft	3/2	5		900
Special	8 ft 6 in	3/2	5/6		810

Fosters of Ashburne

Model	Length	Pieces	Line Weight	Notes	Price US $
The Airsprite	7 ft 6 in	2/1	5		324
The Airsprite	7 ft 6 in	2/1	5		336
The Whisp	6 ft	2/1	4/5		252

Farlow & Co., Ltd

Model	Length	Pieces	Line Weight	Notes	Price US $
Farlows Fife		3/2			72
Holdfast	9 ft 6 in	3/1			114
Parabolic Still Water	9 ft 6 in	2/2	6		294
The Midge	7 ft	2/1	4		240

Everett Garrison

274 Garrison rods are seldom on the market, and I've known some models to bring as much as $6000-
275 $7200 at auction. Over the last few years, the following models have been sold.

Everett Garrison

Model	Length	Pieces	Line Weight	Notes	Price US $
195	6 ft 9 in	2/2			6960
201	7 ft	2/2			4800
204	7 ft 6 in	2/2			4200
206-076-1	7 ft 6 in	2/2			4200
212	8 ft				1920
212 J-80-1	8 ft	3/2			4920
218	9 ft	3/2	8		3000
220	8 ft 6 in	2/2	7		6960

Harold Steel Gillum

Model	Length	Pieces	Line Weight	Notes	Price US $
1-715	7 ft 6 in	2/2			6600
1-803	6 ft 10 in	2/3			7320
1-852	8 ft	2/2			4320
1-858	8 ft 7 in	2/2	7		2460
1893	8 ft	2/2			4680
1-904	6 ft 6 in	2/2			6600
1-917	7 ft	2/2			6600
196-1	7 ft 6 in	2/2		restored	1620
1-963	6 ft 6 in	2/2			6240
Deluxe	8 ft 6 in	3/2			3060
Salmon	9 ft 3 in	3/2	9		3000
	6 ft 6 in	2/2			4740

Goodwin Granger Rod Co.

Model	Length	Pieces	Line Weight	Notes	Price US $
Aristocrat	7 ft	2/2	5		900
Aristocrat	7 ft	2/2	5	restored	744
Champion	9 ft	3/2	6		210
Deluxe	9 ft	3/2	5		390
Favorite	9 ft	3/2	6		510
Premier	8 ft 6 in	3/2	5		780
Special	7 ft 6 in	3/2	4/5		1320
Special	8 ft 6 in	3/2			660
Special	9 ft	3/2	6		480
Victory	7 ft	2/2			1020
Victory	8 ft 6 in	3/2			630

Hardy Brothers Ltd

An entire book would be necessary to list all the models produced by this company – in addition, Hardy also produced a variety of special models in very small numbers. Almost all tapers can still be ordered today. Happily, the company used serial numbers for many years, making the approximate year of a Hardy rod easy to determine.

Greenheart

A.	1900-1916
B.	1916-1920
C.	1920-1922
D.	1922-1924
E.	1924

Split Bamboo

Year	Number		Number
1890	15452		
1900	50745		
1903	94071		
1904	100887		
1906	A 13452		
1927	E 6681		
1928	E 11716		
1931	E 20923	-	E 22183
1932	E 22814	-	E 25141
1933	E 25142	-	E 28698
1934	E 28669	-	E 32102
1935	E 32103	-	E 36204
1936	E 36205	-	E 40002
1937	E 40003	-	E 45445
1938	E 45446	-	E 49492
1939	E 49493	-	E 52331
1940	E 52332	-	E 53664
1941	E 53645	-	E 55130
1942	E 55131	-	E 56090
1943	E 56091	-	E 56399
1944	E 56400	-	E 56855
1945	E 56856	-	E 57900
1946	E 57901	-	E 60708
1947	E 57901	-	E 63386
1948	E 63387	-	E 67200
1949	E 67201	-	E 70990
1950	E 70991	-	E 75100

Year	Number		Number
1951	E 75101	-	E 81000
1952	E 81001	-	E 86200
1953	E 86201	-	E 91000
1954	E 91001	-	E 96202
1955	E 96203	-	E 98999
and	H 101	-	H 4600
1956	H 4601	-	H 10121
1957	H 10122	-	H 14127
1958	H 14128	-	H 20678
1959	H 20679	-	H 27533
1960	H 27534	-	H 35183
1961	H 35148	-	H 48465
1962	H 48466	-	H 52737
1963	H 52738	-	H 58199
1964	H 58200	-	H 62932
1965	H 62933	-	H 69100
1966	H 69101	-	A
1967	S		
1968	J		
1969	B		
1970	K		
1971	Z		
1972	O		
1973	C		
1974	Y		
1975	L		
1976	D		

The serial numbers probably indicate the number of rods made by Hardy. Only about three hundred rods were produced in certain years during the Second World War, but this number climbed to 13,317 in 1961. Assuming five working-days per week, this would indicate a daily production of about fifty-one rods!

In the 1990s, some "classic" models were reintroduced in the USA:

Model	Length	Pieces	Line Weight	Notes	Price US $
Marvel	7 ft	3/2	4		2160
Marvel	7 ft 6 in	3/2	4		2220
Added to these, were "lightweight" models:					
Blue Ridge	6 ft	2/2	4		1758
Catskill	6 ft 8 in	2/2	4		1770
CC de France	7 ft	2/2	4/5		1890
Phantom	6 ft 10 in	2/2	5		1734
Yellowstone	7 ft 2 in	2/2	5		1794

Prices for the new models are between $1560 and $1920. Below, I present only a small, representative selection of the many Hardy models. The note, "post-num.," (post numbers), means that the model was made after 1967.

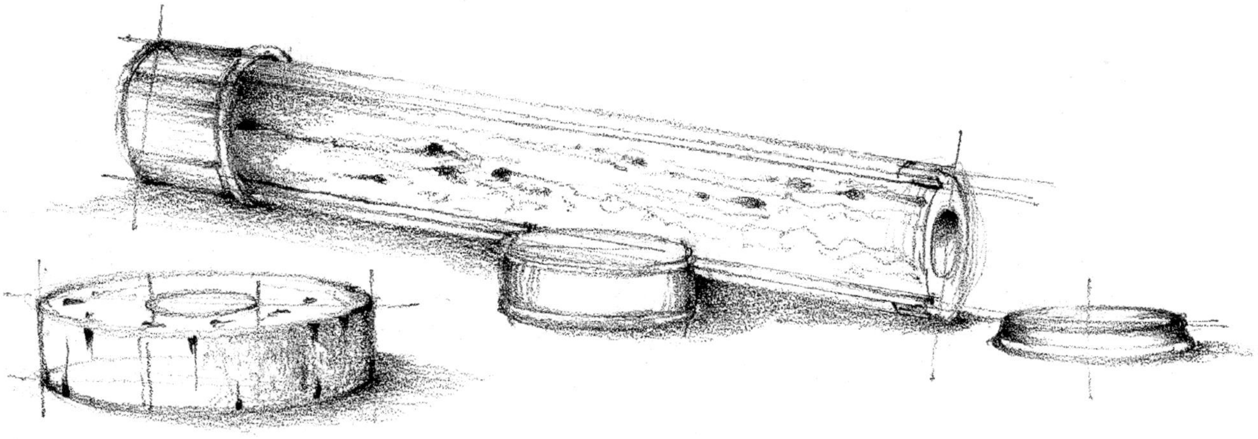

Model	Length	Pieces	Line Weight	Notes	Price US $
AHE Wood	12 ft	3/2			274
AHE Wood	12 ft	3/1			162
CC de France	8 ft	2/1	6	1958	690
CC de France	9 ft	3/2		1952	1020
Fairchild	9 ft	3/2		1954	384
Fairy	9 ft	3/2		1960	600
Gold Medal	9 ft 6 in	3/2		1898	426
Gold Medal	14 ft	3/2		1901	230
Hollolight	9 ft 6 in	3/1		1960	420
Hollolight	9 ft 6 in	3/2		1961	504
Houghton	10 ft 6 in	3/2		1920	246
Houghton	9 ft 6 in	3/1		1955	257
JJH Triumph	8 ft 9 in	2/1		1957	248
JJH Triumph	8 ft 9 in	2/1		1958	300
JJH Triumph	8 ft 9 in	2/1		post num.	600
Keith Rollo	9 ft	3/1			514
Knockabout	9 ft 6 in	2/1		1963	684
L.R.H.	14 ft	3/2		1950	384
L.R.H. Dry Wet	9 ft 3 in	3/1		1959	600
L.R.H. Greased Line	13 ft	3/2		1958	1010
Marvel	7 ft 6 in	3/2	4	1956	1320
Marvel	7 ft 6 in	3/2	4	1958	1800
Marvel	7 ft 6 in	3/2		1968	1542
Palakona	8 ft 6 in	2/1		post num.	768
Palakona	8 ft 9 in	2/1		post num.	684
Perfection	8 ft 6 in				548
Perfection	9 ft	2/1	5	post num.	334
Perfection	9 ft 6 in	2/1		post num.	274
Phantom	6 ft 10 in	2/1		post num.	1200
Phantom Hollokona	9 ft	2/1		1961	514
Pope	10 ft	2/1		1909	282
Special Itchen	9 ft 6 in	2/2			720
Tourney	8 ft 6 in	2/1		1951	770
Viscount Grey	10 ft 6 in	2/1			282
Wye	11 ft	3/1			257
Wye	12 ft 6 in	3/2			384
Wye	13 ft 6 in	3/2			308
Wye	15 ft	3/1			248

Heddon Rod Co.

Model	Length	Pieces	Line Weight	Notes	Price US $
35 featherweight	7 ft 6 in	2/2		Deluxe	996
60	8 ft 6 in	3/2			612
# 10	7 ft 6 in	3/2	5		780
# 20	8 ft	3/2	5		600
# 14	8 ft	3/2	5		240
# 14	9 ft	3/2	6		390
# 35	7 ft 6 in	2/2			1008
Black Beauty	7 ft 6 in	3/2	5		930
Black Beauty	8 ft	3/2	5		690
Black Beauty	8 ft	3/2	5		690
Black Beauty	9 ft	3/2	7		480
Deluxe 35		2/2			1140
Deluxe Peerless	8 ft 6 in	3/2	5/6		900
Deluxe Peerless #35	9 ft	3/2	6		570
Deluxe Peerless #35	9 ft	3/2	7		510
Deluxe Peerless #35	9 ft	3/2	7		660
Deluxe Peerless #35	8 ft 6 in	3/2	5		780
Dowagiac	9 ft	3/2	6		390
Expert 125	8 ft 6 in	3/2			564
Expert #125	8 ft 6 in	3/2			540
Riptide	9 ft	3/2	7/8		420
Thorobred #14	8 ft	3/2	5		660
Thorobred #14	8 ft 6 in	3/2	6/7		450
Troutmaster	8 ft 6 in	3/2	5		450

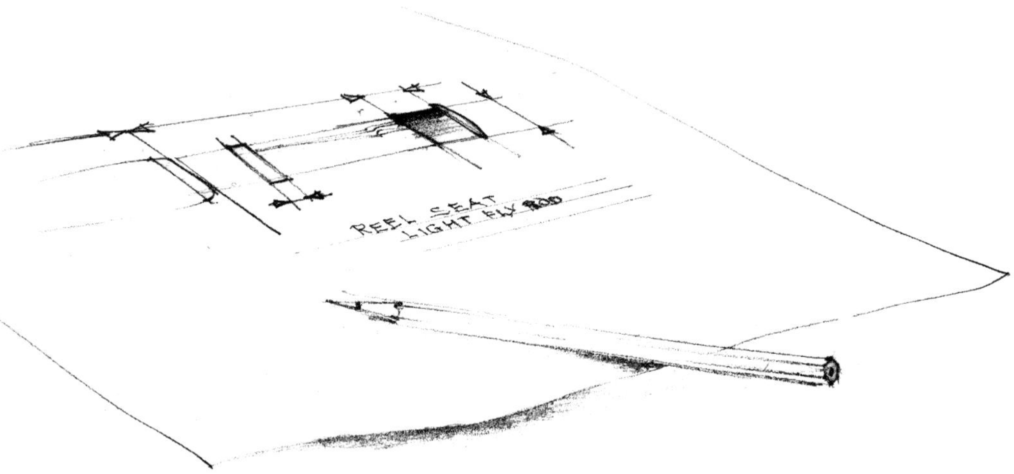

H. L. Leonard Rod Co.

A look through the various catalogs indicates that "pre-fire" models (as well as those built during Tom Maxwell's era) are in highest demand and most frequently sold.

Model	Length	Pieces	Line Weight	Notes	Price US $
36	6 ft	2/2	3	Post fire	3640
36	6 ft	2/2			1170
37	6 ft 6 in	2/2	4		2210
38	7 ft	2/2	4		3250
38	7 ft	2/2	4		4160
50	8 ft	3/2		Pre fire	1716
51	8.6 ft	3/2	7	Post fire	1625
51	9 ft	3/2			533
51	9 ft	3/2	7/8		1073
378	7 ft	2/2	4	Pre fire	1300
388	7 ft	2/2	4		2665
388	7 ft	2/2	4		3250
398	7 ft 6 in	2/2			1950
398	7 ft 6 in	2/2	5		3250
408	8 ft	2/2			1950
668	8 ft	2/2	5	Pre fire	2080
35 Catskill	7 ft	3/2		Pre fire	3380
36-2	6 ft	2/2		Maxwell	2925
36L	6 ft	2/2			2405
36-L	6 ft	2/2			3380
36-L	6 ft	2/2			2860
37-3	6 ft 6 in	3/2		Maxwell	2860
37ACM	6 ft	2/2			2015
37H	6 ft 6 in	2/2			2080
37L	6 ft 6 in	2/2			2340
37L	6 ft 6 in	2/2			2080
38 Baby Catskill	7 ft	2/2		Pre fire	2665
38-3	7 ft	2/2		Maxwell	4030
38-4	7 ft	2/2	4	Catskill	4550
38-L	7 ft	2/2		Pre fire	1495
40-5	8 ft	2/2		Maxwell	2340
40-6	8 ft	2/2		Maxwell	2665

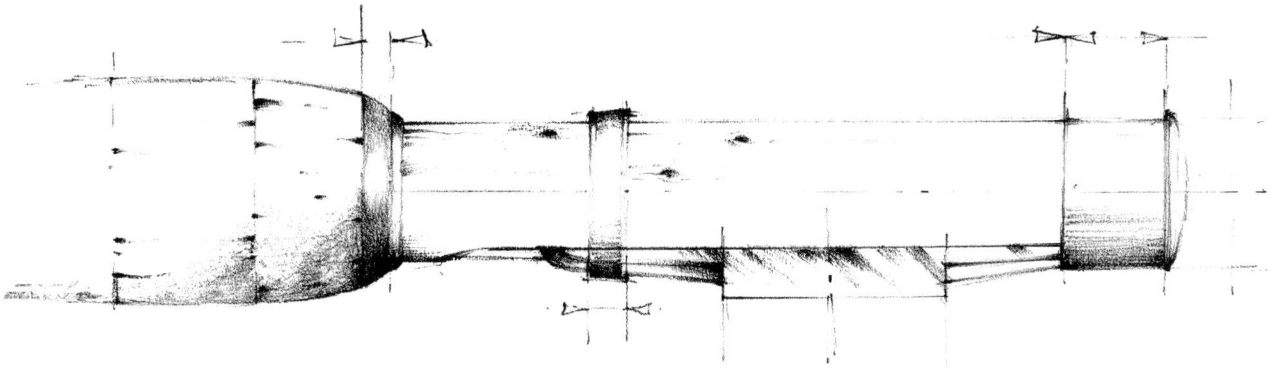

Model	Length	Pieces	Line Weight	Notes	Price US $
40L	8 ft	2/2	5		2600
40M	8 ft	2/2		Maxwell	2340
41DF-6	8 ft 6 in	2/2		Maxwell	2340
48-4	7 ft	3/2		Maxwell	4745
48-4	7 ft	3/2		Maxwell	3640
49-4	7 ft 6 in	3/2		Maxwell	2990
49-4	7 ft 6 in	3/2		Maxwell	2665
49-5	7 ft 6 in	3/2		Maxwell	2730
49-5	7 ft 6 in	3/2		Maxwell	5460
49-5	7 ft 6 in	3/2		Maxwell	3770
49DF	7 ft 6 in	3/2	5		3640
49DF	7 ft 6 in	3/2			2145
49DF-5	7 ft 6 in	3/2		Maxwell	3380
49M	7 ft 6 in	3/2		Maxwell	2340
50-4	8 ft	3/2		Maxwell	3380
50-6	8 ft	3/2		Maxwell	4030
50DF	8 ft	3/2	5	Pre fire	1950
51-7	8 ft	3/2		Maxwell	2405
86 SDF	9 ft	3/2	8		1073
Catskill	7 ft	3/2			1495
Catskill	9 ft	3/2			949
Catskill	9 ft	3/2			650
Duracane	8 ft 6 in	2/2			715
Fairy Catskill	5 ft 6 in	2/2			2600
Leonard Mills standard	7 ft 6 in	3/2	5		1560
Leonard Mills standard	8 ft	3/2	5		1560

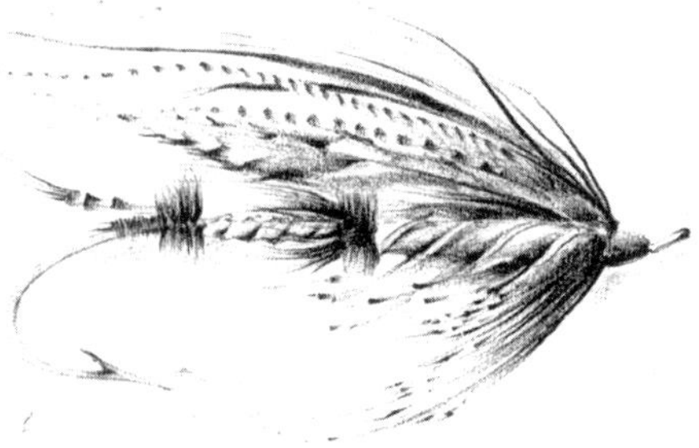

Orvis Rod Co. Inc.

Model	Length	Pieces	Line Weight	Notes	Price US $
99	7 ft	2/1	4/5		450
99	7 ft 6 in	2/2			288
99	8 ft	2/1	6		480
Battenkill	7 ft 6 in	2/1			690
Battenkill	7 ft 6 in	3/2	6		1020
Battenkill	7 ft 6 in	2/2	5		540
Battenkill	7 ft 6 in	2/2	5		750
Battenkill	7 ft 6 in	2/2	5/6		720
Battenkill	8 ft	2/2	5/6		570
Battenkill	8 ft	2/2	6		600
Battenkill	8 ft	2/2	6/7		630
Battenkill	8 ft 6 in	2/2	7		450
Battenkill	8 ft 6 in	3/2	6		750
Battenkill	7 ft	2/2	6		840
Caenis	6 ft 9 in	2/2	4		990
Deluxe	6 ft 6 in	2/2	5		1020
Deluxe	7 ft	2/2	5		720
Equinox	7 ft 6 in	2/1			264
Far & Fine	7 ft 6 in	2/2	5		1320
Flea	6 ft 6 in	2/1	4		510
Impregnated	7 ft 6 in	2/2	5/6		630
Impregnated	8 ft 6 in	3/2	5		810
Limestone Special	8 ft 6 in	2/1	6		690
Madison	7 ft 6 in	2/1	7		540
Madison	8 ft	2/1	6/7		570
Madison	8 ft	2/1	8		540
Madison	8 ft 6 in	2/1	9		480
Madison	7 ft	2/1	3		570
Madison	7 ft 6 in	2/1	5		630
Manchester	9 ft	3/2	8		300

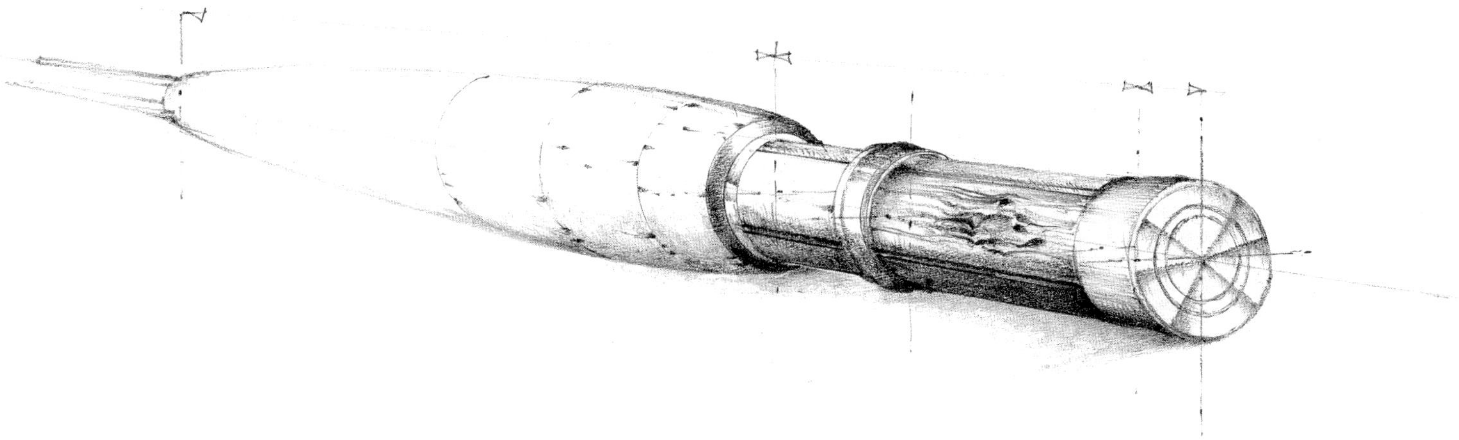

Model	Length	Pieces	Line Weight	Notes	Price US $
Midge	7 ft 6 in	2/1	5		570
Midge	7 ft 6 in	2/2	4/5		870
Midge	7 ft 6 in	2/2	5		930
Midge -Nymph Com.	7 ft 6-9 in	2/2			612
Mitey Mite	5 ft	2/1			504
Nymph	8 ft	2/2	4		870
Pace Changer	7 ft	2/2	5		480
Rocky Mountain	6 ft 6 in	3/2	5		1020
Rocky Mountain	6 ft 6 in	3/2		Fly/Spin	540
S S S	8 ft 9 in	2/2	10		630
Salmon	9 ft	2/2	8		510
Shooting Star	8 ft 6 in	2/2		Salmon	420
Shooting Star	9 ft 6 in	2/2	9		630
Spruce Creek	6 ft 6 in	2/2	3/4		1260
Superfine	6 ft	1	6		750
Superfine	6 ft 6 in	2/2	3/4		1170
Superlight	6 ft	2/2		Fly/Spin	252
Traveler	8 ft 6 in	4/1			612
Ultralight	5 ft 9 in	2/1			480
Wes Jordan	7 ft 6 in	2/2	5/6		984
Wes Jordan	8 ft	2/2	7		810
Wes Jordan	8 ft 6 in	2/2			300
Wes Jordan Special	8 ft	2/1	6		990

Jim Payne

Model	Length	Pieces	Line Weight	Notes	Price US $
100	7 ft 6 in	2/2			840
100 H	7 ft 6 in	2/2			2520
101	7 ft 6 in	2/2			3720
102	8 ft	2/2	5		3360
102	8 ft	2/2	6		2760
102 L	8 ft	2/2			3720
103	8 ft	2/2	5/6		3000
103	8 ft	2/1			1740
103	8 ft	2/2		Various tips	1320
104	8 ft 6 in	2/2			2460
198	7 ft 6 in	3/2			3120
201	8 ft	3/2			7320
202	8 ft	3/2			5340
204	8 ft 6 in	3/2			2460
204 H	8 ft 6 in	3/2		Restored	1500
204 H	8 ft 6 in	3/2			3480
205	8 ft 6 in	3/2	6		2400
206	9 ft	3/2	6		2040
209	9 ft	3/2	7		1800
216	10 ft	3/2		Salmon	2460
410	9 ft 6 in	3/2		Salmon	2340
96	6 ft	2/2			3720
96	6 ft 6 in	2/2			4800
97	7 ft	2/2			4140
97	7 ft	2/2			4080
98	7 ft	2/2	3		4200
Banty	4 ft 4 in	2/2			4800
Parabolic	7.1 ft	2/2			4020
Parabolic	7 ft 6 in	2/2			1860
Parabolic	7 ft 9 in	2/3			3720
Parabolic	7 ft 1 in	2/2			4800
Parabolic	7 ft 7 in	2/2			5220

Pezon & Michel

Model	Length	Pieces	Line Weight	Price US $
Fario Club Super Parabolic PPP	8 ft 6 in	2/1	5/6	1050
Parabolic Chalk Stream	8 ft 3 in	2/1	6	180
Parabolic Competition	8 ft	2/1	5/6	192
Parabolic Normale	8.4 ft	2/1	5/6	192
Parabolic Ritz	8 ft 2 in	2/1	4/5	510
Parabolic Skish	8 ft	2/1	5/6	510
Parabolic Still Water	9 ft 6 in	2/1	5/6	384
Parabolic Supreme Competition	9 ft	2/1	7/8	570
Parabolic Supreme Competition	8 ft	2/2	7	1020
PPP Master Lambiotte	8 ft 3 in	2/1	5/6	336
Ritz Super Parabolic Super Marvel Type Hans	7 ft 2 in	2/1	4/5	750
Ritz Superparabolic PPP Type Creusevaut	8 ft 3 in	2/2	6/7	810
Special Competition	7 ft	2/2	6	1020
Skish	8 ft	2/1	5/6	468
Sterling Normale	7 ft 2 in	2/1		804
Super Parabolic Longcast	8 ft 2 in	2/2	6/7	444
Super Parabolic PPP	7 ft 6 in	2/2	5	1110
Supermarvel	7 ft 9 in	2/2		1020
Supreme Normale	8 ft 6 in	2/1	7	510

Phillipson Rod Co.

Model	Length	Pieces	Line Weight	Notes	Price US $
Heywood Zephyr	7 ft	2/1	5/6	Fly/Spin	330
Pacemaker	9 ft	3/2	6/7		480
Pacemaker	8 ft 6 in	3/2	5		420
Pacemaker	8 ft	3/2	5		780
Paragon	8 ft 6 in	3/2	5		642
Peerless	8 ft	3/2	5/6		900
Peerless	7 ft 6 in	2/2	5		750
Power Pakt	9 ft	3/2	7		390
Premium	9 ft	3/2	7		510
Premium	8 ft 6 in	3/1	6		360

E. C. Powell

Model	Length	Pieces	Line Weight	Notes	Price US $
A-Taper	9 ft 6 in	3/2	7/8	Hollow built	900
Steelhead	9 ft 6 in	2/2			720
Trout	9 ft 6 in	3/2		Hollow built	612
Trout	8 ft 6 in	2/2		Hollow built	1440

Sharpes of Aberdeen

Model	Length	Pieces	Line Weight	Notes	Price US $
Aberdeen	11 ft	3/1	7		216
Aberdeen	14 ft	3/2	10/11		180
Eighty Eight	8 ft 8 in	2/1	5/6		252
Midge	6 ft	2/1	4/5		354
Scottie	8 ft	2/1			360
Scottie	9 ft	2/1	6		180
Scottie	9 ft 6 in	2/1	6/7		168
Scottie	10 ft	2/2			108
Scottie Impregnated	12 ft	3/2	8/9		288
Scottie Impregnated	15 ft	3/2	10		480
Spliced	13 ft	3/2	9		234
Spliced	14 ft	3/2	10		234

South Bend Bait Co. / Cross

Model	Length	Pieces	Line Weight	Notes	Price US $
1500	7 ft 6 in	2/1	5/6		330
24	9 ft	3/2			30
291	7 ft 6 in	4/1	6	Pack rod	240
291	7 ft 6 in	4/1			360
346	9 ft	3/2	6		240
59 -9	9 ft	3/2	7		120

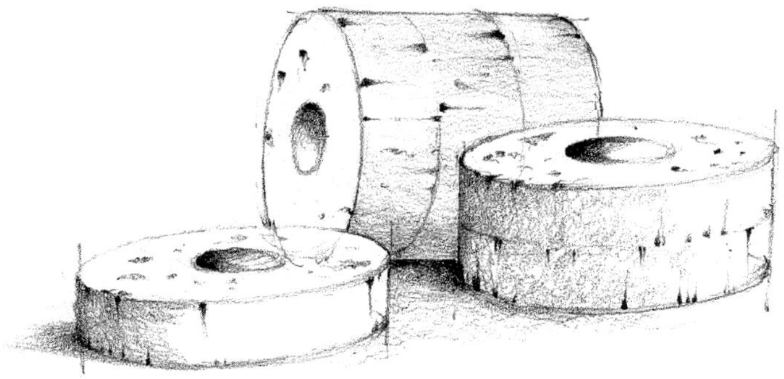

F. E. Thomas Bangor

Model	Length	Pieces	Line Weight	Notes	Price US $
Browntone	8 ft 6 in	3/2	6/7		1800
Browntone	8 ft 6 in	3/2	5		1500
Browntone Special	8 ft	3/2	5/6		1440
Browntone Special	8 ft	2/2			1860
Browntone Special	9 ft	3/2			276
Browntone Special Fairy	7 ft	2/2			1200
Dirigo	7 ft 6 in	3/2	4/5		1794
Highland	7 ft	2/2	4		1800
Mahogany	8 ft	3/2	4		2160
Maine Browntone Special	10 ft	3/2		Dry Fly	492
Maine Special	8 ft	3/2			1200
Maine Special Mahogany	6 ft 10 in	3/2			3720
Special	8 ft 6 in	2/2	6		870
Special	8 ft 6 in	3/2	5/6		1440
Special	7 ft 6 in	2/2	4/5		2160
Special	7 ft	2/2	3/4		1800

Thomas & Thomas

Model	Length	Pieces	Line Weight	Notes	Price US $
10 Anniversary	8 ft	2/2	5	Only 10	4380
Amabilis	8 ft	3/2	5	Only 20	3384
Beaverkill	8 ft	2/2	5		1920
Classic	8 ft	2/2	5		1560
Classic	7 ft 6 in	2/2	5		1380
Classic	8 ft	2/2	5		1380
Classic	6 ft 6 in	2/2			1056
Hendrickson	8 ft	2/2	6		1740
Individualist	8 ft	3/2	5		2160
Kosmic Commemorative	8 ft 6 in	3/2	5	Only 20	3540
Midge	8 ft	3/2	5		2760
Midge	7 ft 6 in	2/2			1440
Paradigm	8 ft	2/2	5		2640
Sans Noeud	7 ft 6 in	2/2	5	Only 20	3840
Special Trouter	8 ft	2/2	5		1170
Special Trouter	8 ft	2/2	6		696
The Fountainhead	7 ft 6 in	3/2	4	Only 20	3120

R. L. Winston Rod Co.

Model	Length	Pieces	Line Weight	Notes	Price US $
Hollowbutt	8 ft 6 in	2/1	8		1020
Trout	5 ft 6 in	2/2	3		1860
Trout	6 ft 6 in	2/1		hollow	1020
Trout	7 ft	2/1		hollow	600
Trout	7 ft 6 in	2/2	4		2220
Trout	7 ft 6 in	2/2	5		1410
Trout	7 ft 6 in	2/2	4/5		2100
Trout	7 ft 6 in	2/2		hollow	1740
Trout	7 ft 6 in	2/2	6	hollow	1560
Trout	8 ft	2/2	6		2100
Trout	8 ft 6 in	2/2	6/7		1194
Trout	8 ft 6 in	2/2	6		1200

Wright & McGill Rod Co. / Granger

Model	Length	Pieces	Line Weight	Notes	Price US $
Aristocrat	6 ft 6 in	2/2	4		570
Aristocrat	8 ft 6 in	3/2	5		690
Aristocrat	9 ft	3/2	6		480
Champion	8 ft 6 in	3/2	5		540
Champion	9 ft	3/2	6		330
Champion	9 ft	3/2	6		210
Special	8 ft	3/2	5		780
Special	8 ft 6 in	3/2	6		540
Special	9 ft	3/2	6		540
Stream & Lake	8 ft 6 in	3/2	6		510
The Favorite	8 ft 6 in	3/2			810

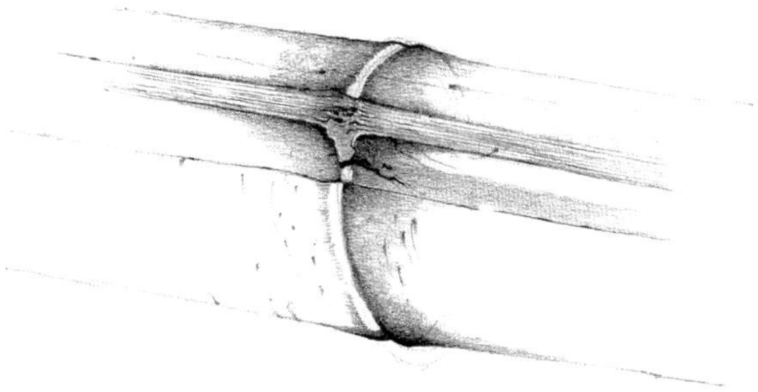

Paul H. Young Co.

Model	Length	Pieces	Line Weight	Notes	Price US $
1943	8 ft	3/2			1440
Boat Rod	8 ft	2/2	6/7		1440
Driggs	7 ft 2 in	2/2		Restored	4080
July 1948	8 ft 6 in	2/2			1320
Little Giant	7 ft	2/2		Restored	3720
Martha Marie	7 ft 6 in	2/2			2040
Midge	6 ft 3 in	2/2			2400
Para 15	8 ft	2/2	5		2640
Para 15	8 ft	2/2		Deluxe	2160
Parabolic 15	8 ft	2/2			3000
Perfectionist	7 ft 6 in	2/2	4/5		3000
Perfectionist	7 ft 6 in	2/2			2460
Special	7 ft 6 in	2/2	5		1104
Special Dry Fly Rod	8 ft	3/2			840
Texas General	8 ft 6 in	2/2	7/8		1800

About the CD

Split-cane rods have admirers the world over.

There are many reasons for the popularity of bamboo rods, but to learn more about the particulars, I found it important to obtain personal input from others. As often as possible, I carried a tape recorder with me, eager for each opportunity for an interview. But, because several of these interviews took place at fly-fishing shows, in hotel rooms, or as we made our way to fish some stream, the recordings are not always of the finest quality. Perhaps the results could be viewed as a "bouquet" of opinions from various points of view.

The CD could only have been produced with the help of my friends. I'm particularly grateful to my friend, Burkhard Hartmann, and his "Ton" studio. Wolfgang Gärtner assisted by providing vital information. The music was written by Burkhard, with Karl Mengel playing the congas, and Burkhard and I playing all the other instruments. For their generosity in providing the interviews, I also wish to thank Leen Huisman, Udo Hildebrand, Günter Henseler, Heinz Weiland, Roman Moser, Christoph Teichmann, Paul Schmookler, Nelson Ishiyama, Ed Engle, A. K. Best, and Thomas Dorsey.

Total playing time:
76 min 27 sec

Part 1. German

1.	Intro German	2:30
2.	Leen Huisman	3:32
3.	Udo Hildebrand	4:04
4.	Günter Henseler	8:07
5.	Heinz Weiland	8:28
6.	Roman Moser	8:29
7.	Christoph Teichmann	8:00
8.	Instr. Interlude	2:21

Part 2. English

9.	Intro English	0:26
10.	Paul Schmookler	5:17
11.	Nelson Ishiyama	3:42
12.	Thomas Dorsey	7:25
13.	Ed Engle	6:31
14.	A. K. Best	6:58

Appendix

Materials:
Accessories:
Arcane Component Works
P.O. Box 148
Hopeland, PA 17533
Tel: (717) 738-7330
www.arcanecomponentworks.com

REC Components
17 Middle River Dr
Stafford Springs, CT 06076
Tel: (860) 749-3476
www.reccomponents.com

Bamboo:
Charles H. Demarest, Inc.
P.O. Box 238
Bloomingdale, New Jersey 07403
Tel: (973) 492-1414
www.tonkincane.com

Golden Witch Technologies, Inc
P.O. Box 159
Hopeland, PA 17533
Tel: (717) 738-7330
www.goldenwitch.com

Bellinger, Inc.
1556 Industrial Way S.W.
Albany, OR 97321
Tel: (866) 371-6151, (541) 926-8266
www.genuinebellinger.com

Wrapping Thread:
Arcane Component Works
P.O. Box 148, Hopeland, PA 17533
Tel: (717) 738-7330
www.arcanecomponentworks.com

Bellinger, Inc.
1556 Industrial Way S.W.
Albany, OR 97321
Tel: (866) 371-6151, (541) 926-8266
www.genuinebellinger.com

Gudebrod
274 Shoemaker Road
Pottstown, PA 19464
Tel: 610-327-4050, 877-249-2211
www.gudebrod.com

Guides:
Snake Brand
13808 NE. 242nd ST.
Battle Ground, WA. 98604
Tel: (360) 666-9928
www.snakeguides.com

J. Stockard Flyfishing
14 Flanders Lane
Kent, CT 06757-0800
Tel: (877) 359-8946
www.jsflyfishing.com

Golden Witch Technologies, Inc
P.O. Box 159, Hopeland, PA 17533
Tel: (717) 738-7330
www.goldenwitch.com

Pacific Bay International
165 Business Park Loop
Sequim, WA 98382
Tel: (800) 272-2229, (360) 683-2080
www.fishpacbay.com

REC Components
17 Middle River Dr
Stafford Springs, CT 06076
Tel: (860) 749-3476
www.reccomponents.com

Bingham Enterprises
12004 Perry St.
Overland Park, KS 66213-1626
Tel: (913) 897-6657
www.angelfire.com/ks/bingham

Reelseat Inserts and Hardware:
Rush River Rods
4864 263rd St.
Wyoming, MN 55092-9010
Tel: (651) 462-3659
http://pages.prodigy.net/pumpkin10/index.html

Wagner Rods
6549 Kingsdale Blvd.
Parma Heights, OH 44130
Tel: (440) 845-4415
www.wagnerrods.com

Struble
300 S. Redwood, Suite 100
Canby Oregon 97013
Tel: (888) 459-1353, (866) 459-1353
www.strublemfg.com

The Brookside Rod Co. (Rodmakers Findings)
37 Brook Street
Naugatuck, CT, 06770-3101
Tel: (203) 729-1503
brooksiderod.tripod.com

Landmark Component Co.
PO Box 7071
Loveland CO 80537-0071
Tell: (970) 278-1311, (888) 557-6561
www.landmarkflyrodtubes.com

Arcane Component Works
P.O. Box 148
Hopeland, PA 17533
Tel: (717) 738-7330
www.arcanecomponentworks.com

Golden Witch Technologies, Inc
P.O. Box 159
Hopeland, PA 17533
Tel: (717) 738-7330
www.goldenwitch.com

Robert Venneri
21 Chuck Hill Road
Saugerties, NY 12477
Tel: (845) 246-5882
www.venneris.com

J. Stockard Flyfishing
14 Flanders Lane
Kent, CT 06757-0800
Tel: (877) 359-8946
www.jsflyfishing.com

Wood Stabilizing Specialists, Int'l., LLC
Ionia, IA 50645
Tel: (800) 301-9774
www.stabilizedwood.com

Pacific Bay International
165 Business Park Loop
Sequim, WA 98382
Tel: (800) 272-2229, (360) 683-2080
www.fishpacbay.com

Bellinger, Inc.
1556 Industrial Way S.W.
Albany, OR 97321
Tel: (866) 371-6151, (541) 926-8266
www.genuinebellinger.com

REC Components
17 Middle River Dr
Stafford Springs, CT 06076
Tel: (860) 749-3476
www.reccomponents.com

Ferrules:
Rush River Rods
4864 263rd St.
Wyoming, MN 55092-9010
Tel: (651) 462-3659
http://pages.prodigy.net/pumpkin10/index.html

Wagner Rods
6549 Kingsdale Blvd.
Parma Heights, OH 44130
Tel: (440) 845-4415
www.wagnerrods.com

Arcane Component Works
P.O. Box 148
Hopeland, PA 17533
Tel: (717) 738-7330
www.arcanecomponentworks.com

Golden Witch Technologies, Inc
P.O. Box 159
Hopeland, PA 17533
Tel: (717) 738-7330
www.goldenwitch.com

Bellinger, Inc.
1556 Industrial Way S.W.
Albany, OR 97321
Tel: (866) 371-6151, (541) 926-8266
www.genuinebellinger.com

REC Components
17 Middle River Dr
Stafford Springs, CT 06076
Tel: (860) 749-3476
www.reccomponents.com

Finishes:
Fultz Rod Co.
10360 Hwy 328
Reyno, AR 72462
Tel: (870) 769-2825
www.fultzrods.com

Golden Witch Technologies, Inc
P.O. Box 159
Hopeland, PA 17533
Tel: (717) 738-7330
www.goldenwitch.com

Pacific Bay International
165 Business Park Loop
Sequim, WA 98382
Tel: (800) 272-2229, (360) 683-2080
www.fishpacbay.com

Bingham Enterprises
12004 Perry St.
Overland Park, KS 66213-1626
Tel: (913) 897-6657
www.angelfire.com/ks/bingham

Cork:
Struble
300 S. Redwood, Suite 100
Canby Oregon 97013
Tel: (888) 459-1353, (866) 459-1353
www.strublemfg.com

Wagner Rods
6549 Kingsdale Blvd.
Parma Heights, OH 44130
Tel: (440) 845-4415
www.wagnerrods.com

Landmark Component Co.
PO Box 7071
Loveland CO 80537-0071
Tel: (970) 278-1311, (888) 557-6561
www.landmarkflyrodtubes.com

Arcane Component Works
P.O. Box 148
Hopeland, PA 17533
Tel: (717) 738-7330
www.arcanecomponentworks.com

J. Stockard Flyfishing
14 Flanders Lane
Kent, CT 06757-0800
Tel: (877) 359-8946
www.jsflyfishing.com

Pacific Bay International
165 Business Park Loop
Sequim, WA 98382
Tel: (800) 272-2229, (360) 683-2080
www.fishpacbay.com

REC Components
17 Middle River Dr
Stafford Springs, CT 06076
Tel: (860) 749-3476
www.reccomponents.com

Tools:
Wagner Rods
6549 Kingsdale Blvd.
Parma Heights, OH 44130
Tel: (440) 845-4415
www.wagnerrods.com

Golden Witch Technologies, Inc
P.O. Box 159
Hopeland, PA 17533
Tel: (717) 738-7330
www.goldenwitch.com

Bellinger, Inc.
1556 Industrial Way S.W.
Albany, OR 97321
Tel: (866) 371-6151, (541) 926-8266
www.genuinebellinger.com

Planing Forms, Mills:
Wagner Rods
6549 Kingsdale Blvd.
Parma Heights, OH 44130
Tel: (440) 845-4415
www.wagnerrods.com

Tom Morgan Rodsmiths (Morgan Hand Mill)
21505 Norris Road
Manhattan, MT 59741
Tel: (406) 282-7110
www.troutrods.com/handmill.html

Golden Witch Technologies, Inc
P.O. Box 159
Hopeland, PA 17533
Tel: (717) 738-7330
www.goldenwitch.com

Bellinger, Inc.
1556 Industrial Way S.W.
Albany, OR 97321
Tel: (866) 371-6151, (541) 926-8266
www.genuinebellinger.com

Planes, Plane Irons:
Golden Witch Technologies, Inc
P.O. Box 159
Hopeland, PA 17533
Tel: (717) 738-7330
www.goldenwitch.com

Highland Woodworking
1045 North Highland Avenue NE
Atlanta, Georgia 30306
Tel: (800) 241-6748
www.highlandwoodworking.com

Lee Valley & Veritas
P.O. Box 1780
Ogdensburg, NY 13669-6780
Tel: USA: (800) 871-8158, Canada: (800) 267-8767
www.leevalley.com

Hock Tools
16650 Mitchell Creek Drive
Fort Bragg, California 95437
Tel: (707) 964-2782
www.hocktools.com

Woodcraft
406 Airport Industrial Park Road
Parkersburg, WV 26102-1686
www.woodcraft.com

Woodworker's Supply
1108 North Glenn Road
Casper, Wyoming 82601
woodworker.com

Ovens:
Green Highlander Flyfishing Co.
(Bret's Ovens)
Tel: (810) 714-5546
www.greenhighlanderflyfishing.com

Measuring Tools:
Wagner Rods
6549 Kingsdale Blvd.
Parma Heights, OH 44130
Tel: (440) 845-4415
www.wagnerrods.com

Golden Witch Technologies, Inc
P.O. Box 159
Hopeland, PA 17533
Tel: (717) 738-7330
www.goldenwitch.com

Fingernail Router Bits:
Eagle America
P.O. Box 1099
Chardon, OH 44024
Tel: (800) 872-2511
eagleamerica.com

Grizzly Industrial, Inc.
P. O. Box 2069
Bellingham, WA 98227-2069
Tel: (800) 523-4777
www.grizzlyimports.com

Sandpaper:
Hardware, woodworking, automotive stores

Internet, Discussion Forums, Other Information

Bamboo Rodmaking Tips
www.bamboorodmaking.com

The Classic Flyrod Forum
http://p205.ezboard.com/The-Classic-Fly-Rod-Forum/bclarksclassicflyrodforum

Computer Program: HEXROD
Can be downloaded from:
www.wcattanachrodco.com

Wagner Rods
6549 Kingsdale Blvd.
Parma Heights, OH 44130
Tel: (440) 845-4415
www.wagnerrods.com

The Rodbuilding Forum
www.rodbuildingforum.com

Power Fibers Online
www.powerfibers.com

Index

Bibliography

A. J. Campbell (Fly-Fishing Tackle A Guide for Collectors & Anglers) 1997

Wayne Cattanach (Handcrafting Bamboo Fly Rods) 2000 Copyright by Wayne Cattanach

Ed Engle (Splitting Cane) 2002 Stackpole Books

Michael Jensen (Mit der Fliege auf Fried-, Raub- und Meeresfische) 1997 Müller Rüschlikon

Kenneth Mansfield (Fly Tying Rod & Tackle Making) 1971 Angler's Library

Jack Howell (The Lovely Reed) 1998

Jamie Maxtone Graham (To catch a fisherman) 1984 Published privately by the compiler

Wes Jordan (Profile of a Rodmaker) 1992 Centennial Publications

Dick Spurr (Classic Bamboo Rodmakers) 1992 Centennial Publications

Michael Sinclair (Fishing Rods by Divine) 1993 Centennial Publications

Ray Gould (Constructing Cane Rods) 1998

Martin J. Keane (Classic Rods and Rodmakers) 1976

Wayne Cattanach (Handcrafting Bamboo Fly Rods) 1992

Dick Spurr & Michael Sinclair (Colorado Classic Cane) 1991 Centennial Publications

Graham Turner (Fishing Tackle) 1989 Ward Lock

Charles Kewley & Howard Farrar (Fishing Tackle for Collectors) 1987 Sotheby's Publications

Luis Marden (The Anglers Bamboo) 1997 Lyons & Burford

Hardy Bros. (Anglers Guide & Catalogue) 1956 Hardy Bros. Alnwick England

John Gierach (Fishing Bamboo) 1997 The Lyons Press

Jamie Maxtone Graham (The Best of Hardys Anglers Guides) 1982 Macdonald Publishers

S. Allcock & Company (Allcocks Anglers Guide) 1938-1939 S. Allcock & Company

Paul Schullery (American Fly Fishing) 1987 Nick Lyons Books

Everett Garrison (Building a Bamboo Fly Rod) 1977 Nick Lyons Books

Poul Buch Jensen (Splitcanestaenger) 1976 Eget forlag

Gerald S. Stein (Dickerson The man and his Rods) 1991 Centennial Publications

Hager Lorenz (Bastelbuch für Sportfischer) 1958 Verlag Paul Parey

Letcher Lambuth (The Anglers Workshop) 1979 Champoeg Press

Ernest Schwiebert (Trout Vol. 1 & 2) 1978, 1984 Dutton

Kenneth Mansfield (The art of Angling Vol. 1, 2 & 3) 1957 Caxton

R. J. Barch, Editor, & Robert Mc Keon (Best of the Planing Form) 1997

Jamie Maxtone Graham (Fishing Tackle of Yesterday) 1989 Published Privately by the Author

Verlag: J. Schück (Fisch & Fliege) 1978 Verlag J. Schück

Charles C. Ritz (Erlebtes Fliegenfischen) 1956 Albert Müller Verlag, AG Rüschlikon-Zürich

Verlag: Creative Publishing (The Freshwater Angler Trout) 1988

Andrew Herd (The Fly) 2001 The Medlar Press

John Waller Hills (A History of Fly Fishing for Trout) 1971 Freshed Press

Dr. George Parker Holden (The Idyl of the Split-Bamboo) 1920 Steward and Kidd Company

G. E. M. Skues (Minor Tactics of the Chalk Stream) 1924

G. E. M. Skues (The Way of a Trout with a Fly) 1949

G. E. M. Skues (Nymph Fishing for Chalk Stream Trout) 1939, 1960

Claude M. Kreider (The Bamboo Rod) 1951 Centennial Publications

Hardys (Anglers Guide) 1962

Max v. d. Borne Fliege, Paul Parey (Angelfischerei 11. Auflage) 1961

Max v. d. Borne (Illustrirtes Handbuch der Angelfischerei) 1875 Verlag von Wiegandt, Hempel und Parey

Max v. d. Borne (Taschenbuch der Angelfischerei) 1882 Verlag von Paul Parey, Berlin

Arnold Bacmeister (Das grosse Lexikon der Fischwaid) Verlag Fritz Ifland 1. Auflage 1969

Allgemeine Fischerei Zeitung „AFZ“ München 15.06.1900

Shinji Takama (Die Wunderbare Welt des Bambus) Dumont

John Orrelle (Fly Reels of the Past) 1987 Frank Amato Publications

Bill Stinson (Do it Yourself Rod Building) 1990 Frank Amato Publications

Vincent Marinaro (A Modern Dry-Fly Code) 1996 The Flyfisher's Classic Library

Stuart Kirkfield (The Fine Bamboo Fly Rod) 1986 Stackpole Books

Silvio Calabi (Antique Fishing Tackle) 1989 The Wellfeed Press

Paul Schmookler & Ingrid V. Sils (Forgotten Flies) 1999

George Leonard Herter (Rod Building Manual) 1949 George L. Herter

Heinrich Hildebrand, München, Preis - Courant

Stork, München, Katalog 1911

H. Hildebrand's Nachfahren, Jakob Wieland, Katalog 1914

Hoagy B. Carmichael and Rolf Baginski, 2007 in the famus New York Anglers Club

二〇〇五年